Trekking Along:

The Pacific Crest Trail

Through Southern California

THE FIRST 700 MILES
FROM MEXICO TO CANADA

Maps
Flora
Water Carriage
Mile Markers/Elevation
Events and People Along the Way

HaL "Green Hornet" Margolis

SILOGRAM

First Edition

Margolis, Harold J.
Trekking Along the Pacific Crest Trail Through Southern California

1. Hiking–Pacific Crest Trail   2. Pacific Crest Trail–Description and travel.

Includes Index

Library of Congress Control Number: 2002094359

ISBN 1-879646-00-5 (pbk.) $14.95
Printed in The United States of America

SILOGRAM CORPORATION
SAN: 254-5403

PREFACE

I tell of my experience trekking north from the Mexican border through southern California to Kennedy Meadows along the Pacific Crest National Scenic Trail.

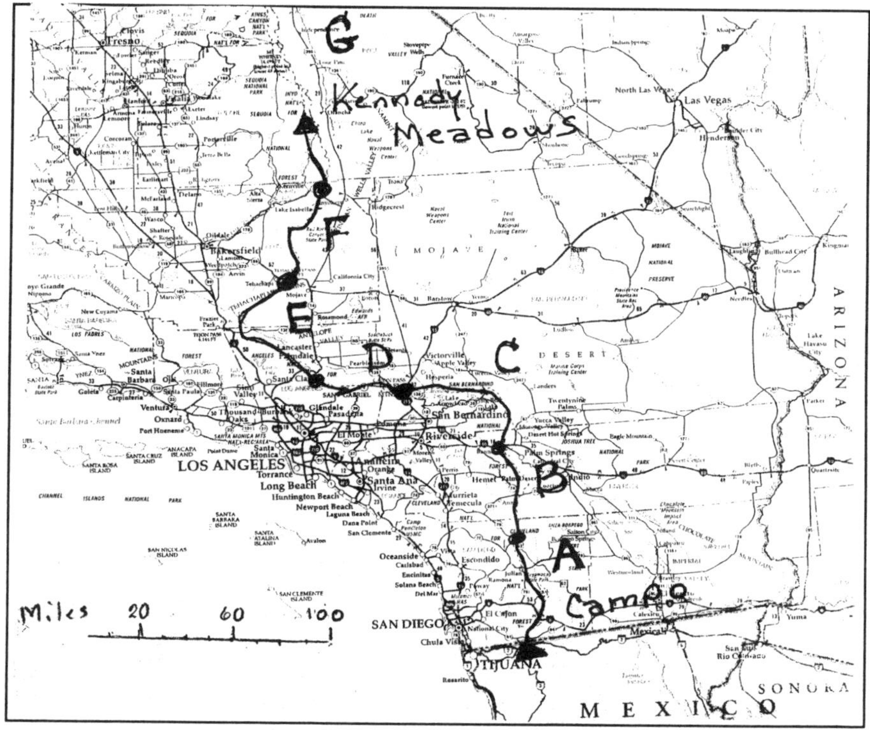

The Southern California sections of the Pacific Crest Trail
Campo to Kennedy Meadows

The narrative follows the PCT trail "sections" as laid out in the *Guidebook*, by Schaffer et. al. The sections, A-G go through thirteen mountain ranges, five national forests, six wilderness areas before reaching Kennedy Meadows, 697 miles north from the Mexican border.

The trek starts at the southern terminus of the PCT at the Mexican border, March 11, 1999 to completion of the San Gabriel Mountains. The following year, April 27, the trek continues north through southern California to enter the Sierra. There are maps and depictions of terrain with landmarks and milage markers. Included are several Supplements on plant identification and matters of safety, particularly on matters of water carriage throughout the southern California area.

Many people were met along the way. I may refer to them by nicknames, first names, or in some cases last names only. My apology to people whose names I fractured and have forgotten. Information about all individuals is incomplete. However, in their totality, I believe they provide an overall picture of the nature of the people drawn to this trail and what the outdoor experience imparts upon their character.

The PCT has its roots going back to 1920 when the Forest Service developed a route from Mt. Hood to Crater Lake in Oregon, named the Oregon Skyline Trail, a first link to what is commonly referred to as the PCT. By 1972 a Citizens Advisory Committee agreed upon a route with standards and markers. For years attempts to follow the general route were hazardous as many details had not been worked out. The trail was finally dedicated in 1993, following Congressional approval.

There is a concerted effort to maintain the trail. Some obstacles in traversing and navigating the trail can be expected from year to year. With some discretion on the part of the hiker, the trail remains safe. For those considering the trek and wanting detailed information about the trail, I recommend contacting the PCTA [pcta.org] and obtaining the latest edition *of Pacific Crest Trail, Volume 1: California* by Schaffer et al. Additional resources exist; they are referred to throughout the text and listed in the Reference section.

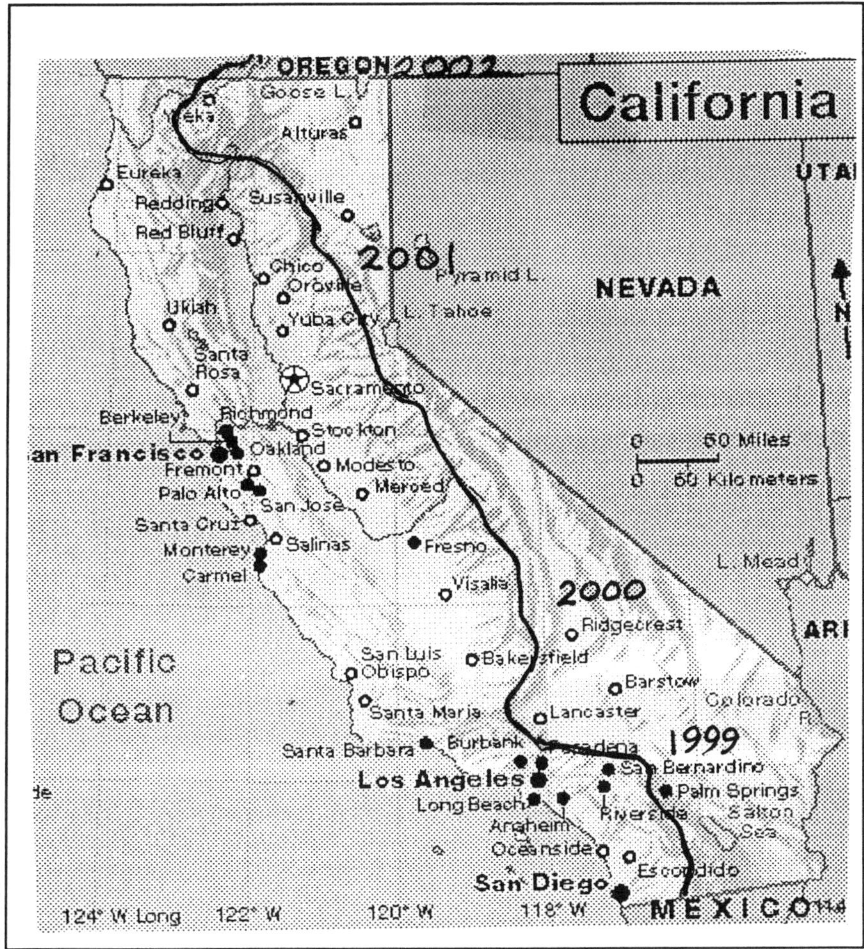

The 1,692 mile route of the Pacific Crest Trail through California

The entire 2,658 miles of the Pacific Crest Trail is wondrous. It enriches the lives of all who are fortunate to trek any part of it. Being connected to the trail – reading about it, working on it, walking on it, supporting it – connects one to it. Any of these connections cause one to become part of the lore of this mountainous trail from Mexico to Canada.

CONTENTS

PREFACE   iii
ACKNOWLEDGMENT   ix

SECTION A: CAMPO TO WARNER SPRINGS

Prologue   1

1. Driving To Campo; Finding the Trail Terminus   3
2. The First Night at the Mexican Border   9
3. The Hauser Mountains & Lake Morena   13
4. Lake Morena to Boulder Oaks Campground   25
5. Up The Laguna Mountains   29
6. Mount Laguna   49
7. San Felipe Hills to Warner Springs   59

SECTION B: SAN JACINTO MOUNTAINS

Prologue   77
8. Warner Springs to Palms to Pines Highwy   79
9. The San Jacinto Mountains   95

SECTION C: THE SAN BERNARDINO MOUNTAINS

Prologue   131

10. San Gorgonio Pass to Big Bear   133
11. Around Baldwin Lake to Van Dusen Canyon   165
12. Van Dusen Canyon to Deep Creek   173
13. Deep Creek Bridge to Cajon Pass   185

SECTION D: THE SAN GABRIEL MOUNTAINS

Prologue   207

14. Cajon Pass to Wrightwood   209
15. Snowed in at Wrightwood   223
16. Blue Ridge & Grassy Hollow Picnic Area   237
17. Grassy Hollow Visitors Center   243
18   Mt. Baden Powell and Islip Saddle   251
19. Islip Saddle to Sulphur Springs   259
20. Sulphur Springs to Mt. Pacifico   267
21. Mt. Pacifico to Soledad Canyon   277
22. Soledad Canyon to Agua Dulce   285

SECTION E: AGUA DULCE TO TEHACHAPI PASS

Prologue   291

23. Agua Dulce   293
24. Agua Dulce to Three Points and Neenach   299
25. Neenach: Jack Fair's Home   307
26. Mojave Desert to Tehachapi   311

SECTION F: TEHACHAPI PASS TO WALKER PASS

Prologue   323

27. North From Tehachapi Pass   325
28. Jawbone Canyon to Walker Pass   333

SECTION G: WALKER PASS TO KENNEDY MEADOWS

Prologue   343

29. Walker Pass to Kennedy Meadows   345
30. Kennedy Meadows   359

SUPPLEMENTS

A. Pioneer Mail to Scissors Junction   369
B. Trip Summary   381
C. Chaparral   385
D. Plant Identification   387
    Wild Flowers and Shrubs   388
    Deciduous Trees   413
    Evergreen Trees   419
    Avoiding Poisonous Plants   426
    Safe Plant Families   427
    Where Plants Were Found   432
E. On Dehydration and Water Carriage   435

ABBREVIATION   443
GLOSSARY   445
REFERENCES   447
INDEX   451

ACKNOWLEDGMENTS

Many thanks to people connected with the Pacific Crest Trail Association, especially to Pete Fish and other trail maintainers, Jeffrey P. Schaffer and others who put together the *Guidebook* and to Benedict Go that put together the PCTA *Data Book* of sites, milage markers and elevations. To Lee Terkel, Ed Faubert and others for sharing photographs, and Peter Rowat for the cover photo. To USGS whose maps I relied on and *TOPO!* for their 2-D computer depictions on CD and *MapTech* for 2-D and 3-D depictions on CD. Beautiful *Topo!* and *Maptech* productions were downloaded. Then with great liberty, I not only fractured them, but reduced them to black and white, but scribbled on them to depict the trail.

To my fellow hikers who told of their adventures, Martin Hutlin "Flatlander", "Meadow" Ed Faubert, Rob Bedichek, Scott Williamson and to authors and PCTers, Cindy Ross, Karen Berger and especially Allen Downs whose work inspired the production of this book.

To Paul Miller in Anza, Donna and Jeff Saufley in Agua Dulce and the late Jack Fair from Neenach who provided facilities and kindness along the way through southern California. To passing motorists that offered rides and unexpected support. To Johann Van Nimwegen (Van) who shared a number of overnights following drop-offs at trail heads and who found time for pickups at unusual places. My son, David and staff at our Green Hornets Aviation flying service at Van Nuys airport provided communications, airlifts, and pitched in during my absence enabling me to do this portion of the PCT. My sons David, Joel and Jon offered transportation. To sons, Joel and Jon who hiked along as good companions for many miles. And especially to my wife, Hannah, for always providing a supportive attitude and the help that enabled me to trek through California and Oregon.

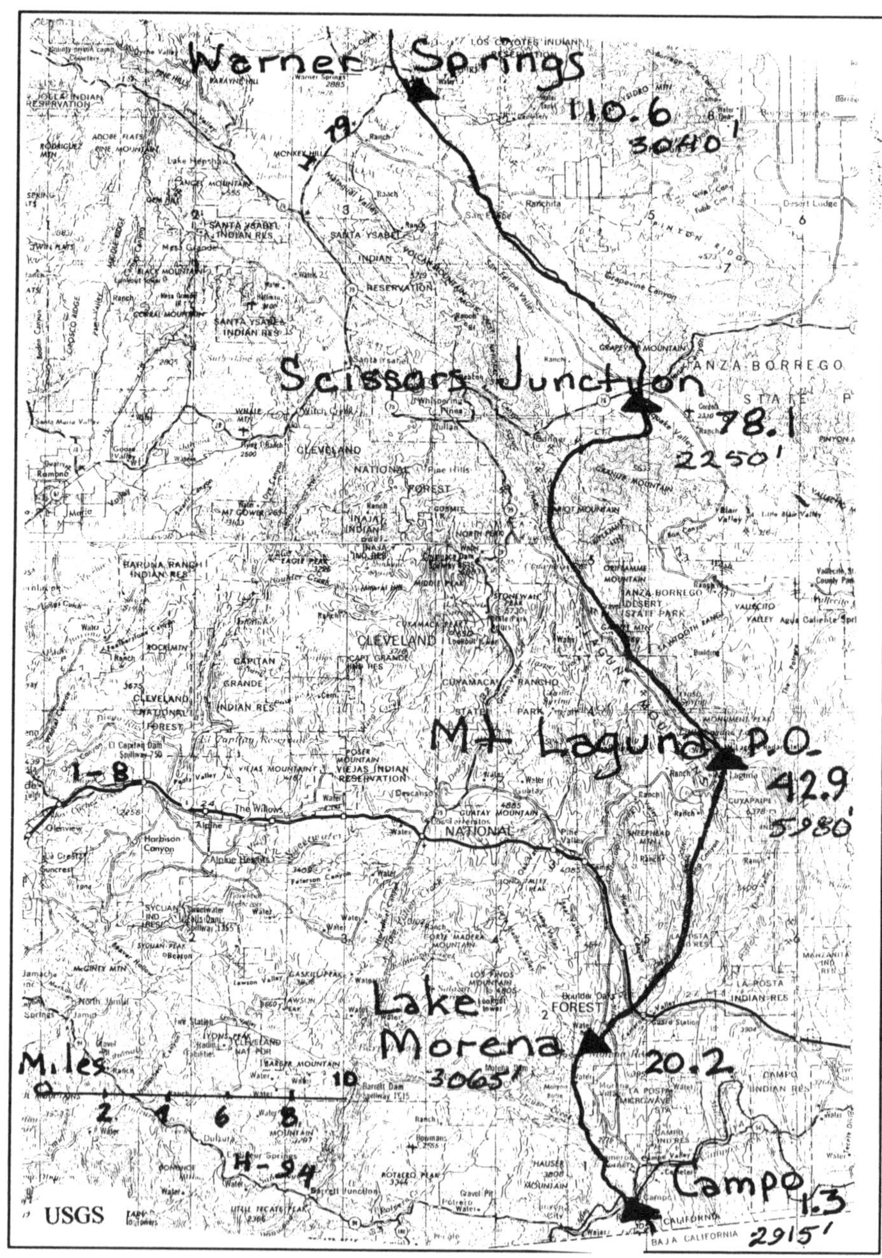

Section A: Campo to Warner Springs
110.6 Miles

SECTION A:
CAMPO TO WARNER SPRINGS

Prologue

Some hikers starting from the south terminus of the Pacific Crest Trail will do an interesting one or two day walk north over the Hauser Mountains to Lake Morena. A lesser number will complete this first hundred and ten mile section to Warner Springs. A lesser number, about a hundred trekkers a year, will make it across the desert to the Sierra, through Oregon and Washington to its northern terminus at Manning Park, British Columbia. Whether one walks a section or walks the entire distance of this 2,658 mile trail, one soon develops a bond to the PCT and a connection with those who venture on it.

Though seasons are never the same, by starting out between April 15 and May 1 keeps the odds more in favor of reaching Manning Park in Canada in the calendar year. Living in southern California, I am but within a few hours of the trail. Anxious to go, I started the hike early in the season knowing that I could readily return home in the event of inclement weather.

This southernmost section of the PCT first traverses 27 miles of high desert including the Hauser Mountains. All is carpeted with the chaparral so characteristic of California. Then comes an ascent to cooler climes of the pine, oak and incense-cedar forest that tops the Laguna Mountains. After 27 miles of mountain forest, the trail drops down to transit the high desert flora which becomes replaced by the unique desert plants of the Anza Borrego Desert. After a day or two traversing the exposed San Felipe Hills, the PCT descends again, but to low rolling hills of pastoral areas dotted with scattered tall oaks. A pleasant walk stream side through a dense riparian growth follows before reaching the 3,000 foot high desert community of Warner Springs.

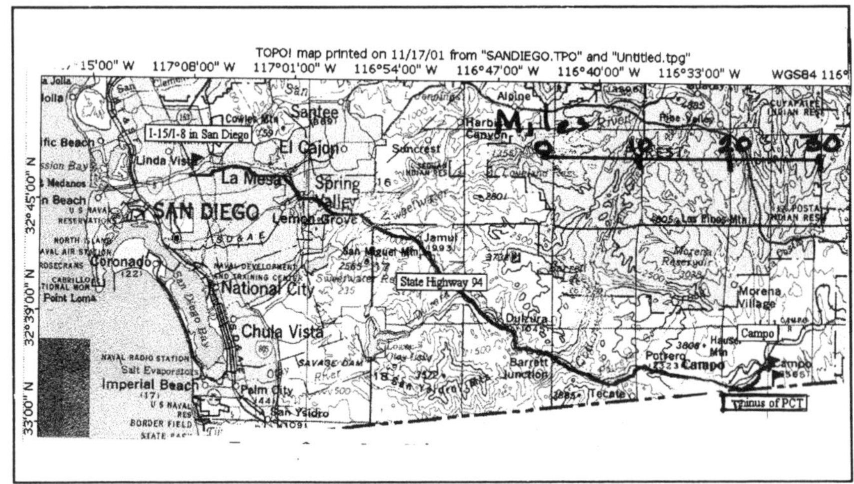

Highway 94 to Campo

Chapter 1

THE SOUTH TERMINUS OF THE PACIFIC CREST TRAIL: THE MEXICAN BORDER

On the way to Campo....Arriving at Campo
....The Mexican border....We're tailed!

March 11, 5:00 PM: On the way to Campo

We go in Joel's car. He selects the route. We'll take Interstate 15 south from Vista to Highway 94, then direct to Campo.   Soon after leaving the busy suburbs east of San Diego, the road begins to take a southerly turn approaching the border. A look at the map reveals H94 approaching the border of Mexico at about a 45 degree angle. The area rapidly appears quite rural as we gradually get closer to the international border.

There is a marked change in the way things look. Roadside businesses become sparse. Traffic is light and the roadside is void of activity. The road is windy and somewhat hilly on both sides. A closer look at the map seems imperative. I see the road ahead depicted as cutting the border at about a thirty degree angle and taking us on a more easterly course as we parallel the international boundary.

There is an air of mystery and a foreboding quality in the air. The sun to our rear has settled. At dusk now, it looks spooky. It's not even dark, yet the road is barely traveled. There are no more commercial establishments. In fact there seems to be no human presence at all. Except for an occasional light by a deserted corner, all is dark. What buildings we do see are neglected, apparently vacant. There is no one to be seen. We now rarely notice a moving car.   U.S. Border Patrol vehicles become apparent as we roll on. Each vehicle is parked a half mile or so apart from one another. A closer look reveals the marked

Broncos are set in strategic places to view terrain. All are in a state of readiness. Engines are running. Darkness sets in the canyons. No movement. All is still.

Throughout this section of highway to Campo, it is but a half hour walk south over sparsely wooded hills to reach the border. It is spooky. The fog doesn't help any. Occasionally, sits an empty vehicle parked alongside the road. Nearly are of an older vintage, sixties and seventies. Some of the roadside structures now are boarded up. All structures are old. They appear as though they had not been improved for fifty years. The light fixtures, advertisements and the highway itself, strangely enough, appear as if time stopped in the 1940's.

The road becomes more spooky as we winds about in the dark. As we travel further east all structures look more neglected. Our headlights reach out of the fog as we get closer to Campo. It seems like we are approaching a hostile frontier. I try to appear calm. Even steady tempered Joel seems to be controlling himself. His affect is flat. Yes, I tell myself, Mexico is really a safe place. I have flown into Baja several times and into the interior and encountered nothing but sensitivity and friendliness from Mexicans. Joel also has had pleasant experiences in Mexico. But, we are not in Mexico. We are in the United States near the border.

We get closer to Campo and to the Border. The road is getting darker. It is cold and quite foggy. It is hard to stay warm in the leaky cab of the truck. We are feeling the fatigue and discomfort of the stressor conditions outside. We do little talking. Also, we have a sense that nothing can be done to offset the distressing mood.

7:00 PM: We arrive at what we think is Campo.

It's dark, cold and even damper here. We see a dim light glowing in the fog. It is Campo, about a mile and a half from the border. The light comes from a small general-grocery store on the north side of the road in what could be the center of town. Like the rest of Campo tonight, the store is closed. The town looks depressed.

We continue on H94 which cuts through the town. It takes a jog northward. In about a mile or so we come across another dim light along the road. Another grocery store appears. We pull into the dirt lot. We stop. We hesitate. Without a word, we step out and venture into the dimly lit store.

It is cold inside. The store is closing. We see a lady proprietor and a large swarthy looking man. Both are heavily dressed. Before I get a chance to say or do anything, the man steps forward and looks down at me. Without taking his eyes off me, he slowly opens his coat. Just enough to display his badge identifying himself as a U.S. Border Patrolman. He must be there for her protection. No doubt about it; he prefers to prevent a crime rather than observe one taking place.

We explain our intent. The expression on her face and body posture suggests she questions our motive. She seems both annoyed and frightened by our appearance at this time, now at night, when she is preparing to leave. Her movements become a little faster giving us the message she would like us to leave so she can shut down and take leave of the area.

She says, "The nearest motel is twenty miles north of here, on the highway about a mile or so east." She tries to disengage herself from discussion. She appears nervous and curt in demeanor. We are told emphatically by the lady. "The Border Patrol does not even let locals in the area to the south."

I look directly at the officer. He avoids the matter but says in an ominous way, neither friendly nor hostile, "The temperatures are sub freezing tonight."

She says with some finality, "The store will be opened tomorrow morning."

Joel looks at me and says, "Let's go outside and think it over."

No more words are said, just a minimal wave from the officer. It's cold. We sit inside the car and discuss our options: The first option is to head 20 miles northeast along the road and leave me overnight at a motel. The second option is for the two of us to stay there overnight and drop me off at the terminus very early. The third option is to try to find the terminus and decide what to do at the time, quite probably punt and go back home pronto before we get into any trouble!

Joel opts for the third option. He chooses to explore Campo. He wants to see and experience the southernmost reaches of the State of California and the Mexican border.

At this point, I figure aborting the hike is but a mute point. Right now it seems as if it's finished before it even began! He winds through the small town, heads south through the mist and fog, makes a couple of turns. No moon nor stars are seen. I pull out my GPS which has the trail terminus landmark already entered manually.

7:30 PM: At the Mexican Border, El 2915, Mi 0.0 - 1.0

It is foggy. You can't see ahead more than thirty yards. Just as the GPS boots up, the car suddenly jolts to a sudden stop. Wow! Before us, illuminated by our headlights in this damp, cold and foggy night, is the landmark monument that I had just seen downloaded from the Internet. That photograph defined this very spot we had set out to find. We are at the terminus of the Pacific Crest Trail! The border must be a few steps away.

7:40 PM: We're Tailed

The concrete monument at the south terminus of the PCT at the Mexican border

We're tailed! Just as I step out of the car, a vehicle appears out of nowhere. It comes to an abrupt stop beside us, a bit to the rear. He turns on his headlights. The blue and red lights immediately identify his vehicle as that of law enforcement. We see before us a lone Border Patrolman, this one in uniform. I say to myself I really need some good words now to explain what we are doing here on the border this cold, misty and dark night.

I have the first word. I surprise myself, and perhaps Joel as well. I spurt out, "I'm considering staying overnight to start hiking northward on the Pacific Crest Trail. My son, here, is dropping me off to return home."

As if he already knew the answer to the question he had wanted to ask, he responds in a matter of fact, professional manner, "The area is very busy. There will be a lot of vehicles that will be constantly driving through this sector. We'll be monitoring you." He then went on to say "We'll make note of your position. Good luck!" He steps into the fog and is gone. Sure enough, engine sounds are heard. Truck lights are sometimes seen through the fog along the 180 degrees parameter north of the border.

It isn't clear as to what to do at this time. I weigh options. Should I follow through on what I said to the Patrolman and adapt to this unplanned beginning. After what seems like a long minute, I explain to Joel, "I'm going to stay over night and get this phase of the trip over!"

Joel seems relieved that at least he accomplished what he was asked to do. It is too cold, damp and scary to do anything but to make the best out of the situation. Like the Eagle Scout he is, he helps set up the campsite.

"I have a plastic tube tent along with me." Neither of us had any experience with such a device, typically used for emergencies.

Joel leaves his car lights on, pointing at the border. He helps to select a spot. We put a rope through the plastic and tie the ends from one of the stronger chamise plant to the monument. Now it looks like a clothesline. Once I unload my pack inside and put weight on the inside corners it begins to resemble a structure, an army pup tent.

The air is getting even damper and colder. The hour is late for Joel who is scheduled to work the next day. We say Goodbye. His tail lights quickly disappear in the fog as he wants to get a good start on the job tomorrow. Yes, gone. I hear a voice inside me saying "You're on your own." I find myself muttering, "I'm on my own."

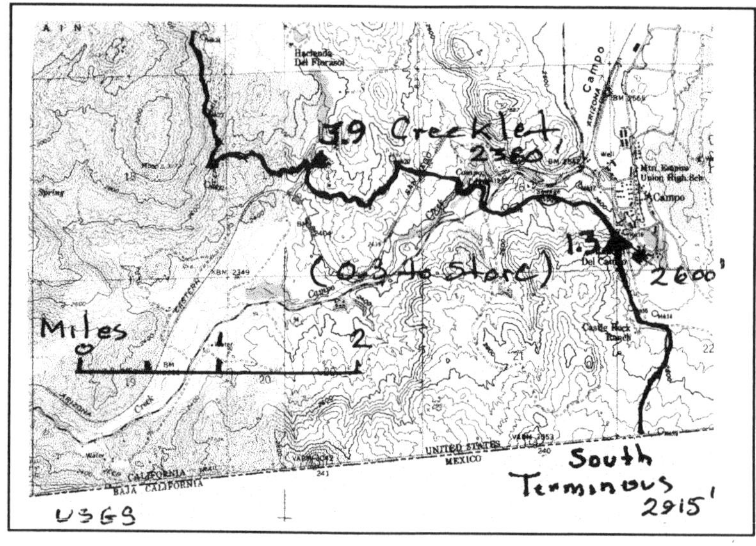

Trail from the south terminus to the Hauser Mountains

Chapter 2

THE FIRST NIGHT

March 11, 8:00 PM: At the Mexican Border, El 2915, Mi 0.0 - 1.0

Damp, windy and cold, near freezing and apparently just starting to rain as I craw inside my plastic tube tent and soon hear the sounds amplified as drops strike the thin, drum-like plastic walls of the tube tent. The buffeting walls complain loudly as the gusts increase. The droning soon became monotonous as I try to sleep. Now some white stuff finds its way inside. The sleet creates a louder drone as the tent continues to flap. I hope it will remain intact. Now, all but the loudest of outside sounds are muffled by the buffeting tent walls. Before the stronger gusts strike the tent, a prelude, a surge is heard off in the distance. The wind comes from the southwest, down a gradual slope of plateau, from heights just adjacent and south of the border in Baja. The surge approaches. Chaparral and terrain respond in approaching waves from various southerly directions.

As the wave approaches, I await the slap. I have a sense there is a person out there rustling through the brush in concordance with the wind waves so as to avoid being observed. As the wave approaches I hear such noises and try to convince myself the knocking on the tent is due from the impact of tumbling weeds or debris.

On the border, I consider that somewhere out there, not far away, people are desperately seeking their way north. Perhaps lost in the fog. How could these people know where they are if it is so dark they can't see anything? A flashlight would reveal their position. What if they were to stumble upon my tent? How might we react to one another? What might be their attitude? How would I deal with them? The thin plastic tube tent continues to flap noisily throughout the entire night drowning out sounds of the human drama outside. I try to decipher what's going on outside. Sounds of movement pierce the muffling effect of the thick fog. Are they friendly or hostile, or are they just desperate?

This is the border, a frontier. People from the south are clandestinely crossing the international border from Mexico into the United State of America. To succeed that night in their venture north, they must prevail over the cold, wet and wind chill factors. Then they have to navigate through the fog. So long as the wind is on their back, they know they are heading northward. But before reaching their haven, they must chance to infiltrate through sectors under heavy surveillance by the United State Border Patrol.

Pitch black out there. Visibility is reduced to zero, too dark, cold, wet and altogether too scary to go outside, so dark I see neither the chamise nor the monument that serve as anchors to secure the line going through the tube tent. What is out there? Should I leave the area and walk a few steps? No. I may not find my way back. So, I'll wait it out. Try to sleep. Then, in the morning when there's light, I'll crawl out. Then I'll see what awaits me. I look forward to making it through this spooky night. I, like them out there, plan to walk north.

I feel stupid for getting into this and developing a sense of helplessness. I slowly come realize there is nothing I can do about it except to stay warm. As I accept this fact, no longer do I place further demands upon myself to get out of this jam. A strange calm comes over me. Now I can sleep. My attention is diverted to matters I might control, such as whether the tent is properly erected and secured. Indeed, it seems so. The tent is secured by one long length of nylon rope. One end is tied to a strong clump of chamise, the only growth in the immediate area. The line goes right through the entire length of the tube and continues another fifteen yards or so directly north to the stone monument which marks the southern terminus of the Pacific Crest Trail in California at the Mexican border. It is too dark to see the rope, let alone to where it is tied.

The selection of the site, the construction of the tent and the way it is laid out is adequate to impede the rain and sleet from falling upon my sleeping bag. But so much condensation forms on the two ceiling walls that I wonder how long I'll be able to stay dry. It doesn't help matters tonight to allow the wind to come through the tent as this only permits more of the sleet to come in. Soon, drops of moisture accumulate on top of my sleeping bag. Yet, I find myself remaining warm and dry inside the bag.   I come to differentiate sounds. No longer do I jump when a nearby chamise branch strikes the tent wall. When something arouses me, I check my Timex Expedition wrist watch, a glow-in-the-dark watch.   It's only ten o'clock. Probably another seven or eight hours to go before this night is over! I try to sleep, but only to be rudely woken by some kind of noise. There it is again! Is it footsteps? I can't tell for sure. I don't know if I am sleeping or if I am awake. Is it getting closer? I admit to myself I am scared. I also figure if I get wet, I'm finished before I begin. But panic, Ah, I won't.

As I poke my head out in the rain, twist around and look north, I Suddenly see in the misty fog, a kind of glow of yellow, blue and red lights emanating several yards north of the monument. It is like an apparition. Not enough clarity to provide a hint of a profile. Yet, I know it is a Border Patrol vehicle. A Bronco on patrol comes by without head lights, unnoticed because of all the noise inside the tent. I am actually relieved when a beam of light is seen barely piercing the fog. The light cuts out almost immediately. Nothing but the rustling of the nearby chamise, the sound of wind, flapping of the plastic and rain upon the tent. I then make out the sound of engine exhaust. The vehicle pulls out with sound of wheels spinning on wet dirt road and exhaust are soon muted after the red glow disappears. But other human like sounds soon recur.

I'll find out that these contingents of Border Patrol rely heavily upon use of heat sensors. These sensors sit on the back of special designed trucks. They look like a cannon with their barrel-like extensions pointing toward unseen living objects. They had me monitored all night. They also monitored illegal immigrants heading northbound. Thirty-two people, perhaps thirty-two lucky people, were rounded up just 150 yards west of this spot.

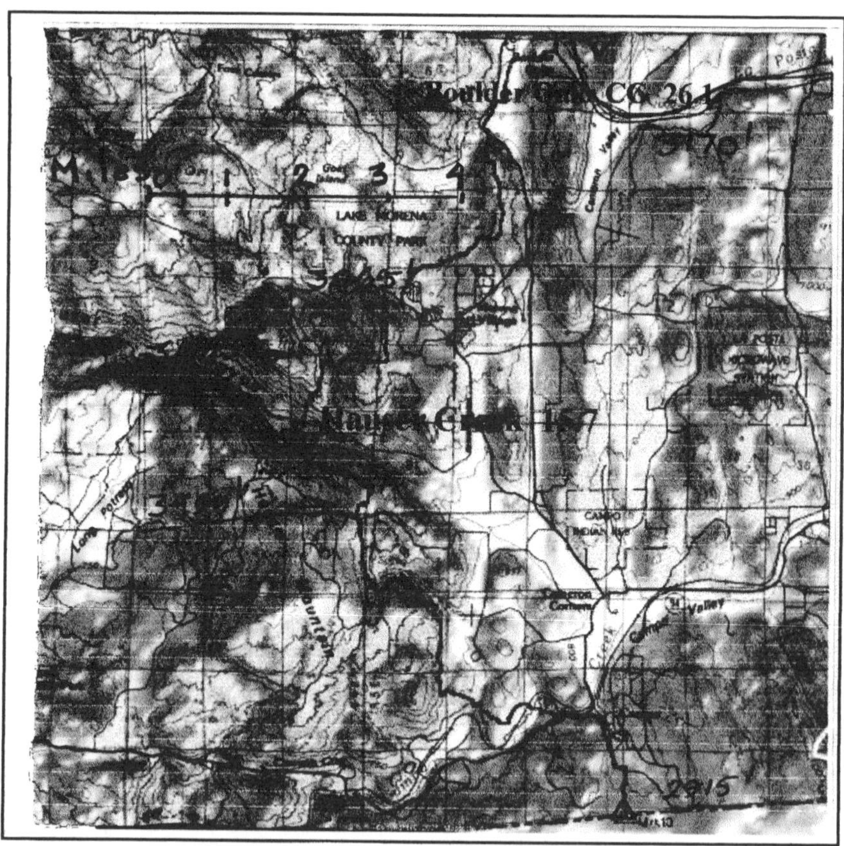

From MAPTECH *Terrain Navigator*

The Mexican Border to Boulder Oaks Campground

Chapter 3

THE HAUSER MOUNTAINS
AND LAKE MORENA

A greeting from the Border Patrol.....Campo
....Hauser Creek ....Lake Morena

March 12, 1998. Friday, 6:00 AM: El. 2915,   0 mi - 1.0

At the very first glimmer at light, about 5:15 or so, I peer out. Only fog and wetness. I can see no more than the monument, just twelve feet away. I take stock of things. I realize I was able indeed to get some sleep and can see and feel that everything on the upper surface of the tent is wet. So is my sleeping bag. I remain warm, dry and comfortable. Though not thirsty, I realize the water bottles are in Joel's car waiting to be filled at that illusive "motel" last night. I quickly emerge and look around. I hear trucks moving about and voices in the distance. The fog mutes everything. I change socks, put on the boots, dry sweater, parka and nylon over pants and mittens I have been using as a pillow. Now there is a little more daylight, but the fog is still too thick to see beyond the monument and south of the border. I begin to feel better as I move about. My morale takes a spiral upward as I realize I survived the night.

I permit myself to look around the very immediate area. The plant that surrounds me is interesting from a number of standpoints. This same plant, a chamise, has appeared in the background of several photographs of trekkers standing before the monument in testimony of their presence here at the southern terminus of the Pacific Crest Trail. Last night, this solitary clump of growth provided me with shelter from sleet and wet gusts of wind of 40 miles an hour. Selecting that specific site for the tent provided a low profile for the evening. The growth helped to keep me from being seen and confronted by desperate people on their own northbound trek.

The area about the monument is largely covered by dirt roads and parking turnouts. A wide dirt road parallels the U.S. side leading to the west and east as far as I can see through the fog. Within six yards of the monument are a number of plants: scrubby chamise, white and yellow daisies, black mustard, white forget-me-nots and/or popcorn flowers, amarinth, and Mexican sage, resembling sage, having a purple flower and a short, lancelate leaf.

A patrolman appears out of nowhere. He steps closer through the fog.

When our eyes meet, he says, "Good morning." He inquires, "Were you cold?"

"No, not as long as I was in my bag."

He asks me," Were you aware of all the activity last night?"

"My gosh, what happened?"

He rather stoically says, "We rounded up thirty-two illegal aliens last night, not long ago." He hesitated, then with a dropped voice, added, "They were in bad shape."

"That's rough. It's sad isn't it?"

He hesitates. Then, with a slight upward turn of his palm and with the same tone of voice reflecting the pathos, he says, "They just keep on coming."

Fumbling for words, I say, "Really pathetic. the wind was so noisy, and it was so dark, I missed all the action. Was anyone hurt?"

"They were cold."

I can see he is getting cold just standing there. I figure he wants to secure this area and get back to his warm car. I assure him, "I'm doing just fine. I'll soon be on my way."

Just as I put everything together and slip on the pack, and as I take my first step north, another patrolman comes by and greets me. I think he's the same man I met the night before.

He said, "I not only monitored your heat production, but I was able to identify the thirty-two illegals with this heat sensor machine."

The machine sits in the rear of his modified truck, a few yards away, the fog is still too dense to really take notice. He goes on to say, "You say you didn't know what was going on?

"It was very dark, foggy and noisy inside my tent."

"I'm surprised you didn't know anything about it." He points westward. "It all took place just over there, over that rise," pointing to an area, still obscured by fog, about 100 yards away."

I say, "The fog and rain muted everything. But I heard strange sounds all night."

It all seems so confusing. So unreal as if from a science fiction story. I don't know whether to congratulate him or console him for his efforts. He nevertheless understands my concern for the whole sorry episode. He probably saved them from further harm from the exposure. He graciously acknowledges my appreciation for his efforts and try to express my concern for the people he caught and rescued. His affect communicates he is stuck on the idea of how all this significant action can take place and this guy, so close to it does not feel involved nor doesn't realize a significant event had just occurred .

Though the conversation gripped both of us, we were getting cold standing in the dampness. We wish one another farewell. He, to go back and get some rest, and I to try get out of the area. A dozen steps into the mist and he disappears in the general direction of the blinking lights of his Bronco.

Appreciative for the opportunity to put some miles behind me, I now finally begin to march northward. The sky has lightened. The fog becomes patchy. The fog now permits to see objects varying from fifteen to fifty yards horizontally. The objective for the day soon appear through breaks of the fog, the heights of the Hauser Mountains.

I look at my compass and begin to hike north. There's a small break in the fog. Now, there is be no immediate need to "walk by instruments." I will walk perpendicular and away from the border wall and look for the Hauser Mountains as a general reference point. I take about a dozen steps north looking for the characteristic PCT marker that I had read about. I see a sign. I head for it. I take a dozen more steps north.

Alas! it reads "TRAIL IS CLOSED." I take a few steps forward and slowly read the sign again, real slow. It doesn't do any good. It still says it is closed! All this and for what! Man! How do I get into these things? I ponder my situation. How am I going to get back? How will I explain this untoward event?

Before I'm able to digest the facts before me, my thoughts are blurred by a sudden appearance of another patrolman again coming out of nowhere. He sees me hesitating and wandering about.

He kindly walks over to me and points in the direction of another marker downhill fifty yards to the northwest defining the PCT. I gratefully acknowledge his assistance. He walks away and disappears in the fog. I hurry to walk in the general direction of where he pointed. Just as I feared! The fog momentarily obscures the sign and I can no longer make it out in the fog. There is no trail nor official markers to provide reference. I soon can't see where I am going, where I am, and where I was. I tell myself, "Hal, you've been on the trek now for five minutes and you're already disoriented." If lost means not knowing where you are and not knowing how to get where you should be, then this is it! I'm lost and I have just begun.

I reach for my compass. Damn it! I tell myself, I'm going to do this if I have to walk by instruments! But just then, before I get a chance to see if it were possible to pilot my way about, I make out a little white sign on a little white post written by an unsure hand. A small and temporary hand-written sign indicates the direction to a trail that leads to the PCT. Now I take a bearing, 290 degrees, magnetic. I first walk northwest to avoid some brush. I take twenty steps before the fog sets in again. What a way to start a hike! But what a relief to start this trek.

The fog begins to dissipate as the sky continues to lighten up. Walking along briskly now, I find myself sustained by the return of internal warmth. Now, for the first time, there are glimpses of places to see. Through the fog I see the first PCT marker. My morale shoots way up. What

a sight! I now am certain that I will indeed soon reach civilization and eventually find a telephone, a store, fill up on water and get some supplies.   I walk along the road and trail. I now can see the area is dominated by chaparral, dominated by chemise, manzanita, scrub oak a multitude of early spring grasses and wildflowers. Soon there are wide stretches of grassy fields with livestock. Then comes scattered one and two-storied structures, mostly governmental. This is Campo.

7:30: Campo, El. 2600, Mi. 1.3 - 0.7

I find nothing moving. I do see a military transport truck parked not far ahead. Across and up the highway, I can make out a small store, perhaps the closed store we saw last night. It seems boarded up. The driver, dressed in Army field fatigues sits rigidly and quietly inside the parked military truck. I ask the soldier, "Is that a grocery store?"

He says without inflection of voice, as if not wanting to be distracted from his stakeout task, "I believe they are out of business."

He is not interested in my response. I head for the store. The small store has boards over its' windows and looks closed. Soon the road parallels a moving stream. Now I get thirsty. I look at the stream and looking for a container that could hold water. I incriminate myself for leaving the water bottles with Joel, but console myself that I have decontamination iodine pills. I look ahead and see a woman opening up the rear door to the store. She doesn't stay very long. As she comes out of the door, I ask her, "Will the store open?"
She says in a matter of fact manner, "It should open at eight o'clock."

My watch indicates 7:20 AM. I decide to wait. I take out my wet sleeping bag and place it on the porch in the full warmth of the rising morning sun. I make calls and collect some empty discarded water bottles should the store not open. I bask in the sun on the warm concrete in front of the exposed southeast front of the store. I pull out my seven and one minute topographical maps of the area and review them once more. I find it fascinating to refer to these maps while walking into unknown terrain. I find it gratifying to confirm by observation what is depicted on a map. I take out my compass and assure myself I can get a fix. I take out my GPS and test it out. Now, in the sun it is delightful. The morale scale goes up.

Just before eight o'clock, a man pulls up and opens the store. He sees that I am a back packer, perhaps the first he has seen for several months. Unlike the tense situation in the other store last night, he offers me the freedom to wander around as he starts his opening chores. I pick up a pint of orange juice and gulp it down. I also buy a package of pineapple coffee cake, some athletes foot powder and two one-liter bottles of water. I then go to a faucet and fill up the empty canteen and the empty orange juice container. I stuff the pastry into my pocket to eat along the way. After quenching my thirst I now have a total of more than three liters of water, contributing to a noticeable increase of weight.

8:30 AM: The Hauser Mountains, El 2,600, Mi 1.3 + 0.3 - 0.7

The Hauser Mountains lie but a couple of miles north of the border. The hills first appear protruding out of the fog as the early morning sun plays on the chaparral that drapes the southern exposed slopes.

The first ascent starts just northwest of Campo, rapidly climbing through a myriad of blossoming chaparral and wild flowers to stay just above 3,000 for several miles before descending down into welcoming Hauser Creek. These rugged hills comprise a small mountain range extending six miles from Campo northwest to Lake Morena. To the immediate west, in view from atop the trail summits of 3,500 feet lies the more extensive Hauser Wilderness Area, one of the smallest in California, created in 1984.

Now it is early Spring. After a rain such as this one, it is especially delightful. There are myriads of wild flowers in the midst of their first blooming phases. Their appearance is intermittent and there may not be a second opportunity to see them this year.

The fog has lifted. My walk thus far had taken me along a route I could not see. I feel a good measure of assurance that the description of the trail is indeed consistent with what I now see.

The trail leads west from Campo to cross H94 where it meanders up across some railroad tracks before reaching the heights of the Hauser Mountains. The PCT then descends to Hauser Creek laying 15.7 miles from the south terminus.   A climb over the ridge to Lake Morena and six miles more to Boulder Oaks Campground.

The maps, the depiction of the geology, habitat and flora is helpful. The description of this part of the trail is quite sufficient for navigation. Though I refer now to my map and take fixes, it is really unnecessary to do so for navigation. Keeping up the skill is rewarding and offers an appreciation to what is seen while walking. The confidence with map reading and navigation skills adds to my assurance.

The trek here is much more interesting and beautiful than expected. Plant life is surprisingly varied and bountiful. Plants are in bloom. The walking is easy. The trail is good. All seems well. The tread reveals a dampness that extends well into the ground. The air smells and feels good. It is warm enough to take off my gloves and parka. What a relief to now feel the warmth expected in this section of California. I pick up my stride. I aim for the heights. I am elated!

Around this bend to the exposed side are seen multitudes of very small flower bearing plants, almost all less than one feet in height. None of which I can recall ever seeing before, not even in drawings or photographs. Even the smallest of plants and grasses, which otherwise would go unnoticed, are blooming with tiny flowers or growths. All possibilities of plant colors are seen. Here are tiny white forget-me-nots and the popcorn flowers, both along much of the trail to Lake Morena. The distinctive long stemmed, blue dicks, yellow mallows, hoary lupine with lavender flowers, California poppies. Bright orange-red paint brush and pinkish heliotrope dot the way as well. In more protective places one finds the larger Majita poppy with its five white petals and yellow center and the kudo vine with its tiny white flower and distinctive spiny green pod of 3- 4" were seen in damper protective places.

This otherwise dry area has a number of creeks and riparian stream beds, all running well this time of year. On the banks of the stream are my favorite trail snack, miners lettuce. There is also some tasty water cress, pepper plant, amarinth and sorrell without flowers. Seen where the area is a bit more dry are stinging nettle, poison oak, vetch, cholla, trailing yucca, and yellow dandelion.

Soon, the trail climbs to just over 3,000 feet as it comes within a half a mile to various ranches and private property. Forming a good proportion of chaparral now are, scrub oak, prickly pair and on top, a lot of manzanita and more chamise. Not far to the south is the west-east highway that Joel and I drove last night. Seeing a road now provides a sense of security.

Water seems to be trickling down all canyons here at the lower and southern terminus of the Hauser Mountains. All this beauty is in contrast to the debris laying along the trail.

The hills provide a refuge for illegal immigrants as belied by foot prints, all heading northbound. Strewn about are fresh cans of food with advertisement in Spanish. Some bodies will be found near here in the days to come, abandoned by their hired leaders, the "coyotes." More trash is strewn along the trail. Earlier, it was too dark and foggy to see the mess. The empty sardine cans, cracker boxes, snack and drink containers are all imprinted with descriptions of its contents, in Spanish. Some are still moist. There is altogether too much trash in this sector for a group of trail workers to recover in an afternoon.

Footprints indicate medium and large shoes with not much weight on their backs. All are recent. All are heading northbound. Yet there is no one around. Nobody. Not a soul. Occasionally, I think I hear something, or somebody. I am still distressed by the thought of their plight.

Soon the trail climbs earnestly in a moderate climb to a rounded ridge. After a short climb around a knoll, the trail descends gently to a large ravine with a nicely moving creek. Willows and cottonwoods and mid-height chaparral with chamise and various grasses and small plants in bloom provide the greenery and the color. Here lies an enticement for a rest and to finish up that pastry I had just bought at the store.

The trail continues to be exposed to the early morning sun as it follows the contours of southeastern slopes of the Hauser Mountains.

This moderate grade is the first earnest ascent along the PCT. There is but little shade, but none is really needed now. The growth becomes more sparse. The soil becomes more dry. The chaparral common throughout southern California dominates this slope of the first ridge of the Hauser Mountains. Soon, I reach the highest point in this sector, 3,400 feet, not to ascend higher until crossing Hauser Creek at mile marker, 15.7. The view reveals Highway 94 to the south and the Mexican border and desolate looking mountains beyond. The border itself is quite discernable. It looks as I imagine the old Maginot wartime defensive line dividing France from Germany, or perhaps the Berlin Wall. There is a lot of excavation associated with the east to west line. The erected wall and dirt roads parallel the north side of the border with dirt spurs leading northward to Highway 94. There is no sign of movement now. All seems peaceful.

There is no let up with the foot prints and discarded food and drink containers. The nature of the trash and footprints indicates that much of the food was shared. The foot prints look as if they are just a few hours ahead of me. The cans of discarded food now appear dry with no sign of recent moisture nor smell about their containers.

After reaching the top of the south slope, the trail leads through the eastern side of the Hauser Hills, providing views to the east as well as to the south. It is now clear how close the highway parallels the border. Not very much is done with the land in this area. It is a frontier and looks like one. About midday now, there is very little traffic nor movement down below on the distant paved roads. How peculiar. Not only are there no people on the trail, but no cars are seen anywhere on the roads below. It is still kind of spooky. But, I don't dwell on such thoughts for long as most of my attention is on negotiating the trail, observing how I am taking the climb, and finding myself so overcome with the natural beauty unique to this area, especially so at this time of year.

The trail meanders up a little with views of a ranch below to the immediate east. After some switchbacks the trail reaches a rolling plateau about 3400 feet plateau marked by a thick forest of 95% chamise; the balance being of scrub oak and manzanita, the only shade for miles. Soon, I find myself on a spot where I overlook the northwest panorama. There, to the north and across Hauser Creek, I see the trail cutting across a corner of California's smallest wilderness area, the rugged Hauser Wilderness, created in 1984. Across the deep canyon, I see Morena Butte, El 3919, protruding and dominating the scene with its granitic cliffs.

Down ahead lies Hauser Creek. Though not the first adequate resting area, it looks quite favorable from this vantage point. Up here on the plateau it is dry, exposed and quite warm in the mid day sun. The trail can be seen meandering down to greet a dirt road on the northeast side of the hill. One can tell from above there is an abundance and variety of plants, larger and greener than those up on top. During the long descent views can be seen of the flowing stream and cottonwoods, willows and other greenery along the stream bed. To the west are distant higher ridges and lakes.

The trail merges quickly with the descending good dirt road. As I head down the road I see the trail tread leading steeply away and down to the creek bed below. Now, on the northeast side of the hill, the flora becomes remarkably highly wooded. Thoughts then are focused on getting to the bottom of the canyon where rest and refreshment awaits.

2:30 PM: Hauser Creek, El 2320 - mi:15.7 - 0.0

This is a great place. No need to rush things. I'll stay overnight! Dinner and camping beside the stream, among the cottonwoods, black oak, willows and sycamores is delightful. Everything is Kosher, the beans, corn pasta, chicken soup and even the beef jerky. It is all put together and heated efficiently to perfection in my small, light weight and inexpensive *Bic* stove. I am using their packaged cubes that easily ignite and can boil a pint of water in about five minutes. A little bit of 91% alcohol from my first aid kit also helps to get some wood started to keep the kettle warm. For my first dinner, I pour out two or three helpings from the top of the small kettle as soup. I eat the remaining pasta, beans and bit of dried jerky for additional zest. On this, my first night out on the trail, I sleep soundly from dusk through dawn.

March 13, Saturday, 6:00 AM, El 2320, Mi 15.7 - 0.0

An easy wake up in contrast to yesterday at the border. Though going through the same routine of dressing as yesterday, it is much easier. This time I am actually having fun and do not care that it may take long to get ready to go. I fill up a liter from the nicely moving stream. As I know there are cattle about, I carefully put two iodine pills in it, and set it aside for a half hour.

I start the climb at eight A.M. The first 1.3 miles is a moderate-steep continual ascent near an abandoned mine to the first saddle, El. 3210. Because of the weight of the pack, my general tiredness from the exercise during the night before last, this being my first leg this year, my age, 65, and open heart surgery in 1992, the ascent to the first saddle requires almost 3 hours. When hiking, all mountains seem higher than while driving. Upon reaching the highest point in this sector, 3,495 feet, the focus of view is now northerly. Ahead and below me, lies my immediate objective, Lake Morena.

Anonymous

Approaching Lake Morena

A few miles beyond the lake the imposing Laguna Mountains dominate the view. The southern spine dramatically rises upwards from Cottonwood Valley to 6,000 feet. I note there is no sign of snow on the higher slopes.

I arrive near Lake Moreno at noon. Because I seem not hampered on level or slight ascent or descent, I pick up speed and finish this leg of 4.7 miles in about 4.5 hours despite the agonizingly slow climb to the summit. The earlier leg, from Campo to Hauser Creek, had some moderate ascents and descents, with altitudes varying from 2300' to 3400', totaled 14.4 miles. Doing this in about seven hours resulted in an overall rate of nearly two miles per hour including rests. I figure, not bad for a guy my age. Perhaps with a lighter load, I can do similar legs with more ease, at least at this altitude, weather and trail condition.

I know I am approaching a large recreation area. I hear sounds of people, mostly children, having fun. Rounding a knoll, I see the kids, then the lake to the north down in altitude by a couple of hundred feet.

Some of the shore is quite bare. All areas of the lake are dotted with small boats. Along the eastern shore is state campground with expansive lawns organized into sectors. There are sections for recreational vehicles of various sizes. There are sections for smaller camper vehicles, another for tents and a subsection for groups of campers, now holding two Boy Scout Troops, one next to the other.

I walk down this pleasant section of trail to arrive at Lake Moreno near noon. Not hampered on level terrain nor on descent, I pick up speed and finish this leg earlier than anticipated.

Anonymous

Lake Morena

Chapter 4

Lake Morena to Boulder Oaks Campground

March 13, Saturday: Noon, Lake Morena County Park, El 3065 Mi 20.2 - 0.1

I make my way to the park ranger station where I make calls to home and to Joel explaining to his machine my intention to stay here over night. I call Green Hornets. I tell the dispatcher of my whereabouts. I imagine I hear them talking among themselves in the background surprised that I was away, let alone on a solo hike. I walk to the two Boy Scout Troops in camp. Both groups appear to having a lot of fun. I settle down in the site on the eastern part of the park, in an area set aside for PCTers. The large park has immense areas of mowed lawn with occasional large shade trees, well set up for camping. A small part of the area, along the PCT is reserved for backpackers. Unlike the other areas teeming with RVs and car campers, I am its sole occupant.

Joel shows up! He pays $2.00 for an overnight stay, pulls his backpack and tent out of his pickup and sets up an overnight camp just at dark. I offer him dinner; not as good as last night, but with his approval nevertheless. We drive to another store and purchase some snacks and refreshments for the night. Joel sets up his tent. After relating our experience at the border, we settle down for the night.

March 14, Sunday 9:00 AM: Lake Morena, El 3065, Mi 20.2 - 0.4

Joel is a late sleeper. He hears me rustling. I offer warm drink. Although a cold night, like the last two, it warms up surprisingly fast. By 8:00 A.M. the warmth of the sun is clearly felt and jackets are off by nine.

We depart to the north together. Soon, he'll turn back to Lake Morena, pick up his car and meet me at Boulder Oaks. About fifteen minutes out, we cruise past some pretty countryside and soon pass through a spectacular glade of manzanita, as thick as any I have ever seen. They have a distinctive reddish and smooth windy trunk. After about another half hour we stop at a high point along the ridge, 3,220 feet, Mile 21.7 and have lunch, a power bar. To the north is Cottonwood Valley and Boulder Oaks Campground lying just south of I-8 as it cuts south around the laguna Mountains. We're sitting on a rocky knoll overlooking the southern end of Cottonwood Valley. To the near west lies sprawling Lake Morena. In this exposed site are many kinds of plants whose names and habits are to me yet unknown. Here I pull out the compass, get a good fix and review the map. Joel does a 180, and heads back to Lake Morena, to meet me at Boulder Oaks at a time when we expect to arrive, he by car, I by foot.

The trail shortly makes a moderate-steep descent. I find myself on Buckman Road in about 20 minutes. I follow the trail below the white

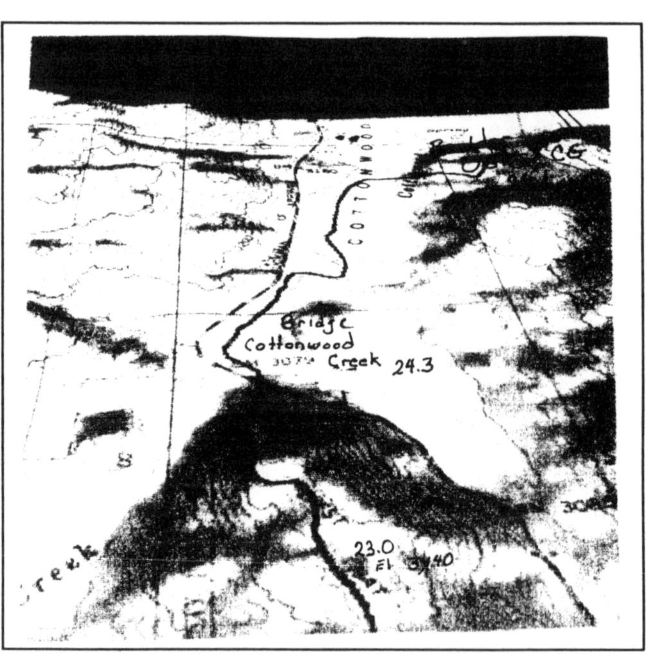

From MAPTECH, *Terrain Navigator*

Cottonwood Valley and Boulder Oaks Campground

bridge where I am forced to cross swollen Cottonwood Creek. I jump over two rivulets. The third rivulet is about seven feet wide, too far for me to jump. I throw my umbrella, hat and water bottles over to the other side. I take out a plastic shopping bag from my pack, place my right foot into it and tie it above my boot. I successfully heave the pack over the stream. I take a running leap, splosh into the water with my right foot, do a quick one-knee bend and spring out on to the other side without a drop of water on my shoe!

Proud of myself I pick up the gait, follow the path which now becomes an old dunged out paved one-way road . I follow it by map as I happily whistle along the way. But not for long. The road soon junctions with paved Buckman Road. There are no PCT markers to be seen. I head back down the dunged out road looking for the PCT turn off. I see a gate. It is locked. A sign posted reads DO NOT TRESPASS. I see cattle, perhaps steers or bulls, but no trail through the over grown area. I spot the campground a few hundred yards to the east, but it seems unlawful, if not unwise to go on through. So I continue along Buckman Road hoping to catch a ride with Joel should he go this way.

I soon approach a school administration site (El 3100, Mi 25.0 +0.5). I chance to meet the transportation supervisor for the local school district as he is unlocking the gate to depart. He cannot advise me as to how to make it directly to Boulder Oaks nor to the campsite, even though he agrees with me "it's just over there." As someone once told Hannah and me when we got lost in a rural portion of Iowa, "You can't get there from here!"

The gentleman tells me his job includes deciding whether to call a school holiday because of rain or snow. He says he is not sure whether to call for a school holiday. I tell him I heard from the ranger at Lake Morena that snow is to be expected down to 2,000 feet throughout the area. I tell him the campground area seems in the process of evacuation earlier. He begins to tell me the coverage of the school district. It includes Campo. He tells me the city of Campo is for sale!

Then suddenly I hear a car. I turn around just in time to wave Joel down. We wave goodbye. We make the short drive around the field to check out the campsite. There is a telephone booth in front of the store, but the store itself is boarded up. We look over the campground. There are several horse stalls. There are tables, water faucets and restrooms. There are no people. The PCT can be seen coming in from the south. Just across the field where I detoured is Buckman Road.

The decision to drive back with Joel comes easy. I'm not equipped for such cold weather. Joel and I drive off. At Joel's apartment he copies some software for me as I put band aids on my toes. I watch reports on TV indicating the snow line will indeed drop to 2,000 feet with considerable accumulations above 3,000 throughout the Laguna Mountains.

Chapter 5

Up The Southern Spine of The Laguna Mountains

Boulder Oaks Campground....Up the mountain....Cibbits Flat
Camground...To the summit; nearby aliens....Long Valley....
Burnt Rancheria Campground....The community of Mount Laguna

March 23, Tuesday; At Home

All pains, real and imagined, are gone by two or three days. No
more blisters, stiffness in the legs, tight shins and calf muscles, vague
upper back and shoulder aches. Joel tells me it snowed throughout the
Laguna Mountains and neighboring foothills. I find myself slipping
into the daily routine. I am anxious to get back on the trail before the
dreaded heat overcomes the Anza Borrego desert and San Felipe Hills.
Van offers to drop me off at Boulder Oaks and to meet me at a car
campground half way up the summit to Mount Laguna.

March 24, Wednesday, 5:15 AM: Van Nuys, The "Safari"

After checking the weather I leave home. It is dark. I arrive at the
rear of Van's house at 5:15 am. It is unseasonably cold. The sun is
beginning to throw out some light revealing the extent of his packing.
He is quickly filling the car with about 500 pounds of stuff. I can't
believe it! The Cherokee is full. I complain as I re-arrange the gear.
"Van, I can't see out of any windows."
Van says, "Use the mirrors."
He has a case of water bottles, four large duffle bags, floodlights,
radios, rope, tent, cooking gear including military food rations for two
weeks, flares, GPS, mobile telephone, radio transceiver, and who knows
what else in those carry bags. He is geared for an emergency.

I mutter in protest, "With all this stuff it sure looks like something will happen to us." I look Van in the eye and ask him, "Do you think we're going to need this?"

He just remains quiet. He sure has a style. I can say nothing more on the subject! His fiancee, Ronnie, sees we're about to go and wishes us well, good luck and all that kind of stuff as if we're going on a safari with an uncertain outcome.

We cannot get any weather information from the radio. All we get weather-wise is radio station KNX. They now claim that "the storm" is coming in, but at a slower rate than expected, with rain not expected in L.A. til tomorrow morning.

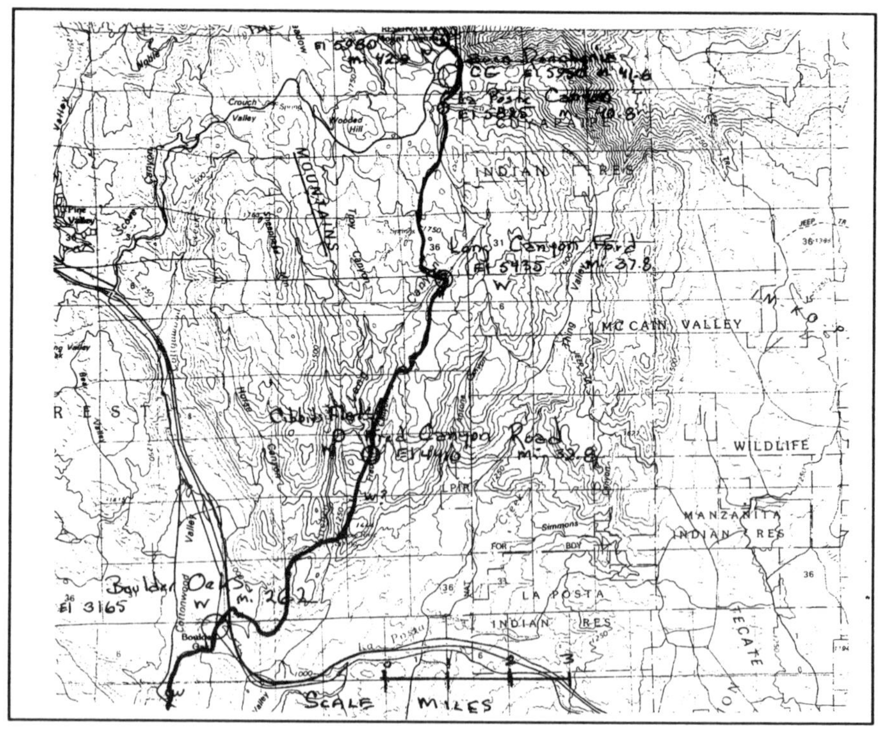

USGS

Boulder Oaks to Mount Laguna

What will be happening to the south in San Diego County remains unknown. We stop for breakfast. We eats as if it is our last meal.

10:15 AM: Boulder Oaks, California, El 3170, Mi 26 -1.0

After a wrong turn, we find Boulder Oaks campground. The aptly named campground is in an area of widely scattered low chaparral, rocks and scattered oaks off old Highway 80 with toilets, table, and water with sites for equestrians. It's cold and quiet. The area is void of cars and people. From the direction of a RV comes a warmly dressed woman in a huge coat giving the impression she is familiar with the area. Van addresses her, informing her that he plans to drop me off to continue the PCT northbound and hopes to meet me at Cibbits Flat.

I ask her, "Have you stayed overnight?"

She smiles and explains, "I've been here for two years; a volunteer with the forest department." She says her husband is with law enforcement in the area. She went on to say, "Temperatures are below freezing at the coldest time of night, about three A.M. in these parts."

I ask, "Do you know the forecast for tomorrow?"

"It'll probably rain tomorrow."

Van asks, "What's the road like to Cibbits Flats Campground."

"It's paved."

Van asks, glances over at me, "How long does it take to walk there."

She looks at me and hesitates.

I save the moment by asserting, "It depends on one's strength and fitness and how much weight one carries. For the most part it's uphill. If things go well, I should probably arrive in about five hours, and another six or eight hours to Mt. Laguna."

She nodded positively. I inquire about permits. I tell her we have an Adventure Pass, but no permit for hiking yet, but am expecting one.

Recalling her experiences, she says, "As far I know permits were never an issue for through hikers." She says to Van, "Just put on your Adventure Pass at Cibbits Flat. You'll be OK."

Van and I review options. We agree to our primary plan, to meet at Cibbits Flat in a few hours. Summarizing, "In the event I do not show up by dusk, we'll agree to meet back here at Boulder Oaks." I explain, "Should there be any unforeseen trouble, the way back is all downhill." I recall seeing the telephone last week. "I'll head up trail a few yards to the telephone.

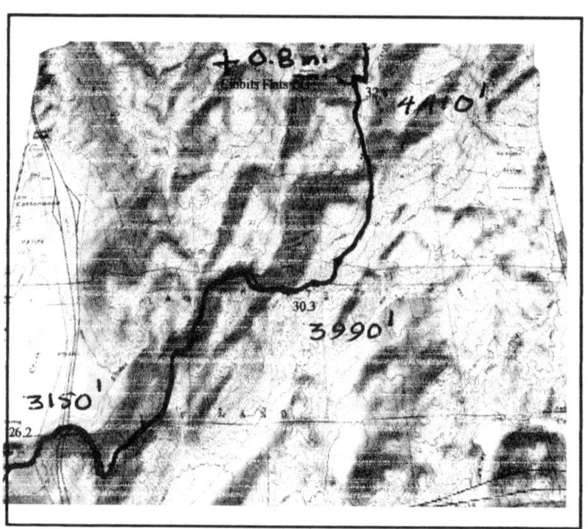

Boulder Oaks to Fred Canyon & Cibbits Flats CG

From **MAPTECH** *Terrain Navigator*

I'll call Green Hornets and let the dispatcher know of our whereabouts and plans for the next two days."

Meanwhile, she points out to Van the way to Cibbits Flats. I put on my pack. Van gets into the car. I head for the trail.

10:15 AM: The Boulder Oaks Store, El 3150, Mi 26.5 - 1.0

Boulder Oaks is a tiny community consisting of mostly scattered mobile homes that supports both a public and private campground lying here at the northeastern edge of Cottonwood Valley at the base of the southern flank of the Laguna Mountains. This picturesque valley comprises of fertile private lands largely inhabited by cattle, a high school and district headquarters serving a wide geographic area reaching southward to the border.

Many of the people in this general area speak Spanish. My reading of Spanish is borderline. But I find that I can readily read and understand all the labels on all the discarded food containers found on the trail. I ponder this situation for a while. I am beginning to get a grasp on the human aspects on this northern migration.

I stop at the closed store. As I approach the phone I see a thin, tall, but rather frail appearing young man standing. He is wearing a distinctive well worn leather hat. He is watching me. I nod as I head for the phone.

I explain to Sean, Green Hornets Dispatcher, of our plans for the next two days. He explains, "It's really pouring at the airport. It's supposed to last all day!"

I ask the man about the store. I had already determined from reading the *Guidebook* that the status of the store was under some litigation with the local authorities and could be expected to close should things not work out.

He says, "I am working at the store.   We plan to re-open it in a couple of weeks."

I respond, "Great."

He says, "I just got in from Canada. I spent three months coming south." He showed me a PCTA pin on his lapel. He looks at my pack and says, "My pack weighed 100 pounds."

"Wow!"

We chat for a while. He says, "Oh, I see you have to get back to work."

He points out the trail. As I head north, I could not help but wonder about his story and how he could have carried 100 pounds. I wonder how many more stories I'll hear. Will I meet others who are doing the trail. Will anyone be attempting to do a good portion of the trail, or even the whole thing. But I am also thinking how can things can be better? If it rains, I have my poncho and umbrella in a car not far away along with 500 pounds of "emergency items" and a good friend waiting. All I have to do is make it to Cibbits Flat.

Because the southern spine forms a sloping shoulder and is attacked directly in line, it now no longer looks steep. The range offers the first transition to the montane forest. I am also excited because I am unfamiliar with this whole area.

The hike continues to feel like a trip of discovery. As is the case of all significant mountains, one can only glimpse one aspect of it at any given advantage point. When one gets close, one doesn't see the mountain at all, you only see the upcoming ridges and hills. I have always enjoyed departing a desert or basin plateau to ascend through transition zones that separate the lower xeric regions to the moist montane forest above.

During the layover I had taken opportunity to study the terrain, the route and local flora. From review of the charts and maps, this excursion through the transition zone should be no exception to the surprises and drama offered by the Pacific Crest Trail.

As depicted by the USGS maps the trail leaves Boulder Oaks and pastoral Cottonwood Valley to under cross Highway 8 where it dramatically encounters the foothills to the southern spine of the Laguna Mountains. The climb appears gradual and generally northward as it ascends the exposed southwestern side. The trail will reach an expansive hilly montane plateau in several miles
where elevation vary little from 5,000 to 6,000 feet in all directions.

A further look at the map indicates the beautiful Laguna Mountains form a desert divide between the relatively moist coastal plain of San Diego and the arid Coachella Valley where lies the Salton Sea. The PCT reaches the beginning of the southern of the Laguna range immediately after crossing Interstate 8 where it immediately strikes upward to gradually reach heights above 5,000 feet, ten miles to the north of here. Once reaching Longs Canyon (37.0), the trail maintains this minimum level for another 17 miles through Pioneer Mail Picnic area (53.0). After leaving the picnic area, the trail leaves the abundant conifers as it winds down through mixed chaparral down to high desert climes of Anza Borrego State Park. The trail then winds down the barren and exposed northern slopes of Granite Mountain to reach aptly named Scissors Junction near San Felipe Creek (78.1) at elevation 2,252'.

From here at the base of the Laguna Mountains, the PCT meanders up sixteen miles to large Burnt Rancheria Campground, then a half mile more to a road 0.4 miles to the small township of Mount Laguna at the highway summit. I had already marked positions along the PCT with distances, elevations and true bearings to landmarks along the way. I find this method takes the edge off being alone in unfamiliar territory.

Because of the late hour, we had agreed to meet at Cibbits Flat Campground. The campground lies 0.8 miles off the PCT at a junction near one of the earlier summits of about 4410'. Near the summit is a dirt road that follows Fred Canyon down from where it crosses the PCT continuing downhill the 0.8 miles to the campground, a total of only seven and a half miles from here at Boulder Oaks.

10:45: Starting Up The Laguna Mountains, El 3300, Mi 27.0 - 1.0

This mountain range has been appearing ahead since spanning the ridges of the Hauser Moutains, now in sight several miles to the south It's a pleasure to head uphill to mountain forests to the kinds of areas I associate with the Pacific Crest Trail. Immediately the trail leads under an imposing large bridge where I find myself eagerly attacking the moderate grades on a surprisingly fast and easy climb. Immediately, I am introduced to a large variety of chaparral, wild flowers, and plants that vary in nature as altitude increases. Here, the flowering of the chaparral is even more marked than when I approached the Hauser Mountains last week. I am now glad that I undertook some reading on the plant life throughout the area.

The chaparral is in a state of change; spring has suddenly started. At the lower altitudes, flowering has just started, more obvious with a sunny exposure where moisture is about. In these moist and sunny exposures, mesquite now shows off its unique delicate off-white beige flowering apparent now upon reaching the foothills. Mesquite thrives here with its delicate off-white flowering spreading out way, velvet-like to the touch. I do not pick up any odor from the flowers. None of the plants about are attracting insects. Nor does the plentiful redberry plants. The redberry plants vary in their productiveness of berries. Some of the fruit looks like bright glossy beads, others more brown and scrub like. Looking more closely one sees occasional brown coffee berries on otherwise unnoticeable plants. Another surprise are the various kinds of spherical brown plant droppings along the trail, the size of golf balls, but very light in wight. These come from the Barberry plant, common to San Diego and Riverside County.

Anonymous

The beauty of early Spring chaparral - Ceanothus in bloom

As the trail winds further upward and reaches into more some northern exposure, I see the dogwood, characterized by their rich green foliage of short and simple, but wide leaves and characteristic white pretty blossoms. I think I see some western azelia with its simple leaf and white flower. Manzanita appears, not in groves as in the Hauser Mountains, but intermingled with other chaparral.

Various kinds of cacti and yucca appear along with the chaparral. The common yucca is also everywhere and in various phases of development, mostly in small clumps. Here, they resemble a cluster of pipes about a foot and a half in height. The common cactus apple, the prickly pear, appear limited to an immediate southwest exposure.

At the lower elevation appears tiny holes in the tread with fine sand forming tiny mounts about. About the holes are occasional low flying insects smaller than houseflies. Other than these quiet critters, there is but little sign of insect life along this portion of trail. The ones moving about are no bother throughout the entire mountain range.

The trail is not only very rich in flora, but dramatically reveals the view to the south and west as the climb continues. Both factors, the view and changing flora provides a motive in of itself to climb up higher! There is now a wonderful overlook to the southward of Cottonwood Valley stretching out below to the Mexican border. Over the immediate ridge to the southwest, that I had just climbed with Joel, lies Lake Morena. Further to the south are the 3,400 foot ridges of the Hauser Mountains. The terrain beyond climbs gradually to the Mexican border. Beyond to the south are the desolate looking mountains in Baja.

The trail traverses a couple hundred feet above a nice running creek with numerous attractive swimming holes. These pools look very inviting to while away the time. Oh, to have the luxury to while away the time in such pools. I would want to try them all! The pools vary in depth. Some have rocks about them where one could rest and enjoy the sensations and sounds of rushing water. But I must not partake or I'll be late to meet with Van. There will be other pools!

Soon, the ridge of the spine is reached. A myriad of colorful plant life. Within a stretch of thirty yards a close look at the chaparral reveals manzanita, laurel sumac, chamise, scrub oak, tumbleweed, amaranth, cholla, yellow mallow, orange paint brush, and yellow black mustard.

Here along the spine is paved Kitchen Creek Road, El 3990. Mi 30.3. A car is being unloaded with a bicycle. One party will probably coast down the hill to be greeted by the driver at the bottom some place. It seems as though they are taking turns. We acknowledge each other's adventure by a wave and a smile.

Once the trail crosses the paved road, the PCT goes around a dramatic bend to pursue a more northerly course. Here there are new views to the southeast, of Indian reservations.

Before long, the trail approaches a very small mini-meadow with a stream gurgling through its midst. Indeed, a very restful spot. What a great place to lunch out and bask in the sun! Here, is a combination of riparian growth, but in contrast to areas more south along the trail, it is more rich and varied, with tall green grasses complementing the deciduous trees and wild flowers beside the bubbling brook. I want to examine the area. But I move on. Too soon, the trail leaves this idyllic area, crosses some drier and exposed hills before meeting the dirt road (El 4410, 32.8) leading down expansive Fred Canyon to Cibbits Flat.

2:30 PM: Cibbits Flat Campground, El 4146, Mi. 32.8+0.8 - 0.6

I leave the PCT at Fred Canyon and easily jaunt 0.8 miles downhill on the exposed road to the campground. What will Van set up?

There is a sense of accomplishment in reaching an unfamiliar destination, like arriving at an airport for the first time. You read about it. You plan your route. You may even time yourself. When you're supposed to be there, you look down and around. There's the field! I get that same satisfying feeling that an abstraction has become reality. That's how I feel now as I approach this campground. Set among large oaks, scattered high chaparral and a flowing stream are picnic tables, fire pits, restrooms and ample sunny areas. But where is Van? I think about our discussed options.

Not until I get way into the campground at its' furthest end do I see where Van set up camp. Elaborate! His tent was erect on a blue tarp set up perpendicular to a slope of a hill. Maybe he is expecting rain. A lantern is hanging on a tree between the tent and picnic table and fireplace. We wave. On the table are various stoves and supplies. We're both grinning. In the car, of course, are the 500 pounds of extra goodies and toys.

Van brings out his emergency dehydrated food packages and catalytic heaters. All are packed in military looking olive drab airtight plastic containers. All you have to do is pour some water into the food pocket and it automatically warms up and you have an instant hot entree. Chicken and rice stew. It wasn't like this when I was in the army! He opens up assorted little packages, takes out crackers and servings of jam. Van spreads them out on the table and offers me samples. On tempting display are the chocolate covered cookies. Van insists I sample them. He shows me his portable, but very heavy, stove. He is anxious to demonstrate how the device works and how quickly it can boil water. "With such a high BTU, it can quickly boil water."

All this is great. But I have the feeling inside that if I give in to all this splendor I would have to rationalize why I had bothered to carry all this stuff on my back and why I am walking instead of driving. In any event I am quite content to prepare my corn pasta, bean and bouillon concoction in a small single kettle over a 4 ounce *BIC* stove. I even surprise myself how efficient it is to have soup, beans and pasta in three different course from one small pot eaten with the help of a Sierra cup and spoon.

Because Van brought his torch of a stove, and in part to placate him, I use his equipment to boil some water and put in some of my dried fruit snack mix into it, prunes, apricots, pineapple, mango, guava and dates. He says he is too full to share any of it.

The outdoor experience provides new perspectives on old concerns. We continued the conversation on matters discussed while on the road as I set up my pup tent. We uncork a bottle of white zinfandel wine and it seems that one problem after another is resolved with plenty of new options. With the wine tonight it is easy to recognize there will be plenty of time to pursue each matter in all their detail later.

Anyway, I tell him of my plans to get up at the crack of dawn and head north. He said he'll be up and we'll figure out what we will do tomorrow. He makes a point of saying that we'll see what kind of weather awaits us tomorrow. I tell him I'll try to find out the big picture of things on the car radio. Van insists on keeping his lantern on all night. Meantime it is becoming colder, the sky is becoming overcast as the stars, one by one, disappear from view.

March 26, Thurs., 5:30 AM: Cibbits Flat, El 4146m Mi 32.8 + 0.8 - 0.8

I wake up and go through the morning drill. As expected it's cold, just above freezing, not much different than other mornings along the trail thus far. While in the pup tent I put on my first layers of clothes, line up the others, then while the hands are still warm, I put on my mittens. Once out of the tent, I alternately take off and put on my mittens as I continue to put on outer layers. In two or three minutes I am comfortably warm again.

Van emerges with his "space" suit. It is a kind of brightly white heavy duty antarctic-like, one piece union suit. He is bundled up so much he can hardly move! He complains about how he slept. He said he left his knife tool and other things in his pockets. Sleeping on a slope, didn't help matters. But he is warm.

The lantern is still on. Although near freezing, I see outside it is cloudy, but not threatening of immediate precipitation. There is little bit of wind and the clouds do not seem to be moving much, nor is there any sign of convection or instability of air.

We plan how and when to meet with all kinds of alternatives and options such as should it rain, should it snow, should I not show up, should I not find him and when he will leave Cibbits Flat and what he would do if I do not show up by 3:00 PM and how he will notify the ranger or peace officers if we do not meet as planned.

I head for the car. The only station I can get is KNX, 1070, from Los Angeles. I don't care very much about the lack of stations because it permits time to sit in a warm and heated vehicle while attempting to get the weather. It is indeed continuing to rain hard in the L.A. area and is expected to last all day. No other weather information is available. No information is available as to the direction and breadth of the storm, let alone what is in store for us.

I will carry my umbrella along with my poncho. If it rains within an hour, I can come back, downhill in no time flat. After an hour, I'll look at the skies and head further north to see if I can put some milage behind me and perhaps try out my new rain equipment.

Except for some experience in the military, on forced marches, I have never had the opportunity to walk through rain or snow. When I did, a poncho seemed to work fine for me and the other 120 others in our medical battalion in handling rain and blowing snow. I figure the main thing is to stay dry and be alert to early signs of hypothermia.

We agree to meet at the southern boundary of Burnt Rancheria Campground. I give him an ETA from noon to 2:00 PM. If we do not meet by 3 PM, he'll head back to Cibbits Flat. If I am not there, he will return to the campground and wait. Should there be no contact by 3:00, he will notify the authorities. We set our watches, repeat and confirm instructions.

6:30 AM: Departing Cibbits Flat, El 4146, Mi 32.8 + 0.8 - 0.9

I walk up the road. I soon reach the trail. Oh! it's so good to be on the trail again. The trail immediately climbs gradually to about 5,000 feet. I am overlooking the campground. I yell "hello." No response. I soon realize by so doing I am alerting any nearby illegal immigrant of my presence. I look at the tread. I see the usual debris lying on and about the trail, enough to draw attention to itself even without knowing there are aliens nearby.

7:30 AM: Coyotes and Large Black Buzzards, El 4500, Mi 33.5 - 1.0

Illegals are nearby. Almost all the printing on bottles and packages are in Spanish. In an area of thick chaparral, obscured to the right and left by mesquite, manzanita, cactus and high grass, I see a baseball cap stuck to some buck weed. Up the trail a few yards are a bunch of fresh footprints. Then I see discarded plastic bags. Then a bright colored dry serape appears lying on the trail. Then a foam mattress. Then, I hear something! I stop. I freeze in my tracks. I listen and look around in all directions and sniff the air. A coyote! The first I have seen so far. He darts off just in front of me. Then stops in his tracks. He peers at me, hesitates and races off. I then see black buzzards flying low in circles overhead! I think I hear some rustling behind me. I take a deep breath. I glance to the rear. I decide to pick up the pace. I look back, but see nothing unusual.   At this point I decide to not worry, as no good will come of it. I'll just jaunt along. Should I meet someone, I'll just try to be cool and collected, and say, "Ola!" The trail continues to have signs of recent footsteps. As of before, all head north.

I try to keep my mind on the flora and continue to get compass fixes on landmarks. I become more confident in my navigation skills. I can always tell my position, altitude and estimate of time to get to my next fix. It is just like long distance flying! It is navigating. After an hour and a half, I find myself a mile high.

Despite the time of day, it remains just as cold as it was earlier. I study the sky. It's become overcast with layers of mostly flat clouds. The cloud ceiling seems to have dropped a little. I now smell that unique and delightful odor that precedes rain. I feel a couple of heavy drops of water. The temperature seems a few degrees above freezing. Looking at the cloud cover and the horizon, there are no signs of squall. There is a build up of clouds far to the north, but no immediate signs of convective activity. I do not hesitate to go ahead.

11:00 AM: Long Canyon, El 5230, Mi 37.0 - 1.0

The trail remains fairly level as it contours into ascending Long Canyon. Soon I hear the welcoming sound of bubbling water. I look in that direction and discover the trail picks up the stream as it cascades gently downhill. The flora is changing ever so consistently. The chaparral remains, but of different species. Here, the wild flowers have not appeared yet. Now, hybrids of large scrub oak and black oak begin to appear. The yucca and cactus are now all but gone. No more manzanita. Grasses are greener and longer, beyond the first joint. Ahead is a single tall pine, a Coulter pine! There are two or three baby pines around it. It is the Coulter Pines that have the distinctively huge yellowish pine cone. If one of these bombs drop on you, you're finished! Here at an elevation of 5,200 feet is the first PCT transition to the montane forest that lies ahead. Further up I approach another similar group of three conifers, again, scrawny Coulter pines.

The stream, small meadow, dampness and scattered small oaks and pines create an invitation to relax and settle down for a while. But because of possible weather changes, concern about uninvited guests and because I do not want to be late, I avoid a well deserved rest. I easily step over the stream and immediately start the last major ascent up the canyon through some switchbacks to the upper plateau. I find this phase somewhat tiring, having to stop and rest for the first time since ascending the

Approaching the montane forest

Lagunas. A short rest permits an appreciation of the changing flora. A glade of Coulter pines is seen ahead. But chaparral continues to dominate the exposed area. Ahead the trail levels off and approaches several mature dry meadows surrounded by scattered pines. Moving along, I see areas used for grazing with several dirt roads meandering through the widely separated pines. No livestock, though. I suppose the herd is waiting for the soil to moisten and subsequent growth of grasses. Suddenly the tread is covered with oak leaves so thick you can't see the trail floor nor any footprints. There are bare oak trees all over. Then, just as suddenly the tread contains maple leaves! Bare maple trees and oak trees are now all over the place. Soon, there are Jeffrey pines, the large stately pines with convoluted dark bark that smells like vanilla and symmetrical lightweight cones. Then come the unmistakable incense-cedars that look like Sequoias. Now, there is very little chaparral. The trail then leads into a thick montane forest as thick as anywhere that I have seen anywhere in the San Bernardino, San Gabriel or Sierra Nevada. I decide this area is understated in its' beauty. It is so picturesque! The trees are thick on this northeastern slope. The trail overlooks a narrow bubbling stream. Because of the darkening overcast sky, the forest is dark. So much beauty is hidden here! The cozy feeling of solitude and oneness with the environment is overwhelming. But I must not stop for I should not be late.

The forest is dark. The skies are overcast. The view north is somewhat impaired because of terrain, tall trees and dark skies. Yet, it is calm and a feeling of inner peace seems to emerge to match the calm beauty of the whole area. There is a sense that I have never been in such tune with the environment and so close to nature's wonders, even when in the Sierra.

12:00 PM: Near Burnt Rancheria CG, El 5950, Mi 41.6 - 1.0

According to my chart I should be approaching the southern boundary of the campground. I see several fairly good jeep roads in the cool deep forest that lead in several directions but hesitate to take them as I choose to remain on the trail, til sure of my position. The beauty is breathtaking now! I find myself distracted by the view of Posta Valley, 4,000 feet below and multiple ridges to the east and the endless deserts beyond.

I see why illegals choose this route. Not only is it hospitable, but the valley to the immediate north is Indian territory. They do not like their area trespassed. Here, the immediate area is hospitable, thickly forested, plenty of water and numerous places for stealth camping.

I Continue on what I hope is the right trail. It continues in curvy jaunts. At first easterly, then northerly. I see stakes with numbers on them. I assume I am on a self-guided nature trail. My compass tells me I am northeast by about a mile from where I should be. To my west is a ridge. I figure I long passed the campground which now is southwesterly of my position by about a mile beyond a steep ridge. If I continue on the trail, I will wind up at the Nike Base where I can take a road down to the highway and walk south a couple miles to the campground. But it will take a while and I do not want to cause any undue concern. So, I look for a route to take in the general direction where I want to be. Then I see a trail leading right in that direction.   Great! There are no signs of recent use. No foot prints. The trail leads off the PCT at a bearing that seems to be the exact general direction where I expect Van to be waiting. I note the time and head down this unmarked trail. In ten minutes I see a very small building

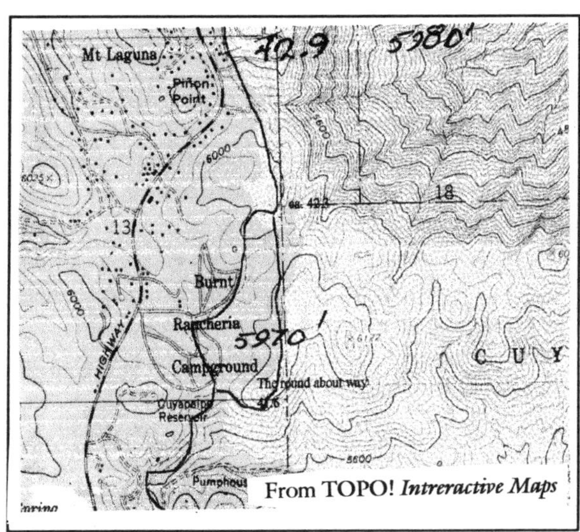

Finding Burnt Rancheria Campground

in the middle of a dense forest. Next, I see an outhouse, then a picnic table. I head down into the campground. No one is around. My compass tells me I am indeed at the most southern boundary of the campground.

I figure I made it to the campground at the rate of about 2 miles per hour, covering a quarter mile every fifteen minutes. With the watch serving now as distance measuring, I am doing well in providing known speed and distance covered over time. I have no time to congratulate myself because Van is nowhere to be seen. There is also no sign of life anywhere either. The whole large campground area is deserted.

The campsites are clean. As it was in Cibbits Flat Campground, no water comes from any of the faucets. My water bottle has about a pint left. I pull off my pack, reach for my stove and food, but alas, find nothing but power bars. I easily down one of them. I rest and ponder the peculiar situation. The storm can break out at any moment. No doubt, the precipitation would be in the form of snow. I wonder if this is the right campground and ask myself if I did anything wrong.

I walk around and explore the area. My compass seems to tell me I am at the southern boundary of this campground. There are no landmarks to confirm my position. I am not even sure I am indeed in the right campground! I recall the events when I was flying south through the Williamette Valley when I was uncertain of my position because of lowering ceilings and could not pick up the VORs. My magnetic compass circled around erratically and I soon lost sense of direction. I soon saw a small airport and landed nicely in very heavy rain. Later, when I reviewed the aerial charts closely I took note that the area was blighted by magnetic disturbance that made my compass useless! Can I trust my instruments now?

I put on the pack, take a tour of the campground, looking for the camp host or headquarters. There is a building. I saw it from afar. But it is closed. I walk around looking for something to identify the building. I confirm that I am in the right campground. I conclude the compass is indeed working OK. Why isn't Van here. Is Van OK?

At the same time I see the Cherokee parked outside a closed entry way. He shows me the note he had just finished to post indicating where I might find him. My watch says 1:30 PM.

2:00 PM: Mt Laguna Post Office and Store, El 5980, Mi 42.9 - 1.0

We drive a mile or so northerly to the center of town. One short block. The post office, store and motel are open. Other small businesses appear closed. I go to the post office to buy some stamps.

The lady sees me, concludes I am a hiker, and directs me to the PCT register. I review the pages. Here, I find the name and address of "Flatlander" whom Hannah and I met at Red's Meadow. It was he who inspired me to take on this venture. Sure enough, he went through here in April of last year. I jot down the information in my address book. There are only a couple of others that registered that El Nino year. This year there is but one entry so far, a solo hiker that just came through earlier today. Some of those foot prints were probably his. Maybe he had food with Spanish labels. Unlikely! The lady postmaster explains he complained of his knees and got a ride down to Pine Valley.

I go next door to the store. This interesting and inviting store is run by a lady who relates easily. She explains that this same gentleman came in a while ago, bought some orange juice and said he was finished hiking.

Her husband is a fire fighter. She says he nightly goes out and puts out campfires around the area. She complains of the hardship of living in the area because of the break-ins to cabins and rescues of illegals. Many are found dead because of exposure. She says the northern movement of illegals is costing us, the taxpayers, plenty of grief and money. As I buy a special map of the area and some cheese crackers, Van and I have a cup of coffee as we discuss ramifications of the northern movement of the illegals.

Though people in the area are largely employed by the government, business in the area is no doubt being significantly affected by problems associated with these clandestine operations. Interestingly, there has been little sign of violence and personal harm to the citizenry, let alone to trekkers. The whole matter of northern illegal immigration is pathetic! The problem, apparent here and in Campo, opens up a lot of serious questions with answers that are not at all satisfying! It begins to rain. Some snow is in the air. We decide to not stay overnight at their inviting cabin resort. Instead we head home.

Mount Laguna Area and Pioneer Mail Picnic Area

Chapter 6
Mt. Laguna

Mt. Laguna Lodge....A hike to Pioneer Mail Picnic Area
....Snowed in at the Mt. Laguna Lodge....The community
of Mt Laguna....A break in the weather and a plan

Monday, April 5,

7:00 PM, At Mt. Laguna Lodge, El 5940, Mi. 42.9+0.4 - 1.0

Hannah and I left home this afternoon looking forward to be being together and perhaps do some walking. We had stopped at the Warner Springs airport and later to look over the Pioneer Mail Picnic area.

The area at Pioneer Mail Picnic Area is covered with about two to four inches of snow with some bare spots. The PCT is partially covered with snow. I think the trail is do-able in this area; to the north the trail drops in altitude. The snow line seems to be about 4,100 feet.

It is dark as we approach the resort town. Snow is all over the place. There is a solid covering of four to eight inches. There are snowdrifts up to a foot. Nearby dirt roads and trails are obscured. The store is closed. I see the sign, indicating night registry. I ring the bell. A small 2 x 5 inch slit opens.

"What do want?"

"I'd like a room for my wife and me, if you have one."

Her attitude changes as she remembers me from last week when Van and I dropped into the store before leaving Mt. Laguna. She hands me a key. "Check it out and let me know if you think it is OK."

The room has the basics. It is quite clean, fresh looking, with a microwave, television, refrigerator and freshly refurbished bathroom.

She opens up the store for us. We are not really hungry, but do buy some snacks for supper. She tells of two young hikers staying at a room next to us that are held up because of the weather. Anyone in the area, she says, should expect cold temperatures, a storm overnight with snow lasting through tomorrow. We buy some coffee cake and orange juice for tomorrow morning.

Though pensive in mood, Hannah and I are glad to be together and comfortable in this romantic spot. We retire not knowing what awaits us in the morning.

April 6, Tuesday AM: Mt. Laguna Lodge El 5940, Mi. 42.9 + 0.4 - 1.0

I peer out the door. The "downtown" area, consists of the Post Office, the Mt. Laguna Store and Hotel, a couple of forest agencies and a maintenance garage across the way, now full of activity.

We meet the trekkers. They are strong looking lads, both having experienced several hikes together through the San Gabriel Mountains. They started at Campo last week. They made it to Lake Moreno where they got snowed in. This was the storm that had begun just after I had reached Burnt Rancheria Campground last week. They wisely decided there was too much weather expected. They were able get a ride here to Mt. Laguna.

They also encountered Mario who told of a story of hiking from Canada, enough of it different to suspect he was perhaps relying too much on his imagination!

The four of us review the Mt. Stephanson 7 1/2 minute topological map. We decide to hike north along the PCT for a few miles, intercept highway S2 and walk back to the resort, thus avoiding cabin fever and at the same time appease ourselves by doing a portion of the PCT. The map depicts our the trail about 300 yards to our east. Should the become too obscured or layered with snow too thick to negotiate, we figure we could turn around and come back, or head west for the road which would never be more than three quarters of a mile away.

10:30 AM: The Hike To Pacific Mail Picnic Area - 0.6 El 5940, Mi. 42.9+ 0.4 - 1.0

The four of us, me in the lead navigating with compass around my neck, seek the trail. A resident in the area points out the way, north on the highway, to the road to Mt. Stephenson, thence up the road a piece to catch the trail. We do so. We see one of the distinctive PCT posts.

The trail winds uphill a little bit, then parallels the contours near the 6,000 foot level, maintaining this altitude plus or minus 50 feet for a mile or so. Meanwhile the trail becomes somewhat obscured with no foot prints along the tread.

As the temperature increases somewhat, the crust is wearing down and we find that we are stepping through deeper and deeper snow. Now, the footsteps are going into the snow at least six inches, occasionally to twelve inches or more when snow drifts into the center of the concave trail. I keep the lead putting in steps with my clodhoppers. Hannah and Rinaldo are holding up pretty well, as is Billy, despite wearing his low tennis shoes.

As we approach the peak overlooking the Vallecito Valley, Rinaldo is looking continually at the sky, pointing to the intruding clouds, saying, "They're coming our way...It looks dark out there...Look, it may snow."

Every time he does this, we find our pace increasing. We work harder tromping through the snow. Indeed to the west, the mountain tops are becoming obscured. The wind is increasing, but the view is incredible as we approach another summit along the ridge. Here, we are kind to ourselves and reluctantly agree to stop, catch our breath and take in the view. To the north, east and southeast, the terrain drops off dramatically 4,000 feet, providing panoramic views over dry looking Vallecito Valley. We overlook a good part of the great Anza-Borrego Desert State Park to Borrego Springs, the Borrego Valley and to the Salton Sea. I also see the San Felipe Hills, what lies before me.

As we stand firm to avoid being blown away, we find we can only tolerate the position for only a minute or so. We step back, turn around and head downhill to where we hope to find the road. There does not appear to be any shortcuts to the

The burnt out ridge top overlooking the desert. The The gale force winds have cleared the area

road. All jeep trails are now obscured. We identify the trail mostly by a few animal prints that were made along the tread before us.

We didn't count on this situation. But we are not unduly worried because we know we will soon be heading westerly in the direction of the road. The snow depth seems to increase as we get into some shaded protected areas.

Hannah is struggling in and out of the footsteps we provide. I am continuing to provide deep wide holes for her to follow. She steps into one of the holes, unfortunately, not one of my mine. She goes through to the bottom to the dirt, twisting her leg as she falls into the hill to her left. I am right there and help her out. She appears somewhat stunned, but mostly surprised and somewhat embarrassed. She says she's OK.

Meanwhile we catch up with the guys at the road. I apologize to her for pushing her on. Our pace slows down as the others forge ahead unaware of our troubles, hoping to reach the road before another snowfall. The path becomes heavily wooded as we switchback down to a stream, cross a very pretty wooden bridge over a frozen stream, then up the other side where we see our friends talking to a forest service personnel officer in a turn out on paved Sunrise Highway, S2.

We rest a bit. It is 1:30 PM. I look at the sky, note that we are now at 5,450 feet with a small but noticeable decrease in snow depth. They are cold and anxious to get back.

I look at the sky, take stock of my physical condition, determine that I am OK and spurt out to Hannah, "I would like to go on north to Pioneer Mail Picnic Area, five miles to the north. If so could you pick me up at 5:00 PM when I expect to arrive?"

She gives me a funny look, agrees, and explains to Billy and Rinaldo that she will walk back with them and return with the Saab to pick me up at 5:00. She says, "If you're not there by six I'll call the Rangers, Sheriffs or Highway Patrol, OK?"

I hesitate, and say, "Let's make it at 4:30, and if you don't see me by 5:30, let them know."

We all agree and wish each other a good hike. They disappear to the south and I head north, solo along the trail.

I miss the trail as it crosses the dirt road to Oasis Springs. I mistake this snow covered dirt road for the trail. Soon the "trail" gets wider as the snow thins out revealing a dirt road. I must have traveled down about a quarter of a mile before I realize something is wrong. I check the map and realize what I had done. I turn around and make it back to where the trail might more likely be. Instead, I find S2, the highway. I decide to walk north along the highway, doing so for about a mile where I find a little parking area. At the east end of the parking area is a sign with an arrow indicating the PCT is eastward. I hesitate. I check the time and decide it would be OK to attempt to continue on the trail. I dropped another one hundred feet or so in altitude. I figure the snow should be getting thinner.

I recheck my map, find my location and decide to go ahead, around Garnet Peak and traverse around Garnet Mountain. Here are astonishing views of the valley below to the northeast. The snow finally thins out a little so that the final two miles are on a tread characterized by intermittent snow of no more than four inches. The last mile or so goes by quite fast as I cruise on. I now notice the road is above the trail to the left. I wonder if I had passed the pickup area. I reluctantly maintain the pace and continue north along the trail. I enter a wooded area, see a picnic table and check my watch. It is 4:30 PM. I hear a car door close. I look across the picnic area, and wave to Rinaldo and Billy. I guess this is the right place! They step out of the car to view the area.

4:30 PM: Pioneer Mail Picnic Area, El 5260, Mi 53. 0 - 1.0

We arrive simultaneously. We're all impressed with ourselves. They actually were only able to rest from their walk twenty minutes before driving north to pick me up. I ask myself if permitting myself to walk another six miles, to be picked up by them after they walked back by road was a selfish act on my part. If so, then is walking the PCT a selfish act? It is! Much to ponder! But I feel lucky, grateful, but a little guilty. I try to convince myself it's OK to feel this way. It seems no one is self-sufficient enough to walk the PCT without support from others. Perhaps I'll have the opportunity to return such favors.

Back at Mount Laguna Resort Hotel, El 5940, Mi 42.9 - 1.0

That evening before nightfall, we select a couple of frozen turkey dinners, some snacks, coffee cake and orange juice for morning. We micro-waved the turkey while we watch the San Diego news on their Channel 8. We discover that it could very well snow for days and wipe out the trail for a long time.

Hannah is complaining about her knee. It hurts when she walks and bends it. She says she's feeling fine, despite her injury, so long as she doesn't move the leg. We spend a pleasant evening together enjoying the moment. We put the turkey in the microwave and settle down for a comforting meal with some White Zinfandel.

April 7, Wednesday Morning: Mt. Laguna Lodge

It is dismal outside. There is no sun to be seen this morning. It apparently snowed all night. There is a pile of four or more inches on top of everything that was here the day before.

I make contact with Van. We discuss the uncertainty with the weather. He says a storm is expected to hit the interior San Diego County area by nightfall, with a good chance of continuing through the LA area through the day. As it is a fun place to be for a while, and there remains a chance, a slight one at that, of a northbound hike, and since he has the time, he says he'll be glad to join us. He tells me he will be coming up alone, expecting to show up anywhere from three to seven.

A car appears marked with "Rescue Squad" followed by Sheriff and Highway Patrol cars. Soon comes a snow plow and Border Patrol Bronco. The fellow with the Rescue Squad tells the story of a rescue of a back packer at Boulder Oaks. A lady had her tent blown away and was experiencing early signs of hypothermia. Another woman was expected to walk up from Boulder Oaks with reservations for the night.

The good people that run the general store also run the hotel. They not only provide services for tourists, but also provide a social center for people that reside in and around this small community. The store is a classical general store. They have a good sampling of common brands of canned, frozen and refrigerated food and drink, including wine and beer. They also have much of the common household type of hardware and outdoor accessories needed for the 200 people residing in the immediate area, and those doing car camping and weekend cabin stayers. The only produce they had today was apples in the refrigerator. In addition to the hardware, they have a collection of clothing and art, some vintage, most for sale. The decor of this store comprises of antiques from the thirties, forties and fifties, with a myriad of older things of this period including old sewing machines, snow shoes, coffee urns, tin cans, old coke and milk bottles and advertisements common to the pre-war period.

I had met these people that run the store a week or so ago. We continue the discussion on the matter of the illegals. Someone from the rescue squad joins the conversation. Another resident sticks in his two cents. We discuss the international scene.

I listen to the group discussing the hardship that the situation brings upon to law enforcement and related agencies. The Border Patrol seems strained in their operations, letting some through, but not everyone.

The shopkeeper points out the money drain to the taxpayer and the hazards confronting the north-bound illegals. I had agreed with Van last week that one solution was to activate an army division or two to patrol the area. I think it would work. After all, I served with an infantry division in 1961-62 preparing for encounters in Viet Nam, the 32nd Infantry Division. It had 300% casualties during the second world war. Our guys alone with mobile tents, vehicles, motor pool and weaponry could readily secure the whole area, and quite likely not hurt anyone in the process. I also slept on the frontier on the border with Mexico. Yeah! I felt qualified to put in my two cents as well!

The manager comes up with a relatively simple solution. She says, "We should re-install the Brassero program of several years ago...Remember that program?"

"Yeah."

"It worked." She went on to say, "Why do you think it was dropped"?

I could not answer.

She replies readily to my silence, "It was because the owners and unions got together and got the INS to drop the program." She further went on to say, "Support for the change was offered by the Coyotes and other smugglers who profit from the illegal activity."

I tell her, "Now I understand some of the causes and what can be done about it."

She thrusts her head back, exhorts, "This is not an unsolvable problem. As Americans, this isn't too difficult for us to solve."

I was stunned with the simplicity of the cure.   "Maybe there's something that can be done about it." I said, "Maybe I'll write some something up. If so, I'll send a copy to you."

We have no tire chains for the Saab. We are snowed in. The whole day goes by quickly as we thoroughly enjoy ourselves. Hannah rests in the room all day, invigorated and sedated by the hike yesterday, but nevertheless tired while nursing her knee. I listened a lot to people and take in the whole scene. I visit the post office again and review the PCT registry of backpackers. We watch the weather on Channel 8. Curiously, the Channel 8 news trucks appear right at the store.

The shopkeeper suggests I present myself to the producer for coverage as a "snowed in backpacker." Although I admitted to myself that I would enjoy the attention, I am too embarrassed to do such. Instead, I intently watch their production on TV describing the outdoor scene here at Mt. Laguna.

It snows all day without let up. Billy and Rinaldo invite us to their cabin where they are preparing a barbecue for steaks. Being nice to ourselves, we go to the store, looking for something to purchase and share with our friends. The store has a small case of frozen foods - everything non-Kosher with too much fat and cholesterol. However we look in the corners and find a couple of rib steaks, at least a kosher kind of cut. We select one we could split. We bought some beans, canned fruit, beer and chips. Billy put the steaks on the barbecue. Just as we polish off our steaks, Van arrives in our Grand Cherokee! As it was again after hours for the store and motel, I help to check Van in. The same lady offers a room next door to ours. She turns on the light to the store and he selects the other steak. He checks in. I put the steak on the barbecue. I introduce him to Billy and Rinaldo and we all have a pleasant evening not knowing what the weather has in store for us tomorrow. We're all tired and we all turn in early.

April 8, Thursday Morning: Mt. Laguna Lodge; A Break in the weather and a plan. El 5980, Mi 42.9+0.4 - 0.0

I awake with the first sign of natural light. While in bed I reflect in the morning twilight what may be in store for us today. As it gets lighter, I look out the window. The sky is clear. There is no wind. Morale takes a skyward leap. Soon, I await the weather forecast on Channel 8. Although high winds are expected, up to sixty knots at times throughout the area, we seem to be in store for at least two or three dry days in the area.

As of last night, both Rinaldo and Billy as well as myself had ruled out a hike. Too much snow and not enough time. They seem to have settled on spending the next two days at Julian where they would be picked up by friends.

Van offers the option to drop Billy, Rinaldo and I off at Scissors Junction at the southern flank of the San Felipe Hills. I check with Hannah and the young men. It's a go! Van and the dynamic duo will follow us to Julian where Hannah will refuel. Hannah will continue west to go home. Van will drive the Cherokee eastbound with Ron, Billy and I in it, downhill to Scissors Junction.

We quickly pack and hop into the cars. There is plenty of snow on the way to Julian, a little left at the somewhat lower altitude of the town. I stop at Pioneer Mail Picnic Area to find the grounds completely covered with a fresh and beautiful snowfall. Over four inches fell on top of the already two to four inches in the area. The trail cannot be seen. I figure, I'll do this downhill leg of the trail later.

This time the service station in Julian is open. We fill up Hannah's car. The operator sees our backpacks, He asks what we are doing. We tell him of our plans. He says in a certain tone we should not attempt such a hike in the area as it is too dangerous now with the cold spell and high winds. Undaunted, we check our water supply and thank him for his fuel and advice.

We wave goodbye to Hannah as she pulls out to drive home. Van, Billy, Rinaldo and I drive off to Scissors Junction. Billy and Rinaldo have a total of four litters of water between them. I have two and one half liters of the precious stuff. As we approach Banner, we find that we have left the snow behind us. Van drops us off at Scissors Junction, at the trail head. We put on our packs and wave goodbye to Van as he pulls off to go home. We're on our own.

Chapter 7

Over The San Felipe Hills & On to Warner Springs

Up the San Felipe Hills....A sandy wash...Up at the first
first sign of light....Crossing the gap....Barrel Springs....
Departing Barrel Springs....Confronting a herd of cattle
....Losing the trail....Warner Springs....At Warner Springs
Airport....Back at Green Hornets

April 7, Wednesday, 11:00 AM: Scissors Junction;
Up the San Felipe Hills, Elev 2,200, Mi 78.1 - 0.0

About 1,800 feet below the snow line, it seems as cold as it was above. Despite the clear skies and calm winds, light and variable, Billy, Rinaldo and I are dressed for winter. I am still wearing my nylon coveralls, parka and snow hat. When will it get warm? Rinaldo finds the trail head. We put on our packs, take a deep breath, look at each other, give a thumbs up sign to Van who had just dropped us off. We immediately start up the moderate to steep grade. As Van drives off, tempered by the company of Rinaldo and Billy, I feel that similar feeling in the pit of my stomach. If my feelings could talk, it would be saying, "I, and now my good company, are both on our own."

Billy and I get ready to tackle the San Felipe Hills

The trail immediately starts to climb earnestly and soon we find ourselves on switchbacks climbing up and around Gold Mountain for the next few miles. We all huffing and puffing. The extra five pounds of extra food, water and clothing now puts on an additional 25% load. We are quite aware of our good fortune of doing this climb with a southeasterly exposure in cool weather. Yet, I am sweating. We climb and climb. Our view over our shoulder of the valley below and imposing Granite Mountain beyond is dramatic.

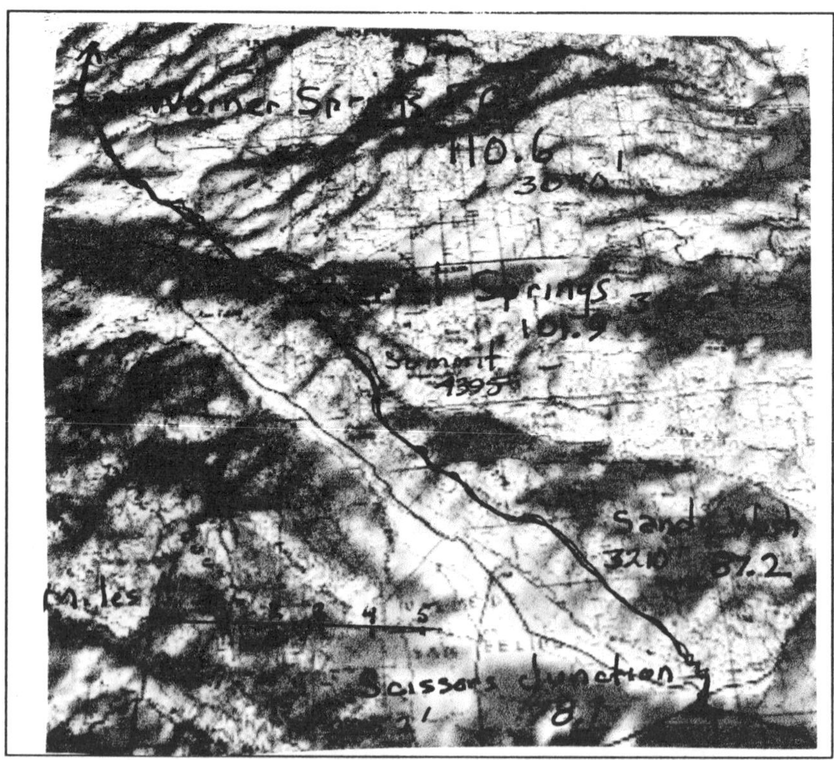

From MAPTECH *Terrain Navigator*

Scissors Junction, over the San Felipe Hills, to Warner Springs
32.5 Miles

We immediately become aware of the change in environment. The peculiar Ocotillo, barrel cactus, prickly pears and the unique low chaparral dominate the landscape. Too soon, after we climb just a bit we find ourselves drinking some of our precious water, This acknowledgment leads to a growing preoccupation with water consumption. We never felt the desire to drink so strong.

The corresponding change in flora with increase in elevation was something to marvel The cactus grows more vibrant. Because of the recent rain, the tiniest of plants are flowering. They are blue, red, white, lavender, purple and yellow. I tried to look them up earlier while we were laying over at Mt. Laguna, but I am at a loss as to identify all but a few. The prickly pair is beginning to issue bright red knobs. White forget me nots appear on some of the recently wet areas. Somewhat higher up, the sumacs were drenched with tiny red odorless cones. Almost all species are showing some sign of flowering. Yet, as before, there is no odor nor obvious insects in this area now.

About three hours into the hike we consider where we may stay. The guidebook indicates only one or two suitable places for the first 13 miles. I can see why. There is no high chaparral to be seen. The trail is narrow, on steep rocky terrain mile after mile up this southern exposed seemingly endless flank of the San Felipe Hills. We are hoping that we will reach a plateau or something within the first few hours. It doesn't happen! The only suitable spot for a good rest or an overnight are in the small, but sharp canyons containing intermittent creeks. All are dry. If it rains, even a little bit, we could get quite wet

3:00 PM:. A Sandy Wash, for the night, El 3210, Mi 87.2 - 0.2

After four hours of climbing and tediously following the meandering trail, we reach a sandy wash that we think is described in the *Guidebook*. We do not know where the next rest area might be. We easily agree to camp here tonight. Not bad after putting on eight miles on such a late start. At the rate we are going, we have a good chance of making it to Barrel Springs by tomorrow for a resupply of water. Because of the recent rains we assume there should be ample water.

The wind begins to pick up as we look for a suitable place for protection in the event of more wind or rain. There isn't any. We compromise. We put our tents under some chaparral, some scrub oak, sage and some fair size juniper. We hope it will not rain; our concern for being washed downhill was compromised by our desire to be protected from winds which are already beginning to blow. We so agreed. We pitch our tents close to one another so as to offer additional windbreak and I guess, to share our fate should it rain hard enough for a flash flood. My immediate task is to secure my *Wenzel* pup tent in the sand while hooking up a fly. I do the best I can with what stakes and rope I have.

We settle down. We show off our cooking gear. Each of us have pride in our individual style. I was impressed with their use of dried tomatoes and Italian style large oval pasta with dried beef in it for additional taste. They were impressed with my tiny stove and how efficient it cooked my usual mix of corn pasta, dehydrated baked beans, and soup bouillon. Rinaldo offered some of his beef jerky. I put it in my concoction. They say it tastes good. But I don't believe em. Anyway, I enjoy the hot wet mix. It just gets colder. I take advantage of whatever light is left in the sky to put everything inside my tent. I had learned to organize the small interior, and went into the evening drill. My pack is placed in the rear right. The soft sweater is laid on top of a pile of stuff including my nylon pants, a fresh shirt, and parka. The towel is nearby for additional comfort of one kind or another. The boots are placed in the corners by the door so as to further protect the tent in the event of winds and to provide access for a quick get-a-way. My first aid kit with an ounce of vodka and sundries are in plastic *Ziplock* to the side, as is my water bottle and tiny AAA flashlight. Candles and a cigarette lighter are on the other side.   My mittens are most handy. I put on a fresh pair of socks as I slip into the sleeping bag. I check my *Timex Expedition* wrist watch. It emits a strong light when the button is pressed, so strong that it serves in a way as a flashlight to light up the interior of the tent with a press of the button. I check the position of my mittens and soon drift into a warm comfortable sleep.

But about eight O' clock I am awoken by winds that sound like an approaching freight train! Not again! The sound would start as if out in the distant, growing louder as it approaches, like at the border. Then comes a swooping sound, the tent shudders. The fly rattles against the top of the tent. The wind soon makes the fly useless.

There is a roar out there that could be heard on top of the slapping of the wind. What's going on out there? Again it is too dark to see much of anything. This state of affairs reminds me of an evening on the banks of Spirit Lake, in northwest Iowa. Several of us GI's that served with the 32nd Infantry Division got together for a reunion in the spring of 1965 to do some fishing. We had just set up our large tent for the five of us just after dusk. As we all were relaxing in the warmth of our sleeping bags we hear what sounds like a freight train coming in our direction. It got closer, closer and as it came upon us. Then the air inside the large tent disappeared. There was no air to breathe. The big tent suddenly collapsed on top of us. The "train" drew away in the same manner as it came. This was my first experience with a tornado.

It now begins to sleet. The gale winds lasts all night. Although basically warm during the earlier part of the night, I began to struggle a bit to maintain a comfortable level of warmth and comfort. The moisture in the air is intense. The wind keeps me awake, not only because of the noise. The hypnotic effect of the sounds momentarily puts me to sleep. But it wears off. Instead it just gets louder and louder. The tent then shudders and shakes with regularity as the wind hits the tent regularly with a speed of probably about 30 or 40 knots and occasionally sometimes up to 60 knots. The faster the approach of the wind as it swirls through the brush, the harder it hits the tent. But occasionally it seems to miss and only shakes the tent. Each time the tent shakes, it sprays a bit of water from the inner walls onto the sleeping bag. After midnight, I was not able to sleep more than a few minutes at a time, producing weird dreams and flashbacks of the experience in Iowa and on the border.

After some sleep, about 2:00 AM one of the blasts wakes me up with a startle. I feel cold and damp. It is pitch black. I come to the conclusion the tent had now collapsed. I note it is raining and sleeting and the wind is blowing hard. The tent and its wet inner walls are upon me and my already dampened sleeping bag.

With the light from my wrist watch, I reach outside, feel the presence of the important guy line extending from the top center of the tent to the ground. It is shaking, but I realize it is secured. This tent is held upright by two poles in front and one in the rear. Even though I am getting wet, this discovery is good news. I reach out, find only one pole, supporting the front. One pole dropped and caused the tent to collapse on top of the sleeping bag. I quickly find the missing pole. With some effort and strain, I am able to secure the pole into position between the bottom corner and the upright slot. The other adjoining pole remains secure in its' proper position. Thus, I find I am able to erect the tent while still lying inside my sleeping bag. What a relief! The sleeping bag is now wet on top because of its' contact with the water collected through condensation on the ceiling of the tent. I take note that I am dry inside.

After all this I have to take a leak! After this relief, I look up and see some stars. This sighting lifts my morale. Upon getting back into the tent I quickly put on dry socks and a warm shirt and pants and curl up inside the bag. I listen to the approaching wind blasts and hope the tent would last til daybreak.   At about 3:00 AM I peer out into the night to see how hard it is raining or sleeting. I see stars. What now sounds like the pitter-patter of rain is but the scrub oak branchlets gently rubbing against the top of the tent actually clearing off some of the accumulated moisture. I realize that by now, that if nothing more happens to the tent I will likely make it without further incident to daybreak. I then fall asleep never to get comfortably warm, only to waken to have to take another leak.

April 8, Thursday, 5:30 AM: At The First Sign of Light, El 3210, Mi 87.2 - 0.0

I peer out and find the sky is clear. No wind. But it is cold. I put on my mittens, readily find my pants, boots, sweater, overalls and parka. It doesn't take long to get dressed and get warm. My tent is frozen. The ground is damp all over.   There are patches of sleet all over the area. I start my little stove and soon make some hot drink. By this time, Billy is up and moving about. Rinaldo prefers to stay in his bedroll longer. Billy left a pan out to collect water in the rain. None was found in it. In the meantime I start to do my chores, including pulling out my bag and putting it on top of a dry scrub oak plant until I could find a place later to put it in the first rays of the morning sun.

Because I am so anxious to keep moving, I limit myself to making some very quick, *Quick Quaker Oats* from a packet. What warm water was is left, I drink. I stuff everything in the pack, damp and wet as it is. I tell Billy and Rinaldo that they will soon catch up with me on the trail as I plan to stop at some place where the sun might provide some comfort and could lay out the bag and tent to dry out

6:30 AM: On Top the spine of the San Felipe Hills: A cache of water, El 3485, Mi 90.9 - 0.0

What a relief to get on the trail. Looking at the tread, a little bit of sleet collects everywhere, becoming thicker as the elevation increases. Hopefully, it will get thick enough to collect enough to drink.

The trail continues to climb moderately as one overlooks the San Felipe Valley and the snow covered Volcan mountain range that parallels the route, three or four miles directly west. I could not identify the actual airplane crash scene, but find thinking about it a distraction from the winding trail that endlessly goes from one canyon to another as the trail widely zigzags in its generally northwesterly direction just below the ridge line. I figure if the trail climbs any more there would be plenty of snow around.

The map indicates the PCT eventually reaches a summit gap of about 4,300 feet where indeed there should be enough snow to eat. But that occurs further up the San Felipe spine, a couple of hours ahead. At the moment I approach a gate, and as I put a sign on the trail with the current time as a marker for Rinaldo and Billy, I look ahead and saw eight large gallons of water, each one connected by a rope. On each bottle, there is an identification with people connected with the PCTA.

There is a label attached indicating to take as much as you need. I have but half a liter in reserve which I now readily polish off in a minute. I fill up my two liter bottles and wait for Billy and Rinaldo who I hear huffing and puffing before I see them. We celebrate our good fortune.

Now, a lot of the pressure is off. I move on to let them catch up and pass through later on. They can move a lot faster on climbs. Because of my relatively light load, I move faster on level or downward tread. The trail continues up. They soon pass.

Dramatically the trail levels off. Up ahead, Billy stops and points to his immediate left. A cave! There, just a few feet from the trail, to the left, is an inviting sandy flat area inside a cave providing protection from wind, rain and storm, or even too much heat, enough room for two or three persons to sit, and for an individual to comfortably sleep without tent. If ever I return on this area, this is where I will attempt a night layover. Such a layover would not only be more comfortable, but save a hell of a lot of time in setting up a site, let alone the freedom of worrying about the tent being blown away.

About 12:30 P.M. Crossing the Gap, El 4395, Mi 96.3 - 0.0

Without warning we suddenly pass through a gap with a dramatic and inviting change in temperature, flora and view. Now, there is a northeastern view. Below is the relatively lush Montezuma valley where Montezuma Road continues on to Borrego Springs and to Borrego Valley. To the immediate north lies Warner Springs. Beyond lies the Santa Rosa Mountains with snow above 5,000 feet. Our trail, dusted with snow, can be seen winding down into now-moist Hoover Canyon to drop us off at Barrel Springs at the road a few miles downhill to our left.

The trail continues generally northwesterly then crosses a gap to follow the north exposure where all flora changes dramatically. The chaparral returns to its richest forms. The chaparral is so rich that the area looks tropical. Even the very large and healthy Manzanita looks unusually green and thick. There are thick groves of tall, healthy and vibrant chamise, the foliage gleaming in rich green hues and is very soft to the touch. Everything is flourishing now on this moist ridge. The entire hill to left of the trail still has a thin layer of wet snow on it, thinning out as we descend. Various species of fern and occasional broad leaf plants add to the tropical effect. The wild flowers add color. The short grass is unusually green. Low lying flowering plants emerge from the snow dust making their early spring statement as bits of water emerge from everywhere.

I find my gait slowing down as I try to prolong the experience of seeing such natural beauty in the height of season. Tiny flowers are everywhere. Everything is coming alive. I see the first bug on the trail, a large black beetle.

3:30 PM: Barrel Springs, El 3475, Mi 101.9 - 0.0 .

Approaching Barrel Springs, the trail winds down towards a stream. The tread then suddenly becomes covered with a carpet of oak leaves. The PCT winds down into a very moist, rich, and pretty oak grove. It looks like a painting. Very Californian! The terrain eventually flattens. There are gates. The huge oaks create a darkness where little else flourishes. Soon a fence and gate appear. Then appears an acre or so of trampled grass and recent cow dung. Up ahead is Barrel Springs. A clean trough with clean piped water is flowing into it. The ensuing water is absorbed by the turf. The trail and the trough are guarded by a couple of cows and calves. They wait and

Approaching Barrel Springs

watch me as I try to be as quiet and unobtrusive as possible. I maintain a steady gait leading down the trail. They seem to sense I am thirsty. Nevertheless they stand firmly in the trail. Eventually one snorts. The other cow turns away and they go off to watch me at a distance as if to confirm another human being wishes to share their turf and water hole. Their behavior clearly shows propriety of turf. It's theirs, but it is also for my use. They need it more than I. This is their water supply. I saw the fence. Fortunately, I notice there is flowing water just up the trail and maybe they'll head that way, but I do not recall if the gate will block their way. Dung is everywhere but there is no odor. I must be adapting!

I try my cellular phone again. No luck. I can't contact Van, GHA, nor the Warner Springs Airport. I again realize that what happens cannot be predicted. This aspect of uncertainty is turning this hike into an adventure. As long as the weather continues to cooperate I will be happy. I am finding out along the trail it does not take really much to make one happy. A pleasant day is enough.

Eventually Rinaldo and Billy Arrive. Before we set up camp we set down together and enjoy the first comfort of outdoor warmth on this leg. A great feeling! The warmth lasts only an hour or so before the sun drops and the persistent damp coldness sets back in. By this time, however, the tents are nicely set up. No need for a fly. I use the fly as a base below the tent. After a pleasant meal, a repeat of the same, we all retire to what we hope will be an uneventful night. I plan to get up somewhat later than yesterday and have some time to dry my bag and tent in the sun before moving on to Warner Springs.

Before retiring we compare notes on how we plan to navigating the leg to Warner Springs. Our notes do not jive. The trail had been modified. I tell them I will put marks along the trail, with arrows and the time of day.

April 10, 9:30 AM: Departing Barrel Springs El 3475, Mi 101.9 - 0.0

I see frost everywhere. It was probably colder than last night. The elevation is about the same. However there was no rain and no winds.

We concur we slept better than the night before. We were cold at night, but not as anxious about it as we have learned how to prevent being cold. Ron and Billy had the same problem, even with a fly overhead. There is not enough ventilation inside the tents to keep the condensation down to tolerable limits. If I am to use this tent, I have to think of a solution as it will re-occur in cold and moist areas.

I wave goodbye looking forward to having them join me up ahead. We synchronize our watches. I am again on my way, and on my own.

The first part of this engaging trail traverses light chaparral with mild ups and downs with very little overall change in elevation. There is always a pleasant view nearby. Soon the PCT winds over a series of valley-like expansive long dried meadows separated by low ridges, each covered with low chaparral and grass. This is quintessentially southern California!

10:30 AM: Confronting a Herd of Cattle, El 3280, Mi 103 - 0.0

As I descend over one of these hills into the next valley, I notice the wide expanse of a meadow ahead. This is one of those large flat meadow valleys extending about three miles long, and where I am, about 500 yards wide. I see before me, along the trail, midway across, several groups of cattle, perhaps six or seven apiece huddling together, about fifty yards apart, comfortably grazing on their turf, a beautiful sight. However, two of these groups were right smack on the trail in front of me. I can not differentiate whether they are bulls, steers or cows. It is too much to expect them to give way without a fuss. Now at 100 yards, I determine they are probably steers with no calves or cows around. For reasons I will ponder later, I decide I will not give ground nor change my direction, nor give them any sign other than quiet confidence so they may have no fear of combat. After all, maybe they'll behave as if I will feed them. Yes, the turf is theirs, more than mine, but I mean no harm at all and hopefully they will pick up such a signal. I hope to pass by in an uneventful manner. Thoughts quickly occur of my possible fate. I envision the newspaper article, "Backpacker Mauled Along the Pacific Crest Trail: in Critical Condition!"

I have no more time to think about such morbid thoughts, because at 80 yards the beasts all turn and face me directly, all twenty of them! They now form a single herd right in my path. I realize I can't run without first jerking off my pack which would startle them, the last thing I want to do. The only time I've ever seen a person close to such animals were pictures of bull fights. I've avoided going to bull fights so as to avoid the melee and subsequent bloody end. My pace continues unrelentingly at 2 ½ miles per hour. We were now 70 yards apart. They continue to slowly move in a clustering attitude right smack on the trail ahead. The distance now is half a football field, about 50 yards. They keep facing me with erect head, ears up and wide gleaming eyes. I can see their eyeballs as I get even closer. I hear their breathing! They do not seem excited, but kind of transfixed on what I am doing and perhaps what I might do next. This state of affairs continues. I am now 20 yards away from the lead steer. He just happens to be the largest!

Then, suddenly, this huge large steer, a black and white beautiful beast, pivots around thirty degrees. He postures himself head on to my intended direction. He then turns a bit, adjusts his posture as I come closer, always head on. He lunges into the air, emits a heavy snort. He puts his weight on his rear feet, stomps down a couple of times on his front feet. I feel the tremor of the ground! He hesitates. He waits for my reaction.

Seeing no reaction on my part other than the maintenance of the same gait and posture, he snorts again in a final protest and backs away. The others follow. I am so scared I do not turn around to look back! I am just listening. As I lose hearing them, I later see they are moving slowly backwards, turn around and stroll lazily downhill. They separate themselves somewhat, then slowly and casually regroup. They continue grazing as if nothing happened!

11:30 AM: I Lose The Trail Again; El. 3400, ca. Mi 104.0 - 0.0

As I get to one more of these rolling meadows the characteristic 4 x4 posts that typically have the PCT marking can be seen one after the other. But the coloring of them are somewhat different and they are without signature. Various trails, some with more footprints lead directly northward to Warner Springs, to a road that now appears visible just 400 years to the north. The map shows this road going directly to Warner Springs. The marker ahead with a unique color seems to lead directly west to Lake Henshaw, off ahead by about four miles, definitely in the wrong direction. The guidebook says the trail is obscured in this area and advises to go by compass headings. I take a bearing. I look at my maps and decide to follow the trail to the road and wait for Billy and Rinaldo to distantly appear, at which time I figure they will see my sign on the trail and head for me. So I head for the road and wait for them to appear on the close horizon.

Toward Warner Springs
By Hilton Osborne, PCTer

Meanwhile I wave at cars, hoping that one will stop and I could determine, more for sure, indeed which way, and how far it would be to walk to Warner Springs. Several cars go by. The people simply wave back.

Way out there at the junction where I had turned off the main trail, I see Billy and Rinaldo. still about 400 yards to the south. They cannot hear me. Obviously they noted the arrows and the time I etched on the trail. They seem to be discussing the matter. We finally make contact. I wave my red Poncho to get their attention. Rinaldo puts both hands in the air as if saying, "What are you doing there?" I can see that Billy is putting both hands straight up in the air, an aviation sign to come directly to me. So, I swallow my pride, cross under the barbed wire fence, leave the security of the road, and head across the field to intercept their course. We concur to continue on with what to them seems like the PCT. The trail climbs, leaves the open exposed fields and goes into a somewhat more moist area of tall chaparral. This trail looks more like the PCT than others. We see the PCT trail marker. Now we all agree we are indeed on the right trail. Soon, the trail becomes enclosed by even larger brush.

Suddenly, before me are two thin, athletic looking young ladies, dressed in very clean, bright white and red pants appearing with matching bright red bandanas over their long blond hair. They briskly approach me southbound, saying "Hi, Hal!"

"Do we know one another?"

"They told us your name; you're doing the trail aren't you?" Some polite words take place.

One says, "You're not far away now." They continue southward, and I, northbound to catch up with Rinaldo and Billy. The trail joins alongside a fast moving stream flowing through a pleasant area called Canada Verde. The stream heads directly for the Warner Springs trail head. This part of the trail, in contrast to the dry plateau, is unusually pretty, damp, cool, and heavily forested with a variety of deciduous trees and high shrubs creating an oasis of hospitality full of possible camping sites all over the place. I visualize this area must be cool even in the warmest of days. Soon the stream widens and forms a wash. I soon see a bus yard and the highway leading to Warner Springs. We rest momentarily. The two young ladies appear heading for their car. They say they look forward to getting a massage at the resort. Ah yes, a massage.

1:00 PM: Trail Head near Warner Springs, El 3040, Mi 110.6 - 0.0

At this point, no one knows what will happen an hour or so from now. Will we party? Will one of us get stuck? Will I go on? We head east towards the center of Warner Springs, hoping to find a phone where we can communicate with our potential picker-uppers. It is now comfortably warm. A mile or so up the road we get to the center of the community where lies a store and gas station next to the post office and a posh golf club facility.

We head for the store and purchase cold drinks. We hear the weather is supposed to deteriorate by tomorrow. We head for the phones. They make contact. Billy and Rinaldo expect a pickup from friends in two and one half hours. They wait to hear of my fate before heading to the restaurant. I call up Green Hornets. Tom is willing to fly down, but there would be no one else to dispatch on this good flying day. Nathan, one of our flight instructors, offers to pick me up in an hour and a half with a student who is being checked out in the Cessna 172RG Cutlass. He offers to pick me up at the Warner Springs Airport in an hour and a half. I point out that this airport is a glider field and it is important to study the directions that I had left with their dispatcher before attempting to come in. I suggest that Tom call the field and tell them that general permission was granted by the management of the field last week for a pick-up and possible activity with the gliders or with the resort.

Warner Springs Airport, El 2930, 110.6+1.0 - 0.0

I walk the last two miles by road to the airport where I had been with Hannah a few days earlier. This place is the epitome of fun flying. One after another they land and become towed off. I am standing right next to the field. Apparently, because of the niceness of day, there had been a lot of pressure to fly. The gliders are all being hooked up twenty yards away. There are several "show-offs" doing aerobatics in gliders, stalls, wing overs, loops, and hammer heads, all very slow and gracefully done. The pilot of one craft lands right in front of me, just where it was towed off for takeoff. I congratulate the pilot for doing such a graceful and wonderful job at what he knew well. It turns out that Jim is an employed instructor at the field. He offers to take me up and do some aerobatics. I turn down the offer, saying appreciatively, "When I am here next time, I'll want to go up with you, but not necessarily to do aerobatics the first time up." I had done stuff in our aerobatic C-150 and was familiar with spins and loops. I know from experience, it is good to have a good first experience while doing a transition to another type of aircraft. Like a short hike, it leaves you to want to do more. We immediately started talking about the ins and outs of glider flying as contrasted to powered craft. We talk about the Cherokee crash. I let him know that I am a volunteer FAA Safety Counselor and had been conducting a study now for over three years on accidents with single engine aircraft in Southern California. I tell him "I am particularly interested in this one." I had talked to Brad, who offered his opinion on the matter last week. Jim, coincidentally, had been monitoring weather conditions during the flight with accurate ground equipment. At the time he was measuring wind speed, downdrafts, time, temperature, etc on their route. He studied the data. He offers his opinion. Jim says he had been flying 1,500 above ground level, got caught in a 3.000 foot per minute swirling downdraft that are common in that area. He should know, I figure, he flies gliders. We draw the crash site on the ground thinking it through together when our Cessna appears in the pattern. He gives me his card. I hope to fly dual some day with this experienced and interesting glider instructor.

Soon, Nathan waves to me as he arrives with his student, David in the Cutlass. I see him negotiating traffic well and makes a perfect landing before the crowd. However, he comes too close to the glider pull out area and is directed by loud speaker to stop where he is and turn around. He stops, but in turning around he calls attention to himself while he blasts parked gliders on the sandy field. I feel embarrassed by this display. Jim drives me in his little shuttle, pack and all, to the airplane. I ask Nathan and Jim if there is time to go for a glider ride. They are in a hurry to get back. Understandably, they are concentrating on the job they are doing and do not want to be distracted by all the wonderful activity on the field. I explain to Jim we'll make sure he doesn't start the plane until he is parallel on the asphalt runway, something very unnatural for a pilot to do at a strange field.

We pull around, but we start the plane in a hurry in a position that is not exactly parallel to the field and in so doing blasts a couple more precious gliders tied down. He then taxies down the runway to run-up. He passes the designated run-up area where he begins the pre-flight in-cockpit procedures. As we take off, Nathan radios the unicom dispatcher thanking her for her patience. No harm done. Polite words are exchanged.

I look at the terrain covered on the ground in the last few days as I rested deep into the seat. It is truly awesome to look down at the route one covered walking. But at the same time it is disappointing as it occurs so quickly flying at one-hundred miles per hour. The trail just whizzes by. Too many memories to recover in a few minutes.

The flight back is a good uneventful flight through very complex airspace. Considering this is David's first chance to fly a Cutlass, both he and Nathan do a splendid job flying as I remain transfixed on the terrain below.

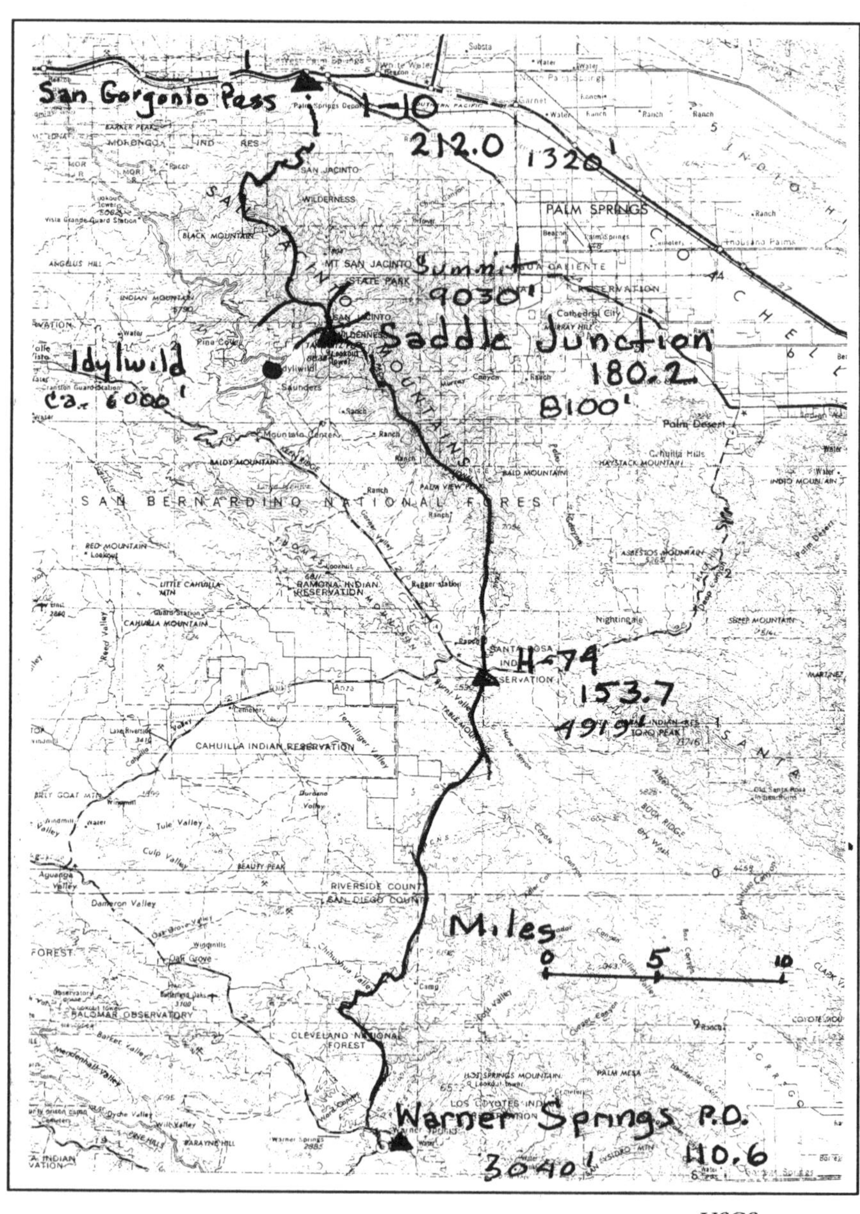

USGS

Section B: Warner Springs to San Gorgonio Pass (1-10)
101.4 Miles

SECTION B
WARNER SPRINGS TO SAN GORGONIO PASS

Prologue

This one hundred mile section covers a wide variety of climates and flora. Starting at H-79, (Mi 112.4, El 2930 feet), near Warner Springs at the second crossing of Highway 74, the rail first meanders through a semi-tropical riperian deciduous forest along Agua Caliente Creek for three and a half miles. Upon crossing the creek, the trail climbs briefly up the western slope through mixed chaparral and streambed plants. Too soon, drier climes of chaparral are reached and traversed for several miles until some relief occurs upon reaching 4000' where some widely scattered pinyon pines provide some cover. Chihuahua Valley Road is reached at Mi 128.3 where an option occurs for filling up on water from a tank not far off trail. Then a brief climb up to the shoulder of Combs Peak for a rest with views under the shade of a solitary Coulter and Jeffrey pine tree. This high point of 5595' is briefly followed by an easy jaunt through a transitional forest that descends into drier chaparral. The trail reaches intermittent Tule Creek near a reliable spring and then to a low point of 3350' at Nance Canyon.

After passing through the transition forests of The Santa Rosa Mountains, the trail approaches the highway summit of the Palms to Pines Highway 74 at Mi. 153.7, El 4919' where an option arises for a mile detour west to the Paradise Restaurant. In any event the trail then pursues a gradual climb, along the pretty intermittent Penrod Canyon Creek. An altitude of 7,000 feet is obtained in about twelve miles whereupon the trail stays this high for the next 30 miles including a summit of 9,030 feet, before dropping dramatically down to xeric San Gorgonio Pass at I-10 at 1195, mi. 210.3.

Most trekkers tend to visit Kamp Anza, 5.8 miles off the trail, about three miles north of Nance Canyon. Another popular rest and

and re-supply point is Idylwild, reached either by hitching along Highway 94 or later taking the Devils Slide Trail down to Humber Park, 2.2 miles from Saddle Junction (Mi 180.2). Once at Humber Park, it is another two or three miles to the center of town. Another option to Idylwild is to trek 4.3 miles down the Marion Ridge Trail to Highway 243, caught just after Strawberry Junction Trail Camp, at mile marker 182.7. In practice, the choice of how and where to re-supply and rest depends somewhat on day to day weather conditions, quite unpredictable through late spring.

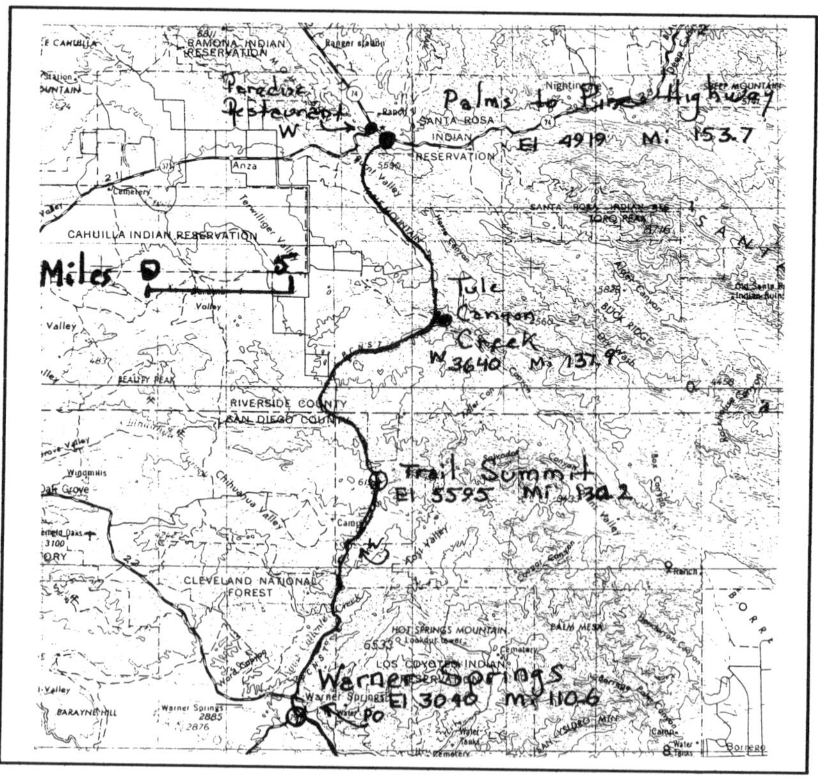

USGS

Warner Springs to Palms to Pine Highway 74

Chapter 8

Warner Springs & Over the Santa Rosa Mountains

....A Campsite near Warner Springs...At the trail head at Agua
Caliente Creek....Confrontation with a rattler....Some
precious water....Overnight on the shoulder of Combs Peak..
Water everywhere, but nothing to drink...An unlikely source of
water at Tule Springs and meeting Scott Williamson....
Nance Canyon....Beating the fog....An evening over Terwilliger
Valley...The Palms to Pine Highway

April 18, Sunday

Van offers a ride to Warner Springs where we camp out for the
evening. But first we stop at the airport and watch gliders pulled off into
the air and visit the Warner Springs Ranch to see the hot springs.
3:15 PM. A Campsite; On the PCT near Highway 79, Near the Fire
Station, El 3040, Mi 110.6 - 0.1

After driving about looking for a suitable campground and finding
none open, I tell Van, "I know of a suitable place, but don't think we
should build a fire there."
"I'll be careful."
"Use a stove. Use mine."
"Don't worry about it!"
"There's a fire station just a couple hundred yards away."
Van is one of those kind of outdoor people that gotta have a large fire.
I guess for the atmosphere. My fires are low; the heat they give is just
for the small pot I use. Upon arriving at the site, Van is quite pleased,
but I am self conscious about camping in sight and so close to a fire
station! I complain. No good. I worry and recall his bon fire at Cibbits
Flat!

After several short hauls from the car, about 100 yards away, across a damp stream, but wet enough to cool down a couple of beers, he discovers his air mattress collapses. He says, "I know what to do." He heads out to the car. About fifteen minutes later, he is seen laboring up with a huge air mattress, probably six by eight feet and about a foot thick. It was so big that if it were filled with helium, he'd probably be floating away! He crams it into the tent. "It fits perfectly! What comfort!"

My stingy foam conventional backpacking mattress just barely works. However, I picked a good soft spot potted with a thick layer of oak leaves.

Next, after moving in his furniture, he brings out his military rations and pulls out an old propane liquid stove that looks like it might have worked during the great depression. "Please, just keep the stove out of sight." Hoping to discourage him, I remind him, "The fire station is right there through the trees."

"Don't worry about it."

It turns out there is a leaky valve. He pulls out a match. As he ignites it, the fluid already under pressure, now with heat causes it to explode with a roar. The sky practically lights up as flames spread all around the stove. He alertly pours anything he has that's wet on it. That accounted for our beer supply. He adjusts the stove. We do use it to heat up our dinners. Van now prepares one of his military emergency rations, stew. I have one. Then comes Italian spaghetti and meat balls. They're OK. We settle down, grateful that we did not alert any firemen.

April 19, Monday, 6:30 AM: The trail head, Agua Caliente Creek, El 2930, Mi 112.4 - 0.0

Soon we are both packed and ready to go. We drive out to the northern PCT trail head on Highway 79 at a small bridge. Van drops me off as I have a last minute snack. We agree that I will call him from the Paradise Restaurant, a mile west of the trail head at the end junction of highway 173. I will call him when I arrive and perhaps he can come and pick me up. What is important is that it is a restaurant. It has food and water and a telephone...I hope. The availability of such facilities, so far, has been quite unpredictable.

We wish one another farewell and we soon are traveling in our different ways. I check my watch; it's now 7:00 AM. I am in long sleeve shirt, sweat shirt, parka, snow hat, mittens, but not cold enough for nylon pants covers. By 7:30 or so I arrive at the campground, a wonderful place for packing with horses. There is a shed there. I assume that it is for private use by the Warner Ranch Corporation, with access available for PCTers. I take off the parka and mittens, stretch out momentarily on one of the clean tables. The trail tread for the most part is level winding along a well moving stream burbling with a pleasant sound. The foliage is largely scrub oak, ceanothus, manzanita, sumac, sages and other common ones I can't name at the moment. As the path meanders back and forth over the stream, there is a feeling of security associated with being outdoors. My 2½ liters of water is untouched. There seems no need to collect water. The trail shortly begins to climb and switchback up the left, westward side exposed to the early sun. The temperature rises quickly. The nearby flora begins to show signs of relative drought or dryness as one leaves the canyon bottom. Soon, I have all my outer clothing inside the pack except for long pants which I wear because of the low reaches of the shrubbery, narrow trail and fear of being struck by ticks. My cotton T shirt soon becomes moist with sweat ascending the western wall. Soon, I find myself again in a dry area with little shade, accomplished at a cost of a good amount of water. It is still early in the day!

About 9:30 AM: A Confrontation with a Rattler

After passing Lost Valley Road, the trail meanders up more exposed territory as it follows the contours. At about the 4,000 foot level as I am pondering matters of water and the next fill up point, I suddenly see a fair size snake, semi curled six feet ahead of me. It seems we notice one another at the same time. This reptile of several feet in length turns his head towards me and freezes. I do the same. This heightened state of arousal lasts a long five seconds. It slithers southward and upwards and interestingly enough, backwards into a low cluster of scrub oaks

rattlesnake

and becomes well camouflaged. However the rattling sound reveals it is only one to four feet off the trail. It now begins to rattle up a storm. I am aware of my snake bite suction cups, tourniquet and incisor inside my first aid kit. The only sound I hear is the increased sound of the large rattle at the monsters' far end. I figure he is in a protective mode and could immediately strike if threatened. I tightened up my pack and made a twenty yard dash for it up the trail attaining some height as expected from a running broad jump in the vicinity of the sound. I catch my breath, sigh with relief, get my composure and trek on wondering what else will happen today.

4:00 PM: Chihuahua Road, El 5050, Mi 128.3 - 0.1

Water is nowhere to be found in its' natural form. As I still have a liter and a half of water, I elected to not try the water trough downhill on the riding trail at the dirt road several miles back. Perhaps I should have given it a try, tiring as it would have been to come back up hill to the rejoin the PCT. To go such distance for only a quart of water, unfortunately, has not been in my repertoire of outdoor activity. Eventually, a non-dramatic saddle is reached at El 4945.

Passing through gaps or passes is often fascinating. The scenery can change dramatically. At this gap, the increase in altitude does not seem to result in any cooling. No payoff, just hard work. There are signs of reaching the lower reaches of the montane forest as there are some scattered pine needles on the trail in the protected areas and a hint of moisture appearing on the north side of hill along intermittent streams. When I see a pine, after a long absence, I'll smell a bark and chew on a pine needle and look for pine cones. But here, there aren't any. Also no sign of nearby water. It must have rained or snowed in this area last week on top of a few inches of already accumulated snow. But there is but little sign of recent precipitation. Because it is so dry, and no positive sign of recent rain, there are but a few budding flowers and only some grass in really dark corners of ravines.

I reach a dirt road, Chihuahua Valley Road, where I come to the conclusion that I really need water, not just for now, but for tonight and tomorrow morning, let alone the rest of the trip. I see the water tank described in the guidebook up the road quite a bit. Not changing direction from the trail, I habitually find myself continuing up the trail to my destination for the evening, the east shoulder of Combs peak, El 5,595 feet.

I can't believe what I see! Before me is an almost full gallon of water sitting under the shade of a sagebrush just to the right of the trail. The container has no notes on it. I take a liter. I want to leave a note, but my pen had run out of ink. I could have easily taken the whole thing, but I limit my greed to the liter. I put in a couple of pills and continue up to the shoulder of Combs Peak.

Up ahead I see a small cluster of pines that surround a tiny plateau marking the trail summit with a broad overlook from the northwest clockwise to the southwest covering a good amount of California Real Estate I have never seen before. Pleased with myself, the site, the view and the time of day, and my luck with water, I take off the pack for a while and take in the sights before dusk.

To the north are familiar sites. Dominating the view is Mt. San Jacinto, 10,800 with no sign of snow. Mt. San Gorgonio, further north and higher by almost a thousand feet, protrudes with a white dome of snow. The trail will only come close to both summits. That's OK with me, I've already been on top of both. Just northwest is Terwilliger Valley lying about 1,500 feet below me from this altitude of about 4,000 feet. Lights from Anza are beginning to appear with dusk. The valley from this vantage point appears studded with widely scattered lights, a semi-desert, but now a growing rural area.

To the immediate east are the imposing Santa Rosa Mountains. They form the southern flank of the San Jacinto Mountains at a height of just over 8,000 feet, certainly high enough to extend the mountain divide south to block moisture to the eastern deserts of Coachela Valley and the Salton Sea. To the southeast lies much of Anza Borrego Desert State Park.

From this vantage point I am aware of the rough and sharp escarpments of the terrain. At higher elevations lay the montane forest. The lower elevations host rich chaparral. Here, in between, is a general transition characteristic of this leg of the PCT. Coulter Pines appear in protected places above 4,000 feet, but in small clumps and widely scattered. Here, at 5,500 feet on the northeastern slope of Combs Mountain, I look up and see rich conifers. In this area the Coulter pine seems to be the most common conifer.

5:30 PM: On the Shoulder of Combs Peak, El 5595, Mi 130.2 - 0.0

I find a fairly nice spot, sandy, protected by scrub oak, manzanita and ceanothus and two large coulter pine logs for sitting and sorting out stuff. I look at my watch. I've put on about ten and a half hours on the trail today and 17.8 miles behind me today. I figure that leaves me with an overnight to reach the Palms to Pines Highway for a late afternoon meal at the Paradise Restaurant if I so wish. The wind kicks up. I lay the fly below the tent, secure the corners of the tent with gear. I note that I am not really hungry, just thirsty. I settle on liquids. I find some tea to help overcome the taste of treated water. I take care to leave a pint for tomorrow morning. As on all previous nights, the winds cause a lot of noise to this tent, keeping me from what otherwise would be a pleasant and uneventful night. The 200 degree view from the campsite is dramatic at dusk. Soon the stars stud the view above. I leave the tent door partly open to enjoy the view and avert internal moisture. It works.

April 20, Tuesday, 6:00 A.M. On the Shoulder of Combs Peak: Water, water everywhere, nothing to drink!

I had a fair sleep. To my surprise I feel alert and refreshed. I put a band-aid on toes and heels. I examine my right boot and find a fault, a protrusion, in the boot in the region above my blistered toe. I examine the boot in the region where my heal is complaining and find that my arch supporter has a course lip just under my sore heal.

The tread meanders downhill on the northern flank of Combs Peak which is a transitional area between a moist montane forest and lower chaparral. The peak rises about 600 feet above and to the southwest. It is solidly pine forested. It is moist above me and dry below. This must be the divide! Occasionally I dig for water, but find none.

Unlike last week when all this was snow covered, there is no snow in sight. None on this mountain. None around. Snow remains on top of Mt. San Gorgonio, protruding far north across Banning Pass. The San Jacinto Mountains, from what I see of them, seem free of snow. I do wonder what lies on their northern exposures at 8,000 feet.

I continue being preoccupied with my water reserves. I soon ration my water to sips, hoping I may find water soon. I determine from the map that the trail descends and finally crosses an intermittent stream in about 2.4 miles at an elevation of 4,710 feet. Because of the moisture along the trail, I am thinking that this intermittent stream has water in it. It feeds intermittent Tule Creek which is supposed to have a year-long spring. I will cross it several miles up trail.

I think I hear water running. Yes, it sound like a mild steady low roar. As the trail descends, I stop momentarily at times to look down and see if there is water in the canyon. I cannot see the stream bed. There is no access down the steep chaparral-covered wall to the water carved canyon below. Continuing down the trail, the bubbling sound contributes to my thirst. The trail descends rapidly. I hurry along to get closer to the stream. The map indicates I am now but a few yards from the canyon bottom. The sound of running water disappears. I take a few steps back. I now can hear it!   Soon enough the trail then dramatically enters the confines of the canyon bottom, at an elevation of 4,710 with only a dry stream bed and no sound nor sign of water. No dampness is found below the surface either. Someone must have tapped the stream for water. I don't see any pipes. Perhaps I was imagining things. At any rate, I feel disappointment when I realize I have only one ounce of water left. I am parched and thirsty. The damper forest was far behind me. I am so parched that my tongue seemed to get stuck on the roof of my mouth.

My map tells me I will cross Tule creek, an intermittent stream in about five miles. At my rate, reviewing the descending trail, I determine it is in a deep canyon. I can be there in two hours. If there is no water there, I will head for Tule Springs further downstream and hope the well is not dry.

11:00 AM: Tule Creek, El 3590, Mi 137.9

Once at Tule Creek, I see a gently running stream of about one foot wide and three inches deep. Wow, what a river! No need to put on the extra milage to the spring tank umpteen yards downstream. I fill up all bottles with that precious stuff, but take care not to drink it until thirty minutes after treatment, then followed by a few minutes of bleaching through a second pill. I bask in this mini-oasis and ponder how many hours or days will pass before this trickle sinks into the ground.

Suddenly a solo back packer appears. His gait is rapid; he disrobes his pack and fills his bottles. He sees me washing my feet and socks. He sits down and does likewise. He says he's on his way to Manning Park and when he gets into Canada, he will turn around and do the trail north to south, "All in one year...I tried it before, but couldn't get further south than Red's Meadows because of weather in October."

I am impressed with his ease at cleaning his small pair of nylon socks. He doesn't seem tired. He rinses them energetically, squeezes them as if he's done it a hundred times, and puts them right back on! I have to keep my thick cotton socks hanging on the rear of my pack to dry out. No more cotton socks and shirts for me! He claims he is doing thirty three mile days. I offer him some dried fruit. He takes a couple of prunes leaving one for me, then insists on taking the trash with him. He left on a polite note, saying he was planning on having a lunch break at Nance Canyon, 3.4 miles ahead. Watching him depart on a steep grade with such ease and absence of discomfort, as compared to me, convinced me this man was telling me how it really is, and what is to be. I yelled out, "What's your name?"

"Scott Williamson."

I am stunned. Here now is the first person I've met on the trail since starting on the Mexican border. He is not only "just" going to Canada, but he wants to make it back to the Mexican border THIS year!

The first pill just made the water more murky. The second pill cleared some of the murkiness, but left a clouded bleached almost opaque quality to the water. The taste of it was terrible, but nevertheless thirst quenching.

About 1:00 PM, Nance Canyon, El 3350, Mi 141.7 - 0.0

Another narrow stream of water, about two inches deep and a foot across is slowly sinking away in the sand. There may be no water tomorrow. There is but little grass along the edge of this creeklet indicating I am lucky today to find even a bit of it. I drink up as much of my processed water I can, then fill up with the new supply of Nances' water. While relaxing in this second oasis, I see a dome tent upstream. I call out from 50 feet away,

"Scott, are you there?"

No answer. I think I hear someone snoring. At the same time I notice the tree trunk that I leaned my pack against is covered with large brown ants. A glance at my pack reveals that my thick wet cotton socks tied onto the top serves them well as a welcome host. The white socks no longer appear white. Much of the back pack is covered with these large black ants. I am very worried about the ants getting inside as I have everything wrapped up in plastic bags in the event of rain. At the moment I am grateful there is no answer from the tent. What an embarrassment this would be. Soon, I clear out quietly letting someone sleep. I'll probably meet this person the following afternoon.

6:00 PM: Above Terwiliger Valley, El 4500, Mi 145.5 - 0.0

I am quite filled with that crummy tasting water now and feel like I polished off an over chlorinated swimming pool or as if someone mistakenly put some Ajax cleaner or bleach in it to make it taste even worse. My pack, now 25-30% heavier, is becoming a burden as the trail leaves the canyon bottom at 3350', to climb out to the ridge top above Terwilliger Valley at about 4900'.

Short of reaching the summit, I spot a delightful place along the trail in a protective sandy clearing made by an intermittent stream. I decide it would not likely rain. If it does rain, I won't complain. No one will listen. I'll just drink it up! I easily set up camp. At first I made some hot tea which successfully covered the foul swimming pool water. As I get into the tent I realize the sand, here in a western exposure, still retains some of the solar warmth accumulated during the late afternoon. Though it was getting cold as the sun is going down, it is comfortable laying on the warm sand. With the same kettle and fuel, I make my usual corn pasta with beans and beef jerky, this time with a little more fluid.

I settle down comfortably in the warm sand overlooking Terwilliger Valley and Anza. I ponder the significance of this area. The area was settled during the late 1700's through the leadership of De Anza when he trekked north to provide aid to impoverished areas of Southern California on his way to San Francisco. He returned with about 200 settlers and some cattle. I think, wouldn't it be great if there were an airfield down there. But then, would it be for them or for me? I realize such thoughts mean I am pooped out. I slide into my sleeping bag and soon drift off into a curative sleep.

April 21, Wednesday, 7:00 AM: Above Terwilliger Valley, Beating the Fog, El 4500, Mi 145.5 - 0.1

Slept late. "No rush now", I thought as I lay inside the tent. My complacency and sense of well being went elsewhere as I peered out of the tent. I saw a fast growing layer of thick clouds rolling up from below in the valley gaining altitude by the minute. The cloud bank, marine in nature, was moving in about 25 knots from the northwest The clouds extended from the valley floor not far below, about 4,000 feet, advancing now to about 100 feet below my position. The fog is obscuring everything below. As I put together my stuff and pulled out I felt a sudden dampness ibn the air.

The clouds were soon at my level with occasional buildups beyond 6,000 feet across the valley. I wanted to make it to the gap ahead without fog obscuring the trail, let alone obscuring the beautiful anticipated view of the mountains to the immediate north east.

The weather soon overtakes me and for a while there is nothing to navigate by except the trail.   Fortunately, the tread is now well marked by familiar footprints.

As I approach a bend in the trail, I see the nearby summit of Table Mountain, El. 4910', looking mesa-like, flat and rounded, appearing ahead through the fog. It seems it could easily serve as cattle grazing. I am sure glad I now can see through the fog. If there is any cattle, I want to see them well ahead of time! No surprises! Trails lead every which way on top. It is too foggy to tell for sure which way to go is best. Foot prints go in different ways. I go slow. That there is a sharp cliff now to the right actually helps me to navigate as there could be no other trail near by in that direction. It clears up. I get to look down. Whew! Scary, indeed.

Allen Downs

Trying to beat the arrival of fog

It cleared up as quickly as it got foggy. This same cloud bank could now be seen to cover the Hemet Lake and the more distant Idylwild areas to the northwest. Way above the cloud bank lay the heights of the San Jacinto Mountains, looming now in a very imposing way. I realize I am coming to a significant point in this northward trek from the Mexican border. I not only know I am approaching mountainous areas, but for the first time I am about to enter familiar territory.

Soon I outflank Lookout Mountain. I check my position with the peak as a landmark, I see a gap ahead corresponding with the map and my position. Once over the gap, I know I will be able to look down at Highway 74. This was confirmed by hearing the sounds of passing motorcycles, then trucks, then cars.

12:30 PM: Palms to Pine Highway 74 and to Paradise Restaurant El 4919, Mi 153.7 +1.0 - 0.5

After a short walk to the monument across the highway marking the entry into the formal San Jacinto Mountains, I reluctantly head down Highway 74, the Palms to Pines Highway to walk the mile to the agreed upon place where I would call GHA and Van. For two cents I would have continued midway through the San Jacintos to come down the Devil's slide again to Idylwild to contact Hannah, Van and Green Hornets. But I am tired, my legs and feet are complaining. I am thirsty and would get great pleasure of

Paradise is closed today!

feasting at the restaurant and drinking something cold and delightful. I'll rest my bones, make a call and make up my mind on what to do.

However, the Paradise Inn is thoroughly closed, for how long no one around knows. People drop in by car, truck, motorcycle and then by foot. All ask me for directions! Unlike the areas to the south, I basically knew this area and could satisfy the concerns of all the tourists. I find a water faucet a few feet south of the restaurant. I empty out what is left of my crummy water and fill up. In moments I polish off a liter, then another as I try out the phone.

It works. I leave a message for Van. I call up GHA and let them know I still exist and my whereabouts. Van happens to be there at the time. He says he can leave the L.A. area at 1:30. I tell him, "Fine, I'll most probably drive back with you."

Motorcyclists were quite busy this day driving eastward to Indio and Palm Springs from San Diego. They were typically on large relatively quiet Harleys in groups of three or four, dressed for cool weather.

Two motorcyclists, each on a Harley, stop by hoping for a late breakfast. They were to meet a third rider. We chat. The rider appears. He slows down, attempts a right turn into the gravel parking area, slips and falls. At first it looked like the exhaust pipe landed on his leg. We offer first aid. A band-aid to his knee sufficed, a minor scrape with the gravel was all that was apparent. In a few minutes they waved as they sped off to Laughlin, Nevada, on the Colorado River. Other people dropped by. All were in the midst of some kind of adventure, were either hungry, disoriented, or both.

Interesting enough people seemed not put back by my disheveled dirty appearance. They behave as if I really know what I am doing here, even though Paradise is closed.   I think the old west motiff of the restaurant architecture which reflects the outdoor grubbiness with its hitching posts, old signs and memorabilia has something to do with it.

An elderly backpacker wanders in. The second backpacker I've met on the trail now since starting in Mexico. His voice is pressured like mine. He can hardly talk clearly. He expresses concern for a young man that passed him along the trail, three miles back before coming to the trail head. He asks me if I saw the young man. He says he was to meet him here at the Restaurant. He also says there is another young man he just met along the way. I explain that I had been here for two hours and have seen no walkers. He is not very communicative, just worried. He takes off his shoes revealing a large blister on one of his toes. I offer him a band-aid. He gratefully takes it and covers the tender area.

"Where did you come from?" I ask.

"From Campo".

"How far are you going"?

He softly says, "I don't know."

I persistently add, "Where might you be going now?"

He says, "I told you, I just don't know."

I enquire about the details of the encounter with the younger man. He portrays a picture of an experienced pretty fast moving hiker. I recall that portion of the trail. I tell him, from what I recall it would be pretty hard to get lost in that area. After listening to him again describes the encounter, I try to reassure him that the fellow probably went straight through onto the San Jacinto Mountains. He finally concludes the matter by saying,

"Aw, I'm probably making a mountain out of a molehill." He puts on his pack and walks back towards the trail head."

About an hour later, the second backpacker, not as young as that described by the older fellow saunters by. He arrives in the same general condition. I direct him to the water faucet. In regards to the missing hiker, he tells me the same story. We both assumed he simply continued through. It turns out that this is the trekker who had been resting in the tent at Nance Creeklet. Would it not have been for those ants I would have gotten to know his name. He says he will be joining a work crew to work on the PCT trail. After filling up with water, he also departs for the trail head.

Tourists come by. A New Zealander drives by and asks to take my picture in front of the restaurant. I find a quarter and buy the last issue of today's LA Times. The front page is covered with the teenage shooting at Columbine High School in Colorado, where perhaps 16 youngsters were killed, as many injured, right on campus. Two perpetrators were believed to have immediately committed suicide. I review the weather forecast. I have time now to consider my physical needs, dearth of supplies and how to arrange a pickup should I return to the trail. I decide to go home with Van. Van arrives at about 4:30 PM. I drive home.

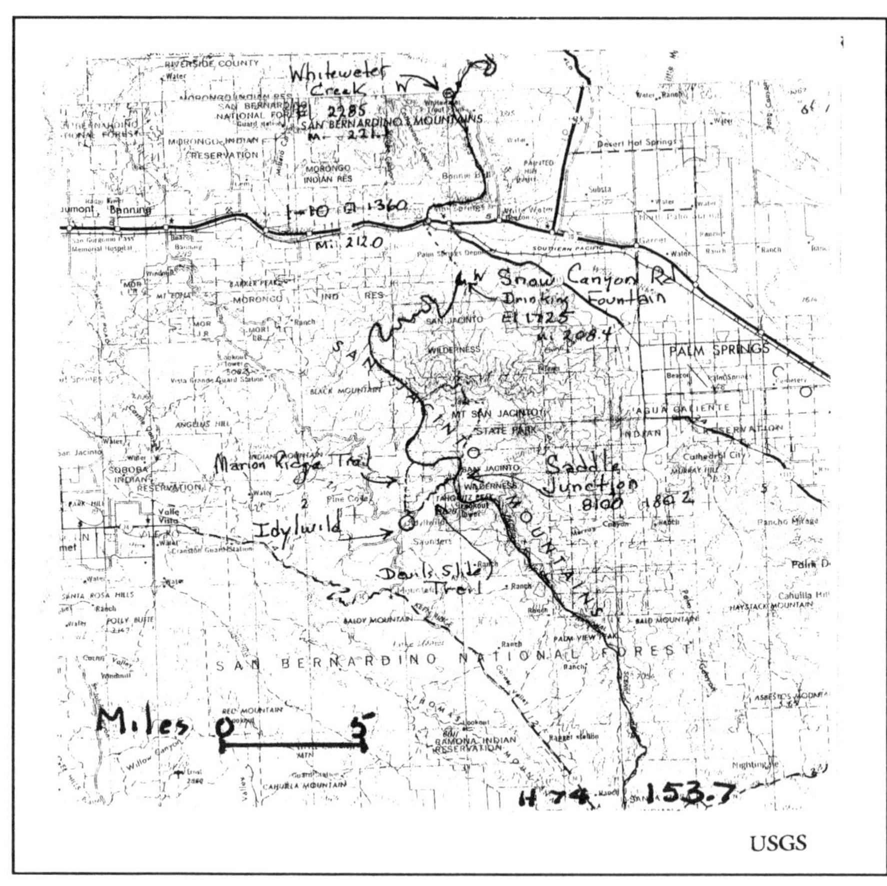

H 74 To Saddle Junction , Idylwild and I-10

Chapter 9

The San Jacinto Mountains

The Paradise Inn...The trail head at H-74....Live Oak Springs...Over Hemet Lake....The Devils Slide Trail to Idylwild....Back to Humber Park....Trail summit on Mount San Jacinto....A snowy stealth site near Willow Creek...Back at Idylwild.....At Van Nuys Airport ....Idylwild State Park....The Marion Creek Trail....Strawberry Junction Trail Camp....Fulller Ridge....Black Mountain....Down to San Gorgonio Pass...The bottom of the hill

April 24, Saturday Afternoon: H-74, The Paradise Inn

It turns out that Van drives me back to the mountains to drop me off at the trail head on his way to Imperial where he will present an address to his fellow Rotarians. On the way up the mountain, near the summit, we stop at Mountain Center at a small general store about 12 miles west of the trail head to purchase a Coke, to use the bottle for water. The manager tells me that it had snowed earlier and the road ahead was a "white out" earlier in the day. Soon we stop at the Paradise Restaurant so I can empty the bottle and fill it up with water. It is cold. It is damp. It is foggy. Now it is open! Faces can be seen peering out from within the restaurant There is no time to go in and see who is there. I dump out the cola and fill it up with water from the outside faucet

2:00 PM, The Trail head, El 4919, Mi 153.7 - 1.0

A minute or so later, we are at the trail head. Van drops me off and whisks off to make his appointment. There are several vehicles there, including trailers for horses. Up trail a bit ahead, just off the parking area, is a monument in honor of a trail builder that died during duty.

I see a man and a woman in their car, binoculars nearby, as if waiting for something to happen. I venture over and say, "Hello."

The man says, "We are waiting for Batch to appear coming down the trail from Lookout Mountain from the south, over there."

"Who's Batch?"

"Batch has been hiking the PCT for many years. He's 77 years old." He pulls out his binoculars and says, "There's Batch now! He's coming around the bend. He'll probably turn left here and head down the road to the restaurant. Let's surprise him and give him a lift to the restaurant."

"It was opened when I passed it coming here."

"Good."

As he prepares to pull out, I say, "See you later, I'm anxious to get on the trail."

Batch is 77 years old, has done the trail before and they want to give him a measure of support. We wish one another luck as they pull out to meet him. Apparently there are a number of people like this along the way that help PCTer's. They may have done the trail, or part of it themselves, perhaps are members of the PCTA, or work on maintaining the trail. In any event, they are volunteers that live near the trail and like to help out.

From here, the PCT generally follows the desert divide. Dramatic views now appear around every bend. At one moment one can look westerly and overlook much of the semi-arid inland basin dotted with communities and over multiple coastal ranges. When walking east of the ridge, one can overlook the Coachela Valley and the deserts to the east. Over one's shoulders to the rear is the mountainous terrain covered in the last few days. The northern exposure varies from hour to hour as a number of peaks are passed.

This southern portion of the San Bernardino National Forest seems protected from the pumping and diverting of the forest watershed. Perhaps as a result of this protection, much of the higher slopes of the Mount Jacinto mountains are drenched with green grass, meadows and ferns covered with a rich forest of conifers, as beautiful as any forest

I've seen in the Sierra. Further along at higher altitudes are small moist meadows on slopes, *cienegas*.

From Wellmans Junction, 9030', San Jacinto Peak, 10,800, can be reached in a few miles. Near the summit is a one room stone cabin. It is kept open and available for hikers. Inside are a few spring bunk beds and wooden cabinets From the summit one can descend the north face and reconnect with the PCT beyond the Marion Ridge Trail.

A few miles from the PCT, reached either from Saddle Junction or later at Wellmans Junction, is the top of the marvelous Palms Springs Tramway. The top of the tramway sits atop an 8,300 foot knoll containing a lounge and restaurant that overlooks Palms Springs and the Coachela Valley to the immediate east. From the bottom, a few miles from Palm Springs, one can ride the tramway stepping off at 8,300 feet. Should one take the tramway, a number of attractive areas, including the PCT, are readily accessible by trail. From there, the 10,800 foot summit is but a five or six mile walk..

Here, because of intermittent fog, visibility is limited. It is moist, damp, but above freezing and sign of snow nearby. But I can easily see the trail. Through the mist appears the equestrians whose vehicles are parked back at the parking lot. They tell me it is warmer up ahead.

I maneuver around droppings that tell of their track. The PCT becomes very interesting as it meanders around streamlets, boulders, and a host of chaparral growing strong in the more moist soil. As the trail climbs, coulter pines appear. It is getting dark, sooner than expected, as visibility is hampered by the moderate fog.

The map tells me I am on the desert divide, with forests on my left and desert on the right. But I see nothing of the scenery. Through the fog I see a gate, then a trail marker at a junction to the trail leading down to the east towards Live Oak Springs.

It is time to look for a place to spend the evening. I opt for Live Oak Springs which is supposed to be on a spur to the east, down about a mile. The *Guidebook* depicts it as a place for camping with reliable water. As soon as I turn down the trail to the canyon below, I pass below the cloud ceiling and see a bit of snow on the side of the trail.

I also see large hoof prints, freshly made, heading down the trail before me, along with very moist large droppings. I have never seen such large footprints with a split hoof. I wonder how large the animal must be to make such a large deep print. Maybe they are big-horn sheep. The trail continues down to the canyon where there is no moving water despite the very damp conditions. I travel down to see the "springs." I find some large oaks but do not see the springs. Maybe it's covered by snow. I set up camp near patches of snow, find myself ready to crawl into the sleeping bag. Doing so, I am rewarded by the comfort of my bag and rapidly fall asleep.

Big Horn Sheep

Abruptly awoken by the sound of footsteps and heavy breathing and deep snorting. Then the rear pole to the tent disengages letting the rear tent top fall upon the pack inside at the rear. I hold my breath and listen! The snorting stops. The unseen beasts walk away. I put the pole back up, have a snack but now find it a bit difficult to fall asleep.

April 25, Sunday, 6:00 AM: Live Oak Springs, El 5400, Mi 160.3+1.0 - 0.3

Up at the first crack of light, I go through the morning ritual and rapidly climb up this spur trail to get back on the PCT. The clouds begin to roll by leaving the trail clear but the numerous mountain tops around are still obscured by clouds.

As the sun breaks through mid-morning I see a back packer, the second one on the trail since I started. He introduces himself as Allen Downs. Allen has found a sunny spot on a knoll and is drying out his sleeping bag. He is taking care of some minor wounds and tending to blisters on his toes. Pointing to his legs he says, "Wherever I go, I find cactus needles!"

Prickly pear

I can see he's tired and hurting. He's been on the trail basically non-stop since he started. But he is in good spirits, nevertheless and is anxious to get on. Before he goes, I ask him to inspect the impact of some tick bites on my rear end. He says, "They don't seem to be much."

His gear is now dry. He starts on well before me. Allen says he hopes to make it to Idylwild for a layover. Other trekkers should be there. I relax in the warmth of the sun and wait for my sleeping bag to dry out.

Now, the weather clears and reveals the grandeur of the southern flank of the San Jacinto mountains. Before me are a series of peaks to be traversed one after another. First, the trail meanders east of Butterfly Peaks, then just below the summit of Lions Peak one approaches a another series of peaks, the next one aptly called Pyramid Peak. Then comes Palm View Peak and Apache Peak, each one looming higher than the preceding.

5:00 PM: A night overlooking Lake Hemet, El ca 7800, Mi 168.0 - 0.2

Before dusk I find a stealth site overlooking Lake Hemet. To the immediate west, down below , is a beautiful expansive montane plateau connecting Idylwild, Mountain Center and Lake Hemet through long Garner Valley. To the southeast it narrows at Santa Rosa Summit at the trail head. Much of the sixteen miles of highway 74 can now be seen connecting Lake Hemet to the trail head where Highway 74 drops off from the summit (4,900) where it will rapidly descend 4,000 feet to the desert floor at Palm Desert in but a few dramatic miles.

At about 5:30 PM I am tending to my delicate dinner in preparation for the evening repast. From the south comes a back packer, smiling broadly as he says "Hello" and utters some words in Aussie that I barely understand. But his demeanor and gestures says it all. He was in the restaurant while Van was waiting for me to fill up with water. He explains he is rushing to get to Saddle Junction and Idylwild before nightfall, a difficult task. He says his name is Chris Dawes. He seems to enjoy knowing I have trouble understanding what he is saying. This fellow is now the third person I've met on the PCT since starting from the Mexican Border.

7:00 AM, April 26, Monday, El ca 7800, Mi ca. 168.0

After a rather pleasant evening and easy night assured by drying out the sleeping bag, I continue up the eastern side of Spitler Peak. To the east through a gap connecting to Apache Peak lies the desert floor.

I go out of the way somewhat to ascend Apache Peak, El. 7567 and look around. I see the trail ahead traversing the ridge line to the northwest several times. I look forward to the view at each bend. It is this ridge that divides the dry desert from the more moist areas to the west. To the north is the snow-clad summit of Mt. San Jacinto. I judge the snow line extends down to about 8,000 feet. I do not dwell on this thought. Instead I ponder the significance of the impact of this mountain range on the climate and weather of Southern California.

From the snow melt here, the intermittent streams go east and west. To the east they form much of the critical water to the booming resort communities of the Coachela Valley. To the immediate west, one can see the fertile land in the Garner Valley below. Immediately here, along the desert divide at elevations varying from 6800 through 7400 feet, I see the upper limit of the Chaparral and the lower limit of the coniferous montane forest. As the trail climbs up further and close to Antsell Rock (7679) and northeast of South Peak (7584), the snow patches began to increase in size and snow begins to appear on the trail as it meanders along the northeast exposure.

I scoop up some clean snow with my bottles and wait for the ice to melt while carrying them in my pack. Ahead, about a mile is Red Tahquitz Peak (8738), where the trail traverses it's eastern exposure.

Soon, a trail summit of about 8,200 feet is obtained. Then, dramatically, the trail turns left through a gap and begins to follow the northern exposure which leads to the dramatic entry to wonderful Tahquitz valley. This pristine heavily forested sloping plateau is characterized by a solidly montane forest with wet meadows and streamlets. Scattered about, between jutting peaks, are the most beautiful mountain forests I've seen yet in all of Southern California, rivaling the more beautiful of the Sierra mountain valleys. From here, one can reach by good trail, 5.7 miles away, the top of the Tramway facility at Long Valley (8600') for a ride down the gondola to the lower station at about 2,700 feet which connects with a good paved road. The upper terminal offers food,

Tahquitz Peak

water and snacks including a restaurant and cafeteria-bar lounge overlooking the Palm Springs area. Hannah and I were there last summer, making it to the summit in an wonderful overnight experience.

Once on the protective north side of Red Tahquitz and Tahquitz Peak, the snow is now covering 75% of the trail, often several inches thick. This condition continues for about a mile or so until it meanders north and away from the steeper slopes into the midst of the valley. Then, a sign appears indicating one is at Saddle Junction (8100).

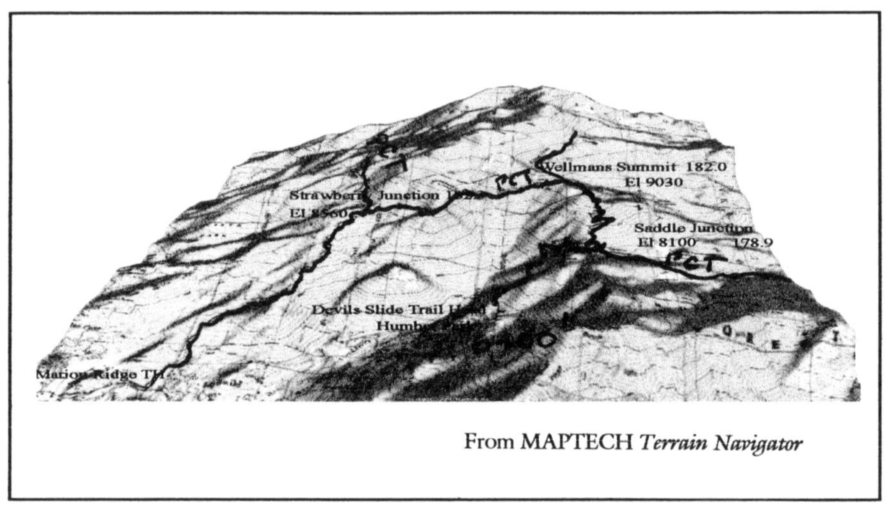

From MAPTECH *Terrain Navigator*

Access Trails to the PCT from Idylwild

To   the
north, the PCT merges with a northbound trail leading to a summit (El 9100) where a trail loop can take one to another summit or gap atop Wellmans Divide, 9,800 feet where one can either continue the loop 2.3 miles up to the peak, 10, 800 feet and catch the PCT uptrail a few miles, or divert four miles through Long Valley to the top of the tramway.

I easily opt for The Devils slide Trail, a side trail that descends about 2.3 miles down to the trail head at Humber Park. The interesting name comes from a period of time over a hundred years ago, when lumber was hurled, then slid down the steep slopes. From Humber Park to Idylwild is another two or three more miles of steep paved road.

April 26, Monday, 6:30 P.M. Idylwild, El 5860, Mi 160.2+5.0

I reach the trail head at Humber Park (6400) and take the exhausting 2 ½ mile walk downhill to the outskirts of Idylwild. I am pooped after this day of 18 miles of up and down, and at times snow covered trail, and now after this final walk along the steep pavement, I feel done in for the day.

My first thought is to reach a phone and make contact with people at home. The very first business I see waking down the road is a bar called "The Roadside." It is a small bar and lounge. Inside are people playing pool and sitting at the bar drinking. I ask for a beer and directions to a telephone. The bartender provides me with a glass of cold tap beer, a wonderful reward after a day or two in the wilderness. The first swallow is wonderful. The men sitting to my left and right soon identify me not only as a stranger, but as someone who is coming off the trail. All kinds of queries arise as the word spreads from one patron to another that I have been waking from the Mexican border. I cannot enjoy nor finish the drink as I am so tired and already zonked before stepping up to the bar. I follow directions, continue further down the hill to a restaurant called La Casita. I enter the restaurant, ask them what time they close and my wish to make a call. They direct me to the phone.

Because of my appearance, the managers speak to one another in Spanish, giving me the impression that they think I am a northbound vagrant asking for a handout. I surprise them by explaining in Spanish that indeed, yes, I am a transient and yes I have come from the border, but I do not want a handout. They call upon a waiter who speaks a good English. He suggests I consider staying at the Fireside Inn, just next door. I thank him for his clarification and suggestions. I make the calls letting Hannah know I have made it to Idylwild and leave a message for Van informing him of my whereabouts.

After showering, I head next door for the motel, register, and in minutes I am back in the restaurant scarfing down a bowl of tortilla chips and fresh homemade red salsa with a bottle of beer while awaiting my entree of chicken tacos with rice and beans.

I am given the key to the "Squirrels Nest", the name of my quaint, rustic, but well equipped room with twin beds, refrigerator and floor heater, carpeting, bathroom and amenities including hot coffee, teas, chocolate etc. It seems like such a "m'chia", a paradise, to sit down and relax after such a stimulating but wearing hike. As I lay down, I drift into never-never land.

April 27, Tuesday, 10:00 AM: Idylwild

Thoroughly rested I walk to the Post Office to review the PCT trail entries and register. I see Allen's note that he is staying at the Tahquitz Motel, a few blocks away. I drop in.

He's still nursing his wounds, his blisters. He says he will rest his feet a couple of days and continue on Wednesday if he can. He explains that a number of other PCTers are also staying here at this motel, while others are expected soon. He says he was there at Lake Morena for the "send-off." He had met a number of PCTers that I had become familiar with through surfing the internet. He says that Rob, Jonathan, Charlotte, Donna, Yip, the "Happy Couple," and Meadow Ed were either in town or right here at the motel. Allen pointed out that he was at the Paradise Restaurant when I filled up with water and when Batch was picked up at the Highway. Batch was driven to Idylwild, staying over night somewhere.

We do some errands. We walk. He favors his left foot. We visit the local Laundromat and the post office where he is awaiting a supply package. We stop in at a pizza parlor where we find out from the owner that he himself befriended Batch and drove him sixteen miles to the trail head a couple days ago. Allen and I are both impressed with not only the owner's helpfulness, but also of Batch's way of getting things done. We both have a "Super-Dooper," a pasta salad, a specialty of the house that fills up the plate.

We walk back to the Tahquitz Motel. I see several sleeping bags and tents laying on the rails. Several of the PCTers are gathered inside one of the rooms. I am asked for my story. Knowing that each one has a story, I limit mine to two minutes, explaining that I am intending to go as far north as I have time and energy to do so.

I must return to the Squirrels Nest, get something to eat, check messages and settle in for the night. While I pamper myself with food and drink, I prepare a list of needed items. I easily settle down and fall again into a blissful sleep.

I am awoken by bright light radiating from out of the windows. Is it suddenly morning? Light floods the interior of the room. No. It's Van. He is working his car adaptive flood beam right through into this dark room. I give him an update explaining I am not equipped well enough to go further north on the trail at this time. We're both tired. We chat briefly and go to sleep.

April 28th, Wednesday, noon, To the trail head.

Unfortunately, La Casita is closed. I bore Van as I drive around to pick up some supplies. But the key store is closed and I am not able to find any suitable cold weather clothing and supplies. But, so long as the weather is OK, I am satisfied that I can continue today through the northern flank of the San Jacinto Mountains. Van agrees to await a call to meet me at a designated time where the PCT crosses Interstate ten east of Cabazon, Friday or Saturday. With Van's indulgence, I am able to purchase enough items to minimally initiate the next leg assuming there is no major change in the weather picture. A snow shower or two would not interfere too much. A final check with the weather, on the basis of the weather channel, NOAA weather, car radio and a final check with the forest service station reveals there is a slight chance of afternoon thundershowers in the local area. The weather channel points to a clear period with no precipitation in the entire Southern California area. I can see no reason why not to go as soon as possible.

Van and I arrive at the Humber Park trail head at about 2:00 PM. Just then, Rob Bedichek and another trekker come down the trail. We swap notes. Van drops me off and drives away with the two trekkers to the Tahquitz Motel, a gathering place not far from the center of Idylwild where they are expected. Van goes home, I resolutely go up the trail.

April 28, Wednesday, 2:00 PM, Humber Park, Trail Head to the Devils Slide Trail, El 6400, 160.2+5.0

Not long after starting the ascent up the Devil's Slide Trail and just after I take my first swig of water, I run into Meadow Ed, a noted PCTer whose presence has been reported by trekkers on the Internet throughout much of the trail, especially southern California. In winter gear, he makes a formidable impression. We both come to complete stop, his bulk blocking the width of the snow covered trail. He looks at me, hesitates, and with a puzzled expression in his frozen white broad-bearded face, says, "Where ya going?" I hesitate, catch my breath and utter, "To Banning Pass, I hope."

"Meadow Ed" Faubert

Upon surveying my boots, shell pants and parka, he comes out with a facial expression, that if it were to be translated into words, would say, do you know what you're doing? He replies, "There's a lot more snow up there. With a tired and relieved expression on his face he says, "I'm sure glad I'm coming down."

"Trying to regain my composure I say, "Yeah, I know there's a lot of snow. I came down a couple of days ago over the desert divide. There was even more snow then."

"Oh, are you doing the PCT?"

"I started out from Mexico in April, taking breaks along the way. How about you?"

"I have done a lot of the PCT over the years and thought I'd do this part again. There's probably others in Idylwild now."

The conversation continues for a while. After introducing ourselves, explaining our motives as to how it is we are in this peculiar place at this time, the conversation returns to the state of the weather. Meadow Ed volunteers with an ominous note, "You know, it looks like it could even snow some more."

Mustering up confidence, I explain, "I've been listening to the latest forecasts. The latest is "widely scattered thunder showers passing through, then followed by dry air.""

With a gesture of his hands, he says, "Well."

"I figure if I wait any longer there may be more to worry about."

Meadow Ed puts his hands on his hips, and repeats the same theme, "There's quite a bit of snow near Tahquitz Peak." He scratches his white beard, and says, "I'm glad I'm getting out of it."

I explain, "Look Ed, I'll see what it looks like at Saddle Junction. If I don't like the way it looks, I'll just turn around, head back and be back down in an hour or so. I'll probably spend the night there, rethink the situation in the morning, and hopefully get a good start in the morning to make it over Fuller Ridge."

He sees that I am determined. We share notes on our experiences, the people we met, and wish one another good luck. Ed lives in Santa Monica and South Pasadena. He has been trekking through much of the trail over the last several years. He is known by some as a hiker and others as a trail angel and by some as both. He is known for showing up anywhere along the route and offering a kind word or deed. His demeanor, overgrown white beard, body posturing, and melodious voice and considerate manner reveal a fellow with much trail savvy. I feel that understanding him may reveal much of what motivates people to attempt such adventures.

I am surprised at my speed. I reach Saddle Junction in an hour and a half at 3:45 PM. I feel great! I figure I might as well put on some more milage before retiring so early. So I head up towards the summit.

4:45 PM, At the Summit, El, 9030, Mi 182.0 - 0.5

I reach the PCT summit at the junction with the trail to Wellmans Divide where one branch leads down to Longs Meadow and then to the tramway where one can ride a gondola down to a station on a paved road leading to Palm Springs. The other branch continues to climb up about 2.5 miles to the 10,800 foot summit of Mt. San Jacinto Peak. From there, a trail can be taken down the other side that connects as a loop spur with the PCT in another couple of miles.

I efficiently find a spot to set up my tent, go through the ritual and retire for the night at 5:30 PM even though nightfall is more than two hours away.

The wind begins to blow and it suddenly snows hard, really hard! I find that I cannot maintain adequate body heat inside the sleeping bag. I re-arrange clothing, cover up the bottom of the sleeping bag with a large plastic bag to further assure dryness. I turn over, put clothes under cold spots, but nothing seems to help. I decide to wait till 6:15 PM. Should I not become comfortable, I will head down the trail to return to Idylwild so as to get to the trail head by dark.

A problem occurs. Before I left Idylwild, I had treated the tent and clothing with water proof spray. Though unaware of the snow building up on the on the outer tent walls, I feel it is difficult to breath as the air seems thick and filled with the smell of the spray. I not only don't like feeling cold, but also feel a need some fresh air. The thinner cold air at altitude does not make me feel better about things.

My watch tells me it's 6:15. I still am not comfortable. I crawl out of the tent. The tent is covered four inches of snow and ice. There is snow everywhere! The wind is blowing hard. The snow is coming down in thick flakes. It is indeed a blizzard. Visibility is limited to about forty feet. The tops of the trees are obscured. It is a white-out.

I head down the trail. In just a few feet, I find the trail completely obscured. I continue in what I believe is a generally southern direction of the trail but do not pick up any sign of the trail. I tell myself 'This is not the first time on this part of the trail. You should be able to find it." Even if I did, I would not be able to follow it through the fog.

I soon become disoriented. I check my compass and as I try hard to read it through the frozen cover. It tells me I am heading in a generally northern direction. I decide I am disoriented, in fact, lost. Here I am lost! It is snowing. The wind is blowing. It is foggy and dusk is approaching. I decide to lose altitude pretty fast scampering down the slopes. However, I do not know where I am nor where I am going.

I find weather becoming less severe as I lose altitude. But still bad. I drop down quickly, believing I am now probably about 7,500 to 8,000 feet elevation. My thought is 'This is indeed panic!' It is getting on to 7:00 PM and starting to get dark, even colder. How far down will I go? If I continue, I'll eventually get to the bottom of the mountain, but where? What lies ahead?   I approach a canyon and a stream almost totally iced up. The snow is still falling and it is about four or five inches deep here.

7:00 PM: A Snowy Stealth Site Near Willow Creek, El 7800, Mi 182.0+2.0 - 1.0

Though a break in the fog I see the stream and a crevice in a large boulder. I quickly check it out and find that it is free of snow inside and dry for almost the length of my body. But it is sloped upward. I remove some rocks inside to create more space. I set up my mattress inside and put my sleeping bag and poncho down to try to keep it as dry as possible as it is lying on snow with more snow falling from the dark sky. I also use my tent as a ground cover. I try to keep warm and figure that eventually tomorrow, with light, if I don't freeze, I might determine where I am, and figure out a solution.

I try to maintain a good fluid level. I eat snacks. I use the paper package as a buffer under my knees which does help somewhat to keep them warm. I cover up the end of the sleeping bag again with a plastic bag.

As I try to remain mentally cool and physically warm, I figure there are major two possibilities where this creek winds up. It either spills into steep Strawberry Canyon on its down flow to Idylwild or it flows eastward into Willows Creek, then into Tahquitz Creek to continue down to Palm Springs through Indian country. A third possibility that I cannot rule out is that my compass is responding to magnetic disturbances and could be pointing in any direction and this stream could be going elsewhere. I ponder such stuff and how could it be that I get myself into such a mess as I anxiously await dawn.

April 29, Thursday, 5:10 AM At the first crack of light, El ca. 7800, Mi 182.0+2.0

Finally, I see some light in the sky. I take stock of the situation. Glad to have sensations! I conclude because I have not yet begun to shiver, I am still in the mid phase of hypothermia. I realize I do have several symptoms that disturb me, including feeling cold, some loss of judgement which I attribute to the drop in body temperature, lack of fluids, exposure and just being scared. I try to collect myself. I easily get up as I am already fully dressed. I tell myself to not mess things up any more. I stretch out in the cold and slowly gain warmth as I move about. I reach for my water bottle. It is frozen! I also note my hands are cold and fingers are numb. I trudge through the snow to the stream, break the upper level of ice and collect a cup of water. I try to build a little fire in my Bic stove. I find a fuel cell and eventually ignite it with help of the cigarette lighter which I attribute to some good luck, as I cannot feel anything at all with my fingers. All but just a tiny bit of wood is not completely wet. With patience, I find the water heating up. By the time I put the water in the cup and add some cocoa mix, it is but luke warm. My stove system is just about ineffective. I drink as much fluid as I can. I drink some of the water directly from the mostly frozen stream. I now figure the odds are now probably somewhat more in my favor and I want to keep it that way! But I still don't know where I am, let alone how to get where I want to go. Realizing I've met these two criteria, I conclude I am indeed lost. I try hard to come up with a plan. The only plan that emerges is to follow the stream down to it's end and hope to emerge from the snow into the chaparral country somewhere below where it may not be drier, but certainly warmer. I sense this is not good. I hope for some other plan to emerge. I begin to have images of what may happen if I follow this plan, stepping through rocky canyons, being in flooded canyons or a quagmire of brush. What would constitute success? Making it through the ice, snow and rocky terrain into Indian territory in one piece and stumbling onto some private property or gambling casino.

There is momentary small break in the clouds. In the small opening I see a peak extending through the tops. I check out the map and identify it as Cornell Peak, near the top of the Palm Springs Tramway. Just as suddenly as I see the peak emerge, it becomes obscured again. I take off my mittens, grab my compass, which I keep tied around my neck and take a reading from where the peak appeared to be. I conclude I will trust the instrument. I now know that I can eventually figure out just where I am and where to proceed from here. I pull out

From MAPTECH *Terran Navigator*

Figuring Out My Whereabouts!

my map and unfold it. I figure out the true bearing "away from the station," the peak. Though I cannot see anything beyond thirty feet, I do know that I am near a stream and a deep canyon. I superimpose the bearing from the peak to a stream and canyon on the map. I now know exactly where I am...if I can trust all this deduction.

I conclude I am on a bearing from the peak along this stream. It has to be Willows Creek at a point near where it intersects the upper trail from Long Valley, from the tramway to Saddle Junction. I do not know if I am beyond this trail or not. Therefore, I decide to follow the general direction of the creek, but not to lose any more altitude. I will remain west and high from the creek.

I decide not to follow the stream down to its ultimate end. If I cannot make out the trail, I will follow the contour around this hill to my right and take it around to the vicinity of where I believe there will be meadows in Tahquitz Valley, then head westerly in the direction of where I believe should be Saddle Junction where I hope to find the Devils Slide Trail back down to Humber Park.

My morale increases. Though somewhat skeptical of my judgement at this time, at least I've got a plan! It seems a lot better than losing altitude at any cost. As I head around the next knoll, avoiding the stream, I see a sign posted to a tree. It reads 'NO CAMPING HERE.' I realize I must be near a trail.

I gain more confidence. I am almost positive that I now know where I am and know generally where I am to go. As I am heading westerly, I look above me and see what appears to be an outline of trail through the snow, the trail I hoped I must have just passed. I trudge uphill through six inches of snow. I get closer.

Yes, it is definitely a trail. No footprints though. Not even animal prints. The trail is covered with about five inches of snow, barely distinguishable from the surrounding terrain. If I were above the trail here I would not have recognized it as such. I catch my breath and conclude I have not done such a bad job and become somewhat less disgusted with myself for getting lost.

I now realize it is a matter of time before I see my new found acquaintances at Idylwild. But first I have to be careful to stay on the trail and not make any more mistakes. I take stock of myself. I'm OK. In fact, my feet are warm and dry. All but my hands are warm. They're achy, still cold and the fingers are numb. My pack is all together, but heavier.

I check my watch. It is about 7:30 AM. I reach Saddle Junction about 8:00 AM. At the junction I see fresh tracks from one person heading north on the PCT where I had traveled yesterday afternoon. I just made a loop! There is still four or five inches of snow on the ground.

I opt to head down, the now very familiar, Devils Slide Trail and reach the trail head at about 9:00 AM.

Right then and there at the trail head is Allen, Yip and Charlotte, being dropped off by car. I was immediately impressed with how they were attired in special materials, unlike mine.

The driver explains he is in a hurry to pick up two more hikers at the motel and could we all hurry along. There are a lot of questions. There was much to hear and explain. I tell them I aborted the trip at the summit last night because of weather conditions and lack of adequate equipment. I explain the snow conditions and about the northbound tracks I noted in the snow. I quickly throw my pack in the trunk and wish them well as they start their trek to Big Bear.

Left to right: Jonathan, Charlotte, Nathan, Jason & Lara, and Yip at Devil's Slide Trail Junction, leaving Idyllwild

PCTA *Communicator*

PCTers snow trekking together to I-10

8:00 AM: The Tahquitz Motel, Idylwild

As we drive down towards Idylwild, the driver explains he is the manager of the Tahquitz Motel. I decide to check in. After making the usual calls I rent a unit. I quickly heat up the room, examine the condition of my sleeping bag and tent. The bottom foot and a half of the bag is frozen. The tent is still frozen. They weigh about three times their normal weight. My pack also has ice and snow inside. My clothing, food and related supplies are all dry as they were protected by plastic bags.

Surprisingly, my boots are dry inside. My cotton socks are only damp in places. Though finally comfortable, my morale is down as I am not able, equipment-wise, to continue north at this time.

Despite some poor decisions, apparently I made some good ones! I will overhaul my equipment and purchase a bunch of stuff including a good mattress, underclothing, consider coveralls of modern material for cold and wet weather conditions, perhaps a different tent and certainly a stove more appropriate for high elevation, cold and damp weather.

I call home and leave a message for Hannah telling her where I am and that I am fine. The balance of the day is spent drying out my equipment, picking up some food and taking a siesta.

I get a call from Jon who says he will borrow David's Cherokee and leave after traffic rush. He says he expects to arrive at about 10:00 p.m. He asks me to be prepared to leave.

The manager knocks on the door about 9:00 PM. He hands me a cordless phone. Hannah tells me Jon had a blowout in Covina and will be late.

Another knock on the door. It's my next door neighbor, Rob, who I met at the Devils Slide Trail Head the other day. We chat. He invites me to join him for breakfast a couple blocks away at 8:00 AM prior to his departing north to Big Bear. During the course of the conversation, we cover cold weather backpacking and some of the ways he had been doing it on his mountain climbing adventures in Washington and Colorado.

I was quite impressed with some of his equipment and ideas, including wearing a jump suit of modern lightweight material, putting plastic bags in one shoes to offset the feet from getting wet and a host of other tips.

Jon arrives. We chat. Rob retires. We decide to stay overnight and get up at the first crack of light. Jon tells me he was hoping he might have an opportunity to hike with me. I told him it was just as well because of equipment requirements..

April 30, Friday, 5:30 a.m. On the way home

While I drive, Jon asks me for two cents worth of advice on several matters of concern to him. I give him a dimes' worth. I am too conventional and driven by my personal motives to be much value this morning. Some of this is confirmed while we discuss matters while breakfasting at Denny's in Glendora. We discuss some possibilities of where we may go hiking on our next trek together.

While Jon deservedly naps in the car, I find myself worrying about the situation at Green Hornets. I wonder how the operation is going on without my watchful eye. I want to continue the hike, but am bothered by my concerns of the operation. Am I plagued by my own needs to control things there? I become apprehensive as I approach Los Angeles .

May 3, Monday, Green Hornets at Van Nuys Airport

I look over the aircraft ramp and notice that there are less airplanes than usual out on our ramp. Alan, our Chief Pilot quietly comes over to me and says, "There are a couple of issues I'm concerned about." He first brings up some kind of inconsequential matter about an airplane, then says, "A pilot is stuck at Fox Field in Lancaster."

"How's that?"

"The FAA called advising us that one of our planes attempted to come in VFR in IFR conditions yesterday and was diverted to Fox Field."

"You mean he tried to make it without getting a clearance?"

"Yeah, he was followed on radar. They also determined he was too close to other aircraft, and probably in the clouds."

.   I asked the dispatcher, "When did he take the plane and could we have prevented it?"

The dispatcher shows me his paper work. It was quite incomplete indicating that our staff had become loose in letting him fly with us. A CFI who knew him said he had burnt out two engines at an FBO across the field and yet on another occasion glided in to Van Nuys Airport making a landing without fuel.

I am really upset. Mindful of our safety record -- no injuries and no major accidents since we started the business, I say, "Well, our first job should be to get the pilot back home. Then worry about the plane and dealing with him."

Just as the dispatcher was explaining things, Van comes in and wonders why things are so tense. Being a pilot, he soon puts together what happened.

He tells me, "Hal, let's get out of here and let them handle it."

"But things are screwed up."

Van tries to be objective, "At least the plane is on the ground; there's nothing you can do that can make things better at this point."

"But I need to look into it and come up with something to prevent such things from happening again."

The problem is basic to implementing my "trek plan." How to avoid commitments necessary so as to undertake such an adventure. I am interested in maintaining a safe and economically sound operation at the airport. I also do not wish any undue burden to Hannah and others. I develop both short term and long term plans to assure continuation of the trek northbound.

I spend the rest of the afternoon purchasing several pairs of wool and nylon white socks, a folding mattress, a bivvy bag to cover up my sleeping bag at night, a small water filter, fleece underpants to serve as extra warmth, nylon undershirts, long gaiters, a pair of over gloves, a small lightweight stove fed by a small propane cannister. Now, I figure if I can cram this stuff into the pack, I won't ever be cold again!

Van is free to leave Wednesday to head for Idylwild, then to stay overnight. The next morning he will drop me off at the trail head that leads up from Idylwild. He wants to meet me at the Black Mountain Trail Camp the next day by taking a dirt road that appears by map to cross the PCT near the camp site.

May 5, Wednesday, Idylwild State Park, El 5850 - 0.0

We arrive at Idylwild about 2:00 PM, hungry. We drive by La Casita Restaurant. It is closed. I wish to buy some more things, especially a lightweight water-proof parka. We drive by the sporting goods store. It is closed. We stop at a Mexican restaurant across the street from the U.S. Forest Service Station. Both are open. We have a pleasant lunch on the porch. Van checks with the ranger about the condition of the road and campground at Black Mountain. The road is open, but the campground is closed. This obviates our plan to meet at this campground, along the way to San Gorgonio Pass. A short trip to the post office reveals less entries by PCTers this week. I don't recognize anyone.

We decide to stay at the California State Park Campground in Idylwild. Van chooses a delightful wooded spot with water nearby, a restroom facility with hot showers and outdoor laundry or cleaning facilities. It is near the highway. The warm afternoon is followed by a pleasant evening. The cars and trucks make a lot of noise on the nearby highway. With all his planning, attention to detail and overindulgence in accessories, poundage of gear in the rear of the Cherokee, I can't help but observe and marvel at the extent of his comfort-seeking behavior.

As I set my pack down and begin to set up my pup tent, I suddenly hear a loud buzzing sound that blots out all sounds birds, animals, of people, nearby traffic. I look in the direction of where it is coming from. I see an electric line leading from the front door of the Cherokee to an electric pump that in turn is connected to the same large air mattress he crammed into his tent at Warner Springs last month. After about half an hour, it seems full and he again crams it into his tent. As expected he immediately goes in and tests it out. He falls asleep. I try the shower. Yes, it is warm. We avoid making much of a supper as we both were content with our Mexican Dinner. I put my stuff in the wooden pantry provided by the Park Service near our table, put some things in the Jeep Cherokee and call it a night.

May 6, Thursday, 8:00 AM: Marion Creek Trail, El ca. 6000 - 0.0

I select an alternate trail route from Idylwild to junction up with the with the PCT. The old Marion Trail route is about the same distance up as is the Devil's Slide, a climb from about 5800 to 8600 feet in about four miles.

The posted forestry service Snow and Weather Report indicates "seventy-five percent coverage of zero to twelve inches of snow above 8,000'. I figure that if I can get to the PCT at Strawberry Junction, 8,070' by noon, and walk the PCT to the junction with the trail to the next summit of trail, 8,800' near Deer Springs by 2:30, I can get through snow filled Fuller Ridge well before dark.

The day's trek should be about twelve or thirteen miles. I will carry minimum water as there should be plenty of snow to pick from and will change tactics by wearing my light jogging tennis shoes and nylon socks with my boots, wool socks and gaiters tucked away in the pack til needed.

This rather direct 4.3 mile trail is one of three trails connecting Highway 243 near Idylwild to the PCT. The trail first follows a poor jeep road for about 1,000 yards then becomes a pleasant tread through a forest of mixed conifers paralleling a burbling creek for about a mile before crossing it.

Looking back now are the lower ridges and plateau of Hemet, Moreno Valley and the Santa Ana Mountains. Beyond is the LA basin obscured with a typical thin marine layer. Views to the south are more dramatic as they immediately overlook Strawberry Valley, the Devils Slide Trail with imposing Lily Rock and snow capped Tahquitz Peak, 8,846' dominating the skyline to the south. At about the 6,900' level is a trail junction. Here is a post and sign indicating a mile to Suicide

Rock, El 7528. It is indeed a plunge. So is Lily Rock. The difference is that Lily rock is popular for rock climbers that carry ropes and clamps, whereas Suicide Rock is for people that do not bother with such things. The trail climbs a little more earnestly, but still at a comfortable mild-moderate rate. Squirrels, lizards, and various kinds of birds are more plentiful. The immediate surroundings increase in beauty as I ascend. Patches of snow first appear on the northeast exposure at about the 7,600' level, not a problem. I soon realize that I left my mittens on the trail junction sign. I leave my pack and check my watch. I soon get back to the trail and take note they are covering up the word, "Suicide!" I leave my pack, check my watch. In ten minutes I am back. I ponder about this matter for a while. I then also realize I left my wallet with my credit cards, cash, ID and trail permit in the car console. Oh well! I just hope I don't get stopped by a peace officer. No point in stewing on the matter. No, there seem to be little to gain by returning down the trail. Van is long gone. Now, I am more anxious to get to the PCT. At least there, if I get stopped, I am where I should be! I don't want to think about what I would do in town without ID or money.

Noon, Strawberry Junction Trail Camp, El 8560, Mi 182.7 - 0.0

Soon, I approach the PCT. It is always a relief to see the characteristic 4" x 4" post identifying the PCT. A nearby sign indicates that Strawberry Junction Campground is 100 yards south along the PCT. I can't pass this up! This is a delightful trail camp, especially today. The sun is shining brilliantly overhead. It is warm. The wind is calm. This is by far, the most beautiful day and spot experienced thus far from the trail terminus at the Mexican border. There are two outhouses there. One is operative, the other is laying on its' side. I do some more pondering. Had I known last week when I got holed up in the snowstorm at the summit that there were these two protective structures, I certainly would have preferred the 1.8 mile downhill walk on the defined trail rather than what I had elected to do last week.

At the trail camp, I see a lone hiker stretched out in the sun by his Walrus one-man tent, reading a book. It turns out his name is Cory, a graduate student in ancient history. He knows Hebrew, Aramaic and Greek. He had completed the Appalachian Trail. He started off from Campo, but had just changed his mind about doing more of the trail. He'll relax today and attempt the summit of San Jacinto Tomorrow. I tell him about the cabin on top and a little about the trail, it's condition and water sources.

12:30 PM On the way to Deer Springs

The trail slowly turns around the mountain entering the northwest and north side. Snow begins to appear more often along the trail, but not deep nor intimidating as yet.

I soon bump into a trekker coming southward along the PCT. His name is Dana. He is looking for his hiking partner, Jason, both thru-hiking the PCT northbound from Campo. I advise him that Cory is spending the day at the trail camp and maybe he has observed somebody come by. He hurries to Strawberry Junction. In ten minutes, another trekker appears coming opposite. I say, "Are you Jason"? He replies,

"How'd you know"?

I informed him of what transpired with Dana and that I had told him that Cory was to be found at Strawberry Trail Camp.

Jason said, "When I got to the junction (the place where I attempted to camp out last week), I turned right and wound up going to Mt San Jacinto."

2:15 PM   At the Junction of the Mt. San Jacinto Trail (El 8800).

Here are two young ladies cooking their afternoon meal, with steam emanating from their large pot. One of them resembled the picture of Rebecca Williams in her web site. I said, "Are you Rebecca"?

"Yes, how did you know my name?" It turned out she was a different Rebecca who happened to know the other Rebecca.

"We just got down from the summit."

I replied, "Did you notice the cabin up there?"

"Yeah, someone was using it, staying all night in it."

They were obviously offering themselves a deserving break after quite a challenging hike up and down from the summit. They explained they will probably find a place to stay prior to completing Fuller Ridge. I explain that I am uncertain of snow conditions there and wish to get through the ridge while the snow may still be soft.

3:00 PM: Fuller Ridge, 8725, Mi 188.3 - 0.1

I see the ridge ahead. I pull out my compass and take a bearing to determine my exact location according to the map. As I do so, a hiker appears to my rear. He rests and tells me he is waiting for his hiking partner. They plan to make it together to the Fuller Ridge Trail campsite beyond Fuller Ridge. His partner arrives and they go on at a faster pace then mine. As usual I can keep up with others so long as the trail does not reach moderate steepness. Jim, a semi-retired attorney from Sonoma explains that he is doing a section of the PCT each year. This trek will end in Snow Creek after starting in Warner Springs a week or so before. I wish them luck and let them know that I also plan to stay at the same campground. They hurry along with a sense of urgency that causes me some concern.

I discover that so long as the trail is on the western exposure, it is warm, comfortable and pleasant. As the trail weaves to the northeastern part of the ridge, it is wintry, cold with the tread typically covered with four to12 inches of some hard and soft snow. So far the running shoes are not wet, nor are my feet cold. The trail then approaches aptly named Castle Rocks, close to mid point of this narrow 8600 foot ridge. The trail first seeks the westerly side. Here it goes up and down, and around and between huge crags and boulders. Just as I catch my breath, the trail goes steeply uphill, requiring a rest. On this west side I overlook forested Black Mountain and the general vistas beyond Hemet, still obscured with a thin marine layer. Everything continues to look like a typical summer day. The trail then goes over another gap to the northeast where the temperature suddenly drops about 30 degrees. Just as sudden, there is snow and ice all over. The trail is also covered with snow and ice and now my feet get wet. Reluctantly, I take off my tennis shoes, put on wool socks and the boots I have been carrying in my pack. It works! The feet feel better and the pack is lighter. Not a bad deal! I realize that hiking with boots create a different approach to walking. I splosh though it all, go faster, but slip more often. There is more of a risk for injury. It is more comfortable, the gait is faster, but more clumsy with noticeable weight on the feet. I now have experienced the merit of hiking distances with tennis shoes.

6:00 PM: Black Mountain Campsite, El 7750, Mi 192.2

Once there, I see Jim and Jack finishing up their supper. As this is their last night, they offer me the extra spaghetti left in the pot. "Sure, I said, I'll do you the favor! I'll be pleased to clean up also."
They insist that I just return the tin to them.
"We'll clean it up at home."
I am grateful that I do not have to cook as I was so pooped. I offered them some hot drinks and did clean their pot somewhat. As we chatted we all realized the temperature was dropping and we decided to turn in for the evening. Being in the tent, with the sleeping bag inside the new bivvy bag, with a new longer mattress, I expect a warm evening.

May 7, 8:00 AM: The Descent to San Gorgonio Pass, El 7750, Mi 192.2

It was so comfortable and warm I hesitated getting out of the bag in the morning. Due to my late awakening, I found myself waving goodbye saying they expect to be at the bottom for a pickup by 2:00 PM. Maybe I can catch up with them.

The trail starts off downhill and keeps on going down without let up for about 16 miles. The weather is picture perfect. I find what seems to be the last snowbank at about 7500 feet and fill up my bottles with snow.

After about another hour I reach a dirt road at an elevation of 6880 that splits up into three directions. I see no trail nor marker. I follow the major set of footprints that heads uphill a while where it goes to a viewpoint. Fine, a great view, but no trail! I go back to where the trail enters the road. I study my map. I realize I do not have the trail guidebook for help. But I take measurements with my trusty compass, identify my exact location and check the map. The map definitely indicates that if I take the road to the left, i.e. northeast, and not the other that goes to Camp Lacky, I will find the trail towards the end of the road, about a mile down. Fine, I do so, but find no sign of human footprints, only tracks of deer, birds, squirrels and coyotes. I figure something is wrong! Can I be right and everyone else wrong? I recheck the map. My map clearly shows the trail leading off about a mile down the road after a few turns. At the end of the road, instead of a trail, is a wonderful spot, with a spring and a most suitable campsite on decomposed granite with large cavernous boulders providing shade and shelter. I pull out my bottles, dump out the ice and snow and replace it with water from the streamlet that I filtered with my new gadget I bought the other day. I drink up! Though tempted to stop here for the night, I feel uncomfortable as I am off the trail.

I pull out the map, take more compass readings, identify my position and determine that if I were to head overland to get back on the trail I would have to leave the security of road and trail, maintain contour and try to avoid slipping down hill as this would get me further away from the trail. I climb up rocks to a knoll where I see the trail down and to the north. The route of the trail must have been changed since 1981 when the map was published. Though photo-revised in 1988, it is still way off. The trail is not far away. But in order to get to it I must take care not to avoid losing elevation. If I follow the contours of the hill, I will eventually get to the trail even though I cannot see it.

I opt to do go off the trail and to keep elevation. But I must avoid slipping down the slope. This is a problem! As I begin to traverse the slope I put a strain on my legs and knees. A lot of sand keeps entering the boot. I slip several times and have to climb up on the steep slope to compensate for the elevation drop. Finally, as I turned around a bend, I do find the trail. What a relief! Though I got some needed water, doing so puts me another hour or so further behind the two men that had departed the campground earlier and more importantly, two hours closer to dusk.

The trail continues to wind, then straighten out, then switchbacks as it descends to leave the transitional forest. The last Coulter pine is seen. Now the area is all chaparral. The plants become lower to the ground and further apart as the descent continues. The dominant plants are small clumps of scrub oak, buckwheat, holly-leaf cherry, yerba santa and poor growing manzanita. All become further apart. Descending further there is only an occasional scrub oak, some scrubby looking manzanita and yucca widely about. Meanwhile, there is continuous unbroken view of the desert pass below and the San Bernardino Mountains looming larger as the trail leads down to the bottom.

About two hours or so of this ordeal, the flora becomes even more sparse as the trail narrows as it follows the contours of a 60 degree slope overlooking Snow Creek Canyon, about a thousand feet down.

Soon I realize I am hurting from the groin on down. I should have exchanged shoes and socks. Each painful area seemed to mask the pain of the other. Both feet feel like blisters are forming on the bottom of both feet caused by back and forth movement through the sandy wool socks. The left knee begins to feel inflamed as I begin to favor the right leg. An irritation in the groin also becomes apparent. Is it another tick? I decide I will not try to make it up to Big Bear once down in San Gorgonio Pass. I'm also thirsty and almost done with my three liters of water I collected at the spring. On top of all these problems lies the sinking feeling inside that I have no money, no ID and no permit to explain my existence. But I do have my cellular phone.

4:30 PM: A Second Encounter With a Rattler

Before I can collect my thoughts to decide what to do about my situation, my feet slide agonizingly forward in my boots as I freeze in my tracks. I hear the unmistakable rattle of a rattlesnake. I look ahead and see before me a big rattlesnake eight feet in front of me. The monster is right in the middle of the narrow three foot wide trail chiseled into the side of the steep slope. The snake is coiled tightly many times forming a circle of about a foot and a half with his head facing me and his rattle behind him making a real lot of noise, about 50 decibels, sounding like rice being shaken inside a bag. The diameter of this snake approaches two inches. The head is larger. This is a monster! He swivels a bit, faces me as his mouth opens from his swollen head. He faces me eye to eye. He is ready to attack! His eyes are wide open and his body trembling. I look around to survey the area. To my left ahead was an upward cliff formed by carving out the trail on the steep rocky and exposed slope. To the immediate right is a near vertical drop a few hundred feet below. There seems no way that I can go around or over that snake and come out uninjured.

I slowly back up and try to collect my wits. I reach down and collect three large rocks. I backup some more. One by one I lobe them toward the snake. I have never killed an animal in the wild. The idea of it bothers me. Though landing close to the snake I avoid making a direct hit. The snake does not change its stance or position. I realize if I were to wait, the reptile could retreat to a nearby crevice out of sight. There is no place, it seems for the snake to go. The slope was too steep. It would be a waiting game. If I were to cross, the snake in panic it would be very likely it might pounce on me when I eventually try to pass. Time is not on my side. The snake seem to sense the reality of what is happening. After all, it is his turf as well as mine.

I reach down and pick up two more rocks, give aim and let them go one at a time. I came closer, but no movement or perceptible change on the part of the reptile. I know next time I will not miss. He had his chance and didn't take it! I reach down for two good size rocks. I let one go! A direct hit.

The snake responds by maintaining its coiled posture, but trembles in a coordinated manner that results, while tightly coiled, shuddering off to the left on the uphill side of the trail. I immediately make a dash for it. I negotiate the narrow, rocky trail and let automatic body control keep me from dropping down the slope to my right as I fix my gaze on the tread ahead. As I pass the monster, I drop one right where I think he will be. I am still watching the tread to avoid tripping and too scared to look back. All this unscheduled motion further aggravates my knees, feet, calves and groin area.

Now that the snake episode is over, some of the endorphins wear off and I find I am really hurting. Once a good distance away, I rest and once more take stock of my situation. The elevation still requires a considerable time to descend down to the pass. It is getting dryer, warmer, though not uncomfortable in terms of temperature I am drinking considerable water. I decide to press on as there is no comfortable place to stop nor even to change shoes. Beside that would take time and the passage of time is now working against me unless I soon find a suitable place wide enough to camp out and not block the trail.

At about elevation of just a hundred feet above dry Snow Creek I find a potential camping spot, actually a pleasant spot overlooking Snow Creek and Banning Pass. I consider options. Being close to six-thirty now and with but little water, just enough for dinner and none left for overnight or for the morning, I decide to press on limping downhill and now find myself pulling up my underwear to stop the irritation to my groin.

6:00 PM: Bottom of the Hill, El 1725, Mi 208.4 - 0.0

Finally I reach the bottom of the hill. To my surprise the trail immediately comes onto two large aqueduct pipes at a paved road which I had been seeing for hours from up high. What I didn't see above up high, nor in any guide book, is a real drinking fountain. It seems newly installed. It works! In appreciation to some people who installed it, I drink up. I fill up my bottles and then drink some more!

Now that I have quenched my thirst, It dawns on me that I should still not go on with my legs, feet and groin complaining this way. Oh, for a two or three day rehabilitative rest! It need not matter whether it be in a tent or at home. Because home is only two hours away by car, Mother's Day is coming up, because I have no ID nor money, and because I have a phone, it is easy to ask to be picked up.

Having trust in the cellular phone, I call Van, leaving a message that I would like to be picked up if he were so inclined to do so. I call home, speak to Hannah and tell her of my intent to be picked up. But because dusk is expected soon and Shabbot cannot be stopped from coming, as I do not proclaim an "emergency," I do not expect her come. As the trail is not well marked, blasted away by water and wind, I tell her I will continue walking towards Highway 111 on Snow Creek Road and call again in about an hour. I discover it is a good thing that I did not wait at the drinking fountain. When I walk down the road a mile, I pass a locked gate. A sign indicates I had been in a private, no trespassing area supervised by the local water company.

6:45 PM: Snow Creek Road, El 1230, Mi 209.6 - 0.0

As this desolate and private paved road reaches Snow Creek Road I see a 4" x 4" PC trail marker, one after another about 300 yards apart heading for West Palm Springs Village leaving Snow Creek Road at about a 40 degree angle with open land between the trail and the road. Not knowing whether to continue on Snow Creek Road as I told Hannah I would be doing, thereby intentionally going off the trail, I decide on continuing the PCT tread and risk the possibility of losing battery power to call. The trail begins to disappear as the sand dunes cover the trail and footprints scatter in all directions.

I follow the general direction by compass bearing which helps to find markers that lead directly to the town in the distance, about a mile or so ahead. It is now twilight and the wind is picking up as I find myself in a real exposed wide flat area in the middle of San Gorgonio Pass. I try the phone. It works. I reach Van. He doesn't know where the town is, let alone the turnoff to get there. We agree to meet at the intersection of Snow Creek Road and Highway 111. He says he'll be there about nine PM.

I now head out on a bearing of 075 degrees to find Snow Creek road. Meanwhile everything continues to ache from the hips on down, more so than before. One consolation, when I stop walking, I feel fine. But as before, I decide I should not stop. I come across another jeep road heading in an easterly direction as it starts to get dark. I opt for the road and eventually come back upon Snow Creek Road. I am walking with one hand on my crotch. Everything continues to ache from the hips down. For a while I stop walking and become reassured that when I get to the intersection I can rest and feel OK. But I don't want to keep Van waiting.

I see out in the distance a stop sign. There are twelve telephone poles between me and the intersection. I count out the distance between poles, about a hundred yards or so. Twelve hundred yards more to go. That's not much, I tell myself. Why that's only about 3 /4 of a mile!

8:30 PM: The Intersection of Snow Crest Road and Highway 111, El 1360', Mi 212.0 + 1.0 - 0.0

I finally get to the agreed upon destination. Fortunately it's dark. I sit low so as to become a low profile. With no ID, no permit and no funds, I become a nobody, a vagrant or perhaps a fugitive in the eyes of a peace officer. There happens to be a three foot high sand dune along the south side of Snow Creek Road near the intersection with Highway 111. This sand dune surprisingly provides full shelter from the ground seeking wind now blowing consistently at about 25 knots. These winds are fine for the wind farms a few miles to my northeast, but at this moment, not for me. I lie low, pull in my legs from the roadbed, rest my body, take a breath and thank my lucky stars that I am no longer in any pain and wait for Van to pick me up. The air is dry, but has some sand in it, and marvel at how it moves so close to the ground. I call up Van at 9:00 PM thinking he is near by. I immediately get him in his car. He's still in Van Nuys. He is filling up on gas.

At about 10:30 I am awoken by a vehicle pulling in from the southbound lane from Palm Springs making a sweeping left turn onto my area with a super bright light on top of the cab. My entire area is illuminated and blots out everything else.

"Aha! Busted!" I say out loud to myself. The vehicle stops. I wonder how I am going to explain how it is I am alone out here by myself with no ID and no permits.

I say to myself, "This is going to be a tough one."

The vehicle remains fifteen yards away with the lights continuing to point at me. It's Van. He was a cop! Once a cop, always a cop!

I barely make it to the car I was in such discomfort. Every step hurts. Everywhere. I chose to drive back to give him a break. I have no trouble once behind the wheel. So long as I do not walk, nothing hurts!

The trip back passes quickly. We talk about all kinds of things non-stop all the way to his house. He is going to Ohio next week to present lectures to the Rotarians, then to the speedway to watch some heats. We discuss Green Hornets, his adventures in Central America, China and Turkey, not to mention the latest in his social life. We are too tired to stop and eat somewhere. I drop Van off, drive home and head for bed.

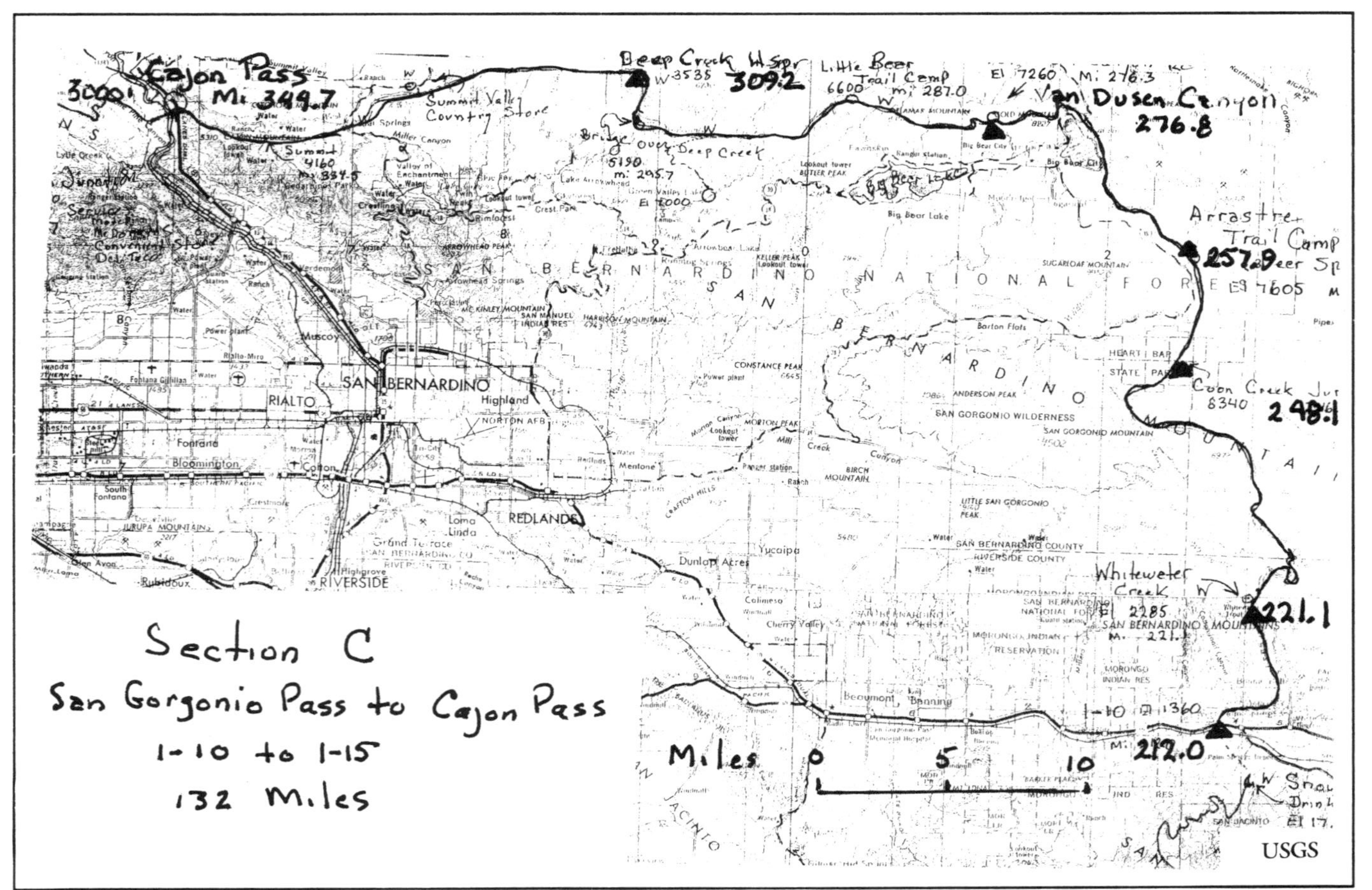
USGS
Cajon Pass
Mi. 349.7
3000'
Deep Creek W. Spr.
W-3535 309.2
Little Bear
Trail Camp
6600' mi. 287.0
El 7260 Mi. 276.3
Van Dusen Canyon
276.8
Bridge over Deep Creek
5190
mi. 295.7
Summit Valley
Country Store
Summit
4160
Mi. 334.5
Arrastre
Trail Camp
257.9 Deer Spr.
El 7605
Coon Creek Jct
8340 248.1
Whitewater
Creek
El 2285
San Bernardino Mountains
Mi. 221.1
221.1
I-10 @ 1360
Mi. 212.0
Section C
San Gorgonio Pass to Cajon Pass
I-10 to I-15
132 Miles
Miles   0   5   10

SECTION   C
THE SAN BERNARDINO MOUNTAINS

Prologue

The trail approaches the San Bernardino Mountains from its most southern reach at San Gorgonio Pass, a low point along the PCT at 1,195'.

The PCT gradually climbs out through arid Gold Canyon. Then by wind turbines through dry Teutang Canyon to eventually greet the rushing waters in Whitewater Canyon, 2,285'. Upon reaching Mission Creek, 3,010', the trail follows the intermittent creek most of the way up to the summit. Here one observe the transition from one dry flora habitat to another, then through mixed forests to soon the moist soils of the mixed conifer forests. Once reaching the forest, the trail remains there for the most part, above a mile high, for 53 miles through the more wooded portions of the San Bernardino National Forest. The montane forest is not left behind til way beyond Holcomb Creek Crossing Trail Camp at the bridge across Deep Creek. Then, after an exposed walk of 9.4 miles, one is rewarded by the wondrous and natural splendor of Deep Creek Hot Springs. A walk through the grandiose Mojave Dam complex is followed by a break at Larry's Summit Valley Store and a stroll through Silverwood Lake State Park. Then, over 4,160' Cleghorn Ridge, down across Little Horse Thief Canyon, then to another ridge overlooking Cajon Pass and the San Gabriel Mountains. The trail then descends through Crowder Canyon to Cajon Pass, a couple hundred yards from McDonalds. Here along the off-ramps are several convenient stores, Taco Bell and a motel.

Whenever the trail crosses though a gap or around a hill onto a northeast exposure the flora changes dramatically, especially at intermediate elevations between 4,000 and 6,500 feet. Doing so, one leaves behind much of the lower chaparral which is replaced by mountain mahogany, black oaks, Coulter and Jeffrey pines, white firs, tall junipers and incense-cedars. Overlapping the two areas are Yerba Santa, Morman tea, pinyon pines, prickly pear and yucca.

Two legs, a loop around Baldwin Lake and the leg from the Summit Valley Store to Cajon Pass, were skipped during the year 1999, both done in the early winter of 2000. The two legs are presented in their logical order.

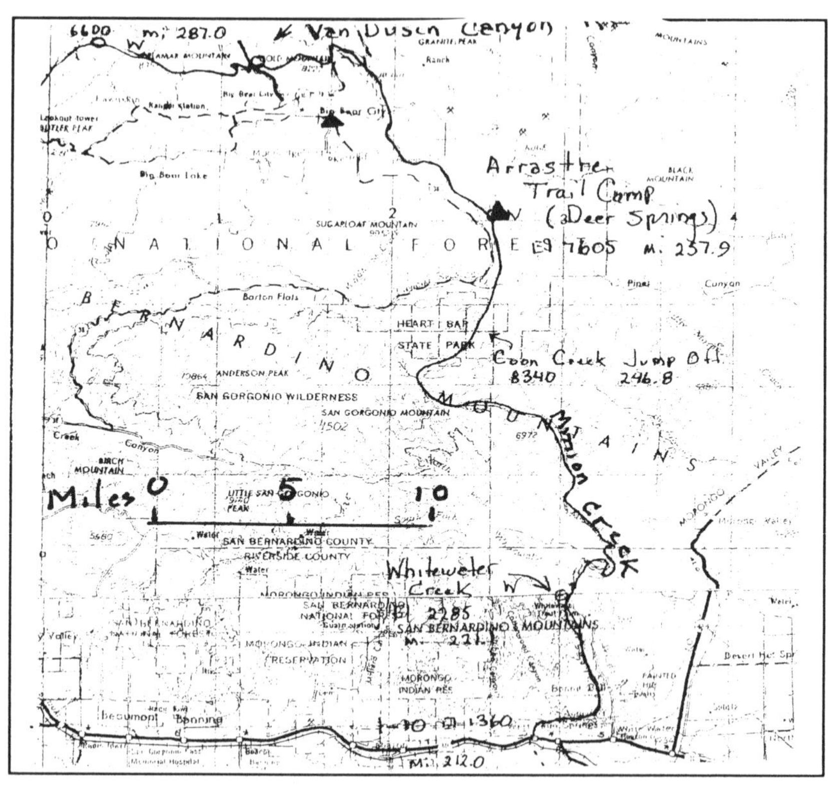

USGS

I-10 to Big Bear

Chapter 10

San Gorgonio Pass to Big Bear

Preparing....Up Whitewater Canyon Road..... Palm
Springs Village....Gold and Teutang Canyons....
Whitewater.....Mission Creek....A stream side dip
....A makeshift campsite....Top of Mission Creek....
Coon Creek Jump Off and the Group Camp....At the
summit; where's Jon?.... Arrastre Trail Camp....Oaks
YMCA Camp...A ride in a Sheriff's patrol car to Big Bear
City....The S.B. County Sheriffs Substation in Big Bear

May 12, Wednesday, At Home, Putting Things in Order

The dogs are the first to hear our sons, Jon and Joel pull into the driveway. The dogs are excited as they watch their one-time masters unload their backpacks from the rear of Joel's pickup. There is a lot to be done in just a few hours. We will leave the house early tomorrow, pick up Hannah in Pomona on our way to the trail head. We find all kinds of duplications, options and things we need. The boys agree with one another that they want foods in addition to what I have, corn pasta, beans, bouillon, jerky and other stuff. We make some calls. We head out to Van Nuys for some socks, shoes, undershirts, socks, fuel bottle, cigarette lighters, some snacks, trail mix, a variety of jerky, some corn pasta, pre-cooked dehydrated beans, all kinds of snacks including packaged foods, cheese and crackers, all appealing to the appetite. We run out of time to do much more planning. We obtain the latest weather outlook for the period. I review my navigation aids and do a final check list of gear and supplies. I now have three check list sources including a copy from the web site of Rob Bedichek. Jon splits up the food and distributes it, all 18 pounds of it. Six pounds apiece! Joel distributes the cooking gear and I distribute the other shared gear, stoves, first-aid stuff and maps.

I pull out the scale. Jon checks out with a load of about 28 pounds all fitting well in his large Kelty external frame pack, but weighted down with a US Army mummy bag, down parka, wool pants, his share of the food plus snacks and stuff. Joel checks in with his very large external pack filled with jeans, wool sweater, and share of food at about 32 pounds. I check in with my usual load plus Joel's stove and fuel, Wenzel tent, bivvy bag, navigation stuff, cellular phone and my share of the food at 24 pounds, producing my heaviest load thus far.

Even with a lighter load I expect to hold them back going up grades. They seem to recognize this expression of limitation on my part in good spirits, but nevertheless seem to deny the need to keep their loads light. Oh Well! We go to bed after midnight wishing we had more time to prepare.

May 13, Thursday Morning; Up and Ready to Go

The dogs seem puzzled, but resigned to be left behind, behaving in a wistful manner, lowering their heads and tails as they watch us prepare. They are highly tuned to signals that foretell intent. They respond with a slight wag of their tail as we tell them Hannah will be home tonight to keep them company.

Jon says, "Are dogs allowed on the PCT? Can we take Max along on the trail? Who'll carry his food?"

I say, "Last summer near Reds Meadows there was a lady forest ranger with a dog like Max trailing her with a pouch over it's back."

"What was in it?"

"I asked her that. She said he carries his own food and stuff."

"That's great."

"But Jon, you're going to have to pull him uphill!"

Jon laughs.

We drive onto the expansive grounds of Lanterman Developmental Center. We drive at the maximum speed of 15 miles per hour through the administrative area where Hannah has her office. Residents are leisurely being wheeled around by staff. Hannah is ready. Like the serene green grounds around the hospital and program areas, Hannah seems subdued.

We leave urban areas and approach Banning Pass. The conversation turns to matters at hand. We discuss our options as to where to be dropped off.

"I was picked up from the last leg at Highway 111 at the junction with Interstate ten."

"Where's that, dad?" says Joel.

"Just beyond an area called Palm Springs Village where the trail passes through. I explained because I didn't know just where the trail crosses the Interstate, I advised Van to meet me at the intersection of Snow Creek Road and the highway that leads off from I-10 to the City of Palm Springs."

"Did he show up on time?"

"No, Joel. He was delayed by a couple of hours."

Jon breaks in, "How much of a purist are you?"

"Do you mean, do I want to be dropped off just where I was picked up, or at the PCT trail head?"

Jon looks over to Joel, "Is dad a purist?"

"He's tried hard to cover the whole trail."

Jon goes on a monologue as to the nature of being a purist, and what that may mean and it's ramifications and of it's importance, and if so, he questions to whom is it important?

I see what he's getting at, and at the same time, I want to give both of them some leeway so as to choose a route to their liking. I say, "There's not much time. We're getting close. We can get off the interstate at Palm Springs Village and drive around until we see the PCT. We should see some kind of marker and then make our final decision as what to do."

May 13, Thursday, 12:30 PM: West Palm Springs Village; On the Trail, El 1580 Mi 212.9 - 0.0

We find ourselves at the deserted West Palm Springs Village area looking for the trail head. We don't find a trail head, per se, but see the trail a couple hundred yards across a barren field. Hannah drops us off at and leaves us at about 12:30, displaying remarkable patience.

As I see Hannah drive off through the dust, we find ourselves in a philosophical mood questioning the nature of things and how it came to be that we are together in this arid and desolute arrea. We conclude that it is best sometimes to do things and not ask too many questions.

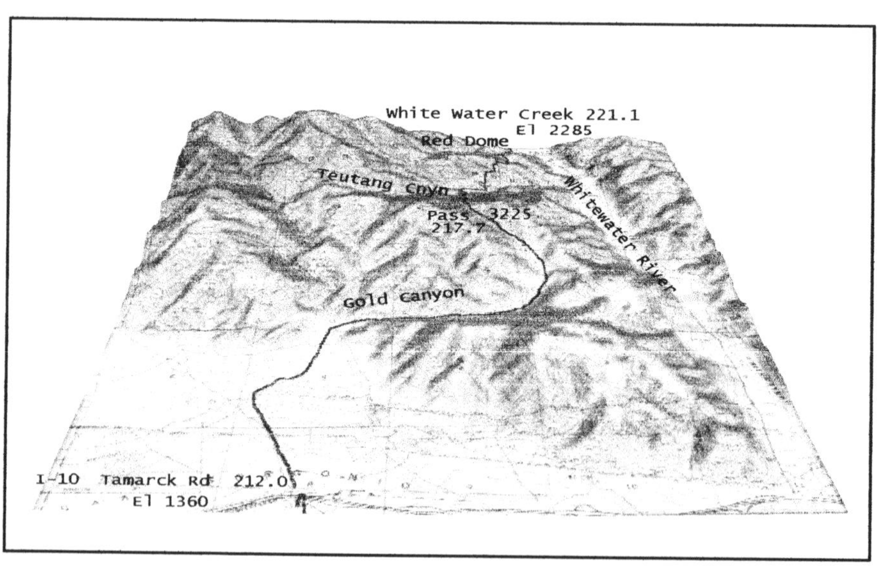

From MAPTECH *Terrain Navigator*

Tamarack Road at I - 10 to Whitewater Creek

The well marked trail from the village first meanders up through widely scattered, low dry chaparral. The 2-4' high chaparral, Mojave yucca, rabbit brush, creosote brush and several species of cacti provide some relief from the parched out clumpy and rocky soil around us. There is but little sign of remaining wild flowers that once brightened the area. Among these are the 2-3' high brittle brush, a round, silvery grayish plant, that when it does bloom from March-June, yielding yellow flower heads almost a half inch wide. Rabbit brush clumps in a similar way, but only a foot or so high, flowering later in late summer.

We soon encounter a dry stream bed. The trail is gravely and sandy as is much of the surrounding area. It looks like months have passed since there was any rain in the area. I suppose it is readily absorbed into the sandy soil. There is an occasional trough, but they are dry.

There are several unusual things to see along the way, for example going up through Gold Canyon we see something to the right that looks like a military bunker with a four foot by one foot barred opening. The concrete bunker is dug in just above the canyon bottom with its opening facing us as walk up the canyon floor.

We get closer to the bunker. We hesitate to explore this spooky man-made structure; perhaps something might suddenly appear or some gas may emit. We read from Schaffer's PCT *Guide Book* (1998) that a drinking fountain in the general area had been removed because of uranium contamination.   But it is so dark inside we cannot determine what is in it, if anything. Anyway, we back off before we can recognize anything.

Soon we began to hear a droning sound, like a squadron of airplanes, T-6's, in the far distance. Ahead around the hill appear large windmills transforming the wind into electrical current. Each of these windmills has its own transformer. As we go up toward the head of the canyon we approach several secured areas where the collected charge was being transformed to higher voltage where it will be efficiently distributed to areas below.

Now, an hour or so along the moderate climb we see a sign near the wind farm. Here lies a bottle of water adjacent to a long-discarded registration platform for sign-in for PCTers.

The canyon head comes into sight as the well maintained trail gradually turns northerly to the left. The tread now accelerates into an earnest climb. And as we climb, more and more wind wheels appear in sight. As the tread increases its climb, I find for the first time on this

Near Teutang Canyon
By Ana M. Gipe 5-15-99

leg that I must stop and catch my breath. The weight of the pack is now being felt. I look around in awe of the hundred or so of these windmills in close proximity to one another, some as close as 150 yards. Climbing the top, the wind is now noticeable and refreshing, consistent with the whirling of the propellers. All but one of them are moving with such a high RPM that you cannot see the props.

There are two types of wind mills. Half of them reveal their steel girders while the second type seem made of concrete, larger and more streamline. With the canyon head now within steps, we rest and take in the scenery and sounds. We are at about the same elevation as the lower windwheels and the wind is indeed blowing about 20 knots.

Narrow Pass Between Gold and Teutang Canyons
El 3225, Mi 217.7 - 0.0

Now, after several switchbacks we are at the canyon head at a gap or narrow pass at about 3,225 feet, 1.8 miles beyond the secured f arm area. Here I can look south and see the snow covered summits of the San Jacinto range, including Fuller Ridge which now seems free of snow. The Coachella Valley and Palm Springs are obscured by haze. As earnestly we went up, now we go down! We cross the dry bottom of Teutang Canyon, El. 2,815 feet.

The flora becomes more rich and the area seems more hospitable. Though mostly shadeless, there are small growths of sumac, chia, popcorn flower and low growing phacelias, growing where it is a little more sandy and moist.

The force of the wind becomes more apparent as we climb up and around the exposed side. Because of the high profile of the backpacks, we find ourselves hugging the upper slope as we go around the various bends. The heaviness of the pack does not help here either. Each time we go through a bend, the force and impact of the wind changes and torques us around causing a sense of panic as we look down the steep slopes. Should a much larger gust come around as we round one of these points we're finished! I conjure up fantasies of one of us becoming a headline, "Hiker Blown Off Trail." We descend and soon leave the sounds of the whirling propelled wind mills.

We reach the bottom of the canyon in 0.7 miles at an elevation of 2815 and not surprised to find no water. The trail soon meanders up a second ridge, then down to the floor of yet another canyon through steep and dramatic switchbacks, typical of many that required a lot of effort to design and construct, and much effort to maintain, because of the evulsion of rock, gravel and sand over the trail. The wind continues to blow hard. Going downhill becomes quite intimidating. The strongest wind force occurs while cornering switchbacks that overlook a 50 degree slope.

Not soon enough, the trail dumps us onto an old jeep road, a horse trail leading from the trout farm where we were just hours ago at the place called Red Dome, a twenty foot rock formation that stands at the foot of the PCT as it enters the wide plains of the aptly named Whitewater River. Now, it is a fast rushing, pure looking, inviting bubbling stream of three foot wide and one or two feet deep. We wonder if the water seems more pure because we walked so far? I wonder if the water is any better than that at the trout farm.

Thursday, May 13, 5:30 PM at Whitewater Creek, El 2285, Mi 221.1 - 0.0

I had read accounts of peoples' experience getting here, recounting events that occurred upon reaching and interacting with this stream. We find the stream is like a magnet, drawing us to its' bubbling and burbling essence of wetness. In so doing I get a chance to meet thru hikers, Andy and Leena, and a solo hiker, Chris, resting while on their way north to Canada. We also get to join in the pleasure of getting wet in the fast moving stream and join others in cleaning our socks. Chris was complaining of his legs and discomfort because of the "agony of de feet." The couple were also complaining about their legs. I shared the experience of making it down the slopes of Mt San Jacinto. Whereas I rested and recuperation at home, these athletes apparently were resting and recuperating along the trail.

Although in good basic shape, Joel, Jon and I were nevertheless tired, but also somewhat demoralized because of our encounter with the people at the trout farm. It just didn't seem fair to us that we had to endure the ups and downs of the several ridges to make it here when it could have been so much easier to pick up the trail head from the trout farm and make it here in ten minutes!

The subject is dropped as we become involved in setting up camp and preparing our first evening meal, beside a rocky cliff among the only plants in the area, scattered pinyon and juniper. This meal is to be prepared by Jon. He quietly prepares a meal of instant mashed potatoes. Although it was satisfying, it was rather boring considering it was our first meal out on the trail together. Collectively we had 18 pounds of food stashed away in our packs. He wanted to serve us potatoes. I didn't offer any complaint.

I was in my sleeping bag in minutes after eating. As I waited for the stars to appear, I took some satisfaction that I had the fortune of being with two of my three sons, but nevertheless could not help but ponder the nature of events that had taken place today and wonder what may happen tomorrow.

Friday, May 14, 6:00 AM

I get up with the first light of dawn. I have a brief conversation with our neighbors as I wait for the boys to wake up. After a brief breakfast we break camp and head off. Chris, as well as the couple, have long gone but can be seen trekking across the stream then up a shallow canyon to the immediate east where they meander up some switchbacks before disappearing at the 300 foot high gap through the ridge to our immediate north. Soon we able to leave. We readily take advantage of the opportunity to follow their general direction. This portion of the trail leaves the 500 yards wide wash of the Whitewater River. Because of the changing position of water flow, there is no tread here. The way is identified by posts that you often see after passing one. But only if you are looking for the sign and not fixated on the next rock in front. The tread becomes apparent as it ascends up to a definite head of this canyon at a dramatic ridge top, El. 3075, 1.3 miles from Whitewater. The view to the south reveals the desolate and miocenic-like area we just transited. The flora changes but little.

12:00 Noon, Mission Creek El 3120, Mi 228.4 - 0.0

After 3.9 miles of more up and downs and after more panoramic views of desert and distant mountains, the trail dramatically puts us down onto the jeep road that parallels Mission Creek, but back down to 2918 feet of elevation. This very long stream that gushes down from the canyon head many miles to the north is dry at this point. The flora, not much different than that seen to our rear, reveals the area has some moisture following rains of

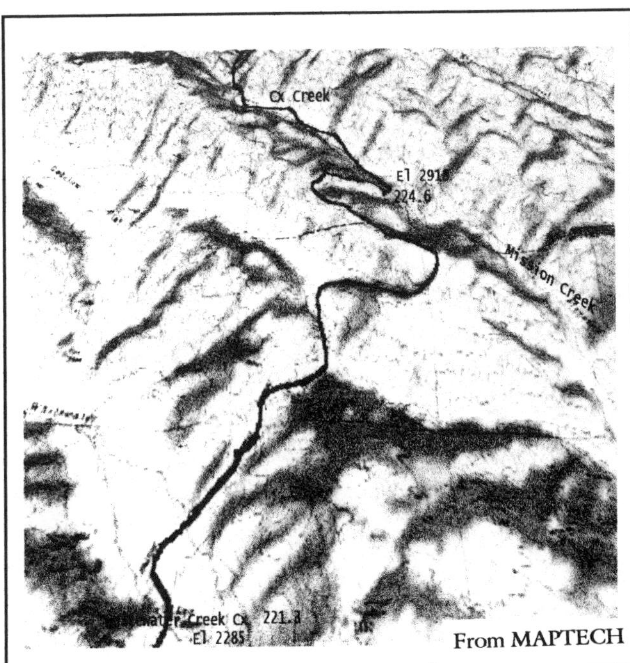

Whitewater to Mission Creek

about a week earlier. But no collectible water anywhere. We look up ahead. We see a large dried out bush producing the only partial shade we've seen for miles. We instinctively pull off our packs, drink up part of our remaining water reserves, soak in what little shade exists from this nameless bush, probably a half dead mesquite, and rest a bit.

The unusually long north-to-south canyon will eventually take us up from this desolate desert to the cool montane forest. Right now there is no sign of it up ahead. For now, even though we are at almost 3000 feet it is still desert. Some vegetation is about us, but everything is scattered and stunted and half alive. We do not anticipate any shade from the high sun for an hour or so until the sun withdraws over the canyon wall with some resultant shade. Perhaps we can reach a gully or find a bush such as this one. We check our shoes for pebbles. We want to get moving and up to more hospitable territory.

We are constantly wondering what's coming up ahead, in terms of streams, viewpoints, interesting places to rest, perhaps a place to eat. I realize how dependent I had become on having access to maps of the PCT trail. The realization of this dependency on maps becomes obvious as I realize I had lost the map of this area, the 7 ½ minute topological map, "Catclaw Flats," which depicts the area in fine detail. We would have to wait until we reach the headwaters of Mission Creek before we have access to the adjoining area. Each of these 7.5 minute series USGS topological relief maps show the area in the scale of 1:24,000 where one inch represents about a half mile. The contour interval for these maps are 40 feet. This map, about two by three feet, shows a great deal of detail including how and where the PCT winds up Mission Creek. The map is of immeasurable aid in identifying, selecting and anticipating objectives, viewpoints, potential rest spots, water sources, camping spots and interesting landmarks.

2:00 PM: A stream side rest; lunch, cleaning and a dip, El 4000, Mi 231.0 - 0.0

The trail gets closer to the stream bed and we hear and almost smell the wetness as we approach an elevation of about 3,800 feet. Here, the two walls of the canyon seem to converge on one another. I look around and find the hills on both sides of the canyon are more vegetated having a more typical look as you might expect of Southern California terrain.

After gaining some altitude the vegetation changes dramatically, the trail takes us into a rich forest of willows and baccharis, alder, and cottonwood trees and a fairly rich undergrowth that signals we are finally leaving the desert community. Anticipation arises for settling down for lunch and a rest in this first hospitable area. The alder, willow and cottonwood, chamise, mountain mahogany near the water and a number of semi-tropical plants in the this riparian growth leave little room to negotiate the trail. Yet, it is a relief from the sparsity of growth that we had been experiencing.

Suddenly, Jon points to the spot where we should stop. He points to some shaded rocks to sit on, takes off his shoes and jumps into the surprisingly cold water. The deepest part is less than a foot deep, but indeed is moving nicely along. Not surprising, it is wet! I take out my sleeping bag, lay it inside out on a sunny warm rock where it will absorb a lot of heat, and air out. Joel and I do not hesitate to follow suit. I take off my nylon socks, clean my feet and socks, take off my clothing and use my bandanna as a wash rag, then as a towel. In this merriment, Jon says, "What if someone comes up?" I say, "Let them come up in five minutes."

Jon asks Joel for his knife and promptly pulls out a pound of cheese and another pound of crackers which he finds residing somewhere in the depths of his pack. He deftly cuts up the cheese with Joel's pocket knife and doles it out to us. Joel collects some water with his filter and prepares a liter of lemonade to supplement the lunch. It is difficult to leave this bit of paradise.

Up at about the 5,000 foot level, somewhat beyond Fork Springs, the flora continues the change from desert chaparral to montane forest. Here, we see both worlds intermingled with one another, cactus, yuccas, ceanothus, deciduous trees, oaks and pines. Near the stream are grasses and blooming wild flowers. Here, in this area, is a good sample of flora from various southern California climes. In one community here can be seen yucca, cactus and Joshua trees of the desert, chaparral of the mid heights, baccharis, willows, cottonwoods and alders of the riparian woodland and the beginning of the oaks and conifers expected of the montane forest. Up on the slopes to the north is a continuation of chaparral all the way to the top of the 7,000' ridge. To the south, it is a different story. A conifer forest appears. Here, at the bottom of the canyon the two environments join together. They mix well.

6:00 PM: We need a Camp Site

We begin to look for an area suitable to spend the evening. But there aren't any in the immediate vicinity. There are no flat areas large enough for three anywhere near. Jon and I are ponder our situation as he pulls ahead. Joel suddenly calls out from behind "I can't go any further"!

"Hey Jon, wait up!" I call.

Joel blurts out, "It's my thigh, it hurts too much when I lift up my leg...I got to stop."

I say, "O.K., we can always sleep right on the trail. Look, there's a spot there for one person, another and another, there," pointing to spots where the trail widens somewhat.

Jon goes down the slope about forty yards to explore the area. He finds a little bit of water, but whatever flat area exists is inhospitable due to either cactus, boulders, brush, insects, poison oak or dampness. In the meantime I go a little bit ahead to look for a more attractive spot. Jon comes back concluding there is indeed water, but summarizes the details concluding there are comfortable areas below, but not safe to set up for the night. I come back reporting a compromise if Joel can placate his leg and walk up a hundred yards.

On faith, the boys agree to go on up the trail. Joel somehow pulls himself together to make it to our home for the evening. It turns out the problem to his leg was due to a cramp probably caused by too much weight and pressure from his pack that is giving a pinpoint pressure onto his left leg. His external frame pack has an extension on the bottom with aluminum bars extending out providing a platform for a sleeping bag or something. These aluminum bars were putting pressure on his thigh, most likely cutting out some circulation and causing a cramp as well as some bruising. I guess endorphins help only so much. And when activated, they only work for a limited time, at least with some systems of the body.

We set up camp in a clearing just ahead and off the trail by a few feet. I set up my tent for Joel and now it is my turn to prepare my specialty for dinner. Yes, corn pasta with dehydrated pre-fried beans, a bouillon of Telma soup. And for tonight turkey jerky and a bit of Jon's dehydrated mashed potatoes. All Kosher! Joel finds he has almost all the bouillon. We split it into pieces and distribute the cube for needed flavoring. I make generous portions, serving it hot. We are all pleased with our supper. For dessert, Jon offers us pieces of licorice which hits the spot at the time. The temperature drops quickly as the sun retreats below the ridge to the southwest. The sky remains clear. There is no wind.

This second night goes rather uneventful once we get settled down. As Joel had complained about being cold in his tent while sleeping at Lake Morena last month, I make a special attempt to assure that Joel will have a warm and comfortable evening. I suggest he tries out my black wicker zip-inner pants while sleeping inside the tent along with his blanket, I think the same one he had when he was a kid! Jon sleeps on my tent fly inside my old, but durable, U.S. Army mummy bag. I sleep inside the bivvy bag on top of two ponchos. We each quietly reflect on the day and personal thoughts. I fall asleep recriminating myself for losing the Catclaw Flats map and therefore contributing to the displeasure of not knowing precisely by map where we are. Neither Joel nor Jon seem as involved with the cartography as I. Nevertheless we all sleep well.

May 15, Saturday, 5:30 AM: Ready to Climb the Mountain! El ca 6200, Mi 235.0 - 0.0

We all seemed recovered from the trials of yesterday. We leave in good spirits, confident that we can find a comfortable paradise-like spot as

Jon found yesterday for lunch. As each hour goes by, the forest grows thicker, greener, richer and darker.

At about 5,500 feet we run into many pretty areas, too many to choose from, making it difficult to decide where to stop. There are the tall alders with their lancelated leaves, willows and cotton trees adjacent to the stream. Tall incense-cedars, Jeffrey pines and live oaks are abundant. Yet prickly pears, yucca and desert chaparral of various species are mixed in! The boulders and rock columns reveal the impact of heat and pressure and uplift. The soil and droppings along the tread varies and reflects the species of the trees overhead. A bit later comes the black oaks, white fir trees and huge Jeffrey pines that seem to announce you are really entering a mountain forest.

From MAPTECH *Terrain Navigator*

A Days hike from near Forks Spring to Coon Creek Jump-off

Soon, at about the 6,100 foot level, 3.1 miles after crossing the confluence of the South and North forks of Mission Creek, and after a rest, we pass a really attractive shady campsite, picture perfect for camping with a bubbling little brook nearby, perfect for camping out on a warm day with tall conifers and huge oaks trees providing almost complete shade. "If only I had that map" I thought to myself. The trail then begins to switchback several times on an earnest climb to the 7,000' shaded ridge above where we cross the boundary of the Bureau of Land Management jurisdiction onto that of the San Bernardino National Forest. This boundary appears on a dramatic promontory in a definite montane forest characteristic of what you might expect in this wonderful national forest. Now it is solidly a conifer forest. Though there are occasional chaparral, mountain mahogany, manzanita and other species, here, the Jeffrey pine and incense-cedar and occasional white fir rule over the chaparral, now limited to the more exposed areas.

2:00 PM: Top of Mission Creek El 7965, Mi 241.5 - 0.0

Inevitably the trail reaches the headwaters of Mission Creek at a trail camp, 4.0 miles after the first really attractive spot. Here the trail reaches several dirt roads. By contrast, the area seems quite hospitable with thick forest and nearby water. There are now occasional dirt roads, small meadows and streams. I note the satisfying feeling inside telling me I reached the matrices of roads on the other side of the mountain, now within reach of familiar places at Camp Angeles, Barton Flats, Hart Ranch and the outback of the San Gorgonio Wilderness area. I feel I am now near and within site of home territory, certainly more secure knowing that if something were to go wrong that we could bomb out, take a dirt road and in no time be on good old highway 38 connecting Redlands, and Mentone with Camp Angeles, Barton Flats to the south and Big Bear and Highway 18 to the east and Green Valley Lake Road which takes us to our cabin at Green Valley Lake, about an hour and a half by car. Yes indeed, we made it out of the desert!

We are disappointed that there is no sign of a trail camp here despite the signs and dirt roads. No toilets, no tables, no piped water, no picnic tables. No, nothing! There was a note held down by a rock sitting on top of a trail marker that someone had recently scribbled describing directions on how to find some nearby water by compass reading. We conclude we have enough water. After no rest at all, Joel and I leave the trail camp, Jon says he'll catch up with us momentarily. In about five minutes, I tell to Joel to stop. I don't see Jon. I blow my whistle and listen. I barely hear Jon call back from a southerly direction, off from where the trail was, and yet off from where it will go. He arrives saying he took the dirt road by mistake and was trying to get back onto the trail. I advised him not to leave the trail without a signal of some kind or another. I hope this won't happen again.

The day and the trail is wonderful here. The view is phenomenal! Over our shoulder to the left are the snow clad summits of highest peaks in southern California, Greyback, Mount Grinnell, Jeppesen Mountain and San Bernardino Peak. Over the shoulder to the right is the Ten Thousand Foot Ridge, also capped with snow. At our three O'Clock position are the mountains forming the eastern wall of Mission Creek. In front of us are the ridges south of Big Bear Lake. Amidst all this skyline are the minor peaks and plateaus we will soon be crossing. I am impressed that just hours before we were in the high Colorado desert transition area. Whereas now, by reaching this area, we are clearly in the montane forest, in areas where we have all been before, not far from familiar trails leading to the San Gorgonio Wilderness Area but also of the mountain resorts of Barton flats and Big Bear.

Here are the tall and stately sugar pine, white pines, Jeffrey pines, incense cedar, all mixed with assorted firs that seem so characteristic of the San Bernardino National Forest. The trail meanders for several miles before finally switch backing up to a minor, but beautiful peak that provides a view of Sugarloaf and Onyx Peaks, guardians of our destination, Big Bear City, where we can be expected to picked up by Hannah, Monday evening. If she decides not to do so, we can trek on and reach our own mountain cabin at Green Valley Lake a day or two later.

Once we get to the summit, 4.7 miles from Mission Creek Trail Camp, Jon blurts out, "I vote for spending the night here!"

Upon reaching this height, we all instinctively take off our packs and rest contemplating our situation. It is 5:20 PM. Dusk will occur in about one and a half hours. Then it will be dark within the hour. We have put on 12.8 miles, mostly uphill. We are tired. There is indeed room for setting up camp and indeed a beautiful view. To the south are the heights of Mount San Gorgonio, the Ten Thousand Foot Ridge and the immediate area we climbed. To the north are the ridges between us and Big Bear Lake. BUT, we have little water. Not enough to comfortably use for supper, thus no reserve for the morning, let alone the next day. We are in an exposed area. We are at the apex of elevation of the trip. It should become cold as soon as the sun comes down and with a wind the chill factor would cause some additional discomfort. Joel argues that Coon Creek Jump Off is but a mile away, downhill, and we should arrive there in 45 minutes. Whatever the scenario, we would be closer to water. There may even be some water about. I argue that we would be safer once in the protection of the camp and adjacent to the dirt road leading to Highway 38. The vote is two to one. We descend towards Coon Creek.

Before we get there we are greeted by a tight group of several adults and several youngsters, the first people we've seen since a couple hikers passed us going up the top of Mission Creek. I ask them if there is any water down below. They say they have gallons of water and invite us to "their cabin" down below for water and food, if we so choose. I tell them, "I'll discuss it with the boys."

Coon Creek Jump Off 6:20 PM, El 8340, Mi 246.8 - 0.0

At the bottom of the hill is a narrow flat area between two ridges, one of which we just came down. The narrow flat extends east to west. The trail enters the forested flat just before it abruptly and dramatically turns at a sharp cliff that overlooking the deserts to the east. This is the "jump off." One step over the side and it's "good bye Charlie."

I barely had time to overview the jump off as I shortly hear and see the group appear. I tell the boys to wait for me for a while. I follow them for some water. They indeed are staying at a cabin, part of a group camp developed and maintained by the U.S. Forest Service. Here, they are preparing skewers of beef with the trimmings! They say they have more than they can eat and hope that they can offer some to us. I fill up my two liters of water and walk off to meet Jon and Joel.

7:00 PM The Coon Creek Group Camp El 8375, Mi 24.0

When I return, I find Jon and Joel sitting on the ground, leaning on their packs propped by a large Jeffrey Pine. They had just had a conversation with a man staying in a recreational vehicle parked but 100 yards or so by the dirt road, the only person now in the area. He had been there for a while and had invited them in for some warmth, music and the like. I tell Jon and Joel of what I saw and what was said to me. I showed them the two liters of water. I figured this should make Jon feel better about the matter.

We pick up our packs and head for paradise. Amidst scattered pines, firs and a montane-type of chaparral, there is an empty cabin for our use. The cabin lies several yards from the main cabin where the folks are staying. The cabin is one room, is a bare shell with

A Forest Service Cabin at Coon Creek Jump Off

Allen Downs

open spaces for two doors and two windows. There is a platform for sitting or cooking. It will be Joel's turn to prepare supper, a mix of couscous.

As I go over to greet the people, the leader of the group hands me three sizzling hot skewers of beef, a skewer of freshly roasted tomatoes and a steaming skewer of barbecued pineapple. I bring these to the boys and we feast on the skewers along with the couscous Joel had made. Even this does not seem to make Jon happy. When Joel returns later with some more food, Jon still seems disinterested and, in a matter-of-fact manner, asks Joel to hand it over as he would keep it for tomorrow.

Apparently these people made reservations with the U.S. Forestry service to stay at the group camp and we just happened along when they realized they had an overabundance of food. They are quite gracious. Their kids seem to really enjoy our presence. It is difficult for them to grasp how far away Mexico really is.

I tell them, "It's up that trail by about 200 miles." The adults say they were informed by the rangers that they would be near the PCT and there was a chance to see people actually walking across the United States from Mexico to Canada.

Jon in the meantime had set himself into my large GI mummy bag on his tarp and is already asleep. To assure that Joel has a warm evening, I offer him my wicker underwear and the tent fly as ground cover. I pull my sleeping bag into the bivvy bag and set it on the mattress setting upon two ponchos. We all sleep well.

May 16, Sunday, 6:30 AM: Coon Creek Group Campground, El 8375 Mi 247.0 - 0.0

I get up at the first crack of dawn, get dressed and make some hot water. Jon and Joel began to stir. Jon sits up. I offer him something hot to drink. He declines the offer. He slowly and methodically gets up, dresses and puts togther his pack methodically. I slowly get my stuff together as I require more time than he to pack away my stuff. I ask Jon, "How'd you sleep"?

He says, "OK."

"Were you warm?"

Jon curtly replies, "Yeah, I want to leave now and head up the trail.

I'll wait for you, and expect you in an hour."

I ask him, "Can you find the trail from here?"

He abruptly says, "Yes."

I tell him, "Make sure to stay on the trail at all times."

He murmurs something. I suggest he take the police whistle along so he can let us know his whereabouts. He shrugs it off and leaves. Meanwhile, Joel and I stow the cooking gear, the remaining shared stuff and depart. We take turns at the outhouse and are on our way, a half hour after Jon had left.

9:00 AM: A Summit; Where's Jon?, El 8610, Mi 249.4 - 0.0

We catch the trail as it leaves Coon Creek Jump-off. The trail immediately climbs, contouring up a steep slope, switch backing several times, more often than not overlooking a 45 degree slope. One slip up and it's over! But the view of the Santa Ana River and it's environs is wonderful and compensates well for the struggle and balance required on the steep gradients of climbing this ridge, one of several to cross before reaching Big Bear Lake. The trail eventually goes around a large shoulder which we carefully follow around. After an hour or so, about 9:00 AM we come to a clearing on a saddle exposed to the early sun. As we approach this delightful spot, Joel says "I bet you he's right there waiting for us in the sun."

I blow my whistle quite loudly. No response. "He's probably playing with us." But he is nowhere to be seen. We decide to continue on a little further hoping we'll soon bump into him. Every few minutes I blow my whistle. I look for his distinctive tracks, but find none. There are all kinds of tracks, but I see none with the distinctive triangle noted earlier during the hike. Joel is not so sure, he thinks he may see his foot prints. We walk very slowly studying the ground. No sign of him really, and no people anywhere to ask of his whereabouts. We wonder what to do. Shall we head back, wait, or try to catch up with him. We decide to head on and look for his tracks. We had taken note his foot print had a unique triangle centered on the heel. We look for his footprints. After another mile we conclude we do not recognize any of the myriad of foot prints as his.

About this time I hear a series of loud deep roars. It sounds as if there may be a lion, tiger or leopard about 200 yards or so away. Joel hears nothing. It occurs again, an even larger and deeper roar, like a tiger. Joel stops and concurs. He hears it too. He's also not so sure what it is.

"Dad, it is something."

We stay frozen for a while and wait. We hear it again. We concur it must be a large wild animal! We start walking real slowly, listening waiting to hear it again. It remains quiet. I refrain from blowing my police whistle and we stop yelling for Jon.

Suddenly, up on the slope to the right about 100 yards we see a lion, then a large white wolf and a huge bear. Lions, Tigers and Bears, oh my! We freeze again.

There is a fence! Fortunately these animals are all on the other side. As we venture a little closer, we see they are in kennels as if in a small zoo. We are not in the mood at the time to explore the area. We now concur that Jon had probably not gone this far. Or, if he had made it anywhere near here, he had hopefully gotten off to Highway 38 where we believe he would head north, either to hitch or walk to meet us at the trail camp or Big Bear. Otherwise the possibility exists for a mishap in the early part of the trail, which would have been on the switchback portion of the initial climb where a fall could explain his absence. We recall overlooking the area as we climbed uphill and do not recall anything unusual.

11:00 AM Along the Trail, at a jeep Road, 8390. Mi 2560.7

We decide to rest and wait a bit to rule out the possibility that we may have passed him and if so, hope he may drop in on us as we' rest and have breakfast. Joel and I have granola, powdered milk and water and lemonade. It dawns upon us that Jon has much of our food and perhaps more importantly, our water filter. He has no maps nor compass to serve as navigation aids. We try to come up with a plan.

Meanwhile there no sign of anyone, let alone, Jon. After considering all options, far fetched or not, we decide the best thing to do is to go ahead to where we think logically would be our agreed upon objective, if we indeed had one! Water, rest and perhaps an overnight. This lead us to decide to go on to ArrastreTrail Camp near Deer Springs. In the event he is not there or does not show up shortly, we will bomb off the trail and seek telephone communications with mom. Should mom not know his whereabouts or is not available, we will contact the Sheriffs' Department or some agency connected with search and rescue.

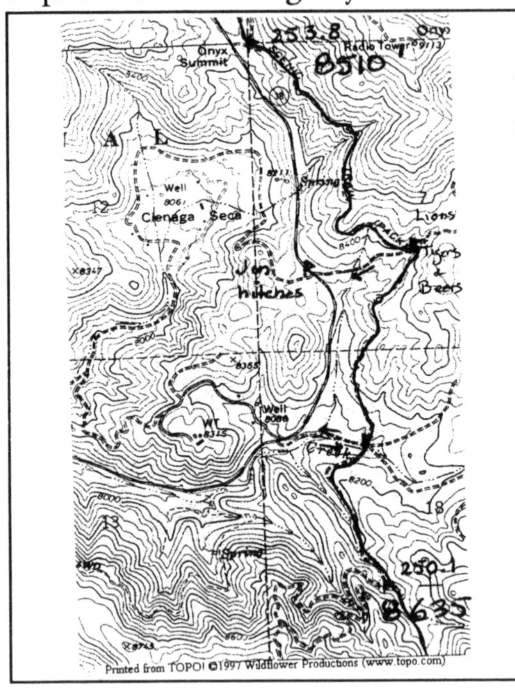

Where's Jon?
Did he turn the wrong way?.

In the meantime the forest remains thick with pines, including the lodge pole and tall scattered junipers. But we are not in the mood to appreciate it. The weather is good. Visibility is unrestricted.

About an hour or so later after crossing several jeep roads, Joel calls out, "There's Jon"! As we get closer, we see a dirt road and a couple of cars with a backpack several yards away leaning against a tree. The backpack, at first, apparently looks like that of Jons'. But as we get closer, we are disappointed. There is an elderly woman sitting in a folding chair and two middle aged adults wondering around.

We ask them if they had seen anyone around. They said they had been there since 7:00 AM doing some practice search and rescue work. They had seen a man trekking by about 10:30 AM and a couple somewhat later. No one else, either way. We thank them for this information. We concur that this could not have bee Jon as it was too early for Jon to be in this area. We continue briskly walking down trail to the trail camp which is now only about a mile away.

Shortly, we meet a couple of day hikers, a young man and woman, coming uphill, southbound. They report seeing no one. Then about a quarter of a mile down, we see three people and a large, friendly brown dog approaching us southbound. They also report not seeing any backpackers. It turns out that these people are connected to the search and rescue training group back on the trail. The dog is a specially trained sniffer-searcher. The leader, Lynn Kyndall asks a few questions. We get in a conversation and discuss the situation with her. She concurs that we cannot expect cellular coverage until we get to the highway, and even then we may not get coverage. She said that when she gets out of the area, she will notify Search and Rescue and the Forestry Service of a trekker that got isolated and could be lost or injured. We tell her of our immediate plan, to continue on to Arrastre Trail Camp where there was a chance that we may meet up with him. If not, we will head off the trail as soon as we can and seek communications with home, and if necessary initiate a search. We told her we would then head for the Fire Station, which I knew provided services for PCT backpackers.

2:00 PM: At Arrastre Trail Camp El 7605, Mi 257.9

The camp ground is amidst white fir trees, conifers, including an occasional pinyon pine, oak tree and a rich undergrowth of plants alongside the passing brook. The campground is empty. Jon is nowhere to be seen. Nor is there any sign that he or anyone else has been here today.

Though the campground seems pretty ideal for backpackers, with an outhouse, tables, fire pits and good shade, we could not get the faucet to work. We rest. Joel looks for water up stream. There is plenty of sun and plenty of shade. But we are too worried to take advantage of this pleasant campground.

We eat a quick lunch, clean up at the stream, replace our socks and study the map to determine a rapid way to get to the highway. Still, no Jon.

Time has now become critical. We leave the trail camp, follow the PCT down about a half mile. We come upon an equestrian team meandering southbound. They have not seen Jon.

The trail crosses the creek a few times before we take leave of the PCT a half mile after road 2N04, at El 7050, Mi 260.0. We head up a steep rocky road that we know goes to Oaks Camp, a few hundred yards up the spur trail which connects by road to Highway 138. We figure we can make a call from there.

Joel starts to slow his space, complaining about his thigh again. We get to this YMCA summer camp at about 4:30 PM. It is still May. The summer camp's large grounds and many buildings and dorms are devoid of people and animals. It is deserted! No telephones around.

We check out the map. We walk about a mile or so. Joel can only walk about three quarters of a mile an hour rate now. We finally reach the highway ahead. We call on the cellular phone. The call breaks up. We get closer. I call again, cannot get through yet. Joel is stumbling. He needs to rest. His rate is still less than a mile per hour. We finally reach highway 38. Joel wants to continue walking. We immediately take turns extending our thumbs. I unsuccessfully attempt another call. Big Bear City is now five miles away. At this rate we will not get there til well after dark, if at all!

We see a "MARTA" bus stop sign a few yards up. Joel says, "it's no use. There's probably no bus. Let's go on!" We pass it up. Just then the bus whizzes by. We wave. But it doesn't stop. Our luck!

Now, about an hour or so walking on the highway in this condition, at about 6:00 PM, I spot an approaching Sheriffs' patrol car. I flag it down. I head for the window. The deputy asks me to come around to the other side. He asks, "How can I be of service?"

I tell him the story. "My son and his brother Jon had left Coon Creek Jump off Group Camp a half hour before us at 6:30 AM and we have not seen him since. Perhaps you can help us by directing us to a phone where we can call to see if he made contact with anyone."

In a professional way, he says, "Do you have reason to suspect he may be lost or injured?"

I say, "The first two miles covered steep terrain. The worst scenario is that he may have slipped and fell. Other than that, he probably is OK. We are nevertheless concerned about his welfare, and hope if we can get to a phone we can find out something." Before I get a chance to mention communications with the Search and Rescue Section, he asks if we have a gun. Joel and I look at one another. I tell him, "We have no weapons."

He assures us that if we carry weapons it is OK, but he is required to know. He suggests we put our packs in the trunk get in the backseat and get on our way. As we drive on, he calls the substation. He seems to be directed to transport us directly there. We tell him the rest of the details.

We slowly cruise along Highway 18, pass through Big Bear City and continue on to the San Bernardino Sheriff's Substation at Big Bear Lake.

6:30 PM. At the San Bernardino Sheriffs Substation in Big Bear,

In the short drive to downtown Big Bear, the Deputy efficiently has the story summarized on the mobile computer. By the time we get to the substation, our image of this Sheriffs' Deputy takes on an image of heroic proportion. We are in the system. At least Jon is. By the time we arrive at the station, the deputy has already touched base with Search and Rescue. I have the strong sense this deputy, out of duty, is doing his best to get us all out of the jam that we had gotten into. We eventually arrive at the county facility as it is getting dark. By the time we arrive, he had already introduced himself by way of card, Deputy Scott

It turns out that Deputy Scott has done some hiking. He tells us about his experience walking the trail along the coastal mountains. He recounted his experience with giardia, caught from water out of a faucet. I become impressed with his training and his familiarity with his job, his outlook towards the community and world in general.

Once inside the substation Deputy Scott escorts us to the squad room and directs me to their phone. He says, Dial nine, then the number."

I say, "I prefer to bill it to our number."

He politely replied, "You've already payed for it."

I call Green Hornets Aviation. The dispatcher says he had gotten a call from Hannah while heading to Redlands to pick up Jon. At Joel"s suggestion I call Hannah by cellular phone. I am surprised to immediately get her.

She says, "I just got an earlier call, but wasn't able to answer it as it was the first time I ever heard the phone ring and wasn't prepared to answer it while driving on the freeway."

"That probably was me trying to get you earlier. But that's a long story." I tell Hannah, "We're at Big Bear, at the Sheriffs Substation; we're OK."

She explains, "I'm driving through Montclair. I had just gotten word from Jon that he had separated from you, then went to Redlands where he is now waiting for me at a Union Service Station."

I figured she would reasonably get to him within an hour or so. We chatted a bit more. I gave her directions and we agreed to meet at or near the Sheriffs Substation here at Big Bear.

She further went on to say, "I'll pick him up and meet you at Big Bear, but where did you say?"

"We're now at the Sheriffs substation near the road to Snow Summit in Big Bear Lake. If you do not see us outside, come on inside and ask for us."

6:30 PM: The Aftermath in the Squad Room

The mood now changes in the Squad Room. Now there is to be no search and certainly no rescue. Deputy Scott explains the complexity of the Search and Rescue operation, including use of vehicles, aircraft and manpower. He knows of Lynn Kyndall and the rescue staff and is familiar with their operation as they work in conjunction with the Sheriffs Department. Scott discusses how vehicles, aircraft, communications and human resources would be set into place if Jon were not immediately located. He aptly points out the San Bernardino Sheriffs Department is nationally known as having a very large, fast and efficient all-out team ready to be out in the field in minutes. Deputy Gartrell orders us some hamburgers, with potato chips, fruit cocktail and soft drinks. Just at the perfect time. Now it feels more like a party!

The Squad Room has various functions. It serves as a day room, an office, a study, lounge, briefing room and control center, probably depending upon demands of activity, whose on duty and who the boss is for the day. There is a long table in the room with ample room for all of us to sit. At this point in time the atmosphere seems comfortably informal. There are computers around for Deputy use, handbooks on the various codes, including criminal, municipal, state and county. There is a vending machine and restrooms around the corner. A self-serve coffee set up is also just outside in the hallway. An occasional trustee, appreciative of doing such good time, comes in to offer service.

There are various bulletin boards with instructions and procedures to follow. On the far wall is a large white board indicating work status of deputies. There are several names. A few are followed by the inscription, "AWOL." Other names are put down for being "Lame." The next line says, "No one watching the jail!" The next line down says, "No one cares!"

A couple of Deputies are writing up reports. Another deputy is consulting with the Sergeant. Now a deputy arrives for duty...limping. Someone says, "See a chiropractor!"

Another deputy looks at me, then says, "See the shrink!"

"Hey, Look at me, see my hand. What's wrong with them...They don't work."

The deputy with the limp just complains more. They act as if they do not believe him. I don't know if he's hurting or not. He does have trouble getting his boots on. A good actor. But once in uniform, his voice and demeanor takes on a more serious role.

It takes more than an hour for the hamburgers to arrive. I don't ask who, nor how they are being made.

In the meantime, I hear the loud speaker blasting away, "Lieutenant Gartrell, wanted at the bridge!"

Deputy Scott clarifies the matter. "Lieutenant Gartrell 'to the bridge' makes reference that he was in the Marine Corps for twenty years before becoming involved with law enforcement." He explains that the call to the bridge is like a roasting where they give him recognition for his service to the country. Upon discharge, Sergeant Gartrell joined The Palm Springs Police Department, then went to San Bernardino Sheriffs Academy, then was assigned here at Big Bear.

Deputy Scott goes on, "Going to the bridge" is the Navy term, also Marine, rather than Army, for the Control Center. "The reason we call him "Lieutenant" is not because he is a Deputy with the rank of Lieutenant but because he was in the Marine Corps and became a Mustang." He goes on to explain that he went through the enlisted ranks to Master Sergeant, then through warrant officer ranks to become Chief Warrant Officer.

By using such terminology, it seems to be their way of recognizing his background while at the same time roasting him. I learn that when he served in Kuwait during Desert Storm as a chemical warfare specialist, he had observed, through mass spectrometry of blood samples of troops, that Iraqi forces were using chemical-biological weapons which he believes to have caused systemic damage to many personnel in service. As the Pentagon was denying such a turn of events, he felt compelled to testify to U.S. Congress on this clandestine operation on the part of Iraqi forces as well as the significance for needed expense to provide medical attention to the GI's so infected. We talked and pondered the significance of risking career to speak out on what we believe is the "truth." I shared some similar kinds of stories, perhaps not as dramatic as testifying to Congress, but nevertheless, risk taking in terms of my career.

Deputy Karen describes her outlook and background with LAPD and their psychiatric emergency team, of her adjustment to the Sheriff's Department here in San Bernardino County, and of her attitude about police work. I listen attentively as she continues. She easily discusses the stressors of the job and what it is like working with male colleagues.

On her tunic is an ID tag with her name on it. But here, you would never believe that this attractive young lady has any other name but "Princess."

By referring to Karen as *Princess*, they are constantly reminding her (and themselves, I suppose) that they are to be constantly on guard to watch their language and behavior while in her presence, pointing out the importance to one another to be always on guard against possible allegations of sexual harassment. The whole atmosphere around the place is quite comical.

In one way or another she tells me that Big Bear is largely a WASP-ish community with a lot of prejudicial ideas among the residents.

Almost as if planned, in comes two calls from dispatch. She gets them. "A barking dog." She looks at me and says, "That's what people get dogs for, to bark. What can this be about?"

I can't help but complain to her about my own dogs and how I put them in jail, i.e. in a kennel inside the house when they act up.

She says, "Oh, now there's another complaint. Of Mexicans drinking on the premises." She tightens her belt, takes a deep breath, and heads for her car to handle this one first.

Another deputy tells me that there was a call last week from an old lady who called because there was a bat that had entered her house. He felt he was treated like a hero. Obviously they like their duty here and morale is high. I really enjoy such an atmosphere in a place like this where stressors do occur, at times intense, but then resolved.

Now a call comes in from a mother complaining that her son's car was taken away for impound. This call was in connection with a prior arrest on a penal code 267 violation which I heard reference to as I came in earlier.

Deputy Gartrell, now on call, explains to the mother on the phone the importance of the Sheriffs removal of cars from a scene of a crime and why they had the car impounded. The deputy senses she is furthering the corruption of her son. Here, the mother was blaming the deputy for taking her sons' car away, even though he was caught dong an unlawful act, a violation of P.C. 267. I look it up in the reference book and discover it is " the abduction of a minor." I sense, by the mother not going along with the police procedure to impound the car and her ploy to quickly get the car back for his use, she was showing how she manages to corrupt her son, saying one thing, but doing another "to let it go."

Finally, the hamburgers arrive. Of course, with the trimmings. In the meantime there are soft drinks on the table and snacks for anyone that wants one. One of the deputies is eating his lunch that he brought from home. I can tell the deputies are used to such snacks. But of course, we're not. And we're quite famished after our ordeal. It seems like we can better understand their ordeal in dealing with the stressors involved in maintaining order after being placed in a stressor situation ourselves.

The "princess" returns. Deputy Karen explains that indeed there were some Latinos sitting on the lawn in front of the high school. But they were drinking Cokes. "There was no laws being broken."

"I told you we live in a prejudiced community here!"

"I see what you mean." I asked her, "What about the barking?"

"The dogs stopped. It resolved itself."

10:00 PM: Hannah and Jon Arrive

The Green Hornets dispatcher informs us all that Jon had called on the cellular phone announcing that they are nearby and ready to pull into the parking lot. It's hard to tell whether Jon is "putting it on" or whether he is just plain anxious about things. But in any event he is announcing his arrival and we are all interested in hearing his story. The deputy that came in limping, was curious. He asks us all, when we're together, how did it happen that such situation like this occurred and how it may be prevented. In so doing, the deputy displays his effective style of leadership and his comfort with such inquiry, demonstrating to the other watchful deputies his method "of getting the facts" so as to facilitate a good report.

The sergeant asks Jon, "I would appreciate it if you were to tell me your side of the story so as perhaps I might learn something about how situations like this can happen." Joel and I are dying from anticipation.

Jon says, "Well, Ah,. It was something like this." Obviously embarrassed but also enjoying the attention. He hesitates and then says something like the following:

> They woke me up. I was impatient. I got up before them.
> I was cold. I wanted to get moving. I got dressed and
> told them I would wait for them after an hour on the
> trail. After awhile, I got tired of waiting and went on.
> Then I rested again. I went on. Rested again. I was
> worried about them. I came upon a dirt road. Without
> seeing a marker or trail, I followed the dirt road for a while.
> It came to Highway 38. I realized I had gone in the
> wrong direction. I came back and got on the trail. I saw
> two back packers going north. They said they didn't see
> Joel and my dad. I went on. I came upon another dirt
> road and decided to take it to the highway to make a call
> home. A car stopped and offered me a ride. They were
> going to Redlands. They dropped me off at the Union
> 76 Station and then I called home.

What we agree upon was that Joel and I had passed the dirt road near the animals while Jon was off the trail. From that point on we were ahead of him only by minutes, but nevertheless he was beyond range of my whistle. Another factor contributing to the fiasco was that I was reluctant to blow my whistle so as not to disturb the animals.

We express our gratitude to the staff at the station, exchange some non-verbal gestures acknowledging all were relieved by the happy ending. I know from this experience, and others in the past, that their role in providing supportive service is underplayed and generally unrecognized by the general public. We drive off to spend the evening at the cabin, forty-five minutes away at Green Valley Lake.

10:30 PM: Green Valley Lake.

There is much discussion on details of how it came to be that we got separated. How come Joel and I could not identify his foot prints. Why did he not write a message on the dirt or write down the time he was at a certain place or why did he not just wait a while longer. We never stopped talking about what happened and what we were thinking about until we went to sleep. We wisely spend the evening at the cabin at Green Valley Lake where we shower and discuss ways to avoid getting lost from one another.

May 17, Monday, Green Valley Lake, El 7000

We wake up refreshed, feeling better, but aching from the day before. We still talk about the hike and the details that led to Jon's separation, particularly what may have prompted Jon to do the things he had done and how Joel and I permitted such an event to occur. This incident prompts us reflect on safety, to come to grips with the necessity to maintain physical fitness, to except limitations on the part of oneself as well as others, for proper planning for each leg, and for all hikers to have access to compass and map and knowing how to coordinate their use on the trail.

We agree that should one leave the trail it is essential to communicate in one way or another by conventional or agreed upon signs. We also agree on the importance of establishing explicit objectives for the day should we separate.

They point out that speed alone does not lead to covering large distances. Jon points out that even though one goes consistently slower (I think he may be referring to me) it is better than moving along at a fast clip. Moving quickly, according to Jon, requires longer rests and causes general fatigue. He points out that when they were waiting for me to catch up with them, I didn't require a rest but just continued going. I noted that they always wanted more rest when I caught up with them. I then would move off and expect them to catch up and pass me.

Chapter 11
Around Big Bear and Baldwin Lake
to Van Dusen Canyon

Around Big Bear and Baldwin Lake to Van Dusen Canyon

The following is an account of the 17 mile trek from near Arrastre Trail Camp to the trail head at Van Dusen Canyon, an area skipped last year.

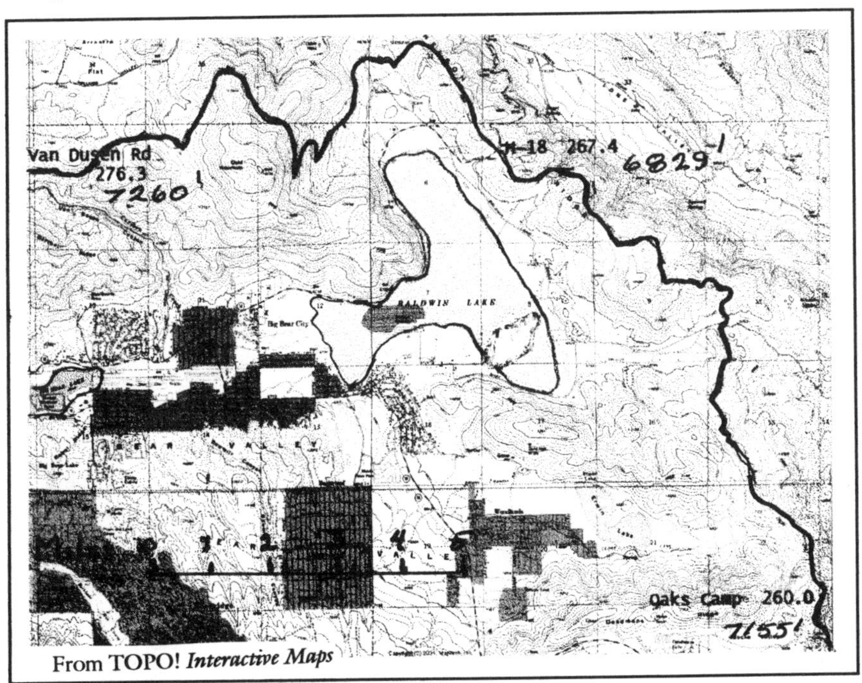

Oaks Camp, around Baldwin Lake, to Van Dusen Canyon

December 24, 2000, 8:45 AM: Oaks Camp near Big Bear, El 7800, 260.5 - 0.2, 25 Degrees, calm

Joel had planned a skiing trip and joined Hannah and I at the cabin in Green Valley Lake. The lake was is frozen over. Though some patches of snow remain by the cabin, the northern exposure is 70% snow covered. My thermometer reads 23 degrees. Joel will follow me in his car to the PCT trail head in Van Dusen Canyon where I park the car. Along the way I notice the thermometer fluctuating from a high of 29 to a low of 21. The snow making machines at Snow Valley are in full blast, blowing frozen steam out a thousand feet out. At the trail head at Van Dusen Canyon, El 7260, the temperature reads 22 degrees. I park the car, secure it and hop into Joel's pick up truck. He makes the drive around Big Bear Lake and before meeting his friends nearby and hitting the slopes as planned he drops me off at Oaks Camp, just off the PCT where we aborted our trek last year. We agree, it seems familiar. But it does look different than it did two years ago. Things often don't look the same while driving through an area that one has walked. Though snow is seen on the nearby slopes to the west, there is no snow to be seen here at Oaks Camp. The flora is dominated by large pinyon pines and sage. There are livestock feeding in their corrals. A few clean, parked cars can be seen. I see no inside lights in the dwellings.

I ask, "Do you remember where the old road is that drops down to the PCT?"

"No, not really, but all you have to do is head down." He points to the east, "And there you'll find the trail."

He's anxious to leave. "Do you know where they are?"

"No, I told them I'd call from nearby. The cell phone hasn't been working around here. I'll have to go back into town to a phone booth."

"I hope you can reach them in time. Thanks for dropping me off."

"Good luck."

Joel drops me off and pulls out.

I look around. All is quiet. It is cold. I put on my extra fleece jacket, and as I check the charts I realize I left the compass in the car.

I head a bit to the east looking for the road and find a recently built beautiful outdoor chapel overlooking the valley below and ridges and mountains beyond. I look down and see no easy way down, nor do I have any assurance even if I were to head down the steep slopes that I would reach the trail. If only I had my compass! I head back up to the parking area, and walk generally southeast to a corral where several horses are watching my movements. I recall the road leading up northwest from the PCT and passing a couple of landmarks, a small pond before reaching this spot.

I head for the corrals and try to not disturb the animals, sheep, horses and mules. I choose to not get too close and head northward. I see a sign indicating the direction to their archery and firing ranges. Their firing range, in the 1994 *Guidebook* is described as adjacent and in sight of the trail. Much has been recently bulldozed, with new constructed facilities, including a firing range. Perhaps for safety reasons, they destroyed the road. It was in real bad shape two years ago.

I head northeasterly along a trail with recent horse tracks. Sparse sagebrush dominates the arid and exposed area. The trail meanders down to meet a canyon and dry stream bed. According to the topo, it heads north-westward toward Sugarloaf and Lake Erwin area, away from the trail. I look for a route to the east. I see ahead an old jeep trail leading directly eastward and uphill to the ridge to the east. I opt for it, and climb up a hundred feet or so to the summit. As I reach the steep summit, right at the top I see a couple of trails and an old post. I look at it twice, take off my pack to decipher the faded out inscription, and to my pleasant surprise, I read that I am indeed now on the PCT as it had just left the stream bed to climb out of the canyon.

9:15 AM: Back on the PCT, El ca. 7,000, ca Mi 260.3

I check my topo. I conclude I am about a 1/3 mile north of where Joel and I left the PCT last year. Around me, atop this arid ridge are but five kinds of plants growing. Sage, occasional dried out buckwheat and/or brittle brush, dwarfed mountain mahogany and up trail to the north a bit, bright green stalks of ephedra, known also as Mormans Tea. Unlike the riparian and transitional forest back alongside Arrastre Creek, the area is quite xeric. The bed of Arrastre Creek can be seen meandering northeasterly towards the desert to the east.

On the trail are bear prints and recent droppings with little moist seeds, like choke berries and/or manzanita. I feel their presence. But what a relief to be back on the PCT. Very soon I see more of the same fresh droppings and bear tracks. I hear some breathing and thumping from about thirty yards uphill and to my rear! Is it my imagination? I see part of a large animal. It is too bulky to be a deer and much too big to be a coyote or mountain lion. The terrain is steep and rocky. It is steeply uphill in rocky terrain. I hear a snort and something that sounds like a horse blowing it's breath in rapid succession. I remember how Larry, from Larry's Summit Valley Store told me that bears don't make growling sound, only a kind of snort. A better look and I make out a trunk of an animal I see greyish-brown hair in clumps. Then two animals. Burros! What a relief! We are eye to eye. They stand with upright heads, both alert, side to side, motionless, absorbed in my action. I wonder if they are lost or runaways. The trail now leads away from them. I look back and they have slowly moved off as well.

The view is wonderful. Everything is crisp. To the south are seven ridges, each towering over the other, culminating in snow covered, Onyx Peak. I can detail the trail and where it leads to Bear Mountain and Onyx Peak. To the immediate west is the shoulder of Bear Mountain. To the north are a series of low mountains forming the length of Nelson Ridge and Gold Mountain and dry Lake Erwin, with it's residential area . To the immediate east is a broadening semi arid valley with Arrastre Creek winding inside generally northeastward. Over the ridge, beyond Arrastre Creek lies the huge desert area of Lucerne Valley and more desert areas and mountains beyond. Indeed, this is part of the greater desert divide. Everything easterly is arid and everything westerly is richly forested. Flora along the tread reveals the remarkable transition.

From here, the PCT continues northerly following the top of the divide. The trail goes through stretches of pinyon pines, some scrubby oak, some with almost full growth, but none much over twenty feet. There are occasional yucca in various phases of development including several Joshua tree to be seen before descending somewhat to strike dirt road 2N02. El 7155, Mi 3.8. This good road can also be seen meandering at a somewhat lower altitude to the east, through pinyon forests near Arrastre Creek. The creek always remains unseen below the lip, deep in the heart of the canyon it carved.

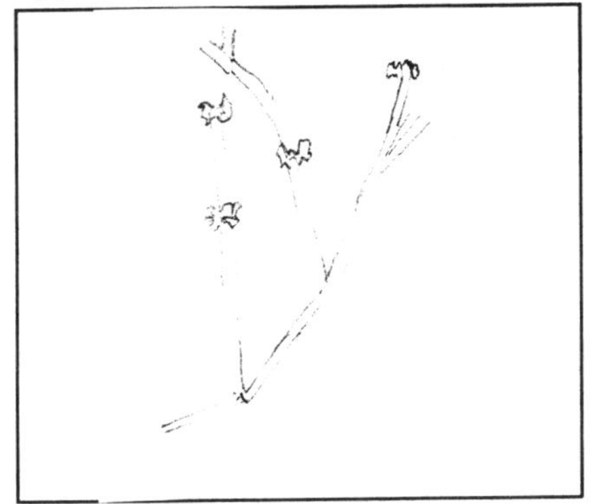

Ephedra (Mormons Tea)

Once on Nelson Ridge, the trail meanders around two of its small peaks. The views of distant terrain remain the same. Here, at the somewhat higher altitude, perhaps two or three hundred feet above 6,700 foot, Baldwin Lake, particularly on the eastern slopes, one finds an occasional lump of scraggly prickly pear, an occasional yucca in various stages of development, widely scattered ephedra, various dried out brittle brush and chia in and between glades of now more healthy looking pinyon pines. From one of the summits overlying an arid section of the trail is a strewn area of burnt down pinyon trees laying about as if rolled down the hill to the east.

As I round the ridge overlooking a new modern ranch-resort facility, I hear the sound of approaching motorcycles. They are getting louder and louder. They might be on the trail. The squeal, roaring and exhaust get's louder. I jump out of the way and let them pass. There are a number of signs posted that limit their approach onto the PCT, but the signs are few and far between. The area has many trails that differ not from the PCT. I follow their tracks to Highway 18. The trail becomes a bit more shaded. As the paved highway is approached, I can see the first sign of tall scrub oaks, signaled by their characteristic oak leaves that carpet the trail. Now, a Jeffrey tree is sighted, confirmed by it's unique egg shaped cones strewn about.

12:30 PM: Highway 18, El 6829, Mi 263.2 - 0.1, calm, approx 32 degrees

Though mid-day, though sweating moderately, I am continuing to wear long pants, fleece sweater rolled up and mittens. In the shade it is cold. In the exposed areas, it is warm. I am warm, but also occasionally feel cold because of sweating at the same time, but overall, comfortable. Once across the road and up the trail a bit, I take the first real rest, about ten minutes. I seek out a cold apple I stored and slowly polish it off. Then an energy bar with a lot of water. I decide to continue on to Doble Trail Camp, where I will take stock of things and decide where I might stay for the evening, or push on.

About a 1:00 PM I reach the turn off to Doble Trail Camp, El 6,880, Mi 269.9. Considering that I have traveled about 10 miles already, I should reach Van Dusen Canyon, up and over near-the-top, 6.3 miles away to my awaiting car about dusk. But I also consider once the sun goes down, because there is a new moon, it will get can dark quickly and because it will get much colder, I must have options for an adequate overnight site. The *Guidebook* and the appearance of things suggest several possibilities for stealth camping, but no campsites of any kind before Van Dusen Canyon. I have a small single AAA flashlight that works. I decide to go on to try to make it to the car. Should it appear that I cannot make it there within an hour after dusk, then if necessary, I'll use my little flashlight.

The trail immediately starts to climb, with some broad switchbacks, up through a 7,700 foot gap to the northeast exposure of Gold Mountain. As the trail climbs, one soon leaves the dominating high desert flora and quickly enters into the montane forest of Jeffrey pines, very large mountain mahogany, very large scrub oaks, wide trunk juniper with its blue berries carpeting the trail. There are small oak leaves and needles from broken twigs of high reaching incense-cedars lying on the tread. There is even an occasional manzanita. White firs of good height appear. Yet, there is a lingering hint of the high desert flora as occasional scraggly low lying prickly pear and an occasional yucca, and pinyon pine appear upon reaching the northeastern exposure of 8,235 foot Gold Mountain and it's 8,000 foot western spine and shoulder. But the magnificent Jeffrey pine and incense-cedars share the throne as they dominate the forest.

The one thousand foot climb up after Doble trail camp is slow going. The trail transverses three or four broad rock slides. They creak and grown as they slip downward in response to my weight, even as I gingerly step from one to another. These piles look as though created by prospect blasting. As I reach the 7700 foot gap, I find that it is now past 3:00 PM, to become dark soon with three or four miles to go.

As expected, the trail levels off and commences a long moderate descent. I pick up my speed with hopes of not having to use my flashlight to find a campsite at dark in the cold. The forest is rich. Many plants overrun one another. White firs are growing amidst clusters of mountain mahogany. Junipers and incense cedars are doing the same thing. The tall odorous Jeffrey pines over shadow most everything.

As the sun is setting, I know I am getting close to the car as I see Van Dusen Canyon and the road a couple hundred feet below. Instead of heading directly for the road, the trail parallels the road as if waiting for the road to reach it's height. Finally, the trail reaches a small wooden bridge at Caribou Creek, and a campsite. I look ahead, I see the road and my car. It is 4:45 PM and now getting dark. I put my pack into the car, take a swig of hot coffee from the thermos, heat up the car, turn on the lights and head down the dirt road to the highway. Now warm, I call Hannah at the cabin by cell phone to let her know I expect to be there in an hour.

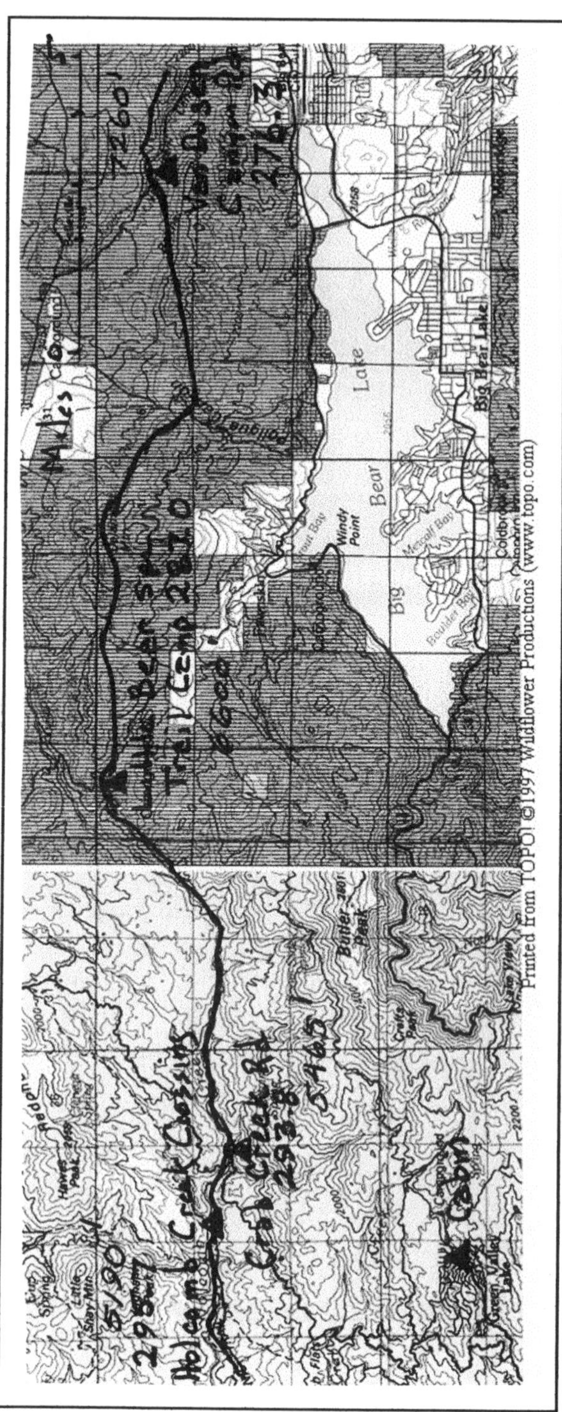
Big Bear to Holcomb Creek Crossing T.C.

Chapter 12

Big Bear(Van Dusen Canyon) to Deep Creek Bridge

Van Dusen Canyon....Little Bear Trail Camp....
Crab Creek Road....Holcomb Creek Crossing Trail
Camp...A stealth camp site

May 24, Monday; Preparing to Return to the Trail

Joel is interested in doing the next leg with me, from Big Bear to Holcomb Creek Crossing. From there a five mile walk will take us to our cabin at Green Valley Lake, a total of perhaps thirty miles or so. We figure it will be great to hike to our cabin and finish a hike with shower, fresh food and a soft bed. We drive the 104 miles to the cabin. We discuss our options. We agree to head for the general area and try to find a connection to the PCT east of Baldwin Lake.

Once we get there, I realize I left my meds at the cabin in Green Valley Lake. I pull out the map. I offer, "Look, let's drive back to Big Bear and drive up Van Dusen Canyon. We can park the car there. From there I figure I can make it to the cabin tomorow and catch up on my meds. And we can be on our way."

"Sounds OK to me", as Joel easily agrees.

So, we drive past the airport and go up Van Dusen Canyon where we easily find the trail head. We park and secure the car.

12:00 Noon, At the PCT Trail Head at Van Dusen Canyon, El 7260, 276.3 Mi - 0.0

Loaded with water, we are on our way. Not exactly as planned, but it'll do. Normally, a northbound departure along the PCT from Big Bear City entails a walk or ride up Van Dusen Canyon Road for about two miles to where the PCT crosses the road. As we parked and secured the car, a shuttle van appears a hundred yards south of us. It stops and drops off two male backpackers, one with an unusually large pack. They immediately head northwest on the PCT. Though we are on our own, we apparently are not the only ones.

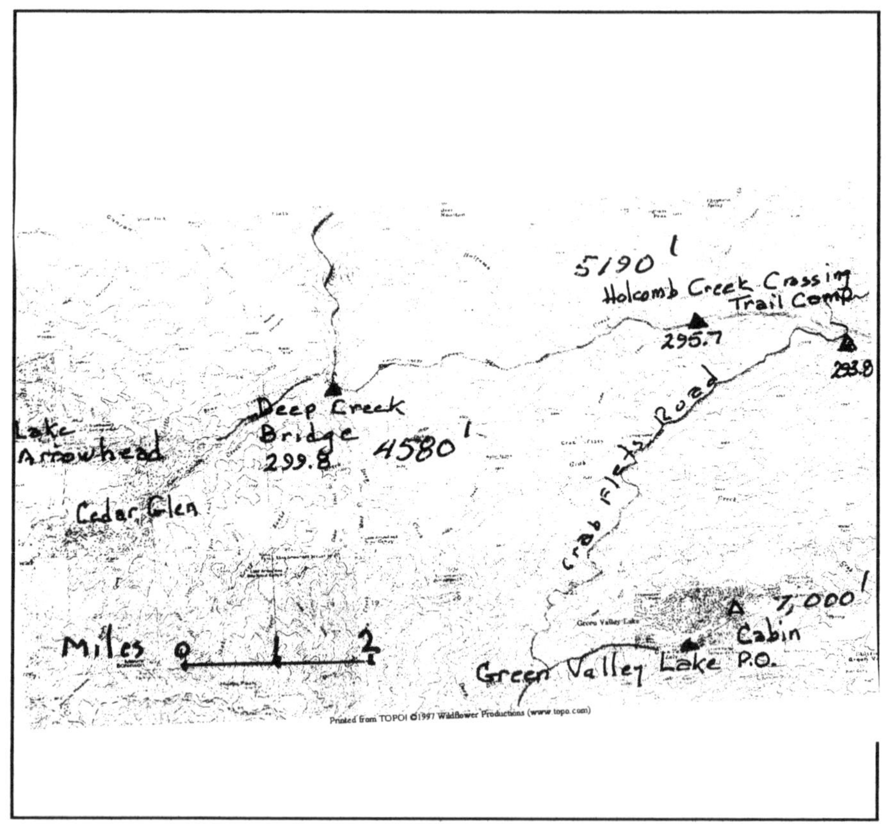

Holcomb Crk Crossing TC to The Deep Creek Bridge

The trail first climbs out of the canyon at a gentle ascent though a typical, but somewhat sparse montane forest. Here, there are a wide number of chaparral–type plants; mountain mahogany, Jeffery pines and junipers catching your eye as you easily stroll through the pleasant, shady and well marked trail leading you up on the side of Bertha Peak. Soon there are dramatic views to the north of Holcomb Valley where only remnants exist of the once booming but lawless town of Bellevue about 120 years ago.

On an earlier trip I had gone through the area and was impressed with the history of the area. The very life of the community was intimately connected to the price of gold. When the rate goes up, there is activity in gold mining in this area. When the price goes down, you don't see very many people panning or digging. I've been in the lucky Baldwin mine a number of years ago, found the caves quite lengthy, intimidating in their dark narrowness.

From here, there is a good distance away to the mines laying below to the right and somewhat behind us. Holcomb Valley looks quite habitable. There are flat areas all over the place with meadows and green grass appearing throughout the broad valley. Yet, no sign of people, animals nor structures except for a few small buildings abandoned years ago during the gold rush.

About this time we come across one of the backpackers that was left off in the van at Van Dusen Canyon. He says he is hiking on to Canada. He's carrying a heavy load including an ice ax in preparation for icy conditions. His pack must be quite heavy. We chat for a minute or so. I say "Cameron, you'll probably pass us soon, perhaps at Little Bear Trail Camp. See you soon."

Suddenly, the trail crosses a minor gap in the ridge paralleling the northern flank of Big Bear Lake, exposing the entire lake. Below, can be seen the southern shoreline communities, recreational areas

Big Bear Lake

and ski lifts cutting up through Big Bears' southern 8,000 foot ridge. The San Gorgonio Wilderness area beyond with snow capped Mount Gorgonio, "Greyback," 11, 530' dominating the scene. The lake down below looks like a map. **The** boats look like toys pulling human like figures producing wakes on the glimmering surface. There is no sound, but an occasional rustle of a squirrel, a squirming of a lizard, or a puff of breeze through the nearby pine needles.

This view is one of the several so far that cause me to stop motion. All thoughts leave consciousness, vanish as I take in and come to grips with the emotional aspect of the experience. For a moment, time seems to stop. I reach for my USGS 7 1/2 minute topological map and enjoy the experience of re-identifying familiar landmarks. I have a sense of serene joy, an appreciation of being able to recall experience of so many summers and winters in this wondrous area I am now overlooking.

It was down there, that I first put on skis, at Snow Summit, in 1955. At that time advanced skiers practiced with short chains connecting their long and heavy wooden skis together, thus keeping them from separating. My first pair of skis, also long and wooden, are now leaning against the wall in the Green Hornets Lounge, usable, but very heavy and long, over 200 cm. The soft leather boots were comfortable but loose even after being securely tied with regular shoe laces. The boot was connected at the toe with the timely "Ski Free" toe binding that released with torque. They had spooling wires that you fit around a groove in the rear of the boot that is secured to the ski permitting an adjustable and springy rise to the heel. In those days one were able to walk level easier as they approached the heel rise of a cross country ski. Because of these limitations to my equipment, I had no alternative but to become an 'advanced' skier the first day out. It was impossible to snow plow even on icy snow, let alone do a snow plow type turn, an intermediate maneuver, because the skis were quite long, the heels rose off the ski and the boots were too loose.

Directly across the lake are the slopes of the old Snow Forest Ski Resort. Two friends of Hannah, two brothers, in the 1950's developed a moderate slope into a resort, with a novel snow making machine, that was clearly designed for the emerging 'intermediate' skier. The top was accessible by T-bars where a wide semi steep slope with numerous turns awaited you and where you could stop at any time and slow down...or should you so choose, to easily pick up speed and race down beyond your skill level.

I also see the area where I stayed with my parents as a kid, back in 1941, where I first confronted steers on a pasture. There is also the area where I went horseback riding for the first time, where I got thrown off sustaining a broken arm.

I can see parts of the lake that for a number of summers were once quite dry. Perhaps the tapping of the streams provide sufficient water now to keep the level of the lake to the dam overflow.

Of course, I see the airport where I had made various landings. But this aerial view far surpasses the beauty of that seen by airplane. I cannot offer an adequate reason for this observation, except that when you are in the air it is difficult to look down. When you are in control of the plane, you mustn't permit yourself the luxury of being distracted by the beauty. From such a height in a man-made machine, the relationship with the terrain below is different than when one is part of the wilderness. Perhaps it is a concern for safety when flying so low to not appreciate the detail seen from above. Here on the ridge, on this well maintained trail, on this picture perfect day, there is plenty of time to reflect on the scenery and reflect on such matters.

Civilization and its' resources are no more than an hour or so away by downhill trail. Though now close to Fawnskin, it seems like another world up here. Nor is it of much concern that a trail camp awaits us a few miles ahead. Actually, the area is full of suitable wayside places to put up for the night.

The trail contours through the north side of Delamar Mountains and begins a lazy descent down the mid and northerly side of the ridge. Across several dirt roads and a few more switchbacks, we approach Holcomb Creek.

4:00 PM: Little Bear Springs Trail Camp, 6600 Ft. 287.0 Mi - 0.0

The trail eventually descends down onto the northern slopes of the 8,000' ridge to reaching Holcomb Creek. Here lies well maintained Little Bear Springs Trail camp. This camp is well suited for horses and seems approachable by jeep or motorcycle. There is a well watered trowel, corral, picnic benches, piped water with good pressure, level sites to set up camp with a slow and quiet stream right there.

Though Joel and I are not tired by the walk, we have had a long day of driving, searching for the trail, frustrated by having to change hiking strategies, grateful that we are here at a convenient time and place.

The weather is great! It is easy to wash up and enjoy the bathing, cleaning and drying out. Joel chooses a soft place, but soon, I hear,

"Dad, there's ants all over. There's an anthill right over there"!

"Try this spot!"

We easily settle down, readily find a good area to set up our sleeping quarters. We pull out our food and plan for supper and evening.

I review the *Guidebook* and topo. I determine that before the PCT gets to Holcomb Creek Crossing, about 6.5 miles away, the trail first crosses Crab Flats Road, about 4.5 miles ahead. I propose, "We part company at Crab Flats Road. I'll go on from there, five miles to the cabin, pick up my meds, and meet you at Holcomb Creek Crossing."

Joel replied, "Yeah, and then go on to the hot springs."

We review the charts and figure out how to plan the trip so as to be at the hot springs at mid-day.

I said, "I'll try to make it back before dark. Let's have a plan of what to do if I do not show up." I further went on to explain, "If I do not show up by 5:30 PM, I suggest you climb up to Crab Flats, take the road a couple of miles then take the short cut to the cabin. You should make it there before it really gets dark.".

Joel thought about the matter, then replied, "How about if you do not show up by 9:00 AM tomorrow, that I return to the cabin?"

I said, "OK." If things go the way I think they will, if I don't get a ride either way, I would expect to be at Holcomb Creek Crossing in about six hours on leaving you at Crab Flats Road. I'll probably stay at the cabin for an hour, then return downhill, about two and a half hours, which should take me to the crossing at about 5:00 PM, way before dark."

"OK."

I say, "Unless something comes up, that's what we'll do." We discussed a number of possibilities that could affect the timing.

We turn in at 6:30 PM, quite a while before dusk. We chatted a bit while in our bags, and had a long night at rest. I urge Joel to consider the *Sleep Screen* Net. He reluctantly sets it up and tries it out.

May 26, From Little Bear to Crab Creek Road,
El 6600, 287.0 Mi

As we were in the sack for almost 11 hours, we easily get up at the first gleam of light. Unlike the trip through the San Bernardino Mountains last week, the evening was relatively warm, requiring fleece hat and mittens only in the very early morning hours. We packed up our stuff and got an early start.

The trail soon climbs up and away from the creek on the northern banks somewhat beyond the margin of mature alders, willows, cottonwoods, green ferns and grasses. Here, above the stream bed we find various conifers including ponderosa and other conifers widely set apart with clumps of scrub and black oak providing most of the shade in the early morning hour. The forest is not as thick as somewhat higher, at least as compared to the immediate northern exposure north of Gold, Bertha and Delamar Mountains.

Below are inviting pools of water formed by a series of makeshift dams forming pools of water. The debris forming the dams are not left not by chance nor by humans, but by beavers. They provide layers of inviting pools separated by heights of less than a foot from one another with water running over and through the dam structure, constructed by branches of willows, cottonwoods, ceanothus, baccharis and anything else that's nearby. I don't see any animals swimming about, perhaps it is too early.

It is quite a nice walk through the area, generally downhill, with some ups and downs mixed in. Here are large groves of white alders of various sizes, Jeffrey pines, white firs, various kinds of oak trees, cottonwood trees with an undergrowth of green pipe grass, numerous grasses and wild flowers. Just above the stream on the north side are the typical chaparral I have seen for miles including an occasional yucca, chia, and ceanothus.

10:00 AM At Crab Flats Road, El 5465, 293.1 Mi
To Green Valley Lake

We rest. We update and summarize our planned separation. I expect to get to Crab Flats Campground on this evenly moderately graded wide light colored dirt road in excellent condition in a little more than an hour. From Crab Flats, I will take the road up for three miles to where there is an abandoned road that goes steeply up to Holcomb Creek Road. From there to the Cabin should require but a fifteen minute walk, a total of about four hours. I plan to stay at the cabin for about an hour, to leave there about 3:00 p.m. to return the way I came, but to pick up a trail that leads downhill from west of the campground more directly to Holcomb Creek Crossing where I expect to arrive about 5:30 PM assuming I cannot hitch a ride.

We reaffirm that should something come up, Joel will camp overnight downstream and wait til 9:00 a.m. Should there be no sign of myself, then Joel is to walk on to the cabin the way I described and arrive there about 12:30 or 1:00 p.m.

Joel will take as much as my stuff as will fit in his backpack enabling me to make it back before 5:30 p.m. For him the 1.9 mile jaunt is a pleasant downhill jaunt for about a couple of miles and he could take his sweet time.

The walk along the dirt road is moderately steep and boring. It requires at least an hour to make it to Crab Flats, a trip I have done last year with Hannah. This time there was a little bit of water here and there seeping down across the road.

The road parallels Holcomb Creek as it climbs. But you cannot see the stream, just the monotonous dry mountain ridge to the north. Whereas the rising hills to the immediate south are montane, the hills to the north are limited to sparse, short and greying chaparral.

The road continues to wind uphill. No cars pass from any direction. No chance for a hitch. The short cut from Crab Creek Road bypasses the Green Valley Lake dam going directly to Holcomb Creek Road at the town. But it is still too steep and rutted for off road vehicles. There are recent tire marks. They indicate they got stuck. It is so steep it takes me over half an hour to just walk up a quarter of a mile or so. Upon reaching the road, I easily stroll down the road, past a number of cabins to reach ours, a half mile or so away.

A stroke of Good Luck!

Soon, I see Bud McPhail's cabin, a popular and long term resident of Green Valley Lake, a contractor that has done some work on our cabin. As I pass Bud's home, a young man is out in front working on an outdoor stove. Bud did some recent work on our cabin, fixing a heating problem. This work had been done several months ago. I had not received a bill from him. At the time he was complaining about his back and legs, that he was in such discomfort that he could not do much work himself and that it might take a while.

I asked the young man, "How's Bud? I understand he had a rough back problem."

"He seems OK to me. He's right inside."

I knock on the door. Out comes Bud. "Bud, how are you. How's your back?"

He goes on to say that it is really his knee that is bothering him. "It seems to slip out of place and causes a lot of grief."

Regarding the bill, he looks in his records and doesn't find anything. He says, "If I find something or can remember what I did I'll let you know."

In the course of the conversation he discovers I must walk back to Crab Flats to pick up the Pacific Crest Trail. He tells me, "I plan to leave here to go down in about twenty five minutes. If you can be here, I'll drive you down to Crab Flats."

"Sure, that'll be great!"

The Cabin at Green Valley Lake, 7000, +5.0 Mi

No time to congratulate nor console myself for making it to GVL from the Mexican border. I rush to make it to the cabin in ten minutes. I spend five minutes there, just enough to pick up my meds, have a drink of water, use the john, and secure the place. Fifteen minutes later I am back at Bud's house, just in the nick of time for a ride back to Crab Flats, fortunate to be spared the walk back to Crab Flats and reduce Joel's wait.

Bud and I chat along the way down. We talked about a friend of his that did a similar trip, from the Mexican border to Green Valley Lake. He lives in Running Springs. He had excerpts in the local newspaper about his adventures from Mexico. We talked about his marriage of two years ago. I also asked him to paint our cabin. Before long he drops me off right at the trail head below Crab Flats.

After a few words of thanks, I head right down the trail with my meds. I was just on this trail last summer with Hannah. It looks much better now. The trail looks like a group of workers had taken down a mobile machine and smoothed out the sides of the trail, making it much easier and safer to negotiate. I am very impressed with the effort that a number of people are doing to maintain trails.

3:00 PM: Holcomb Creek Crossing Trail Camp, 5190, 195.7 Mi

I drop in on Joel. I find him washing his clothes at the now-well moving stream that runs through this primitive trail camp. He seems to have prepared for a long afternoon and had not long been out of the stream. This trail camp is only accessible to hikers. There are no roads nearby, nor are there picnic tables nor any amenities. Nevertheless it is an adequate place for an overnight or rest.

We compare notes. We decide to put on a few miles so as to have the advantage, time-wise, of enjoying ourselves at Deep Creek Hot Springs tomorrow.

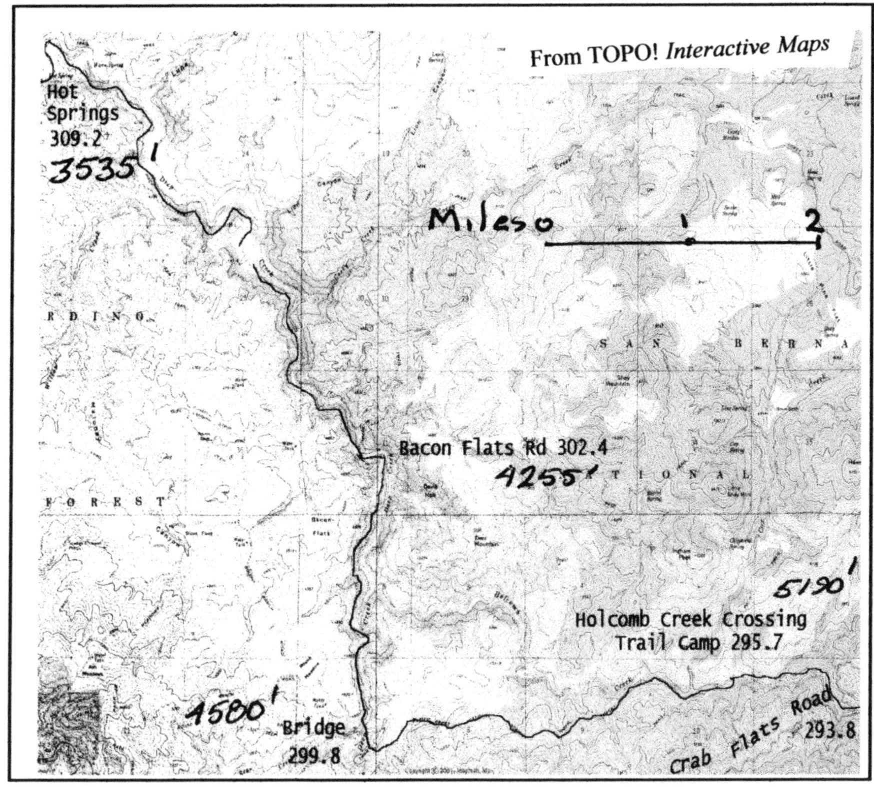

Holcomb Creek Crossing Trail Camp to Deep Creek Hot Springs

6:00 PM: A Pleasant Make-shift Campsite, ca 5000, 198.0 Mi

After a pleasant mile or so walk from Holcomb Creek Crossing Trail Camp, we begin to look for a place to spend the night. We readily find one of several welcome sights and choose a sandy area among some the rocks that seem to invite us to use them tonight as table, chair and counter top for cooking.

After my walk today to Green Valley Lake, putting on an extra four or five miles, Joel and I have no trouble relaxing in our chosen site. I am pleased that Joel volunteers to do the cooking. He makes my brew, incredulously improving the quality of the pasta by carefully not putting it in the boiling brew of dried soup, refried beans and dried beef until they all have cooked well. Then, by putting in the pasta towards the end of the cooking process, he then was able to control and limit the length of time for the pasta to form at its best. We both agreed that this was a great improvement by way of making the mixture. The evening drink was made from a few grams of dried mixture, *Crystal,* when combined with water, forms a liter of raspberry drink. It is remarkable how fast we can polish off a liter of this raspberry drink. We make an another before we almost run out of water. And it is all Kosher! We're off in the sack early again looking forward to see what deep creek looks like, and what the hot springs really offer.

Holcomb Creek before joining
Deep Creek

[Route from Deep Creek Bridge to Cajon Pass is on page 191]

Chapter 13

Deep Creek Bridge to Cajon Pass

A stealth campsite above Holcomb Creek...The bridge across
Deep Creek....Bacon Flats Road at the Creek ....Deep Creek
Hot Springs....The 2nd bridge over Deep Creek....Mojave Dam
....Larry's Summit Valley Country Store....1 ½ Years later
at Larry's Store....Back on the PCT... On the habit of bears....
Trail camp at Silverwood Lake Park...Cajon Pass....Walking back
to Larry's Store

May 27, Thursday: A Stealth Campsite Above Holcomb Creek, El ca.
5000, Mi 298.0

We're off early, at the crack of dawn, refreshed after another long
nights rest. Again we postpone breakfast til we put on some miles at
which time we'll combine a rest with breakfast with the satisfaction we
have already put on some miles towards our objective. We continue to
wind down through a thick mixed conifer forest anxious for a breakfast
break at the bridge, a strategic place because not only Bear Creek
merges into the more active Deep Creek but also the merging of
streams mark the junction of two trails, one leading southeast to Dish
Pan Springs and the other leading to the road to Cedar Glen and Lake
Arrowhead, a few miles away.

Bridge over Deep Creek

9:00 AM: The Bridge Across Deep Creek, 4580, Mi 299.8

Here lies a remarkable 90' span of iron and wood that dramatically sweeps across the canyon providing a wonderful view of the cool and protected watery streambed below. Just at the other side of the bridge is the junction of the short trail that connects the three trails, the Bear Creek Trail, the Trail to Lake Arrowhead and the PCT. What a beautiful spot! It must be an especially welcome site for the south bound traveler, for the miles ahead can be seen exposed in areas with little shade.

From the bridge, the trail follows the general contours remaining high above the stream. Down below, over the lip of the trail, lies the inviting stream below. For miles the trail leads you above the stream, just above the heights of the towering pines alongside aptly named, Deep Creek. The trail, by map suggests it follows the contour at the same distance above the creek. But following it, I am impressed with it's ups and downs, almost as much as going through the San Felipe Hills with rarely a bit of level stretch along the way. Up and down, around dry gulches! The sage, mesquite, cactus and yucca provide little shade. Looking below at the fast moving stream exacerbates the thirst.

The first few miles beyond the bridge puts one immediately into the exposed southwest side of the moving stream , heavily exposed now to the sun to the morning sun. The brush and chaparral is typical of that seen in the low-middle altitudes. There continues to be but little shade.

Just below the trail lies the beckoning greenery of the riparian community out of reach by virtue of a steep cliff that drops down one or two hundred feet to the bottom.

12:00 Noon: Deep Creek at Bacon Flats Road, 4255, Mi 302.4

The first approach to the stream occurs following a descent that junctions with Bacon Flats Road, a dirt road from the Lake Arrowhead region that ends here at the stream. A haven for stream side anglers. There are none here today. Here, as along most of the stream, there are inviting pools of water, perfect for dipping and basking in the sun on any of many smooth boulders amidst the sandy beaches. It is really cool! All kinds of plants are growing down near the stream. It is heavily wooded as boulders, water and sand permit. Alders, conifers, cedars, cottonwoods, ferns provide almost a semi-tropical, yet montane look to the protective area deep in the chasm of the stream bed.

But we are anxious to get to the hot springs area. The trail immediately climbs out of the riparian wonderland to maintain it's tree height distance above the stream. Though we can always hear the stream, we often cannot see it. It is deep and but continues to be inaccessible, 200 long feet below.

The winding chasm soon turns from it's generally northern route to northwest for about three miles. The stream bed drops somewhat as we maintain altitude.

Anonymous

Exposed trail through deep creek

We can see Warm Springs, an area reached from Deep Creek Hot Springs from the other side of the chasm. It is close, but out of reach. There appears no way to get there from here.

The drop in altitude is gradual, not noticeable because of the lowering canyon bottom as we follow it along. But we do drop in altitude and become closer to the desert, hidden from view by the ridge just above our altitude to our northeast. The flora becomes even lower to the ground and more thinned out as each plant competes with another for whatever moisture remains below the surface.

More swimming holes become apparent as we look way down. Water and wet rocks look so good when you are hot and dry! Now, we are so high above the creek we cannot hear it. But as we can plainly see, there is a lot of water running through with considerable growth.

Finally, the trail begins to descend at a faster rate than the canyon bottom. Just as we get near the bottom of the canyon, we look ahead a hundred yards and see a small cienega and the hot springs area.

2:30 PM: Deep Creek Hot Springs. El 3535, Mi 309.2 - 0.0

We're impressed. This is something to behold. The area is accessible only to people hiking in. Approaching the area, I see the popular trail leading down from Bowen Ranch

One of several hot and cold pools

opposite the stream, a fairly steep trail traversing the high ridge to the northeast, perhaps a couple miles. Arriving at the hot springs I see a cienega on a hillside about fifty yards wide with occasional streamlets of water running down, at times through grassy areas and at other places through muddy areas. Some people are covered with this mud!

Several people, mostly semi-dressed adults are lying about moving very slowly through the area.

Before us is an idyllic scene. A person is strumming away on a guitar, overlooking several pools of hot water. All in all there are at least four good size pools where there is sufficient room in each of them for several people to spread out comfortably with adequate distance. The clarity varies from clear to sparkling clear! The pools become somewhat misty as the clean sandy bottom is stirred up momentarily as one steps in and out or moves about on the bottom.

The hottest pool is not one of the above, but a small pool, too small to sit it, "the cooker," Hotter than hell, about 120 degrees, too warm to touch. Hot enough for tea. A pipe runs into this particular area several feet away.

"The water comes out so hot," said a young lady, with a smile, "that you can make tea right there on the spot with mint leaves just a few yards away. But be careful because it is right next to some poison Oak!"

How does it taste"? I ask.

"You have to put a lot in it, especially if you want a buzz from it."

"I'll look for it."

"It's right around those rocks. You can't miss it ."

All I found in the immediate area was poison oak. I wonder what it was she put in it. It sure made her happy.

It wasn't long til Joel and I jumped into the cold water knowing that we could at any time step into a warm or hot pool to soak in. The swimming is good as there is but little current in the pool. Not soon enough, we adapted to the cold water and swam through it. Catching our breath, we then stepped slowly into one of several other hot pools.

This pool, characterized by a nice sandy bottom is much like the pool near Sierra City, where Hannah and I spent the night two summers ago. But here, the pools are maintained solely by volunteers, one of them is sitting right here in the pool beside me. Because the area is so clean and well maintained the Forest Service personnel are somewhat tolerant of the people that camp nearby. Camping is not permitted. At the hot springs. Most people camp nearby up in the private land of Bowen Ranch an hour or so up the trail.

We walked around exploring the area. We find all kinds of inviting pools, some warmer than others, some very hot. Some are shaded. Some are exposed to the sun. Some are near cold water. Some have adjoining creeklets of hot water. What a paradise today! We get closer to the young man playing ballads on a stringed guitar. He goes around from one group to another and serenades them. I do not offer to play. Should someone reveal a hint of disinterest, he'll move on.

We eventually realize we cannot stay much longer. We soon depart so as to arrive at an overnight site where we can meet Hannah about noon tomorrow.   But before we leave, we try out as many pools as we can find. Each has a distinct quality.

While returning to the original sandy bottom pool, I meet up with Larry, the man that was there before. He knows the names of a number of people around.   He tells me about the water. He leaves. He returns shortly with a shovel and plastic hose. He begins to dig out the bottom of the pool. He puts the wet sand nearby to form a sitting and lying platform.

He lives nearby, comes up here weekly and volunteers, as others do, to maintain the area. We take turns digging and smoothing out the bottom. It really does not require digging, but it helps by providing an additional foot of depth. The smooth sandy bottom is about a foot and a half deep with a layer of rock below. Larry designed the pool and provided the sand bags that hold back enough hot water from flowing out to the adjacent swimming hole.

Larry claims personnel form the local university collected numerous samples of the hot water and found it to be quite pure and free of mineral and animal content. He explains the there was a rumor started several years ago of a person who died of an amoebic disease following a dip in the springs. He said it turned out that this man had been in twenty other hot springs during the period preceding his death. Larry claims he fills up large bottles of water directly from the hot springs and takes it home for drinking.

4:30 PM, Leaving Deep Creek Hot Springs, 3535, Mi 309.2

We put our stuff into the packs, heave it on and slowly and reluctantly take leave of this idyllic, but populated area. In less than five minutes we find we're back in the secure confines of the Pacific

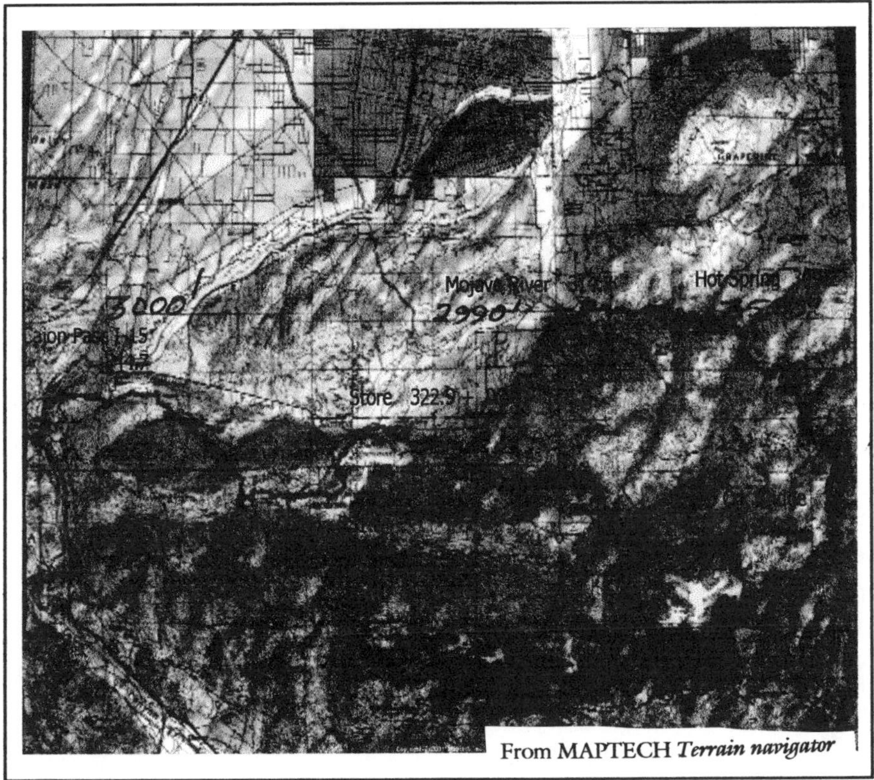

From MAPTECH *Terrain navigator*

Deep Creek Bridge to Cajon Pass

CrestTrail. No one seems to take note or wave as is usually the case when someone treks off. The trail climbs up immediately to regain the contour line above the stream below, continuing now on it's southern side. Though still exposed to the sun, the look of the chaparral now reveals the still lower altitude and proximity to the desert just over the hill to the north and now to the direct west where the stream widens and turns into a wash leading into the desert. The stream bed below now has considerably less water running down stream. From here it looks like the water has taken a subterranean course reflected by the relatively barren flora on it's banks. No more large pines, cottonwoods, alder and willows. Now we just see chaparral brush that has an annual and scrubby look.

A couple miles beyond the hot springs the trail switchbacks down almost to the bottom of the stream bed where it takes you across another bridge, almost as dramatically as the one near Cedar Glen. Here, lower along the river bend a bend we find welcome relief in the way of some growth and coolness emanating from the water flowing below us.

Crossing the bridge, El 3315, the trail then takes us to the even more exposed side of the stream to follow the general contour, but somewhat higher, to about 300 feet above the stream. The area remains barren as the trail follows an abandoned aqueduct. This stretch overlooks the canyon bottom now revealing an intermittent stream with only occasional, but with some interesting looking pools of water. Three miles after the last bridge, the trail descends back down to the stream not far from where it combines with the almost-dry Mojave River that flows through an over-engineered viaduct into a huge dam.. You can't help but ponder how the area might look if it really got flooded. Except for the area near the stream, the entire area looks like a barren desert. Gone now is the river. Now it is not more than a wash. We wonder where all the water went.

At a final high point, on a knoll overlooking the huge dam site before us, I try using the cellular phone to get through to Hannah. Contact is made, but reception is intermittent. We agree to meet at the Summit Valley Country Store on Highway 173 a few miles this side of Silverwood Lake. Arriving at that time should leave sufficient time for Hannah to drive us to Big Bear where we will pick up the car and with time for Hannah to travel if she so chooses to return home, and still have some time for a rest before returning to work tomorrow morning.

The sun has gone down and it will soon be dark. As it darkens we head down a dirt road at the trail head and set up camp beside the faintly flowing Mojave River. The area is generally flat with mesquite growing in patches left by the streams once rushing through not many weeks long. Here, in this area are a multitude of tire tracks, apparently form off road vehicles tearing through the remaining sand piles and brush. One such vehicle can be seen departing as night falls upon us.

8:00 PM: Overnight Near the Mojave Dam, El 3000, Mi 315.7

We make an easy dinner and settle down as it gets dark. Here, the mosquito netting of the *Sleep Screen* turns out to be quite helpful to Joel. Joel is now a believer in the use of the Sleep Screen. This miniature tent-net-dome covers the head with a net layer that covers the upper half of the sleeping bag. The over-the-head-tent enables us to lay out under the stars in comfort despite the numerous flying bugs near the stream.

May 28, Friday, 7:00 A.M. Mojave Dam to The Summit Valley Country Store

We don't see the washed out trail. We know it's nearby. By use of compass we head out through the wash and brush to soon find signs of the intermittent PCT. The trail now takes us through a surprisingly thick jungle-like area through thick baccharis, willows and cottonwood trees with underneath grasses and numerous unidentifiable plants on the bottom of the Mojave River. We can see a little water, a rivulet flowing into the huge opening tunnel through the dam. Maybe it's needed once every fifty years, but for what I cannot imagine.

The trail soon emerges from the thicket and takes us up and down around a myriad of ridges and gullies traversing a larger 4,000 foot ridge, never reaching the top nor the bottom maintaining an altitude of 3,000 to 3,500 feet, a monotonous portion of the PCT. Not compensating enough is a constant view of semi-rural Summit Valley and small ridge to the north that blocks the view of the Mojave Desert.

After about seven miles of this up and down portion of the trail, and not soon enough, fhe PCT comes to a jeep road that will takes us away from the PCT down to Highway 173, to where we will follow the road down west a bit to Larry's Summit Valley Store that I heard so much about.

12:00 Noon: The Summit Valley Country Store, Mi 322.9 +0.5

Here, we find Larry, the owner of the store and a real estate salesperson sitting on the picnic table out on the shaded porch in front of the store. I've heard about Larry from Rebecca Williams and Allan Downs through E-mail. I assume he will turn out to be the character they so described. It was on their knowledge of the store that I arranged to meet Hannah here.

He sees us first trekking down the road. He greets us, "There is water over there and a restroom inside, if you wish to go in." He goes on to quip, "You look like you're really pouring it on, coming down the hill as if you just started, or are you just trying to impress us?"

"Hi!, you must be Larry. No, we're just thirsty."

He says, "I want to hear your story, take a picture of you guys and put it into the registry book."

We easily get into a conversation which turns out to be one way. He talks, I listen. He talks of government policies and his libertarian ways. We try to avoid appearing impolite as we head for the phone. He continues on. All on themes of government's over control of business, the pitfalls of government control, the over burden of taxes, restrictions on small businesses like his and outdoor sports activities in the general area. He points out to us that he believes the federal government should hold back on taxation when a dispute arises. Waiting provides a motive for them to act on the dispute, rather than to let it simmer and drive the citizens crazy.

Larry offers to weigh our packs and take a picture of us to put in the registry book he maintains. Here in the book are photos of several people I recognize. Here can be found the date and weight of their packs at the time.

We lunch out on some of his pre-wrapped sandwiches and snacks. Just as Hannah arrives, he pulls out a huge fish scale and weighs our packs. He pulls out his Polaroid camera and takes a snap of the two us. He writes down our names and the weight of the pack.

Hannah is obviously tired from the trip, but not without a smile and a hug for the two of us. We all, including Larry, exchange some pleasantries. Not surprisingly, Hannah and Larry soon become engaged in a conversation of their own.

But we must say goodbye and depart. I suggest we take the dirt road to Lake Arrowhead. Hannah convinces us that it would be better for the Saab to take Highway 138 through Crestline. Hannah drives along Highway 138 around sun-exposed Lake Silverwood. Soon the road reaches the southern parameters of the lake where the road immediately comes to the steep northeastern flank of the San Bernardino Mountains where a pine studded ridge stands before Lake Silverwood and Crestline. The road makes a quick turn and suddenly we find ourselves back into the spectacularly contrasting area of montane forest. This forest is very rich in its thickness of conifers and cedars and numerous active creeklets send down little cascades of water throughout the length of the mountain side. The road takes us up dramatically up a thousand feet in about five minutes. Compared to what we were had just passed through in the last few days, things appear passing as if in fast-motion. Soon we pass beautiful Camp Seeley, a resort with rental cabins, lodge, and a host of facilities. I recall staying there with my parents sometime during the early 1940s. The buildings and layout looks pretty much the same. The outlying area nearby is now built up as the population centers of Crestline are encroaching the area. We cross over the crest and junction up with Highway 18 where we overlook the populated basin below. We drive up to Big Bear, Van Dusen Canyon Road where we eventually find our car. Hannah decides to drive down to her apartment near work in Pomona via Redlands. We decide to drive back to the cabin where we pick up Joel's belongings. We express our appreciation for the effort put out by Hannah and say goodbye. We drive out and arrive at home, whereupon Joel departs to Vista to feed and take care of his cat.

This next 13 mile was skipped in 1999. The following is an account of the leg trekked a year later.

December 5, 2000, Tuesday, 10:00 AM: Back to Summit Valley, Mi 322.9 +0.5 - 0.5

I turn off the engine to my newly purchased 1993 Dodge Ram 250, and step out in front of the Summit Valley Country Store. I wonder if Larry still has the store. I wonder if he is running things. Would I not be lucky if he were to be in at this time.

Sure enough! There he is, on his cellular phone talking with a vendor.

Hi Larry, "It's been a while."
Larry hesitates in his conversation, "Do you know me?"

I wander around the store and tell him, "Sure, I'll wait for you to get off the phone."

I select a few items, a turkey sandwich, a packaged pickle, and a small package of licorice sticks. I stop over at the counter where Larry is mostly listening on the phone, see a display of cigarette lighters and begin to search for one that has a long flame that may be helpful in starting my gas stove. Larry is still on the phone. I head out to the van and begin to do some last minute preparation, exchanging my cotton clothes for nylon and putting on boots as I wish to be prepared for some rain.

I return to the store in hiking regalia, red neckerchief, wide brimmed hat, short pants, and boots. Now, he places me into the hiker category.

"Are you a hiker?"

"Yeah, I came through here last year on the PCT."

"Did you sign in and had your picture taken?"

"Yeah. I appreciated that as did the others. I skipped the part of the trail from here to Cajon Pass, and now is a good time to make it up."

Larry says, "I don't remember. There were a lot of hikers this year, too."

I ask him if I can park the van in his parking lot over night and return for it tomorrow evening. He assures me it probably will be safe.

An 18 wheeler pulls in. A man steps out with an invoice. He delivers several cases of beer or soft drinks. Larry causes a discussion of bear sightings in the area.

"Not far from here, a woman was approached and really scared by a bear." They have been known to attack people."

I say, "What kind of bear was it?"

Larry says, "A brown bear. You can tell if they are around by their dropping of chokeberries."

"Oh."

Larry goes on to say, addressing the truck driver,"First, you see the droppings, then the prints." He looks at me, "When the droppings look fresh, look around." He looks at the driver, "I've been told what helps is to carry a bell or something as you're walking, so that they hear you well in advance, so that they are not surprised."

"That makes sense. Do you think there are any near here along the trail?"

"Probably not. There was a forest fire that burnt down much of the area near here. You'll see it. They hang out along the Cleghorn range to the west of here, a lot of em."

The delivery man says, "Are they different than black bears?"

Larry says, "They both cause trouble. The brown bear leaves droppings and become more nervous when near their young. So take care."

They have business to take care of, and though I am interested in what they have to say about bears, I am getting nervous just hearing about it all and getting more and more anxious to get on the trail.

"You get to the trail by walking up the road to the top of the hill. You'll see the burnt out area. There's a barbed wire fence. If you cross it, follow the road and trail uphill, you shouldn't have any trouble finding the trail."

I secure the van, throw on the pack loaded with 3 ½ liters of water and wave goodbye.

10:45 AM: Departing Summit Valley

I walk up the road, see the burnt out area ahead. I see the barbed wire fence.   It now blocks entry to the dirt road leading uphill to the PCT. The badly rutted road also has a berm over it preventing cars from passage.

I check my compass, get a bearing and head up the road.   I figure so long as I head southerly, I should soon come upon the PCT. The road becomes obscured with debris and tractor tracks. There are now temporary dirt roads going in all directions, rapidly put in for firebreaks and for access to fire fighters. Some of the area is blighted whereas other areas remain intact with high brush. As I walk southerly, the area becomes less burnt, but there are still a number of trails all over the place leading up and down, from one direction to the other.

11:00 AM: On the PCT Above Summit Valley, El 3480, Mi.323.0

Finally, I see a better-than-average trail that has railroad ties serving to offset avulsion. This must be the PCT! But which way to Cajon Pass. One way heads downward, the other way, upward with no hint as to which direction makes more sense. Whenever I am not sure as to direction, I choose the uphill way, so that if I do a 180 degree at least I'll come back down hill. Although confident I am on the trail, there are footprints going both ways. Not all are human. The trail is first leading generally eastward. I turn around, follow my tracks for a few minutes, then finally convince myself I am heading generally westward, the right way. I become confident as the trail gains some height and I look down and see Larry's store and my van a quarter of a mile to the immediate north. Now, well out of the burn area and feeling secure I am going the right way, I soon clam down, relax, and get well into a cruise phase and start to enjoy the hike.

I look at the passing brush. The area is dominated by low, dried out chia, three to eight foot sage with no odor, four foot high ceanothus, a lot of low scrub oak, some two foot high brittle brush, all dominated now by a lot of five to ten foot high manzanita. The manzanita has berries that are quite mature this time of year. They have turned deep brownish-red or brown. The outer crust is now dry with a separation that easily occurs between the outer shell and the hard, round marble-like impenetrable seed inside. I pick out several. I find that the outer dry shell varies somewhat in texture and flavor. They vary from unpleasant and bitter to a rather pleasing sweet spicy flavor, resembling cinnamon and clove.

But I cannot relax for long. I see a bunch of foot prints, many of them. Not from shoes. I note that the tracks resemble bear tracks and sure enough, there are droppings of "chokeberries."

I conclude that bears must be foraging fruits from manzanitas, with varying success in digesting the outer shells. Their droppings, diagnostic of the palatability of the fruit at the time, suggest they are likely nearby these plants. Sometimes the droppings include partially digested shells and other times the dropping simply look like a collection of children's marbles. The dryness is a clue as to how recent the bears have been around. Because of the recent prints and moist droppings I don't feel like resting! I find myself whistling, singing and looking at foot prints and droppings as I cruise the trail at a constant rate.

The view below to the north overlooks Larry's Summit Valley Country Store on Highway 173. I am also overlooking the middle of pastoral Summit Valley which stretches to the east to the Mojave Dam control site and westward to the hills and low mountains that form the perimeters of Horse Thief Canyon that connects to Cajon Pass and Interstate 15. Across Summit Valley lies an interesting four hundred foot spine-like flat ridge that connects to the dam to the east which protects the valley somewhat from the drier desert air to the north. To the more distant east and immediate southeast lie the heights of the San Bernardino Mountains with their cool and delightful conifer forests and the populated centers of Crestline and Lake Arrowhead.

The trail soon strikes a paved road and a PCT marker, the first I have seen today. The road leads up a couple hundred yards to a dry picnic area providing an overview of Silverwood Lake. I rest and re-arrange my water supply, adjust my pack and look at my charts. I realize that the trail ahead will be difficult to identify. The problem occurs very shortly as the trail drops down to strike a series of dirt roads, each leading to unknown places, and then to a governmental siphon plant on Highway 173. Other than the one marker to the east of the paved road, there are no trail markers to be seen, nor any hint of old ones. My maps reveal a number of trails, but none are identified.

I decide to continue west on the shoulder of Highway 173 and stay on it until being assured of the seeing the PCT, and if not, to continue on to where the highway ends at the junction with Highway 138, and then walk up the road towards the southeast until I can make out the trail. No luck in picking up the trail. Anything, a trail or road, that leads to the south seems private and has no trespassing signs nearby. I walk a couple of miles to the junction with Highway 138, see the sign indicating 3 miles to Silverwood Lake and follow the road uphill to the recreational area.

About two miles into the uphill walk, I feel the familiar pain of developing foot blisters. I see a station wagon ahead coming to stop a hundred feet or so in front of me in a turn out. The driver steps out and introduces himself as Homer, I forgot his nickname. He says he has done parts of the Appalachian Trail. He now has some time off and hopes to be doing portions of the Pacific Crest Trail. We both agree that we are indeed the only ones we've seen this season along the trail.

Homer points out the way to the PCT, just a few hundred yards away. He offers me a local park map revealing the trail. I provide him with a summary of the PCT route in the area and some information about resources in the general area. He drives on to Big Bear and I confidently head out to pick up the nearby trail head at the highway off ramp just a few hundred yards down the hill.

Now at the end of the off ramp, just before the underpass leading back to the lake is a PCT marker and well defined trail, outlined with small rocks, El, 3395, Mi 331.2. As I begin to think about my water resources and wonder how many extra miles I walked, I come upon an empty trail camp with horse corral, hay, stove, picnic tables, outhouse and fire pit. Not far away, I can see one or two group campgrounds, probably empty. I will need water for the next leg. If there is none to be had, I will have to back track a couple miles to the lake.

4:00 PM: A Trail Camp in Silverwood Lake Area, El 3440, Mi 331.6

I decide to call it a day at this point. Should I be sufficiently free of blister pain, secure water, and if the weather holds, I should be able to put on the remaining 12 miles and reach Mc Donald's restaurant before dark. Once there, I can decide to call for a taxi or hitchhike back to Larry's Country Store.

I routinely prepare supper out of the small kettle, a mix of dehydrated pea soup garnished this time with corn pasta, some flavored dehydrated pre-cooked beans and some pieces of peppered beef jerky. After supper there is nothing else to do but crawl into the sack and hope to fall asleep and wake up pain free and anxious to move on.

December 6, 7:00 AM: A Late Start, 3440, Mi 331.6 - 1.0

Sleeping late under overcast skies, I wake up quite refreshed and anxious to get going. The fact that it is close to freezing, adds another dimension of drive to get moving.

But I need water. I have less than one liter left. I decide to wander around the group campground hoping to find some water. After trying several faucets at the first campground and finding no water, I go down to the more distant and lower group campground to try a few more faucets. I get to the last faucet, near the shower, by an outside sink. I turn it on. Lo and behold, out comes water, though somewhat dirty and heated. I let it run til the water clears up. I immediately fill up my bottles. Then the water stops entirely! I suppose the water had been turned off at a more proximal location uphill but able to draw a residual of water collected in the local pipes. Trail magic indeed! I have a stroke of good luck. Now I can finish the hike!

A quarter mile into the walk the trail strikes a steep paved road leading up to a water tank. Once passed the road I see it is surrounded by barbed wire.

The trail continues to climb over to the top and through a gap over Cleghorn Ridge. The trail here takes one through a very interesting growth of plants that characterize the lower transition from a chaparral clime to that of a montane forest, but not really making the change.

During the climb out, I see to the direct south, less than a mile away, the thick conifer forests bordering the north west side of the Crestline area. To the immediate southwest is a transition area that has a mixture of large conifers, oaks, incense cedars and a lessor proportion of deciduous trees.

The path first leads through a glade of various kinds of oaks, scrub and canyon types, and I believe, hybrids thereof. This happens a few times. It is so dense that this shaded trail is carpeted with different types of oak leaves and acorns. A few yards away is the first pine tree seen since the bridge near the trail to Cedar Glen. Now, at about the 4,000 foot level, it again appears as if re-entering the montane forest. The chaparral is now limited to large chamise, sage with a blue tinge, rich manzanita, and a number of hard to identify wildflower plants, some with hints of yellow flowers, perhaps brittle bursh. But then the top is reached, the gap is passed, and the trail quickly descends down somewhat following the contours overlooking aptly named Little Horse Thief Canyon to the north. The canyon was a hideaway area, connected to Horse Thief Canyon to the east, both aptly named. It is narrow, flat and grassy on the bottom, with steep walls on three sides with a stream running through. The larger trees no longer appear on the hillside. The chaparral is in transition where now I see some dried out moss, dandelion, and mustard.

Suddenly, there appears a very strange looking plant. It is low to the ground, quite green, with tight, circular collections of drooping, leathery leaves, seven inches long. The closest resemblance is to yerba santa, but the plant is lower, clumpy, and succulent in the way it looks.

A small stream, not inviting at all, sometimes dry, is soon crossed just above Little Horse Thief Canyon. All around are animal foot prints, including our friends, the bears. It seems clear, now, that wherever there is manzanita, I find signs of bear. Again, I don't feel like resting. Here, even in December, where it is moist, there is some hint of flowers on the stalks remaining. They could be brittle brush, ceanothus and dandelion, but certainly not pretty this time of year.

The trail soon crosses the western extreme of Little Horse Thief Canyon, then immediately climbs the other side to reach another summit at a high tension line, the last ridge before descending down to Cajon Pass. Once atop the ridge, I can see the high dramatic ridges beyond Cajon Pass forming the eastern extension of the rugged San Gabriel Mountains and the designated wilderness areas. Connecting them to the canyon below is the gradually increasing spine of Lyle Ridge that climbs to 8,000 feet before adjoining beautiful Blude Ridge. The peaks protruding behind the ridge are Wright Mountain, Pine Mountains with Mount San Antonio, known locally as Mount Baldy, 10,080 feet. The PCT will follow Lytle Ridge, then Blue Ridge, before climbing 9,399 foot, Mount Baden Powell.

After hesitating and digesting the awesome view of what lies ahead, I start the 1,000 foot descent to the pass below. The trail first leads through the top of some very steep and intimidating cliffs caused by the shifting of the San Andreas Fault with sheer drops of a few hundred feet. There are remnants of a fence that at one time might have been effective to prevent an animal from slipping over the vertical cliff. Looking down reveals a sheer drop. One step over and it is also, "good bye, Charlie." I wonder where that expression came from. The trail takes several switchbacks down over a heavily exposed area with sparse chaparral before one reaches the bottom. The soil looks light in color and worn out in texture. Not much is growing. Nothing seems to be doing well.

Just before the bottom, the trail strikes Crowder Canyon, with a small amount of water trickling toward the depths of the canyon towards Cajon Pass. The canyon bottom gets more narrow as the canyon walls get steeper. Soon, there is no water to be seen.

Except for the riperian growth, it seems like wherever I find myself on the trail, there are about ten or twelve plant species that seem to account for about 85% of what I can differentiated from one another. Before the trail strikes the paved road at I-15, I can see dried out grasses, mustard plants, dandelions and moss, as well as scraggly looking mesquite.

3:30 PM: Cajon Pass, El 3000, Mi 344.7 - 0.8

Now, at the bottom, I realize that my walking for the day may not be concluded so easily. I head up the side road towards commercial enterprises. I stop momentarily at the memorial to the California Pioneers that first traversed Cajon Pass on their way from Salt Lake City and over the Santa Fe Trail. I surprise myself by not stopping at McDonalds to continue uphill a mile to Highway 138 where I find myself standing on the corner trying to hitch a ride.

Just before twenty minutes pass, my cut off time for attempting to hitch, a pickup comes to a stop. He offers me a ride to the Summit Valley Store. But before reaching a shortcut turnoff for him, an LED lights up on the dashboard indicating engine problems. He opts to take the shortcut home to Hesperia and drops me off several miles short. My map indicates it is now about six or seven miles from Larry's Summit Valley Country Store.

At the junction lies a similar store to that of Larry's store with a gas station part of the business. I go in the store and inquire as to whether there may be taxi service from here. In so many words, the manager explains that it would take less time to walk to Larry's store than it would be to wait for a taxi.

6:15 PM: At a Junction to Hesperia. Back to the Summit Valley Country Store, Mi 344.7+13.0 (a 7 mile walk)

I head out and walk the seven miles to Larry's store, but not before it starts to rain. Because it is dark, the first sign of rain is the overwhelming change in quality of and smell of the air. All of a sudden, there is a pervasive odor of horse pasture and chaparral. Then comes the drops. Then comes the change of clothes and the walk through the rain.   On getting to the Summit Valley Country I find it had been closed for an hour or so and Larry is nowhere to be found. The van starts up readily. I take a deep breath of relief, turn around, and cover some of the ground I walked before turning up Highway 138 through Crestline for a quiet restful evening at our cabin at Green Valley Lake.

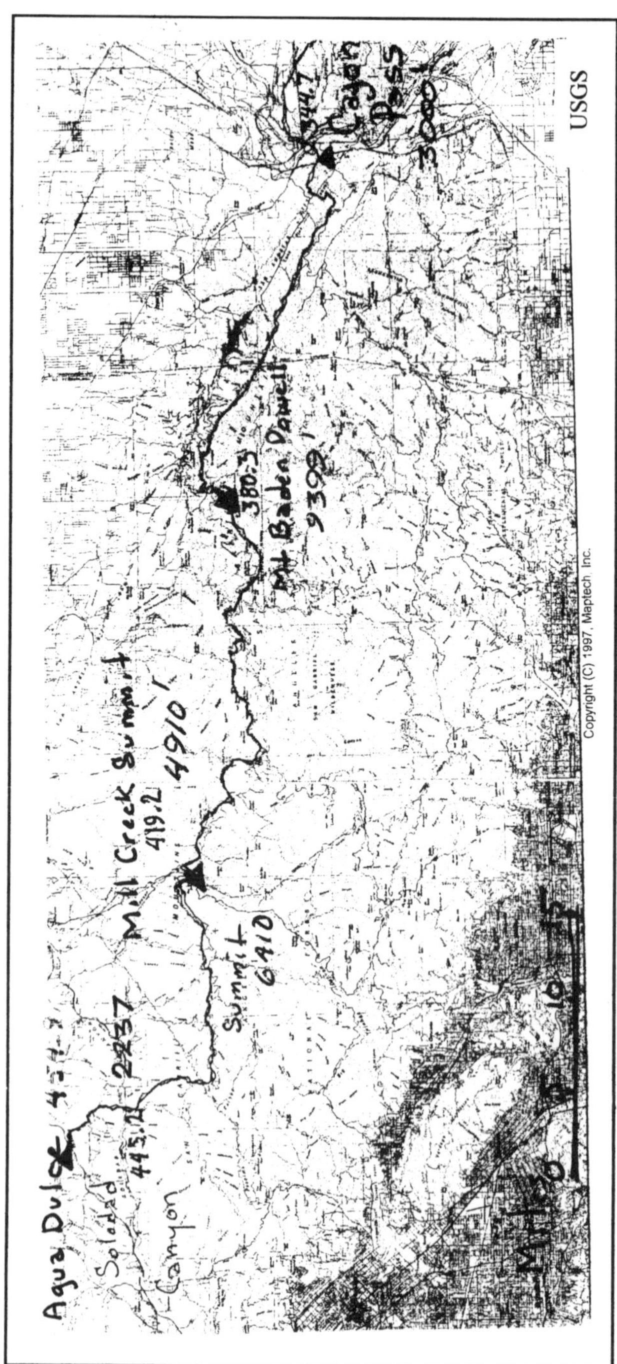

Section D: Cajon Pass (I-15) to Agua Dulce
The San Gabriel Mts.   110.2 miles

SECTION D
THE SAN GABRIEL MOUNTAINS

Prologue

John Muir reported this range to be the most formidable mountains he had ever trespassed. In his book, "California's Mountains," he alludes to the difficulties he had in navigating the steep terrain above the San Gabriel Valley and how blocked his view became as he traversed the heights of the slopes carpeted with chaparral so thick and high he had to crawl beneath them to cover any distance.

Though close to a metropolis, there remains a distinct, wild quality to the entire area. This primitive aspect is noticeable even when driving through any of the dirt or paved roads. This uncivil characteristic is more distinct than any other large mountain range I've seen throughout the state.

There are two major paved roads cutting through the area. There is California 2, the Angeles Crest Highway, that goes up the mountain north of Los Angeles, at La Canada, to follow the crest eastward to Wrightwood and then connects with State Highway 138, then a few miles down to Cajon Pass. The other road forms a mountain route northward from The Angeles Crest Highway at a more moderate altitude where it connects with Callifornia 14 that goes north to Palmdale and Lancaster through the Mojave.

Other roads lead up from the San Gabriel Valley, but end short of the crest. All the roads are subject to closure due to too much growth, snow, ice, rock, dirt and snow slides, flash floods, fires and earthquake. While overflying the area, I saw the effect of a mere 5.0 earthquake, an after shock a couple of days after the main Northridge quake of 1996. A cloud of dust arose from the entire ridge as the land shifted below me! These natural events, for a good many years, resist efforts to tame the area.

Much of it is still wild; the PCT traverses 101 miles of this wildness from Cajon Pass to Acton, only to pick up another 51 miles of wilderness through the northwest section of the Angeles National Forest beyond the Sierra Pelona Valley to near Three Points. The San Gabriel mountains form a new mountain range, dominated by the San Andreas Fault and unusual because it transverses the state, going generally north and west. There are many escarpments, steep gullies, cliffs, gorges, waterfalls, streams and springs along the way.

Southerly exposures are dramatic, but too often, steep, , dry, windy and exposed. Whenever the trail seeks a north or northeastern exposure, especially when there is a secondary ridge to the north, the area can be expected to be more moist, more moderate in slope and richly forested. Such conditions occur often while on the trail. The flora and views in all directions are wonderful and compensate for most inconveniences. Almost all the plants described in Supplement C are seen within this range.

The PCT immediately attacks the San Gabriel Mountains from the 3,000 foot level of Cajon Pass, to eventually strike up along the spine of Lytle Ridge that butts up onto 8,000 foot Blue Ridge. There, many PCTers opt to take the Acorn Trail down three miles of trail and two miles by road to Wrightwood for a well deserved rest. Once on top of Blue Blue Ridge, the PCT crosses the top of several ski runs to remain at or above 8,000 feet for a while and not to descend below a mile high for 70 miles until the trail descends rapidly down to Soledad Canyon.

I have known these mountains since the 1940s. I've experienced them in the summer and in winter. I've hiked from Pasadena to Mount Wilson and the Mount Lowe area several times in all seasons. I skied at all the resorts and know the runs. The area is dotted with attractive car campsites; I've been to them all. I have volunteered to fight forest fires and have pulled water lines. The mountains are indeed formidable and vary a great deal, not only from one season to another, but can be counted upon to present many surprises for anyone attempting to traverse them.

Chapter 14

Cajon Pass to Wrightwood

At home.....A spooky evening in Cajon Pass....The Economy
Inn Motel....At the trail head....An overnight on Lytle Ridge
....The descent to Wrightwood

June 1, 1998, Tuesday 7:15 PM: A Spooky Evening in Cajon Pass, El
3000 Mi 344.7+ 1.0 - 1.0

Jon agrees to drive me to Cajon Pass. The plan includes dining out
at the restaurant at Cajon Pass, the one described in the *Guidebook* as "a
hospitable place for trekkers." Maybe he'll stay overnight.

The newspaper, The Weather Channel and local television concur
that the forecast includes widely scattered showers for the next day or
so, followed by a period of what seems like typical June weather, fog
along the coast but otherwise clear with no indication of precipitation
in the coming seven days.

We look for the restaurant. It is dark. An old building appears out
of the fog. There is long large line of just legible lettering at the top of
and length of the building spelling out "RESTAURANT." In somewhat
smaller print, it says "Tiffanys." We approach it. It is dark. We pull
into the fair sized restaurant parking lot. It is empty inside. The
restaurant probably served traffic on old highway 395 passing through.
The lettering everywhere is faded. The windows are blocked. We shine
our light on the door. There are several small signs pasted on the inside
explaining to their friends that they are sorry, but they had to close up
as of September eighth.

Jon says, "Yeah, it's sad...maybe it was Del Taco and MacDonald that
did them in." After a sigh, he continues on. "At least I have credence
in the authors of the *Guidebook*."

"What do you mean?"

"I didn't want to believe the "twenty-four hour, fine restaurant" described in the *Guidebook* was McDonalds."

"Really?"

"I hoped they couldn't be so cynical?"

"Hikers rely heavily on the *Guidebook*. Every Trekker carries copies of it with them. When conflict occurs between maps and the *Guidebook*, it is the *Guidebook* that turns out more accurate."

8:00 PM: Cajon Pass, The Economy Inn Motel, El 3050, Mi 344.7 + 1.0 - 1.0

Through the dense fog, behind a service station and Del Taco-convenient store, appears a sign indicating a motel. The fog clears momentarily. The only way to get to this motel is by driving through this gas station and mini-mart. The motel was probably constructed before the service station and was left intact. There's a Caltrans servicing center at the opposite side with nothing but desolate wilderness off to the west, where I will be heading in the morning.

Jon says, "Is this where you want to stay?"

I respond, "It's described in the *Guidebook*."

"It's spooky."

"Yeah." I don't really know why, but it reminds me of the movie, *Psycho*, superbly directed by Alfred Hitchcock. Yet, it is quiet. There is no scary music. Instead there is the drone of the freight trains close by, trucks and cars on the freeway and occasional blasting of music from the cars as they wait in line going through the self-serve Del Taco line. All this is going on without us being able to see any of it. We're in a thick fog bank. The unreal atmosphere permeates the environment creating a feeling inside of me that something unpleasant can happen soon.

I head for the office. I enter a small cubicle, four feet by six feet with a window and button. I press the button. I hear nothing. I see nothing except a semi-open door and a semi-lit hallway leading to another door that is closed. I press the button again. A red light near the button goes on, then off as I release the button. I still hear and see nothing.

Jon says, "It is spooky. Do you really want to stay here?"

"Wait, wait a minute. What options do we have?"

He says, I'm waiting outside....What if the door doesn't open?"

"I didn't know you were claustrophobic."

"I'm not. This place is just spooky. There's probably no one here."

I ring again. The red light goes on. I go outside. Jon and I look at each other. "Maybe the manager had to go to the john." I go back in and give it another unsuccessful try. Jon waits impatiently outside. I come out. We walk around the building. I note a cold swimming pool. But the Jacuzzi is letting out steam. "Aha!," I say, "The place must be active."

Jon spurts out, "But there are no cars around. Look! None of the rooms are lit other than the office."

I try a door or two. None open. I suddenly see a door right next to the cubicle. I pull it. It doesn't budge. I push it. It slowly opens. Real slowly. "Shall we go in?"

Jon doesn't say a word. As I enter this dim lit room, I realize I am in a lounge before a registration desk. Suddenly, a very short, dark complected woman dressed with a shawl around her head and a deep red spot on her forehead comes quietly into the room behind the desk. She stands at some distance away from the desk and with a forced smile and soft voice, highly accented and in a pressured voice murmurs, "What do you want?"

She scares me. I put my wits together and say "Uh, I'd like a room for the night."

"Oh", she says, as if surprised, "For the night? How many?" I figure, I just told her.

"For one night." She looks at Jon.

"Just myself. He's dropping me off." I realize I might be confusing her. I quickly explain, "He's not staying overnight. He'll soon be leaving. I plan to go hiking tomorrow, unless the weather gets bad."

She seems perplexed, but generally seems to feel more at ease as a man enters from a passageway to her rear. He smiles in an understanding way, then leaves without saying a word. I think now, maybe she's being trained.

"She's strange," I say to Jon,

Jon comes back with, "It's a strange evening, and it has only just started."

Just then, a man comes in and stands behind us. I figure he also wants a room. I hurry and fill out the forms. She gives me the key to the room. I almost feel as if I don't know what to do with it. I ask her, "Where is the room?"

She says, "right next door. " She points out and around.

The man behind me just stands there motionless.

As soon as we take a step outside, I see the room. It is indeed, right next door. Before, I leave, I ask her "Has any other hikers come through recently?"

"Yes. There are a couple of young hikers in Room 118."

We make the few steps to my room. The key fits. I go in first. Once inside, Jon points to a door leading to the south, in the direction of the managers' office.

He spurts out, "Don't open that door!"

I respond curtly, "Had you not mentioned that, I would not think of trying it! But now, you planted the idea, and all I can say is that I'll make an attempt to not touch it!"

We explore this rather conventional small room. As I put my backpack inside, I say, "Let's get something to eat...but where?" He had picked up a menu at the registration desk lounge area from a restaurant in Hesperia. It describes some boring meals.

Jon looks at the menu. "Where's Hesperia?"

I answer, "About ten miles north."

"It's too far." He goes on to say, "Let's go to Del Taco."

We walk out the door. We're taken aback by the darkness. It is foggy. We look in the direction in which we came. We barely make out the lights from Del Taco, just a few yards away. We walk in the direction of the lights, avoid hazards like fences and trash cans and approach the drive-in line from the rear. We walk around the store and now blinded as we enter the well lit front side. We carry our evening meal back through the fog to the motel. We scarf down our meal in the confines of our room. As Jon prepares to leave, I hear that internal voice saying, "You're on your own...I'm on my own."

June 2, Wednesday, 6:00 AM. Economy Inn Motel, El 3050, Mi 344.7 + 1.0 - 0.8

Being restless I wander about the area, now being able to see what the area looks lie. It still looks kind of spooky. I walk over to Room 118 and introduce myself to the two trekkers. Joshua and Chris are up, but still in bed, watching television. They started out from Campo and are on their way to Canada. They explain they were up late and plan to get a late start. We discuss the weather and what it may be like later in the day. We wish one another luck. I tell them I expect them to pass me near the top as I am sure that their gait is considerably faster than mine.

I walk to the store for some coffee. I realize it is cold, damp and windy with an overcast ceiling of only about 1,000 feet. An hour after starting up the mountain, I'll be in the soup. It is like intentionally going into IFR conditions. I figure I can always do a one-eighty and come back after an hour or so.

The *Times* reports widely scattered showers for today, clearing out tomorrow. People I talk to indicate the same. A man coming down from Wrightwood tells me it rained hard last night. The manager of the store offers a suggestion, "It's a crap shoot." I head back to the motel, pack up in the room and return the key through the window.

But still not committing myself to the hike, I trek down the half mile road to a mini-market and buy two Top Romans soups, a pint of water and a small package of dried apricots. I fill up on water and head next door to McDonald's, at the PCT trail head, for a "Big Breakfast."

Still undecided, I sit by the window, study the air mass outside and review charts of the immediate area. I notice that now, two hours later, the ceiling has moved up another five hundred feet or so and has now become broken, revealing the unstable characteristic of the air mass. I am entranced by its beauty and how the clouds react to the flow of air in the pass and how the mass of air descends down from the mountains to the east and west.

After the "big breakfast" I muster up the inspiration and resolutely head for the trail head, just yards away.

June 2, 9:10 AM: Cajon Pass: The Trail Head, El 3000, Mi 344.7 - 0.9

A decision is made. Care is thrown to the wind as I am overcome with a secure feeling that I will indeed be on the trail, a well maintained, congressionally approved trail that extends from Mexico to Canada. It is like knowing that not far ahead is the omnipotent Scoutmaster that knows everything about anything outdoors. I know that it is trafficked by competent people, and thus being on it makes me feel competent. I know how quickly such a feeling can dissipate.

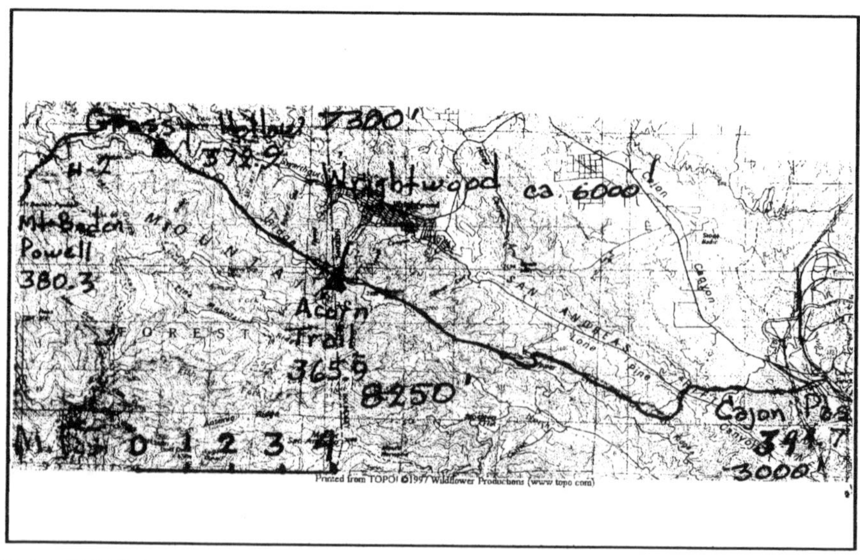

Lytle Ridge, Blue Ridge, The Acorn Trail and Grassy Hollow CG

Immediately the tread heads downward to a stream that surprisingly heads into a large dark curving tunnel. The trail is not marked. The question immediately arises, why would a trail follow a river through a viaduct without a marker? One could get overrun by the water and never know whether they were on the trail or not! The stream, though shallow, is never more than an inch deep, but it is from side to side of the dark tunnel. My feet are already wet. I head on. The tunnel makes a turn. Whew! I see light at the other end. Now, across the freeway, it is a jungle. The trail is obscure. There are footprints. All in the same direction. Emerging from the swamped out area is indeed a trail. It soon becomes marked with signs describing plants. Is this a nature trail? I recall such a note in the *Guidebook*. No trail markers yet, but it is consistent with what may be described in dryer times. A sense of security returns much faster than it left, but it doesn't really set in because it seems so illusory. I figure, it's just been a few minutes, I can always find my way back. I convince myself, this isn't <u>really</u> being lost because I know how to easily get back. Oh, for a marker. The trail passes some private land, and continues through the nature trail, as described. Yet no markers. The trail passes a couple of railroad trestles and power lines just as the *Guidebook* describes. Eventually the trail climbs out of the pass onto higher terrain away from the thick growth. A dirt road. A marker appears. Morale is up a few points. Now the Interstate is about a couple of hundred feet below. Clouds are moving about, obscuring the higher ridges above and across the pass to the east.

The trail climbs further near Mormon Rocks. A grotesque series of uplifted white rock appears. I also see the cloud cover swelling about beyond the confines of the pass, moving out and expanding to the higher terrain on both sides of the pass. An hour later as I attain another few hundred feet higher, I notice the clouds covering some of the ridges I had just passed. Another hour passes. I am now about elevation 4,000 feet, a thousand feet above the Interstate and I notice clouds are now covering more recent smaller ridges that I had passed. The cloud cover is expanding upwards and westward in my very direction. I say to myself, I really don't want to go back. What's a little rain. I locate my poncho and satisfy myself that a little rain might

even make the day more interesting.
But I am concerned that the fog may
become so thick that I lose the trail.

The trail takes me through the
chaparral in Swarthart Canyon that
joins up with larger Pine Canyon. To
the northwest of the head of Pine
Canyon lies Wrightwood, El ca. 6,000
feet. But first I cross dry Swarthart
Canyon. A marker identifies the trail.
The trail immediately starts an earnest
climb up through flora influenced by its
northern exposure. The Mojave Desert
can n ow be seen over the ridge to the
nearby north. Long switchbacks lead up
in a generally westward direction to Lytle
Ridge.

By Dana P. Lemieux

The PCT follows Lytle Ridge which rises westerly to connect with
Blue Ridge at about 8,000 feet. Now I am beyond half way to the
summit. At 5,500 feet, the nearby clouds are seen expanding in air that
seems very unstable. The summit lies ahead at 8,200 feet where a trail
quickly drops 2,200 feet down to Wrightwood.

5:00 PM: Overnight on Lytle Ridge, El 6350, Mi 359.0 - 0.8

I get to a suitable campsite without water. It is cold in the shade but
still some warmth in the direct sun when the nearby clouds part. I find
a place to set up the bivvy bag where, should it rain, it will not get
flooded. I keep my ponchos nearby. I head for a sunny spot where I
prepare a variant of my routine dinner. Along comes Chris and Joshua
going uphill at a good clip. Because they are short on water, they will
press on beyond the Acorn Trail in the hope of reaching Guffy
Campground where they expect water. One of them said, "We plan to
be at Guffy by 7:00 PM." My information reveals Guffy is 7.8 miles
uphill from here at 8,225 feet, a climb of almost 2,000 feet. In an

hour? Should the weather not deteriorate and if they can maintain an average speed of two and one half miles per hour they would still require more than three hours to get there. Dusk is about 8:00 PM. It is likely to be dark by the time they get there. Because of the weather, I am a bit worried about them. But they seem competent enough. I'll look for their tracks tomorrow.

It turns out to be a very pleasant evening watching the cloud formation, the buildups and passage through the mountain crevices, occasionally exposing the higher peaks and ridges. The meal turns out great. I readily clean up. The sun goes down. I take off my clothes and get into the sleeping bag. I quickly get warm and fall into a blissful sleep watching the stars and waiting for the moon to appear through the clouds as they pass over the ridge.

June 3, Thursday, 5:10 AM El 6350, Mi 359.0 - 0.9

I was in that bag for about 11 hours. I had to get up about three time to appease nature. When up, it was cold, but clear, with but little wind.

Peering out from under the bivvy bag I see a glimmer of light. For the most part I am warm, but parts of the bag are very damp and seem to permit some cold air come in. This is not a surprise as I realize the outside air temperature is cold and damp, a hair below freezing. Last night the bivvy bag was not able to compensate for the weakness in the old red sleeping bag. I guess, from now on I must consider it a summer bag. It will not be summer for two more weeks! I get up with the "morning drill" of getting dressed while in the bag. I put on my mittens after putting on every other item so as to assure my hands would stay functionally warm. There is frost around.

The view is spectacular. Here is a 6,300 foot knoll overlooking a panorama of 270 degrees. To the west is the Cugamonga Wilderness and the jagged northern escarpment of Telegraph Peak, Mt. Howard and Mt. Baldy ridge, lining the horizon like a saw blade, climbing east to west from 8,900 to 10,080 feet. I take note the entire ridge is covered with a recent snow cap. To the east and below is Cajon Pass and the mountains beyond that hide Crestline. To the immediate north is Pine Valley and Highway 138 leading up to Wrightwood, which lies out of sight. Beyond is the Mojave Desert. Build ups of nimbo-cumulus clouds appear with thunder heads in various phases of development. The view is absolutely dramatic. The view is much like what is seen while flying through a squirrely storm. As I scan the panorama, beautiful clouds quickly roll by. A breeze. Then it is foggy. I am not inspired enough by the view to remain settled and wait for the clouds to clear. I am cold and want to get out of there. I need to get moving

The clouds dramatically return with the next breeze. The trail is now hard to follow. I hope this storm system will go away. Trail markers in the last several miles were few and far in between. I do not want a repeat experience of being snowed in as I was last month on the southern shoulder of Mt Jacinto. It doesn't help morale to recall the disorientation that could easily come about with poor visibility. Feeling cold knowing I have limited resources to deal with impending hypothermic conditions is not a pleasant thought. However, for the moment, though somewhat hungry, I feel overall comfortable and warm. But this is how I felt before settling in for the snowy night below Mount San Jacinto.

I am anxious to ascend, to break through the overcast into the sun and experience the transition. I am hoping for higher terrain to appear like islands protruding from the ocean of clouds from below.

Instead, less than a quarter of an hour upon departing, I begin to see frost over unexposed areas. The sun must have broken through at times as the frost reveals signs of melting, revealing the dark soil underneath. At about 6,800 feet I begin to notice that this "frost" is turning into little patches of snow in tiny mini drifts.

About 8:00 AM, at 7,500 feet, it is getting colder despite brief moments when the sun breaks through the overcast. I can barely see through the fog. There! I believe I see the connection from Lytle Ridge to Blue Ridge, but with another ridge leading to the left to higher elevations. I suppose, here in the dense fog, three ridges join. I am hoping the trail soon veers off to the northwest, not southwest up to the higher ridge which is thick with snow. Good! I think I see the trail meandering to the right away from the higher ridge. Is this a wish? Just as I see the two impending ridges, the fog becomes more dense, obscuring the view, but nevertheless not seriously affecting negotiation of the tread, now layered with inch of fresh snow. I realize it can start snowing any time, and potentially quite heavy. I recall how it was near the top of Mount San Jacinto when it snowed six inches in one hour and totally obscured the trail.

It has been three hours now since leaving the knoll. It's too cold to stop and study the map. Besides visibility is too poor to confirm location. With my gait at about two miles an hour, I figure I must be soon approaching the summit at the head of the Acorn Trail that leads down to Wrightwood, about a half mile still out of Guffy Campground. Should I opt to continue on the trail, Guffy would be my objective for a rest stop and brunch.

Approaching the summit now, I am in for a big surprise. I see a sign emerging from the fog. It reads "Acorn Trail" with an arrow. Right below the arrow it clearly reads, "PCT 2 Miles." Nuts! I cannot believe what I see. The sign is telling me I am not only off the trail, but two miles off course.

Dumbfounded, I stop in my tracks. I rest a bit and try to decide what to do. I realize I am warm so long as I am moving. I find my body turning cold from the accumulation of four hours of sweat while ascending to this point. What trail? It is too foggy to enjoy whatever view otherwise exists. It must be spectacular. I find there is no point in resting. I just get cold and besides there is no comfortable place to sit.

I take lot of my situation. This is likely the start of an 8,000 foot ridge. I've been near here before, downhill skiing on the top of the lifts of Holiday Hill and Mountain High and have even driven through it on the nearby dirt roads in the summer. I know its' beauty and know where the trail goes. Could the sign be a mistake? Could I be on the wrong ridge. Could I be lost again? If I am indeed on the PCT, by going ahead, I will follow the slowly descending ridge to two campgrounds on the ridge before being dumped off at the first trail head on Highway 2 at about 7,600 feet, in about six miles. Although a short distance by ski, and hardly anything by car, it is now quite intimidating to contemplate trekking through deteriorating weather conditions with tennis shows and no tent, and with no more layers of clothing to put on to maintain warmth. I cannot count on the sleeping bag for warmth as it is quite damp. To take a few steps down this trail to the right, if it is the Acorn Trail would lead to the security and relative warmth of lower elevations on the way to Wrightwood. I know the Acorn trail is steep, characterized by a multitude of switchbacks quickly dropping in its first 2,000 feet. I realize that if I were to take a few steps, I would not want to change my mind and head back up this steep trail.

There is time to decide. But I am getting cold fast just standing about. I act on the assumption the sign is placed in error and that indeed I am not really lost.

With this kind of reluctance, I decide to continue on to Guffy Campground with the attitude that if I do not like what I see, or feel uncomfortable, I will, without reservation or further thought, do a turn around and head back to what seems like the Acorn Trail and head down to Wrightwood for a layover in the comfort of a motel. If it turns out it is not the Acorn Trail, it would surely take me down to lower elevations in the general direction to where I would want to go and at the same time, avoid the colder air and snow. But I am not unduly concerned because, after all, it is not even twelve noon yet and I tell myself the situation is not really dire, even if I were off the trail by two miles! I hope this is not a deja-vu of the experience at Mt. San Jacinto last month.

Momentum leads me to continue on toward what I believe will be Guffy Campground. The trail has but an inch or two of snow on it. Yet the threat remains of a sudden flurry and another bout of experiencing an obscured trail. And now I am assuming this is the right trail. I realize the situation is different than that of San Jacinto. Here there are dirt roads nearby and the distance to civilization is only an hour away, assuming that trail back there was the Acorn Trail. Imagine that, a sign saying the PCT is two miles away! Am I losing my judgement! I know doing so is but one sign of hypothermia and dehydration. But I do not feel that way at all. But I do take note that I cannot maintain warmth unless I am moving. Perhaps I am indeed experiencing an early phase of hypothermia.

Suddenly, my thoughts are interrupted by seeing the tracks that I identify as belonging to Chris and Joshua imprinted in the two inches of snow on the ground. I follow them along the trail, pondering the situation as I gaze onto the snow covered tread. Could they also have wandered off the trail? Did they see the sign?

Soon, I have a partial answer, I see the two sets of tracks wandering in circles culminating in a complete turn around heading back on this trail. Then the tracks are obscured by the more recent snowfall. I conclude that either I am indeed on the right trail or I am not alone in being lost. But, for whatever the reason, these two trekkers decided to go back and head down that trail towards Wrightwood. These were fresh tracks!

It takes just this much information to cause me to turn around and head back and soon reach that crazy sign. By now, every pine needle and every flower and bush is white with either ice crystals or fresh snow. I set my watch and quickly head down the trail. The clouds part momentarily. I see the trail below and its many switchbacks heading down towards Wrightwood.

11:00 AM, the Descent to Wrightwood, El 8250, Mi 365.9 - 0.95

The trail starts descending immediately, first in a gentle forward manner, then getting steeper as it leaves the ridge summit, but not leaving any of the cold and icy conditions behind. The trees and plants and fallen logs along the way remain covered with snow. Every pine need and every flowered petal is white. It is a winter wonderland.

The clouds part momentarily. Looking down trail, I see I will shortly leave this spectacular wintry scene. The trail descends at an increasingly accelerated rate to begin a long series of short switchbacks of the trail, perhaps twenty pair of switchbacks, together following the fall line directly to the upper heights of Wrightwood. As I get down to about the 7,500 foot level, the snow on the trail gets less and less. The pine trees soon became free of the white stuff. But it is still cold. It does not get much warmer as might be suggested by the lack of snow on the trees. The trail continues to drop down really fast. Traveling at about four miles per hour, the rate of descent could be near 35 feet per minute. It takes but less than an hour to drop the 2,000 feet to the narrow valley below. After one long switchback the trail reaches its terminus and ends abruptly at Acorn Road, paved, and with houses along the sides.

Now I realize that some joker must have picked up that sign from here, carried it uphill and planted it just to spook someone like me. It worked! It caused me to bomb out and abort the trail. Would they have done it had they known the grief it would cause? No use to ponder this one.

People and cars are moving about as if nothing unusual is going on. The walk now requires another two miles to reach the center of town. I immediately head for a café where I order ice tea, a double veggie burger with fries. The knowledgeable waitress advises of a motel a block away, the Pines Motel, a popular stay for PCT trekkers.

Chapter 15

Snowed in At Wrightwood

Taking leave of the friendly people at the café, I stroll over to the small one story motel. This motel looks like it was active during the 1930's, probably on the main highway at the time. Here, in those days, as opposed to hotels, resorts and lodges, motels were a risque kind of place to go. Attempts were made to keep one's identity private or to perhaps meet someone for the evening.

I head for a sign indicating the office. I see the small office door. I press the button. Out comes someone acting like a manager. Beyond the door are family quarters, a dog and twelve year old boy looking on as if bored with the routine. There is no waiting room except for this uncomfortable tiny foyer leading to the living quarters with their dog looking on. The area is but three feet by five. Arrangements for renting the room is made standing in this little alcove.

"Cash only," I am told. "You'll have Room F. I'll show you where the telephone is." He takes me around the small three room building to a back of another row of rooms where there is a small room, three by six feet that has a wall phone. Fortunately, it has a light inside, but no chair nor desk. I call Green Hornets, informing Sean, the Dispatcher, of my whereabouts and ask him to have David give me a call. I also leave a message with Van.

It doesn't take me long to settle into my room. My baggage is on my back. I settle down long enough to figure out the bed is so soft that I'll have to lie on my back. While in the supine position I wonder what I'll say to the people in L.A. I'll have to tell them I have no plans for the moment except to wait out the storm. I know that Hannah is at work.

I look about the area and see that I am not the only trekker held up by the storm. Here, there are five rooms, all connected to one another.

Four of the rooms are housing hikers snowed in for the duration. There are several other trekkers in town that occasionally drop by. This motel is strategically located to draw the PCTers as it is one block away from the center of town, several blocks to the post office and hardware store.

It is but a short walk to the hardware store which keeps the PCT register. Here, I make an entry and note who passed through and when, and review comments about their recent leg from Cajon Pass or Big Bear. The names are becoming more and more familiar with each registry. I can guess where they may be at this time.

I know of some that have taken time off the trail for one reason or another, mostly due to the "call of the domestic life." My guess is that most are ahead, but not far. The word around is that it is too difficult to head through the southern flank of the Sierra Nevada at this time. June 22nd is going to be a time where there is likely to be a hiatus of trekkers going through Kennedy Meadows, the gateway to the high sierras. the numbers collecting as they wait for the time they can make it safely though the central sierras. It ought to be a great scene. It could very well be the largest group of through hikers to ever be together on the PCT.

I first meet up with Neal and Malcolm staying in room C, their second day in town. Both started from Mexico last month. These are the first through hikers I meet from Southern California. As it turns out Malcolm finished John Marshall High School, my Alma Mater, in the late seventies. Malcolm plans to leave the trail next month and head for a trip to Australia. Neal wants to finish up in Canada. We share notes about the local weather, concluding it should be reaching its climax this evening, then improving and clearing out entirely by Saturday. On this basis they are planning to leave at a convenient time mid morning tomorrow. Meanwhile, we see the clouds over the ridge. We hear that it will snow here in Wrightwood by four O'clock. I say, "In a way I'll be relieved." They understand. We wait for it to snow. In June! In southern California. Our home area. We can't believe it!

I meet Jennifer and Marlene, two young ladies from northern parts of Virginia staying in room B. They're cooking outside their room.

They arrived yesterday, actually planning to stay and resupply here on packages sent to the post office from Virginia. Jennifer says, "We started following a flight to Palm Springs Airport. We took a taxi to West Palm Springs Village where we hiked on to Big Bear for a layover there. We had to stay there for three days waiting for our supply packages to arrive." They explain the delay was due to the fact that they used UPS as the vendor. They explained that the U.S. Postal Service acts faster when they themselves do the delivering.   During the afternoon we all get further acquainted with one another and share information about a myriad of details, about foods, dealing with poison oak, dealing with water purification and the risks of contracting Giardia, about foods, boots, need for ice axes, and a myriad of other topics that appear vital to doing the upcoming legs. They will call off the trip in mid July, wherever they are and fly back to Virginia.

I take several cat naps in the security of the room before stepping out to cook my usual evening meal, this time on the steps of my motel room. A very positive feeling builds up inside of me towards these hikers, the party of the two young men and these two young ladies. A kinship easily develops on the trail, as it did with Alan Downs, Rob Bedicheck and Scott Williams during the trek through the Santa Rosa and San Jacinto Mountains. Because they are so responsive to others, I relate easily to them, even though we are perhaps a couple of generations apart.

The young ladies are both graduates in biology and are interested in social work. We soon get into a conversation about social work, what Hannah is doing, and about their ideas in regards to social work and how it is that they want a change in that direction in terms of career objectives. I point out that I am a psychologist, and in fact, had given some thought to some major psycho-biological problems.   They expressed an interest in what I thought about this area.

They are indeed good conversationalists and good listeners. I find it easy to describe the complexities of the theory I developed, finding it easy to simplify it in terms they could understand and perhaps appreciate as biology majors with an interest in social work and a curiosity of what drives people to do the things that they do.

We bask in the sun during the fleeting moments when it breaks out. We also wait for it to snow. During this time we talk about the nature of small town and rural living and their impressions of Southern California. We explore the differences between the small town and large town experience. The conversation just doesn't seem to stop as we sit outside trying to soak up whatever warmth the sun offers.

Marlene is reserved, revealing little about herself. Yet she flows with the conversation at hand. She gets by with it as she easily draws personal stuff from other people, like my thoughts about southern California, these mountains here and my interest in psychobiology. Jennifer, on the other hand is expressive and is an open book. They explain they are both majors in biology and are considering going into social work as opposed to further graduate work in biology. She freely talks about her concerns, feelings, attitudes and motives. We agree, should we get the chance, we'll talk about some pscyhobiological issues that interest them. Jennifer stops on the trail every hour and a half and makes something to eat. Her pack is heavier than that of Marlene's. Unlike Marlene who is slight in figure, Jennifer is five foot, eleven inches. They distribute their weight in proportion to their weight and strength. I lift up Jennifer's pack. It must weigh about fifty pounds or more. She carries about fifteen pounds of food, including three pounds of various cheeses. Yet, I am impressed with their discipline. Jennifer and Marlene make a complex pasta. Jennifer takes out a pound of cheddar cheese, cuts it up in a multitude of tiny pieces and puts it into the heating pasta. Her discipline appears by not sampling any of the fresh cheese. I am really impressed! So are Malcolm and Neal as we watch and drool!

As I'm cooking my dinner, into the area walks in two middle aged men to their room, E, adjacent to Malcolm and Neal. They are very business like and seem to insulate themselves from everyone else. They also started from Campo. From their appearance, they seem to be very goal oriented. They hope to make it back home in Canada. They are from Canada and maybe that's why they do not seem intimidated by the cold weather. I offer them something to eat or drink. In a business-like, but polite way they turn down the offer saying they had already eaten and wish to get to bed early for an early start in the morning. They point out that it is not the snow that is the problem, but it is the cold weather that is "the killer."

For the most part, the PCTers I meet are a sociable lot and easily engage in any topic that comes up. Our focus is in our world of the trail, the weather, clothing and gear, and food. Everyone seems to have their unique approach and style of approaching their adventure. At moments like this, one's style is shared intimately with one another.

Only a few flakes fall that afternoon. I easily get to bed early and drift off into another pleasant evening of sleep, but first wondering what adventures await us all tomorrow. I think we have all developed our own criteria of what becomes a "go" and what conditions constitute a "no go." For me, it is largely a matter of the likelihood of precipitation and lack of sun. For without the sun, there will be little chance of me maintaining a minimal level of comfort commensurate with my equipment and my constitution, notwithstanding my recent experiences being caught in the cold. I do conclude that I will purchase a fleecy sweater or shirt to provide an adequate and versatile layer to the torso, to carry a tent to protect from exposure, boots if I have any indication there may be a good amount of snow on the ground and a new pair of mittens to replace mine that are now torn. I will also purchase a sleeping bag as I am concluding that mine is short on feather down now and has usefulness only as a summer leg.

June 4, Friday, 6:00 AM. Pines Motel, Wrightwood, El 8250 Mi 365.9 + 4.5 - 0.85

My pack is ready is go! I don't know if I am ready to go. The Canadians appear outside, dressed up for the ascent to the summit on the Acorn Trail. They'll be off soon. They leave in a business-like manner, without saying a word to one another, nor to anyone else. I step outside and wish them well. Quite preoccupied with their attire, gear and equipment, they seem to ignore me at first, then wave goodbye as they walk up through Wrightwood to the trail head.

I soon polish off my orange juice, cup of home made coffee and Danish as I relax trying to figure out from television what weather lies ahead in these parts. The big picture is one of an unseasonable cold spell characterized by a passing unstable and unseasonably cold mass of air from the northwest, causing dramatic snow showers in nearby mountain resort areas such as Running Springs, Big Bear, and Frazier Park. Heavy rain is falling upon much of the Los Angeles Basin. More is told to be on its way from Santa Barbara, now experiencing very heavy rain. I look outside. There is broken to overcast level about 1,500 feet above us at Wrightwood. It covers the ridge to the immediate south that hosts the PCT.

I head down to the café for some eggbeaters for breakfast. I scan the headlines. There are peace prospects in the Balkans. I seize the paper, not to buy it, but to open up the Metro section and review the recent weather reports and forecasts. Now, they are reporting wintry-like weather throughout the area, including the San Gabriel Mountains. The area is expected to have significant snowfall above 7,500. This mass of unstable, wet air is expected to pass over today and become clear, but with continued unseasonably cold temperatures generally increasing, approaching normal by the end of the week.

I see a backpack and a hiker sitting down scarfing down a huge breakfast. It is the size of the breakfast that identifies him for sure as a PCTer. I introduce myself. The waitress suggests I move from my table to one closer to him. I sit down. Immediately we exchange information about the weather picture. David Long, he is. David came from Mexico and is on his way to Canada. We are engaged in immediate rapport and exchange a bunch of information. He will register at the Pines Motel after breakfast. He leaves before my breakfast arrives.

After finishing the small breakfast, actually my second breakfast, the waitress kindly offers me a hot muffin-like pastry to carry out. I walk out eating it.

As I arrive at the motel, Malcolm departs about 10:00 AM. Neal about a half hour later. I don't see the girls. Perhaps they left. Into the area comes David Long waiting for a room. He accepts my offer to use my room until he gets one assigned, or in the event that I keep mine, he can have it or share it. He puts his household belongings next to mine and does some more errands about town. Soon after he leaves, the manager comes in, asking me if I know a David Long, and could I secure the packages sent to him.

When David returns, he is anxious to get into his packages. He opens up his drift box received from Big Bear. He takes care that this supply box follows him from one post office to another. The plastic case contains all kinds of stuff in a highly organized plastic box, including foods, medications, first aid stuff, and remedies for poison oak. He has been expecting the other package which contains his new white backpack. David spends the entire afternoon studying this mountaineering pack and prepares for his next leg. We are both impressed with the new Kelty pack. He calls up Kelty for some advice on its functions. I ask him to inquire as to how I may get one too. He finds out from calling Kelty that I have to go through a distributer. There are a very limited number of these packs available now. I think I'll eventually get one of these lightweight internal frame packs.

I make telephone contact with Hannah. I share with her my ambivalence on continuing, explaining that If I do so, I would have to wait another day or two, thus prolonging the trip. She volunteers to pick me up with the proviso that we go to the cabin, then sometime this weekend take a drive and hike to Deep Creek Hot Springs. In the meantime she feels she should stay at home while the plumbers work on our septic tank and our leaky shower faucet. She says she'll go to Pomona, pick up her outdoor gear and expects to be in Wrightwood by 4:00 PM. She says she'll call just before she leaves. I go to the manager's office and seek an extension of time. She says OK, but if someone needs it, I will have to leave. I tell Marlene and Jennifer, if Hannah comes, I am pretty sure we could provide a ride for them up the road to Grassy Hollow Campground.

1:00 PM: We wait for Hannah; Some Theorizing to Pass Away the Time

They seem to appreciate that I had some notions on the matter of stress and inhibitory processes and had written a book on the subject. There's not much to do but talk the while away. Marlene asks "What's the theory about?"

Oh boy, this will take up some time. Why not, I thought. I said, "OK, I spent a lot of time putting it together, it may take a while to explain it, OK?"

"Sure," says Jennifer. "It seems interesting."

I thought to myself, great. A chance to talk about my ideas with a couple of interested people.

"I've never had the occasion to explain in just fifteen minutes or so. But I'll try, OK"

They both nod affirmatively.

"I developed two models, then put them together to form a theory. The first model explains the nature of body reactivity to stressor events in way quite different from contemporary theories on stress. Mine is quite simple. When a stressor event occurs, there are two body reactions, excitatory reactions that directly ameliorate the impact of the stressor events and inhibitory reactivity that permit excitatory reaction to do their job--which is to reduce the impact of the stressor events upon the body. These reactions occur at the sub-cellular, cellular, tissue and system levels. Got that?

Jennifer says, "I've never thought about stress this way."

"How have you thought about it?"

"That stress is something that tests the body and can causes harm, something that should be reduced."

Marlene asks, "Are you talking only about humans?"

"No, but all the writing is geared towards human application."

Marlene says, "Go on."

"OK, the other model is a signaling or communicative model. The model offers a couple of hypothetical constructs so as to account for four classes of body signals. The fourth class signals are subcellular, like enzymatic communications.   Third class signals are intercellular communications. Second class signals consist of third class signals that can interface with nervous centers and even conscious processes. First class signals have the properties of second class signals, but have the propensity to interface with linguistic properties to affect conscious processes directly through language. Got that?"

Marlene says, "It is quite complex."

I go on to say, "Stimuli, whether immediately originating from outside the body or whether originating inside the body, can operate as stressor event. Stressor events always lead to either excitatory and inhibitory reactions." I hesitate. Even at the risk of seeming professorial I go on, "Remember, memory occurs at all levels, from the sub-cellular to the highest of complexities of nervous system operations. I extensively reviewed the literature on the nervous system, specifically the anatomy and physiology of how outside environmental stimulation affects sensation, thought and activities of the highest of psychic processes including memory, consciousness and unconscious processes."

Marlene says, "Are you talking about humans?"

I say, "I believe this stuff applies to animals with brains and vertebrate, at least frogs, dogs, cats and humans. My book, "Inhibitory Control theory," discusses sub-cellular, cellular, tissue and systems as they occur in lower and higher animals, particularly humans. The starting point in experimental research starts with Russian experimentation with frogs during the middle and late 1800s."

"Go on."

"The work in this area began with frogs, with work by Sechenov, back in the middle 1800s. It was this Russian neurophysiologist that demonstrated the phenomena and called it Central Inhibition."

"What did he do?"

"I'm glad you asked. He discovered after a frog was decorticated, the frog demonstrated faster reflexes. By conducting such experiments, he established for the first time that a function of cortical activity slows down and inhibits body reactions."

"You mean when part of the brain was separated from the spinal cord, the reflexes were more pronounced?"

"Yes, but not only more pronounced, but faster in occurring. He took measures of speed of reaction.

"Much of what I write about is not original. The beginnings are found in the work by Russian physiologists during the latter part of the 1800's from Sechenov, through Pavlov and Bechterov through the 1930s and did not get into American universities until the 1950's and still doesn't seem have caught on anywhere, except perhaps in immunology and pharmacology. Besides, all contemporary concepts of stress lead nowhere and are holding the reins on the advancement of progress in stress research."

"I've heard of Pavlov," says Marlene.

"Much of this work on inhibitory process was not accepted at first, both in Russia and later in the west. I argue, that although excitatory reactivity gets things done, it is most important to understand that direct action to repel or ameliorate the impact of stressor events come about only through effective inhibitory action."

They hesitate to respond.

"Have you learned anything about the nature and importance of inhibitory body action?"

Jennifer says, "Some things. But nothing comes to mind now."

I explain, "I argue that body components permit the body to react to stressor events."

Jennifer says, "I haven't done any research, But, go on."

I do continue on. "The key concept in the book is that body control, whether we are talking about cellular activity, system activity or psychic activity, lies with the effectiveness of inhibitory action."

Jennifer asked, "How long is the book?"

"About six hundred pages with a glossary and a very large list of references cutting across a lot of fields. I took special care to make reference to anything that was not original. Once I reviewed the literature on inhibitory processes and stress, I came up with the formal structure of the theory. I spent a lot of time applying the theory to explain a number of things."

"What's the book about?"

"It presents the foundation for the theory, argues the theory and then presents applications of the theory to explain body functions and some of its dysfunctions."

Marlene asked, "What kinds of applications are there?"

"Ah…I just didn't want to stop at the point of espousing the theory without attempting to see how it comes to explain some human functioning. So I continued to write chapters on human blood pressure reactivity and some of my research in the area, reviewed the literature on biofeedback, again with a little reference to some of my research, eastern methods of treatment, human shock reactivity, for example, analeptic shock. I took it upon myself to write a chapter on hypertension, mental retardation, schizophrenia and affect disorders, to see whether or not the theory has anything to offer to the solving of any of these human dilemmas."

"Marlene asked, "Did you finish the book?"

"Oh, yeah, I got it out in 1991."

"What do people think of it."

"I really don't know." As soon as the book was printed, I got involved in business. The book was never really circulated nor marketed. Marketing a book is much different that creating one and simply getting it published."

"Did you teach and use it as a text?"

"No, I had just gotten into aviation, purchased an aviation business at Van Nuys Airport and got too distracted to continue teaching at the local universities."

Marlene replied, "I bet, if you had the book as a text, the outcome would have been much different."

"I guess so."

3:00 PM Getting a Stove to Work

In the meantime Marlene and Jennifer cannot get their mini stove to work. It seems clogged. They're only able to let out a little bit of flame. We've been working on now for a couple of hours. No doubt, this is why we were able to carry on with my psychobiological theory. Marlene and I are trying to make sense out of the manual while Jennifer calls up Jim, her husband, for help when we identify a source of the problem. Fortunately, there is a diagram of its' construction and a little package of parts. After several calls to Jim, and with the help of David, who returns and rents a room, I identify a malfunction of the component that governs and releases the pressured fuel. Marlene reviews the manual, finding the components that serve the pressure release. David looks for a substitute O-ring and Jennifer removes the old ring and replaces it. Marlene puts it together and Jennifer fires it up. It works! Jennifer calls up Jim and tells him we had success with it, a team effort!

Meanwhile we are all getting edgy. The manager wants me out. The girls are getting edgy as they want to push on to Agua Dulce and get to the campground before dark. I am worried about Hannah. They do not look forward to carrying their heavy packs up the Acorn Trail to the summit. Should Hannah be willing, I am sure we'll offer them the option of a ride to Grassy Hollow Group Camp, up the road a bit, at elevation 7,600 that also serves as one of several trail head for the PCT in the San Gabriel and San Bernardino Mountains.

Four O'clock passes, but Hannah does not show. Nor are there any calls. The expected snowfall turns out to be a few flakes. The sun shines breaks out every now and then. When it does appear, the warmth is immediately felt. As soon as it disappears in the wavering overcast, the temperature plummets. I call home. No answer. I call Hannah's apartment, no answer. I call Hannah's cellular phone, also no answer. I assume she may be in a remote area, like nearby, and may soon appear. The manager requests I vacate the apartment. David had just left to do some more errands. It is now six O'clock and we wait in the cold for Hannah to arrive. Jim returns. He returns the favor by offering us a refuge in his room.

Marlene and Jennifer reluctantly decide to make dinner for themselves. Just as they are ready to eat, in comes Hannah with the dogs filling up the car. I introduce Hannah to the group.

We chat while the girls finish their meal. They quickly clean up. Hannah takes the dogs for a walk while I drive Marlene and Jennifer to the campground, a few miles up Highway 2. We get to Grassy Hollow

Campground just before it is completely dark. There is just enough light for them to select a site and make camp for the night. I drop them off leaving my headlights on for a while for help. I think that if I were to leave within a day or two, I'll pass them somewhere along the trail.

Back now at the Pines Motel, I discover that Hannah and David ordered pizza and salad from the local pizzeria. We decide to put the dogs in the car and walk down a few blocks to the store. The quality of the salad and this vegetarian pizza was the best I recall. We talked endlessly from start to finish.

David Long plans to leave tomorrow and trek on through to Agua Dulce. He feels that he is one city and supply point behind schedule on his way to the Canadian border. We walk back to the motel. We wish him well, fill up the car with our dogs and drive off to Green Valley Lake, about twenty miles away. On the way we wonder how we can drive close enough to Deep Creek Hot Springs tomorrow for a day hike with our two dogs.

The next day Hannah and I drove to The Summit Valley Store and got directions from Larry on how to best reach the trail head to the Hot Springs. Hannah enjoyed herself down at the springs. But by the time we made it up and out of the canyon, over the hilly terrain to the car, we were as pooped out as the dogs. We had dinner out and drove home together, dogs and all.

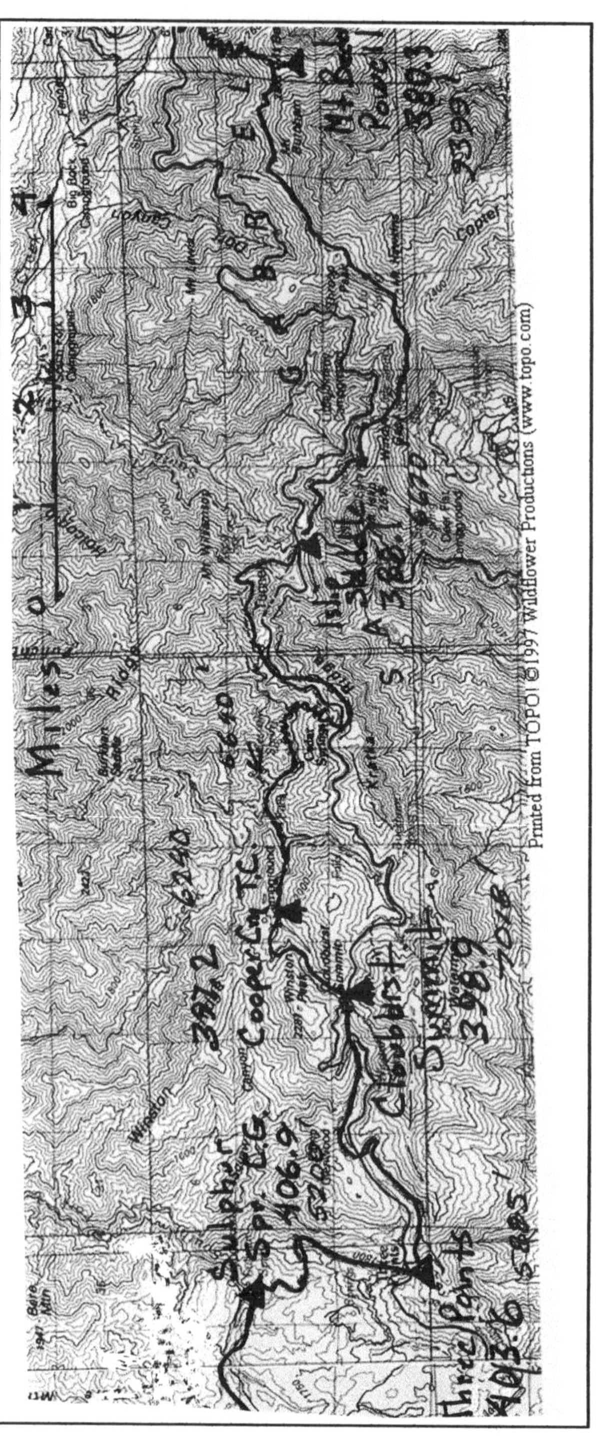
Mt Baden Powell to Sulphur Springs C.G.

Chapter 16
Blue Ridge

The Wrightwood Café....Guffy Campground....
Grassy Hollow Visitors Center

Joel and I firm up our plan for the hike the PCT through a good part of the San Gabriel Mountains, leapfrogging, from car to car. We'll each take our cars and meet at Wrightwood. We'll then know if Jon can find time to join us during the upcoming weekend and do part of it with us.

June 11, Friday, 8:00 AM; The Wrightwood Cafe, El. 6,000

Arriving a little early, I do some errands about town. All these errands require a bit of standing in line. People are dressed lightly, anticipating a warm and nice day. The weather should be good. Business around town is on the up. Weekends are quite busy now. If one listens more carefully, you can even get an idea of who is getting along well with whom and their feelings about matters in the Balkans.

Soon after returning to the corner cafe, Joel appears. While eating breakfast we plan the details of the leg. We plan to meet Jon at the parking lot at Vincent Gulch Divide on Highway 2, at the trail head to Mount Baden Powell, Sunday morning at 9:00 AM.

We decide to travel in two cars through Big Pines to a parking lot on Highway 2 at the next PCT crossing and trail head at Islip Saddle. Such a drive takes us only about 20 minutes or so. We leave the Grand Cherokee at Islip Saddle with re-supplies awaiting for us. We drive back to Blue Ridge in Joel's car where we pick up a good dirt road to Guffy Campground near where the PCT enjoins the Acorn Trail down to Wrightwood.

In marked contrast to last week when there was near blizzard conditions with snow and poor visibility and signs of the trail becoming obscured, it is now warm with clear skies. In fact, it is beautiful. It seems like it just can't get better than this!

10:00 AM; Guffy Campground, El 8225, Mi366.8

Joel secures the car and we are on the trail again. The tread takes us west along the top of beautiful Blue Ridge, now familiar to us from our drive east. The area was struck by a large forest fire two years ago which was obscured by the snow cover and fog last week. Guffy Campground, Blue Ridge Campground and the ski area facilities of Mountain High were all spared. The extent of the fire is more noticeable by trail. The PCT generally is off to the north a hundred yards or so and seems to follow the route of the fire, all the way from near Guffy, along the top of Blue Ridge even across Highway 2 and somewhat beyond Grassy Hollow visitors Center and Jackson Flat Campground. Fortunately, the fire spared these areas as well. Much of the low ground cover has recovered, but hundreds of blackened conifers, oaks and deciduous trees stand bare as reminders of the debacle. There is but little sign of re-growth of the large trees. The fire seemed to travel in a checkerboard manner, skipping large areas then hitting others real hard. We walk for a mile or so through thick and completely intact forest. Then suddenly, for another a few hundred yards anything higher than ten feet is blackened.

The overlooks are dramatic. Every turn of the trail brings another surprise. To the immediate east and behind us is the continuation of our ridge which generally slopes down reaches a gap at the junction with H2. Here at the gap, a couple are looking out impressed with the heights of Wright Mountain, now with no sign of snow. Last week all this view was obscured. To the south are Pine Mountain and Mount Baldy, with but a little left of last week's snowfall. To the immediate southwest and below is the east fork of the San Gabriel river and the obscured valley of the same name. The whole area is covered by the common marine layer extending form the Pacific, seventy miles away. This marine layer and some smog from the L.A. basin and local areas totally obscure any view of the extensive valleys below, and permit only a hint of the extent of the mountains and peaks to the distant south, some of them I climbed. To the west is Mount Baden Powell extending up to 9,400 feet. Every turn and bend gets us a little closer to the well defined peaks with somewhat different perspective of the terrain and summit areas. There is still some sign of snow near the top on it's northeast exposure. I trust that means we may find some water on the way up.

Unlike the neighboring peaks, Mount Baden Powell seems more volcanic in shape. We cannot make out the trail, but we know it zig zaps through countless short switchbacks generally allowing the fall line from Vincent Gap, the saddle below, to the very top. To the northwest we see H-2 winding out of sight. Overlooking the ridges to our north we can see the Mojave Desert floor today, but not the Sierra beyond.

The predominant pines are the Jeffrey variety. Here, there are also mountain mahogany, at times in bloom with their whitish-yellowish mid-size flowing, juniper, large black oaks and white firs becoming more apparent as we trek westerly along the ridge top.

Flowering is abundant. The floor of the entire ridge is dotted with the foot or two high Western Wallflower, characterized by it's bright yellow clumps of petals forming its' several inches, sometimes a whole foot or more, of elliptical shape, the lower lying wild onion with its' small pinkish flowering, occasional lupine with its characteristic blue vertical stalk of layered flowing. These wild flowers are outnumbered by ones I have yet to identify.

The trail takes us directly to the upper reaches of the ski slopes where a number of lift drop-offs appear. Seeing them now in the summer time, in slow motion as we walk though them, provides a much different perception than offered by skiing through the areas in the winter time. Now, appreciation is given to the extent of preparation and maintenance required to develop the areas. The ski runs appear like cienegas with a foot or so deep green grass holding the soil down in wait for snow to fall on their browning stalks. The grassy slopes now go to the very top of the ridge where there are signs appropriately alerting skiers of drop offs and of many dangers to the south of the ridge.

There are several ski lifts now throughout much of this length of the ridge, perhaps a few miles. All look new and well maintained. There are occasional huts for staff and emergency use along the top near the runs. The slopes are generally wide and moderate in their steepness as they gradually curve around the fall line. The road at the top of the ridge now provides a connection to the several runs, starting at their highest elevation to the east. We find ourselves gradually walking downhill westerly where it seems a downhill skier would have to produce but little effort to help him glide down from the tops of the higher lifts in the east to the lower lifts to the west. The area seems perfect for Nordic, cross country skiing, permitting the best of two worlds as one could very readily spend the whole day going up and down and hardly ever being required to do the same downward slope a second time. In fact, even going east from the westward terminus should be a piece of cake.

Soon, we pass through two reservoirs that hold water required for artificial snow making that greatly extends the downhill ski season here. They are the only unattractive features around. The water seems murky. The two reservoirs are surrounded by a high fence.

The trail along the ridge is wide and remarkably easy-going as it meanders gradually downhill. The trail here is largely shaded by pines and is quite pretty now with the flowering of many low lying plants. Were they not flowering at this time, such growth would appear unremarkable as it blends into the common undergrowth on the forest bottom.

Joel and I see an occasional car, recreational vehicle, but very few people appear along the ridge in the campground areas. Very few people are experiencing the advantage of the beauty. In each of the two campgrounds there is a couple camping in or about their vehicles. The trail itself goes very near the campgrounds, Guffy and Blue Ridge, but not through them. We are close enough to wave as we go by, but the calmness of the day and the unspoken desire for privacy dictates we are too distant to exchange words. We soon reach the paved highway and stroll over to Inspiration Point, a rest point and parking lot with a description of the overlook over the east fork of the San Gabriel River to the valley below. We see a small structure across Highway 2. I notice it serves not only is a restroom but can offer a shelter for hikers should there be inclement weather, like there was just last week. A number of unanticipated places of overnight shelter appeared in unanticipated places. Had I known of them I might have not had to endure cold and wet or snowy conditions. Lake Morena had varied facilities including shower rooms, forest service porches and lounges. Cibbits Flats Campground and Burnt Rancheria Campgrounds in the Laguna mountains had open restrooms despite the fact that the campground was closed. A perfect trail-side cave for one or two on top of the San Felipe halls was passed just short of descent at the final gap. There was a discarded wooden outhouse existing at Strawberry Junction Trail Camp in the San Jacinto Mountains. Another surprise was our luck in finding a vacant public U.S.F.S. cabin near the campground at Coon Creek Jump off.

A pleasant approach to Grassy Hollow

1:00 PM: At Grassy Hollow Family Group Campground and Visitors Center 7300, Mi 372.9

We arrive thirsty with barely enough water reserves to get us through the evening. Perhaps water would have to wait until we reach Jackson

Flat Campground, not even a certainty, a couple of miles away. The nearest snow patch seemed a couple of thousand feet above our elevation and a few miles up the Mt. Baden Powell trail. Jon will not arrive until tomorrow morning.

Disappointed in that we could not find a faucet anywhere in the campground, we are about to write the matter off until we approach the structure housing the visitors center. We find the building entirely secured and bathrooms locked. We find the drinking fountain near the bathrooms working.

Our water troubles are over. We fill our bottles and drink. Once our thirst is quenched, we look for a camp site for the evening, not realizing it is indeed a picnic area. At the picnic areas, the tables and barbecue stoves are on a slant finding a sleeping area a challenge. We agree on a spot and leisurely set up camp and cook supper. There is plenty of time to study the charts and plan the next day or two.

We had not been able to effectively communicate back home. We are able, only at times, to get through by cellular phone, and when we did, the call tended to break up before long. I can not count on Jon receiving my calls on his answer machine, let alone assume that he could comply with our requests. In any event, we are planning to meet Jon Sunday morning at nine in the morning at the trail head at Highway 2.

We realize we could easily reach the trail head tomorrow morning, but there is no point in arranging such a meeting. We realize that we have a whole 24 hours to while away in order to be at that point Sunday morning. I suggest to Joel that we offer Jon a ride from Islip Saddle should he wish to continue the hike from the summit of Mt. Baden Powell. Joel agrees. Now, it is a matter of confirming plans or merely relying upon his commitment of last week to show up at the right time. Joel and I do not discuss the situation that occurred on the way to Big Bear City when Jon separated himself from us and messed up the trip. In this case, we make it clear to Jon that if he does not show up by nine in the morning that we will leave a note indicating the time we started out on the trail, then wait a bit for him at the spur to Lamel Springs. Just as leisurely as we set up camp, we cook our dinner. We casually slip into our bags and go to sleep.

Chapter 17

A Wedding at Grassy Hollow Campground

Grassy Hollow Family Picnic Area....A wedding party arrives ....The clergyman arrives....More people show up....Excitement grows....A mood of anxiousness....Indians lead the procession ....The posse arrives...A woman from the Cantina...The bride appears....Man and wife....Pictures are taken

June 12, Saturday, 8:00 AM: Grassy Hollow Family Picnic Area and Visitors Center, El 7300, Mi 372.9

As there is no reason to get up early and no place to go, we take care to sleep late. I look out. The bright morning sun is casting it's light all about. It is warm. No gloves nor fleece hat required today. No need to get dressed while in the sack.

Upon getting dressed I spot a man nearby at the adjoining picnic area. He is casually dressed in shorts. He is moving about in a methodical way, pacing up and around the adjoining picnic area. Strangely enough, he puts a blanket over the outdoor barbecue stand and moves it about as if to try make it neat. He then carefully picks up a bunch of pine cones placing them to make a large rectangle, about twelve by fifty feet in front of the barbecue as if it were a podium in preparation for a ceremony or lecture.

I walk over to him and ask him if he's preparing for something.

He says with an broad smile, "There's going to be a wedding right here at high noon.!"

"Really!"

"Yeah, and it's going to be mine, an old mountain one at that." He takes a step aside. He explains, "It is not necessary for you to move. "After all it's first come. You were here first."

I don't know what to say. Maybe he's nuts.

He walks off.

I walk out to the restroom. It is now open.

As I return, the man appears with a lady in forest service uniform. I am wondering about all the things I might have done that were wrong! As I was by the restroom I discovered that this area is limited to picnicking. I try not to look worried. I have my PCT camping permits in my pocket. A lot of good that'll do! Anyway, the two of them come by. I overhear them talking like some people do when they actually want you to eavesdrop.

 "Well, OK," says he, "We won't shoot off any weapons."

She says, "That's good. I hope you all have a lot of fun."

Now, I realize that there indeed will be a wedding, but is it for real? Will there be a bride? Will there be a clergyman. It is Saturday. Will it be a Jewish, Catholic, protestant or civil?

Before she takes leave she offers me the word, "It's OK to stay there where you are, you'll have a ring side seat."

Wow, not only can I not believe I am not in any trouble, but indeed there will be a wedding right next door to watch to while away the time. I suppose the barbecue will be a beema, pulpit or something. There doesn't seem to be much room for a scroll. I go over to Joel who is sitting about 50 yards away at an observation point overlooking Mount Baden Powell. I explain, "Joel, there will be wedding here, yes, right here at noon."

He doesn't blink an eye. I say, "Let's stay till then and then leave for Jackson Flats after noon."

In a preoccupied way, he says, "We have nothing to do today. We should have gone up to Mount Baden Powell today."

I say in a questioning way, "Well, I assume you'd rather go up with Jon tomorrow."

Joel retorts, "I don't care about the wedding. If you want to watch it, I guess it's OK by me."

I remind him, "We're planning to go up with Jon. We'll plan on going up tomorrow at 9:00 AM. If he's not there, we'll leave a note. In the meantime, let's see what happens here.

He gives a shrug. No doubt he has the itch to get on with the hike and make it up to the top and doesn't care about the wedding.

10:00 AM: The Wedding Party Begin to Arrive

A group is forming about forty yards away. I can only hear the loudest of conversations. The same young man seems to be directing the activity, with the five or ten other adults around following his directions. Just as a few people arrive, I realize I don't see the young man anymore. One or two men in costume of the 1880's appear, each wearing white shirts, a wide brim hat, string ties, an open long coat, very high boots with spurs. Each man is armed with two pistols, each in large holster connected to a low lying belt. Another one comes in wearing a similar outfit of the period. Soon the young man returns. At first I do not recognize him. He is wearing a fresh looking formal outfit of the period. Unlike the other men flourishing weapons, he has none. He moves around nervously, now looking like the groom he is, ready for the wedding ceremony.

11:20 AM: More people arrive.

Now there are about twenty people, most of them in authentic looking garb of the period, including four or five youngsters also dressed in the period. A couple of women now appear wearing long dresses and head gear of the period. Families with youngsters appear, varying in age. Most of them are in costume expected of boys and girls a hundred and twenty years ago. The girls are more formally attired, but in period dress. The other adult and children not in costume are wearing outdoor, comfortable and casual clothes. About a dozen light chairs are facing the rectangle outlined by the pine cones.

11:25 AM: The Clergyman arrives

A small sedan arrives and parks in the lot just a bit away from our area. He steps out of the car. He is wearing contemporary slacks and short sleeve conventional shirt. Because he is carrying a large red book without lettering in his hand, I assume he is an official to the ceremony. As he gets closer, it looks like a bible. Because of his informal attire and the manner he is carrying the bible I assume, he is not Catholic nor Jewish, but most likely Protestant.

Someone calls out, "The preacher is here."

A feminine voice calls out, "Yes, it's Reverend Hurt."
The crowd merges to greet the minister.

Soon, a well dressed young lady appears with a child, most likely her daughter. Both mother and daughter are stunningly dressed in their long bright dresses that bring out the highlights of their blond hair and fair complexions. She strides up nearby holding her daughters' hand, offers a smile and continues to walk up the hill the several yards to merge with the group ahead.

11:30 AM: More people show up.

Snap cameras and video cameras appear. People in small groups are asked to pose together, some with the groom. The "preacher" seems a little impatient or agitated. He is trying to confer with the groom.

11:35: A couple of hundred yards to the east, two or three cars appear in line.

Someone calls out, "Here comes a caravan!"

The groom calls out, "And if there's no bride, I'm calling the whole thing off!"

There is no movement. Another male voice rings out, Anyone wants a beer?" as he downs a Corona.

As more ladies in costume arrive, a voice calls out, "Is Valerie here"

The groom calls out, "If she doesn't show, it's off!"

Another voice calls out to the groom. "Can you wait?"

He yells out louder than before, "I waited for six months already." More confidently, he yells for everyone to hear, "I already made up my mind months ago."

11:45: The parking lot is now full.

Now there are 24 cars and the wedding party has now increased to about 40 people. Someone announces loud enough for me to hear. "The bride has arrived."

Another feminine voice calls out, "She's getting dressed now." I see someone pointing to east.

Meanwhile several youth groups, Boy Scouts, and a couple groups of girls arrive at the far side of the parking lot. The boys are noisy. One kid continuously blows off a police whistle. It sounds over and over again. Meanwhile the girls are quiet, sitting in a small group listening to one of the adults who seems to be offering some structure as to what lies in store for them and how they are to behave. The boys are all over the place, the adults trying to supervise them. Finally, I hear a woman's voice to the east calling out, "Stop that whistling, right now! No more whistling." In my years of working with kids, I continue to marvel at how docile girls are as compared to boys of their same age.

11:48: Excitement grows

As the bride now is believed to be near by. Voices get louder. I can now hear a lot of the conversation. Joel and I have our gear prepared to pack. As I pack up my gear, I take care to leave the table closest to the wedding party empty, providing a sign that they are free to use the area. People become more animated and expressive in body language.

Someone calls out, "We have a podium right here."

The party now grows to about forty as more people arrive. Three men in full garb arrive, two in full black beards, all armed. One wears a badge indicating Sheriff. Many of the women are dressed in the era of the day, long home made dressed with tight waists and bodices. Someone raises a large black book into the air. He calls out, "Everyone's gotta sign in the book."

I hear the groom utter again, "I made my mind up months ago. This is only a formality."

12:00 PM: A Mood of Anxiousness

More pictures are being taken. Women are busy entertaining and controlling the kids, mostly boys, running around releasing energy. There must now be about twenty kids around. A four year old heads for our area. He falls as he is being chased by his mother. Some inventive parents are playing catch with the kids with whatever wood or pine cones there are around. Meanwhile about a hundred yards to the east appears to be the bride's party.

But it turns out that several cars are arriving with more guests. Several of the men in garb come by to our empty table. As they become closer, I see the immaculate detail to their garb, the engraved belts, authentic looking boots, shiny spurs, garters on their sleeves, the various kinds of stylish hats of the period, some wide brim, others black and round. The shirts and pants are well made and stitched quite well in a hand made style. They explain they are the "Mule Skinners," a group from Barstow, California. They offer regular skits at Calico, a ghost town in the Mojave Desert. They explain they also do skits and programs throughout the area. Their number is 714-815-6958. As for today, the groom is part of the group and this event is for themselves!

12:20 PM: Indians Lead the Procession

from the east comes a black sedan of the early 1920's, well refurbished. It seems out of place. It turns around and goes the other way. Then comes a small group of three women dressed in American Indian attire, probably Chumash, the tribe that resided in this area. They move slowly and deliberately and without visible display of affect or mannerism. There seems to be no response from the growing crowd, even as they arrive and quietly congregate amongst them.

A man sits down on one of the chairs. He pulls out a guitar and warms up. I can't hear what he is playing. More is seen approaching from the east. Heading the procession now is a lone man dressed in full Indian garb. Again, probably Chumash. He approaches silently. This time the noise of the group softens as he slowly approaches.

12:30: The posse arrives.

About a dozen men, in two wide lines, in pairs, now appear. walking casually. As they come closer I see they represent the Sheriffs' Posse in full garb and weaponry. I recognize them as being at our table not long ago.

12:35: From "the cantina,"a tall, stately woman appears.

As the posse arrives, or shortly thereafter, I see a young woman behind, by herself. She is tall, thin and of dark complexion and of remarkable stature entering slowly and quite poised in her long bright red dress, perhaps of silk, with a one or two inch border on the low hemline of dark cotton lace. Over her shoulders is a long scarf-like fluffy addition in red and black coloring matching the outfit, probably about eight feet in length. Her long black hair is partially covered with a thin and matching black net. Around her neck is a simple necklace. She looks like she came right out of the past! From a cantina. She walks about very slowly in black shoes. She is absolutely stunning!

12:35: The Bride Appears

Far out, being escorted by some more men dressed as deputies appears another group. At the head of the group is a uniquely attired bridesmaid, sauntering in, carrying a broad natural smile. She is wearing a dress that looks like formal attire from Western Europe of that same era, kind of "Old Hollandish" in a well cut blue and white dress and large bright white shoes.

12:40 PM: The group awaits the bride.

The posse forms about the rectangle, about eight on each side providing an arena for the bride. The minister is standing in front of the group, informal in his dress and demeanor. The group now, about fifty or sixty in number, quiets down. The bride appears about a hundred yards to the east. Now I see her. She is wearing a long shiny, bright red dress with two thin red straps holding the almost-low cut dress up around her shoulders.

The minister asks the groom to stand by her side facing him. The crowd of about sixty is absolutely quiet. The other people in the camping area seem to be paying no attention to what is going on, yet they are also quiet. You can hear a pin drop. I forget we are in a public campground. The whole campground is quiet. The minister is talking quietly, as if directly to the couple. Even though I step out closer, I can only make out a word or two. I hear him talking something the symbolism of the ring.

12:50 PM: Man and Wife

There is a slight cheer. The couple move out a few steps, and a few yards to the east though the posse. Rice is thrown all over them, to some annoyance to the bride. No gun fire, but a loud cheer and a burst of conversation emerges from the group.

1:00 PM: Pictures are formally taken.

The bride and groom greet a line of well wishers. Gifts are piled on a table nearby. Food is now being prepared on a nearby table. More pictures are taken as the groom cuts the large wedding cake and offers his bride and himself a piece. They offer a piece to one another real slowly. The bride takes a bite then shoves the piece, frosting and all, right onto his face. They kiss one another.

Joel and I meanwhile have everything in our packs. We stay long enough to congratulate the bride and groom. I tell them I took notes and will be glad to send them my written impressions, this chapter. We put on our packs and head northwest to Jackson Flats and Mount Baden Powell.

Chapter 18

To Mount Baden Powell and Islip Saddle

Departing Grassy Hollow...Jackson Flat Campground....
A stealthcamp site overlooking the desert...At Vincent Gap
....Mt. Baden Powell....Over the ridge to Islip Saddle

June 12, Saturday, 1:15 PM: Departing Grassy Hollow

We ponder the significance of the event as we head out of the immediate area. We wave goodbye to various people as we stroll through the picnic area and exchange some pleasantries. We head north to pick up the PCT on the way to Jackson Flats Group Campground. The trail immediately meanders through a dark forest. Myriads of flowers and plants appear as soon as we leave the boundaries of the picnic area and get back on the PCT. Sometimes the PCT tread is carpeted! The area opens up as we approach several burned out areas. Although the burn is noticeable, it is of less devastation than areas to the southeast. Soon we get to the environs of Jackson flats. We pass through a nature trail with some explanations as to how a forest maintains itself, with emphasis on regeneration of the soil from fallen trees. Unfortunately it has been neglected and much seems to be missing.

The campground is quite impressive with its rich glade of pines, firs and cedars. The campground has several improved restrooms with flowing water. Each group site consists of several tables with a central serving platform with two cement stands near two barbecue cooking areas. We find the only empty area and shortly set up for a rest. The group area next to ours is filled with about 30 people. They are enjoying themselves, pitching horseshoes, listening to music on the radio, and generally making a lot of noise. We take off our socks and clean up with water from the local faucet. We stretch out on the empty tables. Then after preparing and eating supper we depart to find a quiet place to spend the evening, somewhere out on the trail.

 6:00 PM: A stealth campsite and above Vincent Gap; El 6585, Mi 376.0 - 0.0

We wait til the last moment before we decide on a site to spend the evening. We wish to be close to the trail head, yet not on the road and hopefully at a spot where we can place a call by cellular phone. As we approach a knoll, overlooking Vincent Gulch, the gap where the Baden Powell trail head lies, we find an adequate place on a small plateau overlooking both the mountain and the desert to the north. I try to make a call, hoping that I could get through either from the north to the desert or to the south through the gap to the San Gabriel Valley. I do get through and leave a message for Jon. I call Green Hornets and speak to David. The call breaks up. I try other calls but do not get through anymore. Joel tries later, but without any success. We set up our bags, slip into them and succeed in getting not only a long rest, but a good night of sleep.

June 13, Sunday, 8:30 AM: Vincent Gap; The Trail Head to Mt. Baden Powell, El 6585, Mi 376.5 - 0.0.

We're up at seven, put our stuff together and head down the mountain. The trail takes us immediately down hill directly to Vincent Gap to the trail head. Just before the trail comes onto the highway at the gap, the trail enters into a very thick and dark glade of live oaks. It is so dark, we can barely see. This cave-like experience lasts but for a few minutes. Then we break out and there is the highway. I look at my watch. It is 8:30. We carefully cross the highway. We do not see Jon. As planned, we will wait til 9:00 AM. We while away the time by resting and leisurely prepare our breakfasts. There are about half a dozen cars and some people milling about preparing to ascend this popular trail that will take them to the mountain top.

At 9:15 I prepare a note giving the time, our immediate plans, including where our next resting area will be. Our hope is that he will soon arrive, see our note and catch up with us shortly.

Jon then appears. He agrees to consider walking with us to Islip Saddle; our minds to be made up upon reaching the top. We are anxious to start. We start our ascent at 9:30, reaching Lamel Springs,

Thirty+ switchbacks to the top

just off the trail, El 7765 in about an hour. The tiny spring has but little water seeping out. We take out our hand spade, dig out an area and find we are able to filter out several quarts of well needed water from the water hole. The immediate area is on the side of a steep canyon, with barely enough space for us to sit or stand. We look out below. I count about twenty cars now parked in the lot directly below. The trail is busy with people coming up and going down. As we get higher, we begin to recognize people coming down that had left the trail head earlier. The trail switches back and forth about thirty times or so before reaching the short spur trail to the summit. The trail is well marked with signs indicating milage and altitude. These signs provide feedback as to rate of climb and progress towards the top. We crossed a snow patch about the 8,900 level, easily negotiated. There was only a patch or so on this northeastern exposure today.

Here are seen the limber pine trees discussed in various mountaineering books. These trees seem to resemble both the stunted conifers trees commonly seen at the timber line and the bare and twisted trunk, ancient bristle cone pines seen on White Mountain, east of Bishop, California. Like the bristle cone pine, they are widely separated by one another with no sign of growth between them. They are said to vary in longevity from one to two thousand years.

Anonymous

The rare limber pine tree

1:15 PM: at the summit, El 9299, - Mi 380.3 + 0.3 - 0.0

Anonymous

Approaching the summit along the crest

Though I expected to require five hours to make it to the top, I surprise myself by making it in about three hours and fifteen minutes, well before our cut-off time of 2:00 PM, a time I set aside as being required to make it to Islip Saddle.

Because we got there so efficiently, we are able to spend some time at the summit and reflect upon the view and the monument to Sir Baden Powell, set up several years ago in memory of the founding of the Boy Scout movement. Here engraved are statements produced by Powell, A scout is "trustworthy, loyal, helpful, friendly, courteous, kind, brave, clean and reverent." On another side of the monument is an explanation on his part as to what is the essential value of scouting for a young man. Essentially to provide ways for each boy to attain on his own part, a sense of fulfillment, success and confidence in the skills needed for life. I must tell you my eyes begin to feel very salty as I leaned on the rail and became engrossed in reviewing my experiences in this great international movement.

The summit here is also the eastern terminus of the Silver Moccasin Trail, Scouting's 53 mile trek though the Angeles Crest of the San Gabriel Mountains. The trail is congruent for about twenty three miles westward from here, separating from the PCT at Three Points, a mile or so up Highway 2 from Chilao Flats.

While at the top, Jon shares two of his three peanut butter and jam sandwiches with Joel and I. This lunch does surprisingly well with a raspberry drink made up by Joel.

There is sufficient time for us to overlook and appreciate the 360 degree panorama from the top. To the immediate east is the expanse of Blue Ridge, the 8,000 foot ridge we had just completed. To the east of Blue Ridge, lies the sharp shoulders and escarpments leading to Wright and Pine Mountains, now free of apparent snow, but very intimidating last week when I was approaching them from the east. Clockwise, looking two miles to the southeast is the broad shoulder of pine mountain ridge reaching up to Pine Mountain and aptly named, Mt. Baldy, 10,080, both showing minimal sign of snow. Immediately to the south and directly and steeply below us lies the upper part of the east fork of the San Gabriel River where if we look further to the south we would see the San Gabriel Valley. But the marine layer is so thick today we cannot even make out the mountains of the Cleveland National Forest. To the west lie the peaks and ridges we will soon traverse, Mt Burnham, 8997, Throop Peak, 9138, Mt Hawkins, 8540, to the south of Mt Islip, 8250 down to Windy Gap, 7360. The trail leads through Little Jimmy Campground to wind down to Islip Saddle at 6670 where our car awaits us to transport Jon to his car at Vincent Gulch. I planned the route so that we must be at each of these points by a designated time assuring sufficient reserve time of about an hour, to get to the car before dusk. To the north we can easily make out the Mojave Desert and can barely see the southern flanks of Sierras where eventually the trail leads.

Before we leave, I make an attempt to call again on the cellular phone. With 360 degrees of view, I figure I might get through to a repeater. I get through to Green Hornets, speak to Tom, and say hello.

2:00 PM: The eastern ridge of the San Gabriel Mountains; on the Silver Mocassin Trail

Jon decides to leave the summit with us at 2:00 PM. The walk is easy. Time goes by quite rapidly as the PCT, still congruent with the Silver Moccasin Trail, is now basically downhill. The view remains quite dramatic with surprises at every turn. The trail is typically covered with welcoming shade of pines, firs, and incense cedars, with a pleasant ground cover of thick manzanita, whitehorn, and flowering sagebrush.

Whiling away the time, we find we get involved in a discussion on the relative merits of cotton t-shirts compared to nylon or polyester types on hikes. As the conversation continues, it becomes apparent that Jon and Joel are at it, arguing strongly as Jon argues the case for cotton and Joel argues the case for polyester. I decide to take on the role of moderator and score keeper. The conversation goes something like this:

Jon: "Cotton is better because it is more comfortable."

"Jon gets a point."

Joel, " Nylon is more comfortable because it doesn't hold on as much to moisture produced by perspiration."

"A point for Joel."

Jon: "Perspiration on the shirt causes coolness which feels good."

" Now, two points for Jon."

Joel: "The coolness of perspiration on a shirt interferes with the body's cooling system."

"Now, two points for Joel. It's even."

Jon: "Nylon shirts prevent water from cooling the body."

"Now, three points for Jon."

Joel: "Well, nylon is better because it is lighter."

"Ok, three points for Joel."

Jon: "How do know it's lighter? You're just guessing."

"Personal attack, minus 1/2 point, down to 2 and one half."

Joel: "You see... It's better because it dries faster when it does get wet."

"Aha, now three points for Joel."

Jon: "Cotton is better because when it does get wet, it cools you off faster."

"An old argument restated, half point off again, now two points."

Jon: "That's not fair. You're biased on this issue. You already said you prefer nylon shirts on hikes.

"Out of Order: Another half point off. Now, down to one and a half points."

This nonsense goes on until the tread goes uphill at such a rate I can't keep up with them. After a while, the tread levels off and I catch up with them. They are still arguing the same matter. This "debate" goes on for about three miles.

Little Rock Creek is very inviting, but we choose to look at it from a distance, preferring to continue on to Little Jimmy Trail Camp for a needed rest. Here there are outhouses, picnic benches and firepits. We rest but a few minutes, then continue downhill to eventually get to Islip Saddle at 5:00 PM, El 6670, Mi 388.1 where our car awaits us with transportation and supplies if we so need them.

We arrive uneventfully and drive Jon to his car at Vincent Gap. From there, he follows us to Inspiration Point at Blue Ridge, whereupon he waits about forty minutes for Joel and I to return with the two cars. We agree to head down to Wrightwood and find the pizza parlor that Hannah and I raved about following our experience there last week.

7:00 PM At the Pizza Parlour at Wrightwood, El 6000

We scarf down a veggie pizza. Unfortunately, it was a busy weekend and they ran out of lettuce so they were not able to provide us with a salad nor antipasto. Here the cook is so preoccupied with two attractive young teenagers, holding hands with one of them that he is barely able to attend to our hungry needs. Yet the pizza is every bit as good as the one Hannah, David Long and I had last week. Soon after eating, Jon leaves for home. Joel and I head out for Jensens Market for some late snacks, then drive off just after dusk with two cars westward to find a place to spend the night.

Chapter 19

Islip Saddle to Sulphur Springs

Driving west from Wrightwood....Buckhorn Campground....
All kinds of ways to do the PCT....Out of Islip Saddle....The
bottom of Cooper Canyon....Cooper Canyon Trail Camp....
Cloudburst Summit....Sulphur Springs Campground

June 13, Sunday, 7:45 PM: Driving west from Wrightwood

It is past dusk as Joel and I leave Wrightwood in two cars. We head westward along the Angeles Crest Highway and wind up at Buckhorn Campground. The camp host, Neil, draws out a map revealing our intended course and points out two waterfalls along the way. I make a couple of calls from the new booth and we settle in for the night.

June 14, Monday, 7:30 AM: Buckhorn Campground

Before we make breakfast we wash up and clean our socks and underwear right there by the quick moving passing streamlet. Breakfast is routine. Before we get a chance to move out, two men camping downhill ask us for a battery jump to start their car. After complying, we leave for Three Points where we plan to drop off a car, to then return to Islip Saddle to continue the trek westbound along the San Gabriel Mountains. The name "three" points refers to the confluence of the three trails, The Mt. Waterman trail starting immediately up towards Mt. Waterman, the Silver Moccasin Trail continuing to Bandido Campground, then further west along the San Gabriel Mountains and the PCT that we will later take to Sulphur Springs Campground. The parking lot serves the three trail heads.

When we arrive at Three Points, Joel decides he wants to see Sulphur Springs. So we follow one another the three or four miles to the campground. We arrive there and find the camp a mess with debris scattered about, most flying out of the trash cans with their lids laying about. We pick up the trash and secure the trash cans. There is some water flowing. There are picnic benches, an outhouse and corrals for horses in an adjoining area. We easily decide to drop off the Grand Cherokee and return to the trail head at Islip Saddle with his Toyota.

8:00 AM. There are indeed all kinds of ways to do the PCT

As Joel is driving down the road immediately out of Sulphur Springs we see before us on the road three elderly men and a woman walking down the road. As we pass, we stop to say hello. They are wearing T-shirts emblazoned with the logo of the PCTA. They indicate they are walking the Pacific Crest Trail from Mexico to Canada. They explain they live in the Chino area and do a portion of the trail every Monday, starting last year or so from Campo. One of the men engages us in conversation while the others troop on back to three points. We offer him a ride to catch up with the others who deliberately walk ahead. He squeezes in to my right. Although we cannot secure the door, he insists that Joel drive on. He sticks his legs outside as we drive on slowly. He asks us to pass the group and drop him off about fifty yards in front of them. We do so. It requires him about a minute or so to climb out as he is so arthritic. He timed it right because by the time he was able to make it out of the car the others had caught up with us. Scott Williamson told me a couple months ago at Tule Creek, "There are all kinds of ways to do the PCT."

9:30 AM: Out of Islip Saddle, El 6670, Mi 388.1 - 0.0

We drive on to Islip Saddle where we secure the pickup. We find it quite windy here. Gusts are up to about thirty knots. We find a shady nearby, down a trail that leads to the north, find a place to sit and have breakfast, leftovers from our purchases from Jensen's Market last night. Filling up on water we continue our trek.

The first 1.6 mile takes us up the dry southern exposure of Mt Williamson to the trail summit of near 8,000 feet. The chaparral is low and the trail offers very little shade going up. Along the way of this tiring section are views to the south revealing the poor condition of Highway 39 that used to connect the mid San Gabriel Valley and beautiful Crystal Lake with the Angeles Crest Highway here at Islip

A narrow trail along the slopes

Saddle. The growth is sparse along the climb but with occasional firs for shade. Once at the summit the view to the north now get our attention. Here we overlook The Devils Punch Bowl. The trail down traverses and switchbacks down a very steep sandy slope for a while, then drops off finally back on the Angeles Crest Highway short of Kratka Ridge, at 6,700 feet.

Across the highway, the trail immediately climbs well above the road through pleasant forest characterized by white firs, the tall sugar pine, a choice pine for lumbering, tall ponderosa pines, oak and mountain mahogany. Soon, in about a mile we reach Eagles Roost Picnic Area (6550) where we cross the highway again, this time to descend down to surprisingly pretty, Rattlesnake Canyon.

Here, the scenery changes dramatically. As it reaches the bottom of the canyon, the trail meanders through gullies moist with water. The whole area below seems semi-tropical with a quite wide variety of flora including much poison oak. But no rattlesnakes.

Joel and I get into trying to identify the various kinds of plants, now perplexed by the differing kinds of conifers. Here we try to differentiate firs, spruce and pines from one another. We discover that the white pine changes its appearance as it grows older and taller. Here we find the younger white firs aptly named and easily identified by their white trunk. However as they get older and taller, the trunk, develops, from the bottom up, with a dark bark resembling pines. This development is seen about the branches also. The older branches become dark, with the newer ones on top, still white. According to Belzer (1984), the white fir is the most widely distributed fir in the United States and the only true fir in the Southern California. It grows on moist slopes between 4500 and 8200 feet. They have bluish-green needles. The cones are described as pitchy, having a sticky substance used to produce laquer. The needles are flattened and the cones are upwardly erect on their stems. We think we see other kinds of firs.

2:00 PM: At the bottom of Cooper Canyon. 5730, Mi 395.7

We continue down to the bottom of Rattlesnake Canyon where it takes us to the eastbound stream coming down from Cooper Canyon. At that point the two streams merge and head northwards, down towards the Mojave Desert.

Here at the confluence of the two streams our trail takes us right to the bottom of the canyon where it is absolutely beautiful, the epitome of what you hope for when approaching a small mountain stream. There are several small pools in the immediate area, deep enough to wade through, filled with fish, many over six inches long. The growth extends over the stream producing a cool, shady oasis,

Anonymous

A waterfall up Cooper Canyon

in marked contrast to much of the above southwest exposures. In the area are western azaleas, manzanita, broad leaf lotus, various vines and low growing plants. Joel and I rest here, take off our socks and rinse them in the stream. For sure, this is one of the more beautiful stream side spots I have seen north of the border.

Soon after departing this wonderful spot the trail climbs to a close overlook of a series of waterfalls and cascades After too brief a look, we continue the 500 feet ascent to eventually reach Cooper Canyon Trail Camp.

4:00 PM: Cooper Canyon Trail Campground, 6240, Mi. 397.2 - 0.0

We reach the pleasant and well arranged trail camp way before dusk. Again, we are the only ones around. We wander around the camp site looking for a flat area to lay out our bags. In so doing we find one of the fire pits still warm.

We take advantage of the lowering sun and put our socks out to dry. The stream to the east is running well enough for use, there is an outhouse, several fire pits, picnic benches and ample shade. I take out my sleeping bag, lay it our on one of the many tables to air it out. The wind kicks up sporadically again and blows it off several times until finally the wind settles down. We leisurely prepare supper before turning in early. We both use *Sleep Screens,* a small tent-like net construction that fits over the head and the upper third of the sleeping bag.

June 15, Tuesday, 6:00 AM: An early start, 6240, Mi. 397.2 - 0.0

We leave with the advantage of an early start. We find the trail climbing up to an old jeep road that deteriorates to become a trail, then adjoins another old road, then becomes a trail again. The sector is generally dry with a mixture of conifers and chaparral. Flowering is taking place on many of the lower plants. The lupines get our attention, the plant with the characteristic clump of eight spatulate soft leaves with an occasional flowering of a bluish-lavender stem of flowers. They are found only in moist areas and seem to cohabit with other kinds of plants that thrive in moist areas. In the meantime, the tread takes us another 700 feet higher before reaching Cloudburst Summit, at 7,018, where we cross Highway 2 again.

Once over the summit there is another noticeable change in terrain, view and flora. The dominating view is to the southwest, of the Chilao Flats area. Here the trail generally follows the road, but a good distance below it, then across as the highway curves downhill around a number of bends. The trail meanders around large boulders, providing a number of resting spots, one of them we choose to settle down upon and have breakfast of *Tang,* cereal consisting of granola, powdered milk, and water.

After breakfast, we find we continually have to stop to take pebbles out of our shoes. Perhaps next time around, I'll wear my gaiters. The trail then traverses a forest service dirt road traversing a northeastern slope, as such, providing occasional and adequate shade.

We pass several tiny streamlets with metal structures covering faucets where the water can be tapped. One of these we find leaking. We open up the top, adjust the faucet and in so doing find we are drawn to taking a shower in the sprits. We secure the faucet, close the metal lid and continue on the way, content with the unexpected shower and gratified that we provided a good deed for the day.

Soon we enter the grounds of deserted Camp Glenwood, consisting of a rectangular wooden structure, now empty, with a number of picnic tables, an outhouse and a water faucet. We fill up only one bottle with water as there is a sign that says "Unsafe for Drinking." We continue on to an overlook of Camp Valcrest. Joel and I recall our stay there perhaps fifteen years ago during a winter weekend for snow play with Troop 137.

We soon get to Three Points. We are the only ones around. We hesitate for a moment reflecting on the significance to us of the three trails, the Mt. Waterman Trail, the Silver Moccasin Trail, and the PCT.

3:00 PM: Sulphur Springs Campground, El 5240, Mi 406.8

We continue on to where our car awaits us. The terrain and flora changes again as we head north to Sulphur Springs. The are a is more sandy with a number of small ravines covered by chaparral. The tread meanders among small dried stream beds, gently up and down, mostly down, to eventually get to a small inviting stream that we follow to the campground. We relax for a while before getting into the car.

We drive out of the area to Islip Saddle to where Joel will pick up his Toyota. We agree to meet at Newcomb's Ranch for a snack. We arrive there finding it closed. The place is open Friday through Sunday for weekenders. The place provides a good shelter with its overhanging porches and has some vending machines outdoors.   Though disappointed we agree to meet further down the road at Chilao Flats. We do so, stop and snack a little. We soon say goodbye as we each travel down the Angeles Crest Highway on our way down the mountain where we soon engage the freeway. Joel speeds along to his apartment in Vista and I to Benedict Canyon.

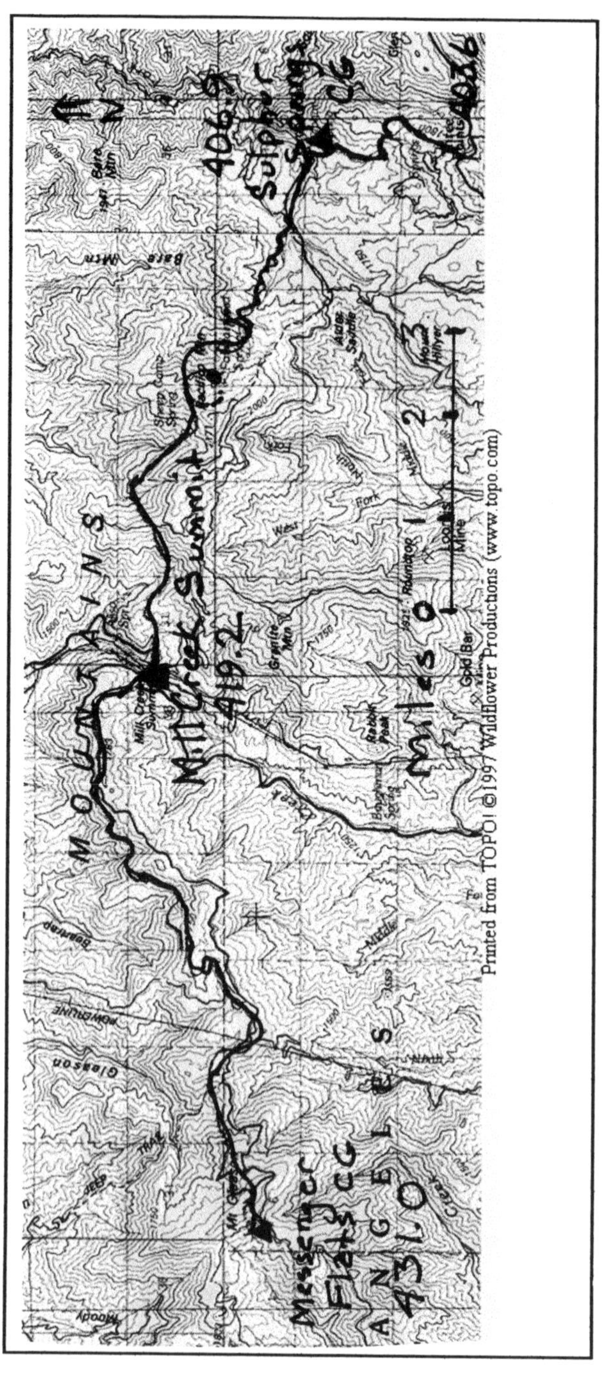

Sulphur Spr. C.G. to Messenger Flats

Chapter 20

Sulphur Springs to Mt. Pacifico

At home: preparing....Sulphur Springs Campground....
Licked by the storm....Back home....Stepping out of a car
onto a Mountain Peak....A night on top....The next morning:
finding a needle in a hay stack

July 11, Sunday, 9:00 AM: Home

Jon arrives as planned to drive me to Sulphur Springs. I feel I am as prepared as I can be for the next jaunt northward. I am prepared to hike straight through from where I left off at Sulphur Springs as far north as I can get til August 1 to get home before Hannah retires from state service.

The Weather Channel and the L.A. Times point to a likelihood of widely scattered showers and/or thundershowers along the route throughout Sunday, Monday and possibly Tuesday. The area is expected to be free of precipitation by midweek. I look outside. I see some thunder heads in the direction of the San Gabriel Mountains.

Joel, staying for the weekend and a ten year high school reunion, accompanies Jon and I for the trip to Sulphur Springs. Despite the weather, we decide to go. Jon takes our joint dog, Max along. Max sits in front while he and Joel sit in the rear. Max seems to enjoy the choice seat as he leans out to his right and sticks his snout out through the top of the window. As we approach La Canada at the base of the mountains, we see thunder heads in the direction we are headed. The thunder heads do not go away. In fact as we get closer to the mountains, we are impressed how they gather to such heights.

Jon says, "It'll be a great experience to drive up through a thunderstorm." Then suddenly he spurts out, "Did you see the lightning? Max doesn't seem to mind the thunder and lightning."

As we head up the Angeles Crest Highway, I say, "Who wants to go up to Sulphur Flats through the Angeles Forest Highway. It's eight miles by road from there and we'll pass Mt Pacifico."

Joel says, "Let's go the same way we came when we drove down."

We head directly to the area where Joel and I terminated our hike three weeks ago. Once we're on the mountain road, the temperature drops somewhat and it starts to rain. At about the 3200 foot level, near Switzers' Camp, we see an accumulation of hail on the side of the road. The temperature dramatically drops to about 59 degrees, down from 93 degrees in the San Fernando Valley. Campers, hikers and bikers are seen rushing to their vehicles to escape the rain and hail.

3:30 PM: Sulphur Springs Campground, El 5240, Mi 406.8

Arriving at Sulphur Springs Campground, we find the area wet. But unlike three weeks ago, there is no water in the stream. We are greeted by a Forest Ranger.

Between the thunder claps she tells us, "The campground is closed. You must not park here." She informs us "The weather should be like this for three weeks." Pointing to the trail, "It's real nasty up there." She makes a point of saying that we should leave the stream and wash area as soon as possible.

Jon, anxious for a hike confides to us, "I can't see why we can't park near by."

Joel says, "There is no place to park nearby ."

I say, "It probably is not smart to park the car anywhere near where the stream may rise."

We drive out a quarter of a mile or so looking for the PCT crossing back up the road. The rain stops.

Joel and Jon see the marker. It is about fifty feet above the wash and dried stream. We park off the road. There are dark large clouds to our immediate south, east and northeast, but no clouds directly overhead and to the west where the trail will take us. We discuss the precursors of these thunder showers. First the warm wind comes. Then as the wind is thrust upward, the temperature drops as the lightning and thunder appear.

There's a loud clap of thunder. We count off the seconds between the lightning and the onset of the thunder, five seconds, 1.6 miles. We clearly see the squall just off to our southeast over the first ridge. It first sprinkles with large drops. The wetness feels good. The temperature is still near 75 degrees. We conclude, if the storm continues, the temperature will probably drop markedly with the shower and with a 15 knot wind, we'll soon forget it's summer. Soon, we'll be looking for the sun to dry us off.

4:30 PM: Licked by the storm, El 5830, Mi 409.8

The storm center gets closer. The lateral visibility to the southeast drops to less than three miles. The thunder clap occurs soon after the lightning. The storm center seems quite close, yet it's still very warm. We';re all sweating as we ascend to the first gap exposing the summit of Mt. Pacifico. I ask myself, Do I need this? Here, I know the weather is poor and I have the opportunity to drive back with the boys. If they return home without me, I'll be on my own. My feeling is that I'll regret that I did so. So, I tell them. "I think I'm going to go back down with you guys."

Jon says, No, wait a minute. All this way, and now you want to back?"

I say, "What difference will it really make for you? You're going to go back anyway."

Joel responds, "Jon, see! We could have just dropped dad off and gone home without walking."

Jon says, Yesterday Larry flaked on me, now it's dad. I think it was what the ranger said."

"Yeah," says Joel.

I say in hope of changing my mind, "Wait, while I go up the trail a bit and see what's ahead around the bend." I go up the trail for a few yards, step out from under the shade of the hill and trees, look around, see the buildup of clouds and the gap ahead exposing the 1,000 feet or so ascent ahead to Mt Pacifico. I hear the thunder and see the huge build up of clouds. I return with no change in my resolve to turn back.

Joel comes up with "OK, let's go back down. But we'll drive out to get some sushi"

"OK, I'm not eat'n it, but I'm buy'n it."

The mood changes. The boys are anxious to get down off the mountain as they are also heated up. I'm the first to move. I put on my pack and reluctantly head down the trail to the car. We get down to the car in fifteen minutes or so with but a sprinkle produced by the storm cell that merely outflanked us. The cell passes uneventfully. No one gets wet. Soon, without a word, we climb into the car and head down the hill. But as soon as we start to drive downhill another large thunder head develops out of nowhere and it soon begins to rain. It pours! The temperature drops about fifteen degrees with the approach of the cell. The rain falls in heavy drops for a few minutes, then stops just as suddenly.   This pattern continues as we drive down the mountain.

When we get near home, the weather seems picture perfect; the streets are dry. It is warm. The sky above us is clear with no wind.

As we approach home, Jon, perhaps in an attempt to stir up the pot and to get Joel's attention, asks," Dad, what are you going to tell mom?"

I stay quiet.

Joel says, "You can tell her there was a great flood."

Jon says, "You can say it snowed."

"It did hail," I quickly replied.

Jon says, "What's a little shower!"

"I'll just answer her questions, if she has any."

5:30 PM: Back Home

We arrive home. I'm not surprised to see Hannah. But she is surprised to see me. In fact, she's startled.

"I thought you had gone! Well, what happened?"

No one helps out. I can't handle the silence. "We were confronted with a series of thunder cells while we were going up to Mt Pacifico. Jon broke in, "Max wasn't concerned, but ah...the Ranger we met said it would be nasty like this for three weeks."

Joel says, "Besides, we're going out together and dad's going to get us some sushi."

The mood becomes festive. Hannah and I get dressed. Soon we're all on our way to Beverly Center to find the sushi place that Jon recommends. We easily find Today Restaurant. Not only do they have sushi, but the large restaurant has a buffet that offers about a hundred items other than sushi. We had so much fun eating that little was made of the short hike.

July 21, Wednesday

It had been raining off and on all week. Now it has finally stopped. I act on Van's offer to spend the evening atop Mt. Pacifico.

We take the same route as Jon, Joel and I took last week past. Beyond Three Points just before Sulphur Springs Campground we leave the paved section and turn left to continue on the unsigned dirt road 3N17 leading westerly. Unlike the inclement weather Jon, Joel and I experienced last week, the sky is now clear and the view of the central San Gabriel Mountains are superb. We reach the junction with the spur road that leads up a mile to the summit. About half way up I see a marker identifying the Pacific Crest Trail in a shady glen of pines and firs. I step out of the car and confirm the existence of the trail head.

7:00 PM: Stepping out of the car onto a Mountain Peak, El 7000, Mi 413.6 + 0.5 - 0.0

We continue carefully to the very top of the mountain where an empty campground awaits us. It appears just as it did twenty nine years ago when I came up here seeking solitude to study and prepare for my comprehensive doctoral examinations at U.S.C. At the summit are a few campsites with a picnic table, fire pit, amidst Jeffrey pines, firs,

some oaks and a little chaparral and a lot of large boulders. There is still
no water here, but there is an outhouse with pitted toilets. Some of the

Jeffrey Pines and boulders on the summit of Mt. Pacifico

boulders are configured to provide shelter in the event of rain or snow.
Although the peak is just over 7,000 feet, the feeling is that of being
much higher because the view is so dramatic. One can see in all
directions, over the top of everything near by and over the wide desert
expanse to the north. Thus the peak is comparable to peaks thousands
of feet higher. This one, however, can be approached by stepping out
of your car.

Van pulls out his pocket radio transceiver and calls out. An
acquaintance, another ham operator from the L.A. area, with the help
of a repeater station, permits him to carry on a conversation as he
purveys the view. Indeed it is a view to remember.

The sun has long dropped below the ridges to the west. It is getting
dark. The sun setting beyond the ridges to the west is breathtaking.

Both of us rush to our respective sites to set up some new equipment.
Not soon enough, we construct our sites by flashlight. Van sets up his
new stand-up 3-man tent and tries out his new sleeping bag and
mattress. He efficiently pulls out the tarp and lays it out on a flat area
near a picnic table that I had once used for study. The wind starts to act
up a little. He's struggling with the construction. "I just set it up at
home, so it should go easy."

The tarp corners are rising with the wind. He's trying to get the stakes into the ground. "Where's some rocks?" Now it's dark. I get some rocks and set them on the corner of the tarp.

Van cries out, "I'm going to get it!" He goes to the car and pulls out his lantern. As he puts one set of poles into the center piece, the other corner fall downs. I don't wait for him to ask for help. He asks, "Should you leave in the morning, leave a note."

"Ok, I'll do that if you are still sleeping."

We install the tent. He stands up, stretches and heads for the car.

"Where are you going?"

"To the car to get something." Van disappears in the darkness. He soon emerges with a seven inch thick air mattress and stows it inside the tent. He lays out his sleeping bag on top. He secures the tent loosely to the ground and poles and he is off to bed.

I set up my new bivvy bag on the same tarp extending out from his tent. My bivvy is a variant of the one I had bought two months ago, but has a larger net and two tension poles that fit into established sewed tunnels and uniquely holds up the entry way erect enough so as to provide space between the upper torso, head and the top of the bivvy sack. The front overhang is adaptable for inclement weather and on warm evenings, provides an outdoor, but bug free environment.

Having stopped in La Crescenta for supper, we take in the evening view then quickly sack out. I await a pleasant evening of rest as I slip into the bag and begin contemplating the day that awaits me tomorrow. But this state of relaxation lasts only a moment before the wind kicks up again. It blows the sides of Van's tent causing the unsecured loose sides to vibrate, flap and hit the poles, sounding like a bass drum leading a parade. This orchestration goes on for several hours waking me up periodically before the wind finally quiet downs. I occasionally awaken to pleasantly gaze at the star studded night sky.

July 22, Thursday AM: Finding a needle in a hay stack

Up before dawn, I catch the sunrise as I organize my pack for the remainder of the trek along the ridge of the San Gabriel Mountains.

How far I will go today, tomorrow and the rest of the week will be decided as I continue northbound. The sky is clear. No more wind. It is quiet. Oh, What a wonderful way to start a trek.

Van stirs. Every move is heard. Van gets up and stretches, yawns, gazes at the morning sun. Then, for sure he breaks the morning silence with a huge sixty decibel sneeze.

He calls out, "Hal, don't move!"

"What's up?"

"I don't know where it is!"

"Where what is?"

Van points to his mouth, "My tooth."

"What's that?"

"It's gone." He quickly reaches down, picks up a stick and draws a line in front of him. He outlines an area on the dry flat sandy ground.

The front tooth he glued on a few weeks ago flew out.

"I spat it out when I sneezed. It's got to be in this area somewhere."

We get on our hands and knees. We look for the missing tooth. After about a few minutes of silence, he says, "I'm not going to give up so easy on this. The dentist warned me not to glue it back in. He's long term friend of mine. He warned me all-right!"

I said, "You mean if you don't find it, you'll put yourself on your own shit list?"

"Yeah, something like that. It's about half an inch long with a spike in it."

We're eye balling the ground on our hands and knees. I find all kinds of interesting little things. Some are moving. But no tooth.

"We'll find it if it takes all day." Van says, "It's got to be in this area," as he redraws the perimeter.

I take note that I had lost a filling cap several months ago. Van then had suggested that I stick some glue on it and put it back in. As we were hunting for the tooth, to kill the time, I asked him, "How did you clean the tooth and area by it?"

Van says, "I boiled it."

I say, "Well, how did you prepare the area in the mouth?"
He went on to say that he remembered how the dentist did it. As we're

scanning the soil, I say, "Perhaps, there is a lot more things we can do than we permit ourselves to do."

Van is silent for a while, he scans and searches the area.

"Van, we'll find it."

With an angry tone, as if recriminating himself, Van questions, "Why be charged so much by someone if it can be done yourself? It's easy to do, anyway. I don't want to go in there and ask him to make another tooth. I know what he's going to say!"

Pressing the point, I say "Isn't it interesting that at times it seems there is little that someone else can do that one can, with some training and experience, do oneself, just as well."

He says reflectively, "With confidence we'll come up with the missing tooth."

He affords himself enough distance from the problem to be somewhat self analytical. Not quite ready for a philosophical or psychological analysis and being more interested in finding his tooth and solving his own immediate problem than pondering the nature of man, he offers a practical solution. He says, "I saved a lot of dough by doing it myself."

I pick up something that looks like a tooth. But it turns out to be a small rock.

He says, "To replace this tooth will cost about twelve hundred dollars."

The sun begins to shine directly on the area. "That was some sneeze, I'll extend the search area." I take a stick and draw another line about ten feet further out from where he was standing when he sneezed. I focus in on more distant sectors from where he was standing. I ask, "How much do you think it would have cost if he had done the re-installation?"

Van replies, "Maybe about fifty dollars. Maybe nothing."

I am at the outer perimeter looking. Van is methodically searching the area by the inner line. We're both trying not to disturb the earth while we look.

Suddenly, Van stands up, lifts up his arm clasping a rather large tooth with a tiny spike in it. "This is it!"

I say, "Are you going to put it back in yourself?"

Van says something to the effect, "I don't know. I'll worry about it later."

We both turn to other matters like putting our gear togther and throwing it all into the jeep. As we're about finished stowing the gear, I reach for my sneakers. I easily find them in the mess. To my surprise I find two left shoes. This means I have to either use my sandals or use my back-up pair of boots which I have stashed in my supply box. These are the pair of boots that provided my toes with blisters a couple of months ago. I decide to use the boots and will take preventive action at the very start should the toes start complaining.

Finally, we hop in the jeep and drive down the dirt road a short distance to the trail head. With my pack on my back, I thank Van for his effort and wave goodbye as he slowly drives down the rutted and narrow road.

Chapter 21

Mount Pacifico to Soledad Canyon Near Acton

Leaving Mt. Pacifico....Mill Creek Summit....Messenger Flats ....TheWest Fork Ranger Station....Down the Hill....Soledad Canyon to theRobins Nest Recreation Park

July 22, Friday, 7:00 AM: Leaving Mount Pacifico, El 6645, Mi 413.6

The dust settles after Van pulls out of sight. The trail is immediately pleasant as it winds easily down through the thick forest. Though no

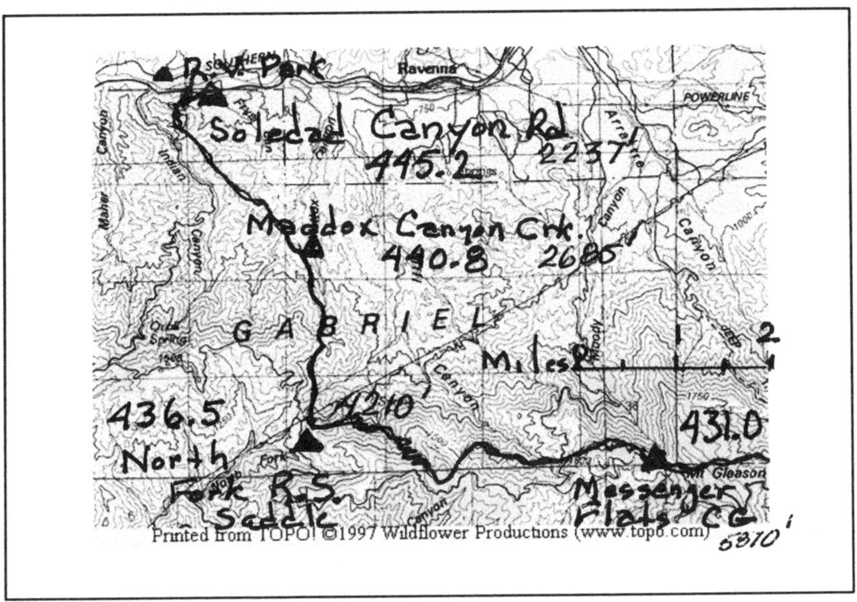

Mt. Pacifico to Soledad Canyon Near Acton

immediate water is apparent, there are mixed conifers with a lush undergrowth to on both sides of the trail. It's seven-thirty, still cool. I am wearing a wicker jacket. For the moment, the weather couldn't be better.

Time passes quickly and the trail "pulls me along" in a gradual descent through the montane forest, westerly along the more eastern ridges of the San Gabriel Mountains.

Soon, I take off my over clothing and pull out the charts. I cannot find the copy of the guidebook, but pull out the topo map and review my progress and visualize the route before me. I see that I will soon reach a dirt road, follow it downhill to the north for about a half mile where the tread continues to follow the contours through a reforestation area, then to the Mill Creek Summit area where water, an outhouse and picnic tables are available. Just then, a tired back packer appears coming up the trail. We converse for a few minutes. His name is Bob. He tells me he is doing a back and forth from Three Points to Soledad Canyon. He says he has been on the trail doing this now for four days. He looks at my exposed water supplies telling me that it seems "About right." He informs me that he has been loaded up with a gallon of water. We conclude there is sufficient water along the way should one load up with three liters. He also tells me, "The ranger at North Fork Ranger Station is very helpful and friendly." He further tells me the trail down the mountain to Soledad Canyon is difficult, especially going back up.

There is not much for me to tell him as he had just made the loop. I do tell him I have been hiking up from Campo and doing as much as the PCT as I can this season. I tell him the summit is a wonderful place to spend the night; water is supposed to be a half mile or so away. We easily get into a conversation.

He volunteers, "I do this kind of thing to clear my mind and get a perspective on things." He explains he really likes the outdoors and would like to do more of the Pacific Crest Trail, especially the southern part of the PCT as he enjoys going through the desert.

The trail begins to head north now following the route depicted by the charts. The tread steepens as it turns, then as expected, picks up a jeep road, then turns eastward following the northeast exposure of the jeep road, then turns eastward following the northeast exposure of the ridge. Here, it is very pretty as it follows the northeast exposure and contours of the ridge. After passing a forest plantation of young trees, it soon meanders down to Mill Creek Summit

12:00 Noon; Mill Creek Summit, El 4911, Mi. 419.2

Here there is a ranger station, a large forest service area and parking and picnic area for tourists including tables, water and restrooms.

Here, at the picnic area, cars stop as they transit the summit on the Angeles Forest Highway between Palmdale-Lancaster to the north and La Canada and Glendale to the south. The summit provides a bit of fresh air and relief after transiting the Mojave, but a few miles to the north.

An elderly couple driving southbound stop for a rest bit. They appear somewhat handicapped. He immediately goes wandering slowly around the perimeter of the area as she sits down nearby. I carry on an interesting conversation with her. She volunteers that her husband has often wished to so some hiking, but never seemed to have done much about it.

After a pleasant lunch, I drink til satiated and fill up. I cross the Angeles Forest Highway and immediately head up the rather steep and exposed trail where it is as hot as it looks. For the first hour or so, there is very little shade until the trail meanders near the spine of the rising ridge overlooking at times the nearby paved road that also traverses the upward climbing ridge.

The air is warm, dry and clear. The views to the south and southwest provide some compensation for the tedious task of climbing up the ridge. Numerous ridges of various lengths and heights can be seen before the final ridges to the west that overlook the Crescenta and San Fernando valleys. For the most part, the area appears relatively barren, but with low chaparral. The area seems incongruently primitive considering it lies close to a large metropolis. The view to the east reveals the pine forested ridges leading to forested Mount Pacifico that dominates the skyline. The view ahead is a hillside of dry chaparral.

Upon approaching the top of the ridge, the trail reaches the road whereupon the trail is difficult to identify. I soon lose the trail. I opt for the road which parallels the PCT not to find the trail until reaching Messenger Flats Campground.

5:00 PM: Messenger Flats, El 5870, Mi 431.0

Here, I share the pleasant, occasionally pine-studded site with a small party of motorcycle riders taking a rest. A single faucet serves the entire campground. It is quite sufficient. As I set up my campsite, they soon leave. Then into the campground comes a car with two young men seeking a rest from their adventure exploring the area's dirt roads. They offer me a can of Dutch beer warning me it's strong. I set it aside for dinner. It turns out it is indeed so strong I cannot get half way through it, even with the help of the meal.

July 23, Friday AM: Departing Messenger Flats, El; 5870, Mi 431.0

Following a relaxing breakfast, I find that, despite the last tough 12 miles of the 18 mile trek, I am easily off on another part of the PCT that is just as pleasant as it was yesterday morning. In fact it is prettier. The trail immediately crosses a gap to follow the northern slopes where the forest is rich. The chaparral remains rich with color as it might occur in early spring. The hillside seems a bit moist. The trail becomes narrow as the shrubbery slaps me gently on both sides. It is very pretty and a contrast to areas on the southern exposed side of the mountain range. I look down slope to the north and find the slopes becoming drier and drier as the desert area is reached. I try not to think about that. But know I will soon have to endure the heat. Too soon, after about five or six miles of very pleasant walking, the trail comes to a flat ridge and an exposed dirt road. But it leads a hundred yards or so to a shaded picnic area adjacent to the West Fork Ranger Station. From here, the trail descend directly to the north into the high desert below.

11:00 AM: At The North Fork Saddle Ranger Station

The ranger station sets beside a little knoll overlooking the desert below. Here is a parking area and pleasant, well groomed shaded picnic area with tables and benches. I immediately head for one of the tables and settle down for a good drink and casual lunch. I look over to the ranger station and conclude that the location here is quite idyllic, with mountain views to the north, east and west and a desert overlook over Soledad Canyon, Escondido Canyon and the Sierra Pelona Mountain range to the north. I then see a young man stepping out of the ranger station. He introduces himself as Todd, a volunteer caretaker of the Ranger Station. He discovers I am doing sections of the PCT and invites me inside. He offers me a coke and a shower inside.

The conversation turns to the trekkers that passed through the area this last season. He shows me the pile of slips of paper where many entered a note or so about their trek.

We recalled many that we met. Many arrived quite drained. Some were exposed to the cold, damp and recent snow storms. Upon learning of the troubles befalling some of the trekkers through the Sierra, he calls up Donna Saufley, a "trail angel" in Agua Dulce. I explain what I heard about the fall and death of John Landers and of the several injuries up north in the area. I explain my Internet source of information to Donna who in turns boots up her computer and gets the word first hand. We share sad moments on the phone.

Donna offers her home in Agua Dulce as a rest bit. She points out that this is a very poor time to attempt the desert crossing and should I wish to continue on the trail, to continue on from Walker Pass or Kennedy Meadows to avoid the blighted and dried out areas to the near north. I explain my situation, that I live nearby in LA and will finish my northbound trek either at Soledad Canyon or Agua Dulce where I expect to be picked up to return home.

I consider staying over night here at West Fork, to continue down in the morning, but decide, despite the heat to continue down the hill.

2:00 PM: Down the hill to Soledad Canyon

After a great shower, a good cold drink and pleasantries with Todd, I open up my umbrella and head down the exposed trail to Soledad Canyon.

For the first mile or so, the trail meanders moderately downhill over shoulders and ravines. Soon, the trail deteriorates and follows a difficult steep descent along a firebreak. No real danger unless while walking you purview the scenery immediately below and over Vasquez Rocks to Agua Dulce over the hills and lose some footing and slip into some cactus or ravine without an end. Even though it is downhill, The work is too hard to appreciate the multitude of plants and flowers.

Soon after four miles of continuous downhill work, the trail reaches the bottom of Mattox Canyon (El. 2685) where a creek is suppose to run this time of year. Alas, There is nothing to ford except dry sand and hot rocks. Though some grass remains near the dry creek and indeed there are some nice cottonwood and sycamore trees that provide some inviting shade. It is still hot, even in the shade at this time of day. There is no moisture anywhere, I opt to sit down in the shade and remove the sand and pebbles from my shoes, drink a good deal of my water and continue on.

Surprisingly, the trail takes a southerly and upturn route gaining a ridge top of somewhat over 3,000 feet in sweltering heat. Then it levels off, strikes a dirt road, before heading down to Soledad Canyon. Not soon enough the trail finally meanders along Indian Canyon Road, but instead of heading directly for Soledad Canyon, the tread parallels the paved road below, before it finally and slowly drops down to the relatively inviting canyon below, a long four miles after crossing dry Mattox Canyon.

6:30 PM: Soledad Canyon; The Robins Nest Recreation Park, El 2237, Mi 445.2

Upon reaching Soledad Canyon, I realize that I have a large assortment of blisters on both feet and I am quite fatigued from clambering down the firebreaks. I head a couple hundred yards west on the road to a recreational vehicle camp site where I am directed to a tenting area to sack out and nurse my aching feet. Walking to the area, I realize the discomfort in my feet. Upon reaching the grassy shaded area, I find a picnic bench and examine my feet. The whole rear of each foot has a blister covering up the whole heel and much of the external edges of the two feet. I look inside the boots and find the cause. Both boots have parts of tacks or nails protruding in the worn out area of the sides and heel areas corresponding to the affected areas of the feet. I call home and arrange a pick up, here at the closest point of the PCT by car from home, about 30 miles.

Hannah comes over the following morning, picks me up. We have a pleasant breakfast together at Denny's in Canyon Country before heading for home.

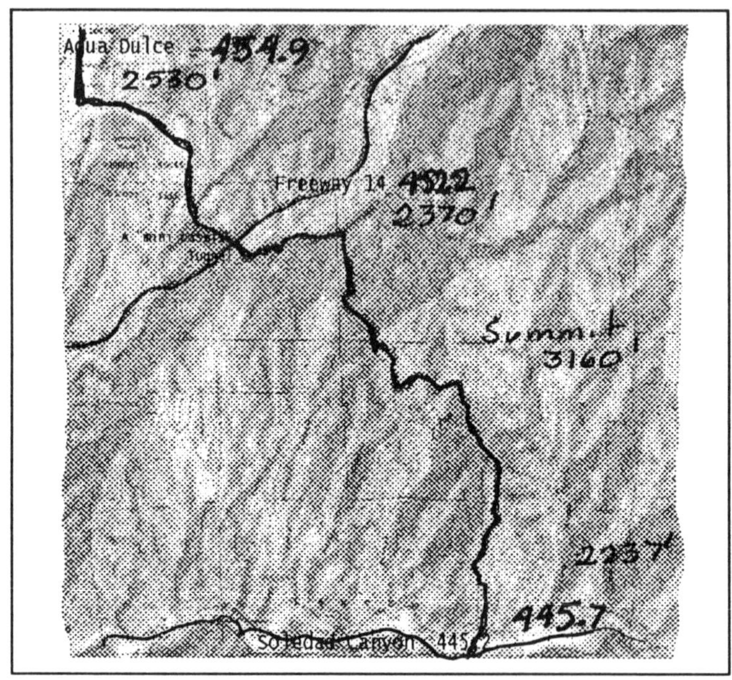

From MAPTECH *Terrain Navigator*

Soledad Canyon Near Acton to Agua Dulce

Chapter 22

Soledad Canyon to Agua Dulce

Soledad Canyon....Vasquez Rocks....Downtown Agua Dulce

Thursday, April 27, 2000, 6:35 AM: Soledad Canyon, Acton Mi. 445.2, El. 2237 - 0.0

Hannah drops me off at the trail head in Soledad Canyon at 6:30 A.M., ten long months after picking me up from this same point, the furthermost point ventured northbound last year along the Pacific Crest Trail. It is here that I ended the trek starting from the Mexican border last year. I try to express my gratitude to Hannah. I do not ask how she can put up with me doing this.

We wave good bye as Hannah adroitly turns the Saab around at the very point where the Pacific Crest Trail leaves the San Gabriel Mountains. I enter the high desert at the base of the San Gabriel Mountains at the lower terminus of Indian and Mattox Canyons. Once again I congratulate myself for completing the San Gabriel Mountains and thankful to attempt another year northbound on the trail.

Soledad Canyon follows the northwestern base of the San Gabriel Mountains where the Santa Clarita River flows faintly from its source at Action, at Soledad Pass, elevation 3,180 feet, generally westward as it picks up some water as it gradually trickles down through Acton to Canyon Country and Saugus. From there the river bed continues down through Santa Clarita, Fillmore, and Santa Paula to eventually spill out what remains, or water it nay accumulate, on its way to the Pacific Ocean near the city of Ventura.

Soledad Canyon Road can be considered the old road to Palmdale-Lancaster, not only before Interstate 14 was developed, but even before its predecessor became a thoroughfare. There are numerous rustic recreational sites and scattered ranches along the Santa Clarita Riverbed as it's persistent waters trickle through this distant and southern part of growing Acton.

The PCT passes Soledad Canyon from atop the San Gabriel Mountains at North Fork Saddle, from an altitude of almost 5,000 feet, plunging down on a terrible trail through Mattox Canyon to meet the Santa Clarita River just east of Robins Nest Recreational area where the PCT then traverses the minor mountain range lying between Acton and Agua Dulce.

I Figure I could, if necessary, stock up on supplies in Agua Dulce. Starting so close to home, I nevertheless find myself loaded up with three and a half liters of water and five days of food. The pack checked out at thirty pounds. The food and water accounts for about a third of the combined weight, or, about twelve pounds beyond "empty weight." The pack weighs only about 18 pounds with only gear and clothing, a feat in itself for me to get a pack to be this light.

I step out now looking for the tread to the Santa Clarita River. I reflect a little on what I am doing and again wonder why I am doing this. I recall how I felt when I arrived here last year - tired, sore and with feet full of blisters from the descent because of having left my trusted running shoes at home causing me to wear boots that had damaged insoles.

I've tried to apply what I had learned last year. It's the details that count. I've given up trying to keep the feet and toes dry with foot powder. I now have my toes completely moistened with *Tinactin* gel to provide moisture in hope to offset the development of blisters to the toes as well as to discourage development of athlete's foot. Another detail is that I am carrying a pair of old and tried out light running shoes as backup for a newer pair. I have a lightweight Kelty Cloud backpack and a lightweight dry loft sleeping bag. I am carrying a lightweight Bic stove and bivvy bag. My sundries and first aid bags are varied and I am carrying a cellular phone. The total is lighter than when I started out last year, even the phone. I won't receive calls, but will try to reach Hannah should an occasion arise.

So, thoroughly rested, prepared as best as I know how, I am now off to try to make it to Tehachapi, about 130 miles northbound on the

Pacific Crest Trail. But, first, I gear up to make it over the first seven mile stretch of hills to Interstate 14. The modest goal for the balance of the day is to reach Agua Dulce, another three miles or so beyond Vasquez Rocks. From there, should I change my mind about matters, I can perhaps get a ride by car, bus or even an airplane ride out by one of our pilots who can drop by with one of our airplanes.

The terrain is no surprise as I recall seeing the area from the air and from over looking the terrain while trekking the heights of the San Gabriel Mountains. Outside of the weather, little changes out here. The flora doesn't look much different than fifty years ago when I used to drive my Dad's two-ton truck delivering wholesale groceries out to the outlying desert areas. The area does not appear much different from that seen along the trail at similar elevations in more southern parts of the state. The shallow and narrow flow of the Santa Clara River carries sufficient water to host varieties of shrubs and trees typically associated with Southern California low mountain streams. The stream is easy to traverse without more than dampening the bottoms of the jogging shoes. The area around the river at this point, more dry than most other running streams, reflects the desert-like low mountain conditions ahead. Nevertheless at this time in the morning, the air feels damp in the immediate area of the shallow river. Though the river is running slow but surely, there are no sign of any two or four legged creatures anywhere around.

Prompted by the *Guidebook*, I head for the railroad tracks. Cued by a commuter trains that rushes by carrying a few cars of passengers from the Palmdale-Lancaster area to Los Angeles, I wave. No one waves back.

Crossing the tracks, the trail quickly climbs away from the classic California stream side flora up into the exposed southern side of the hills into the already familiar grey-green chaparral so typical of Southern California. The initial climb proves more interesting than expected as it provides views to the south where the dramatic cooler San Gabriel Mountain range dominates the view. Views to the east and west are dominated by sparsely covered knolls and minor peaks. All are less than 3,400 feet but high enough to block out the distant terrain.

I overlook a deserted RV recreation area below. There continues to be no activity of animal life except for an occasional lizard and familiar crawling bugs and certainly no sign of people anywhere except for an occasional lifeless mountain-desert ranches dotting the hills above aptly named, Soledad Canyon.

Before reaching the summit, the appearance of the characteristic rock formation of Vasquez Rocks soon appear. This morning they appear pinkish in its igneous and metamorphic rounded knolls and peaks that protrude several hundred feet above the chaparral. I find the weird rock formations, the sparse vegetation, lack of water and the resultant lack of animal life providing a feeling of loneliness and desolation.

The ups and downs of traversing the ridges, none above 3200 feet are soon completed. The trail reaches the final gap revealing Highway 14, Vasquez Rocks, the Sierra Pelona Valley and the next mountain range, the Sierra Pelona Mountains beyond. I think Pelona means hairy, from the Spanish word, *pelo,* hair. From this vantage point they do look hairy, rather than forested or bare.

Once at the summit, Mi. 449.6, about 3,160 feet, I realize my neckerchief is already solidly drenched. I am cooled now only by the wet scarf, wet t-shirt and slipstream of the air. The cooling effect increases as I now finish off the gradual descent at a faster pace. I look before me to the welcoming sight of Escondido Canyon, Mi. 452.1, El. 2,400 feet. Though just a few miles on the trail, I realize that I am already preoccupied with the thought of water as I feel so relieved to discover a bit of running water below.

The trail parallels the canyon, gradually dropping into the depths of the moist canyon, typical of many of the waterways of Southern California with its abrupt change of flora with thickets of willows, cottonwoods and other somewhat broadleaf trees and shrubs. Upon approaching the extensive waterway, it first seems that the whole waterway is blocked by the massive development of busy Interstate 14 directly in its course. As I approach the grade of the highway I am surprised to find the stream is channeled immediately under the highway through a long cavernous ten foot wide tunnel, long enough to provide darkness in the middle, thus providing a good measure of relief from the sun and heat. The water running through late this morning is only about six inches deep and can be traversed easily today by traversing along the widely curved side of the channel. The realization of being cool in the middle of this man-made tunnel, in contrast now to the heat, is awesome. I linger a bit and cool down considerably. The sight and sounds of the trickling water is tranquilizing.

10:00 AM: Vasquez Rocks, El 2335, Mi 452.8 - 0.0

Emerging from the tunnel, to the north side, El 2335, Mi 452, is like entering another climate! The environment becomes suddenly moist, cool and damp. Here, the narrow stream collects and widens in an idyllic site sufficient even for some bathing. There is ample shrubs and trees. Willows and sycamores are among the greenery outlining the stream with immediate canyon walls lurking above. A short rest is called by the inviting rocks alongside this cool collection of water that is slowly bubbling out to form a stream. The shoes seem to come off by themselves. I dip my super heated feet into the wet coolness of the water and bask in the cool air in this mini oasis.

Soon it is time to move on. Here the trail is not well marked and I get nervous about the possibility of getting lost. In spite of my concern, I immediately make a wrong turn. I climb out too enthusiastically to the northeast following horse and foot prints thinking I am following directions in the Guidebook. I note the trail is surrounding the park and leading to a number of widely scattered homes and ranches. Soon, I turn back, wisely avoiding seductive short cuts and follow the unmarked PCT in its more logical course up and along the cool stream bed. Now in the depths of the Vasquez Rocks, the trail leads through very impressive rock formations. These smooth rocks are characterized by grotesque limestone-like deposits with caves and caverns of various sizes imprinted. They seem to overlook this rather pleasant portion of the route going through Escondido Canyon. Down in the canyon it is cool with lots of water bubbling around.

There is a lot of green growth that provides contrast with the stark formations above. The unique formations are a fantastic array of pink covered multilayered overhangs generally of various shades of pink.

I've been through here a number of times with our Scout Troop 137. I can almost hear Mario Baur, Scoutmaster, telling the boys spooky stories of Tirburco Vasquez 150 years ago as he hid from his enemies here. I could improve these ghost stories a bit by bringing in elements of dehydration, poor judgment, heat exhaustion and thirst.

By Lance Davis

In Vasquez Rocks County Park

Soon, after ascending from the depths of the wet canyon, I approach the dry park center where lies a picnic area and nature trail, El 2300, Mi 453. The trail rounds the parking area, avoids the people nearby and the water fountains, and leads through very hot exposed areas adjacent to some attractive private property. The trail soon reaches Escondido Canyon Road, which I follow for about a half mile to exposed Agua Dulce Canyon Road 454.4, El. 2470. A northward turn is made that leads up the hill directly to the center of Agua Dulce.

1:30 PM: Downtown Agua Dulce, El 2530, Mi 454.9

Here, a small shopping mall offers a grocery store with cold drinks and sandwiches and post office combination and several inviting small businesses. These facilities are very inviting after a walk of two miles on the exposed highway. I immediately head for the mall which houses the combination post office and general store.

Section E

Agua Dulce to Tehachapi Pass

Prologue

There are several climates to walk through. The first quarter consists of walking over 3,500 foot ridges, high enough for breezes and views, but not high enough to provide the coolness, shade and hospitality seen in most national forests in California. The second quarter is reached after attaining the heights beyond Lake Elizabeth Road. The growth is transitional in nature with the trail meandering at times through forested areas. The trail then drops down to pass through sparse chaparral of the Mojave Desert. The final section is culminated by a climb out of the hot desert chaparral through a brief forested gap before slowly dropping down through more chaparral, to reach scattered oaks and grasses that provide shade near the cool waters of Oak Creek.

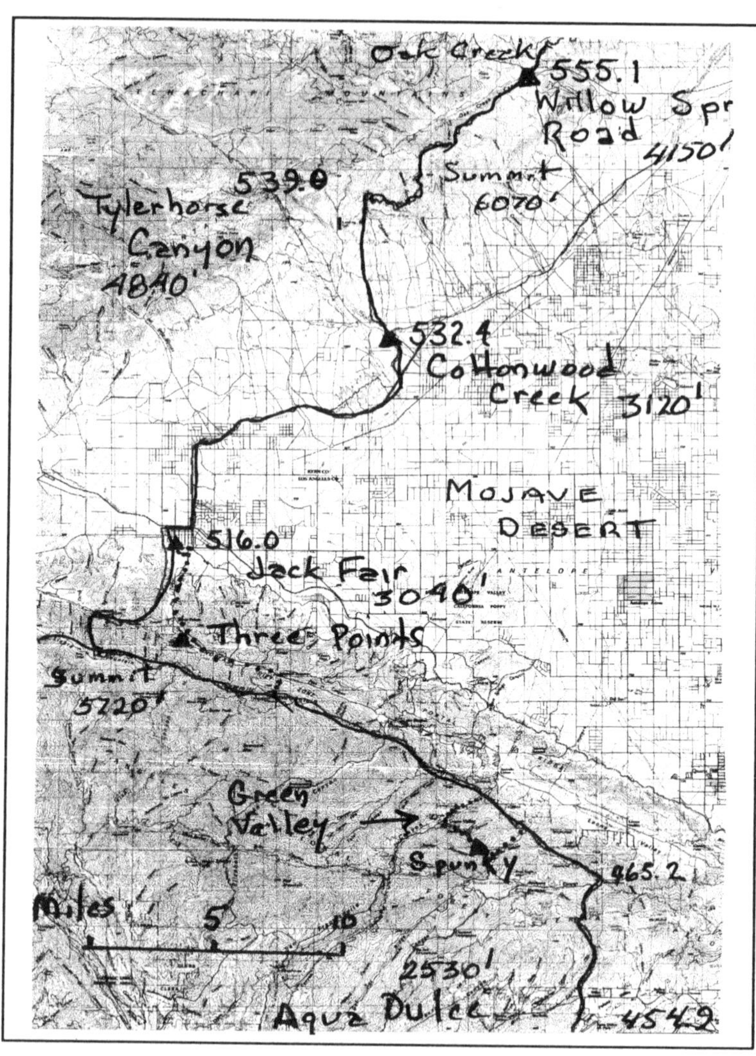

USGS

Section E: Agua Dulce to Oak Creek at Tehachapi Pass
96.2 Miles

Chapter 23

Agua Dulce

Downtown....At the Saufley's home....Their dog declares war on me ....Lucky wants us to stay longer.

1:30 PM: Downtown Agua Dulce, El. 2350, Mi 454.9 - 0.0

I register at the post office, inside the general store. I discover entries immediately before mine are that of Scott Williamson and Doug who stepped into the store yesterday on their way from the Mexican border to Canada. Their plan, once they step into Manning Park in British Columbia, is to head back to the southern terminus at the Mexican border. Though Scott has completed the PCT a number of times, Scott is known for attempting this "yo-yo" a number of times. All their walking is to be completed this year. I also find a note by Donna Saufley, who resides in Agua Dulce, inviting PCTers to call her. I do not hesitate. She tells me that Scott and Doug are there right now.

After scarfing down a turkey sandwich and a very large diet Pepsi, Donna appears. Donna is one of the more popular trail angels to be found along the entire Pacific Crest Trail. We immediately recognize one another. I hop into her car. She whisks me away to her home. In five minutes we are there. The conversation covers our E-mail communiques over the last year and of the people we've met.

2:30 P.M. At the Saufley's Home

We arrive at her property. We enter her mobile home set aside for guests to the rear of their house. As we step in I see Scott standing, holding up a huge half watermelon cut lengthwise with a spoon in one hand. He is totally emerged in the process of polishing off what little is left, slowly and systematically enjoying each spoonful as if it were the first and the last delicious portion.

"You've done pretty good!"

"Hi Hal."

Scott and I recognize one another immediately. We recall meeting last year at Tule Springs, between Warner Springs and the Palms to Pines Highway 74. We recall how it was that we washed our socks in the unexpected water hole above Tule Springs, thus saving ourselves a bit of time and grief. I recalled how he offered to take my "trash" along with him after we polished off my remaining package of dried fruit.

He introduces me to Doug, his trail companion who he met last year on the trail. Scott explains he ended the hike last year in Big Bear after learning that there just was too much snow and ice up north to make it from Mexico to Canada and back to the Mexican border in the calendar year. To make it up to Canada in one year was a feat he had already done. In 1998, After reaching the Canadian border, he was able to make it back to Reds Meadows, south of Yosemite before the snows impeded his progress in the fall. Last year marked the second or third time he had attempted the "yo-yo." This year he is hoping to do it with Doug who appears ready to do it. Scott eventually finishes up the huge half leaving but a thin bowl of green skin which he now can easily hold with one hand.

Scott keeps a vegetarian diet, whereas his partner, Doug scarfs down anything that may appeal to him at the moment. Doug seems somewhat weather beaten and fatigued as you might expect after a month of walking through desert and mountains, whereas Scott appears energetic and enthusiastic as if he just got started on his adventure. I guess this is what watermelon does! I hope one day to try it out.

Their packs are similar to one another. They are small, light, quite compact, and well trimmed to their stature, obviously packed with a great deal of foresight and without waist nor chest belt. The scale indicates Scot's pack weighs about 24 pounds with food but without water, a pound less than mine. However, mine is probably twice the volume, not so trim on the back. They are somewhat tall, thin and muscular in physique, like 220 runners, probably weighing in about 165 pounds. The contents are carefully prepared for their style. Their daily food packages are pre-wrapped and measured.

I know that Scott travels fast and light. Doing so they are not required to carry as much water, food, nor other supplies as otherwise might be the case. They can reach their intermediate objectives in surprisingly quick time. Whereas I now expect to travel an average of about 14 to18 miles a day, they can put on almost twice that amount if they so choose.

The difference in their rate and mine becomes pronounced when the tread ascends. Compared to most trekkers along the trail, I am carrying a light load, even considering my weight. I am impressed with their preparation and style, their overall physical condition, mental state and congenial and inquisitive nature.

Each leg I learn a little more about long distance trekking. Putting on long milage leads to the development of a mind set to cut down the weight of the pack, shoes and clothing. The selection of pack contents and impact of the overall weight is moderated by the physical conditioning that takes place. Confidence comes with learning how one's body reacts to the unique demands of long distance hiking in differing environments. The faster the rate, the easier the leg. The easier the leg, the more enjoyment and self confidence; an attitude that alludes the novice. Even though I have climbed up a number of mountains and put on hundreds of miles, I feel a novice when I am around such long distance hikers.

3:00 PM: Lucky Declares War.

Jeff and Donna Saufley have taken in several small dogs. They each have their "personalities" which flourish in the loving environment provided at their home. They adopted one they felt so sorry for. His name is Lucky. Sometimes, I am told, Lucky becomes mischievous. As soon as I sit down, the small dog saunters over to me wagging briskly wagging his tail. We instantly become friends. But I make the mistake of taking off my shoes. Upon sensing my friendly nature, little Lucky makes a swift move! In a swoop, he takes off with one of my shoes, runs about the inside the mobile home, sits down and methodically removes the insert, displays it and plays with it. He momentarily drops it and looks at me in the eye. Before I can grab it, he runs off with the shoe and out the door. He relishes the chase. It takes all our skill and coaxing to get the dog finally quieted down. I immediately shower.

The evening passes with little silence. All of us, the two Alaskans, the dynamic duo and I spend the night snacking away on delivered pizza and listening to one another's adventures and growing philosophies of life. The Alaskans, father and son, decide to go to LAX tomorrow morning to return home early, after putting on 454 miles of the PCT this year, but not before sharing this enjoyable evening together. It's so much fun!

Friday, April 28, 2000, 7:00 AM: Lucky tries to keep us from leaving.

Donna, Scott, Doug and I prepare to climb in her car for a ride back to town. But first we line up for a picture. I take off my mittens. Suddenly, up comes Lucky as if to appear in the picture, but instead grabs a mitten from my hand and darts off. This time he runs around the perimeter of their very spacious and graded backyard. We're anxious to go. But the chase is on! During this episode, we all finally gang up on the hapless dog and corner him. We all surround him. Donna, Jeff, the Alaskans, Doug, Scot and I converge on him. The circle narrows.   As we form a circle not ten feet wide, he alludes us all. He scampers. Under pressure he decides to hide under Jeff's low riding truck, staying in the middle just waiting for someone to try to get him. We surround the truck. He escapes again. Our efforts result in Lucky putting on a good amount of milage scampering about their acreage.

Someone calls out, "You're a psychologist."

I think of distraction, positive reward, and getting a gun! I yell out, "Just watch."

As everyone watches in disbelief, I get on my hands and knees and take a few steps to the low water faucet. I turn on the outside water faucet, sit before a water dish and noisily exaggerate the pleasure of drinking and swooshing water. It seems to work! Lucky slowly comes by, and sits beside me and heads for the water. But he's not thirsty. He won't drop the mitten. I try to grab it, but he's off again. He just continues to run through and between us. Now, we're all beginning to lose our patience.

"I don't need the mitten," I claim out of desperation.

"Jeff says, We'll get it."

We're ready to hit the trail and it's getting warm already. We each come close to catching him again. Finally, Jeff reaches under his truck, comes up with the mitten, and to our delight, holds it up in the air for all to see. Jeff then triumphantly hands it to me. Lucky watches us leave, seemingly in want to come with us or come up with something to cause us to stay longer.

We climb into the car and soon Donna drops us off at the mall at the exact spot where we were picked up. I put on my pack. Doug says they're going to get some water. I tell Doug and Scott that I'll be splitting now, but expect them to be passing me pretty soon on the grade uphill. Donna drives by and offers a wave. Soon, in about fifteen minutes, looking over my shoulder I see Scott and Doug closing in on me as the road increases its rate of ascent to the foothills of the Sierra Pelona Range. As we cross the entrance to Agua Dulce Airpark, we walk together momentarily, exchanging pleasantries.   I purposefully slow up. Out of habit, they pick up their speed and gradually put space between us. Upon reaching the ascending tread going up the Sierra Pelona, they can be seen a quarter of a mile in front of me.

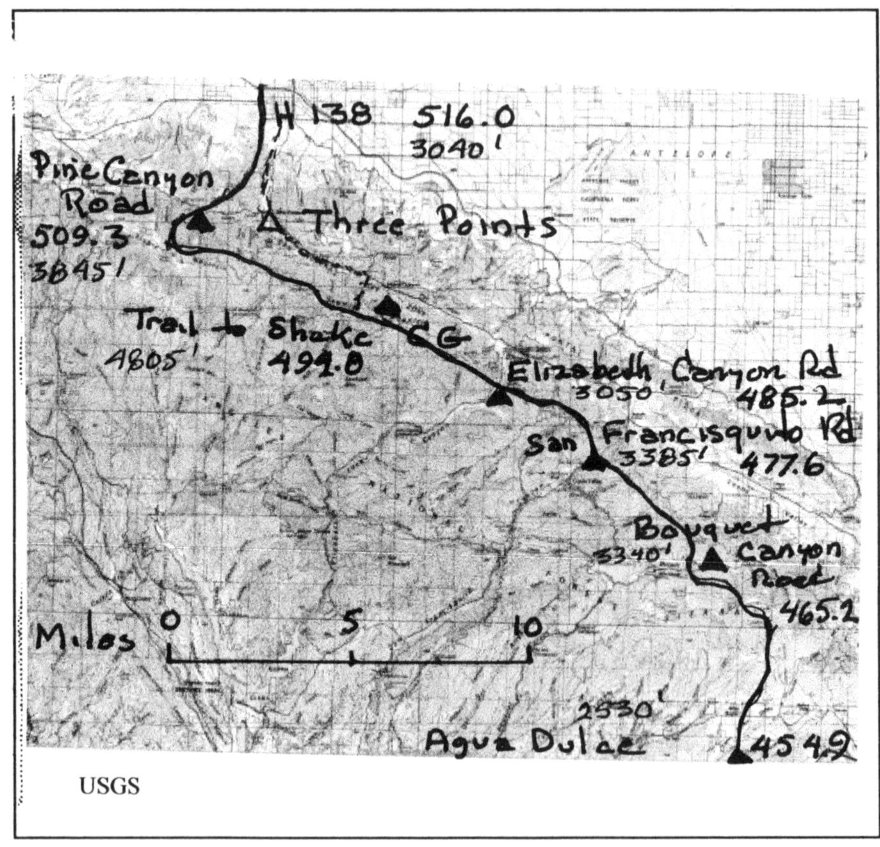

The NW Section of the Angeles National Forest
Agua Dulce to H-138 at Neenach

Chapter 24

The Northwest Sector of the Angeles National Forest: Agua Dulce to Neenach

The Sierra Pelona....Bear Springs....Bouquet Canyon
....Spunky Campground....Green Valley....San
Francisquito Canyon....Elizabeth Canyon....Upper
Shake Campground....Three Points Roadhouse
Jack Fair's home

This sector of The Angeles National Forest lies atop a west-by-northwest escarpment from south of Lancaster to near Gorman. The ridge is interrupted by a number of canyons with paved thoroughfares that do provide resources a few miles away. The PCT enters this forest north of Agua Dulce where it follows the higher ridges northwesterly. The more westerly areas are topped by inviting transitional and mixed conifer forests. The course of the PCT veers west around private Tejon Ranch before descending to the western extension of the Mojave Desert near the small towns of Three Points and Neenach.

April 28, Friday, 8:30 AM: Up Into The Sierra Pelona Mountains, El 2905, Mi 457.4

Soon after crossing the bottom of Mint Canyon, I see a register and enter my name after Scott and Doug's. There is no evidence of other PCTers passing through. The trail climbs to the first ridge top, Mi 462.0, El 4500' revealing striking views. To the immediate south lies the Pelona Valley and Vasquez Rocks. Beyond lie The San Gabriel Mountains; now I have a reverse view of what was seen from the ridge by The West Fork Ranger station. Here, there is a breeze and some shade. The trail then follows this good and well graded dirt road right on top of the ridge for a hundred yards or so, then meanders down the pretty north side to approach cool looking Bear Springs.

Bear Springs, Late Morning, El. 4350, Mi 463.0

Though the area is pretty and moist, it is small and contained. I see no easily visible water, nor any sign of bears! There is a small cienega with grasses and vines growing about. Without looking for the water, I continue passing the spring area, then easily cruise down the moderately descending trail to paved Bouquet Canyon Road, about a mile north of the large reservoir of the same name that cannot be seen from here.

Bouquet Canyon Road, El. 3340, El 465.2 - 0.0

Here, across the road, under the shade of welcome greenery, is a recently placed cache of water bottles, several multi-gallon containers of Arrowhead bottled water, compliments of the Saufley's. I am the first to fill up. I drink some of my water then fill up, taking two liters, taking note that in the last ten miles I had downed two liters. My total capacity is just a bit over three and one half liters, almost a gallon.

The trail climbs up over several minor view points and by deserted mine shafts. When a level of about 4,000' is reached, the trail goes through a gap followed by a shaded area on the northeast side of the ridge where a bit of trickling of water is seen in protected areas. Here, a cool rest is definitely in order. I can't resist picking up and nibbling away at the prolific minors lettuce, a two to five inch plant, resembling clove, but with a wide oval flat green head. The flavor is a cross between lettuce and dandelions. I gobble it up.

Around the first bend, the trail becomes exposed again. In about a half hour or so the summit, 4300' feet is reached. Here, the trail descends through a more pleasant area down to reach a dirt road, El 3725, Mi 471.3. that goes downhill about a mile or so to Spunky Canyon Road. I consider taking it to Spunky Campground, another mile or so down the paved road. I note my dwindling water supply, consider the distance traveled and the state of my condition. With but little hesitation I opt to leave the PCT to go down the road to find Spunky Campground rather than continuing on to where there may or may not be water.

Spunky Campground, 8:00 P.M., El 3200 - Mi 471.3 + 3.0 .

It takes longer than expected to reach Spunky. The milage seems longer than described. I arrive not until dusk is about to end. It is now cold. The almost vacant campsite seems inviting with large oaks scattered throughout the improved National Forest Campground. Just beyond the entrance are three elderly large size men huddled closely around a fire pit. One of them, Dave introduces himself as the Camp Host. He in turn introduces me to two other gentlemen. Though they clearly wish to socialize, they recognize that I am tired and anxious to settle down for the night. Dave points out several nearby campsites with picnic tables and fire pits.

As I am setting up my bivvy bag, he comes over and offers me the use of a small trailer. I don't hesitate and take him up on the offer. It is a very small, but tidy and complete trailer with everything miniature, two small beds, sink, pump for water, refrigerator and working gas range. After sharing an inch of brandy with the gentlemen, I easily cook up some of my special soup-pasta stew and very easily retire in this cozy den to a sound and refreshing sleep.

April 29, Saturday Morning: Green Valley, El 3000, Mi 471.3 + 5.0

Everyone is gone. The campground is empty. I make an effort to tidy up the place, pack up the gear and head down paved Spunky Canyon Road towards the center of town. While doing so I become impressed with the prospects of having a camping van of my own. It was so comfortable in comparison to cooking and sleeping outside in the cold. The mile or so stretch is marked by a series of small homes on fairly large lots, all with a rural quality in this unique town. Green

Valley, another "secret hideaway" seems known only by the residents and some visitors. Many are on motorcycles. Green Valley is one of the many places in Southern California, tucked away from the routine hubbub of nearby greater metropolitan Los Angeles. Once in the area, it seems as though you could be hundreds of miles away.

As I enter the center of town I spot the restaurant, the only café in town. It is next to a mini-market liquor store and filling station, also the only ones in town. They are all fairly busy with patrons. I feel as if I am being watched as I take off my pack and lay it outside the door of the small café. The café offers a delicatessen behind a large case and a varied menu. My breakfast , though simple, seems terrific. I really feel awkward as I can almost sense the averting glances from the few patrons of the restaurant as they avoid direct eye contact. I am convinced I am being quietly observed and seem to put them on guard. I soon realize that backpackers are quite rare this time of year. They react to me as if I am a transient bum. It could very well be that I appear as one. I step out to the mini-market liquor store next door by the gas station. A sheriff deputy sees me and follows me into the store. I think once he realizes I am backpacking and not a trouble-making bum, he leaves the store in favor of discussing some matters with a small group of motorcyclists attired in flashy costumes and small bikes.

Too soon, but without adieu, I drink more water and leave town in some admiration of their effort to prepare for an art-like flea market this morning, but also how they attempt to prevent unpredictable trouble from occurring.

Assured now I am filled with water I head down the road another mile to San Francisquito Road, turn northward and trek uphill in search for the Ranger Station which is near the trail head of the PCT. Finally, after a long mile or so, or even more, I see the Ranger Station. It is not open and there seems to be no obvious water source. Here, even before getting on the trail I find myself sweating up.

Mid-morning: The PCT Trail Head at San Francisquito Canyon, El 3385, Mi 477.6 - 0.0

A water source is not apparent. Not yet thirsty, I don't bother to look around for water, nor to knock on someone's door. I immediately spot the trail head and head northward bound. Going to Green Valley was a longer diversion from the trail then expected, but a lot of fun.

Now the trail ascends up Grass Mountain. Already, whatever grass there is, is brown. The day is getting hot and the trail is rather steep and exposed as mid day approaches. Nevertheless the top is reached soon enough at Mi. 479.2, El. 4,275 feet, where views from this vantage point are quite dramatic. From here one can see Lake Hughes, the Mojave desert, the Tehachapi Mountains and the Sierra peaks beyond that I hope to reach this year.

Suddenly, just upon leaving the summit, coming up the now shaded trail, appear two day hikers. They explain they are preparing for an upcoming Marathon race and are walking the trail here in hopes of conditioning themselves for the event. They also explain that two backpackers were seen walking eastbound on Lake Elizabeth Canyon Road this morning heading for the PCT. This information confirms that Doug and Scott are putting on the speed in covering distances. They are already a full hiking day ahead of me.

4:30 PM: Elizabeth Lake Canyon 485.2, El 3050

Upon reaching the bottom at the Lake Elizabeth Canyon Road, I am surprised to find water flowing in the creek. Grateful that I have no need to detour to the town of Lake Hughes for water and supplies, I decide to settle down early for the evening looking forward to a fresh start in the cool of the morning through the next series of summits. I find an isolated area in the sand near the flow and have a pleasant evening, including a wash of cloths, self, and a leisurely cooked supper. Here, along the streambed are but a few scraggly deciduous trees protruding from the sandy wash, baccharis and willows, sufficient for shade and strong enough to serve as a clothesline.

April 30, Sunday, 6:00 AM: Departing Elizabeth Lake Canyon, El 3050, Mi 485.2

As expected the trail aggressively attacks the eastern flank of Sawmill Mountain, the next hurdle along the way. It soon becomes quite hot and I am sweating more water than I can drink. The trail soon reaches an exposed dirt road that follows the ridge, crosses it and parallels this dirt road in a rather monotonous manner. The road and trail are both exposed to the sun, except for a few isolated shaded areas that call for a rest from the heat. Though the breeze is light, it has a marked cooling effect on the drenched T-shirt, especially when the pack is removed.

As the trail approaches the 5,000 foot level, the coulter pines, cedars and other conifers appear thanks to a reforestation project with a duff of needles on and about the trail.

Soon a trail emerges that branches off downhill 0.6 miles to Upper Shake Campground which is supposed to have year long water. I take stock of my situation and decide to head down for water and a late morning break. The trail down is delightful. It soon takes me to a nice campground with tables, pits and outhouses. It is deserted. Alas, the water is turned off and the johns are locked and the stream is dry.

I rethink the situation and decide to follow a trail that heads for the stream that goes down and north. I soon reach the stream and indeed it has a lot of water running. I fill up. Instead of going up trail, I decide to head north along the trail that parallels the stream to lower Shake Campground on the option to head back to the PCT another way. Once there, I decide to continue the trail down to Pine Canyon Road where I will walk westward a few miles to the Three Points Roadside Inn. Maybe I'll catch up with Doug and Scott. I walk for about six miles, mostly uphill, alongside the sparsely shaded paved roadway. Once reaching some shade, I stop and momentarily, check progress on the map. I decide that if I had to do it again, I would remain on the trail. I enjoy the temporary coolness, then move on.

5:00 PM: The Three Points Road House, El 3800, Mi 494.8 + 7.0

The tavern appears around a bend in the road at the junction with N2, the road leading to Interstate 5 and Gorman, not far from where the PCT crosses N2. It is recognizable by the large Harley Davidson cycles parked in front. Though hopeful to meet with Bob Moyon, the owner, with whom I communicated by E-mail, I enjoyed a wonderful cold beer and a delicious makeshift supper of a chicken sandwich with fries. During supper, I shared an interesting conversation with a young man who assists the business in a number of informal ways. He notes my topo maps and tells me he utilizes these maps to find remains of antiquities and leftovers in abandoned sites.

Though invited to stay overnight, I felt some need for discretion. I decide there is time to make it to Jack Fair's place in Neenach before dark, an additional trek of about four miles down Pine Canyon Road, then a mile or so west on Highway 138 to his place, steps away off the Pacific Crest Trail.

8:00 PM: Jack Fair's Home, El 3040, Mi 516.0

After a high pace, I walk through peach orchards, horse training ranches, and semi-unimproved desert properties, I make it, after putting on more than 23 miles today to the house described in the Guidebook by PCT friend, Jack Fair.

Ed Faubert

Chapter 25

Neenach: Jack Fair's Home

Sunday, April 30, 8:00 PM: Jack Fair's Home, 516.0, El 3040

I timidly walk up through the open gate, enter his acreage, and before knocking on the door take note of the many unusual signs with original sayings nailed onto the exterior wall near the front door. It is dark but I grasp the flavor of the signs. They are characterized by a poetic and existential problems. Many deal with how to get along in a hostile world and focus on the inevitability of death.

I knock on the door. A tall thin, somewhat gaunt grey beared fellow about 80 years of age appears. He has the first word. Something like,

"What in God hill is this?…Well, just don't stand there, come on in! Don't mind the dog, Missy, she's OK. I was a guard dog trainer and she knows how to behave herself."
He goes on to say, "I see you're walking. What a mess you are. Come on in and get something to eat or drink." He keeps on rambling on. I don't have a chance to say anything.

Before long, we settle down on one of his couches with a soft drink munching on some snacks. Each time I would start to say something, he interrupts with some sort of confronting remark.

I ask him, "Did a couple of young men come by in the last couple of days?"

He quickly replies before I describe them, "O yeah, those guys didn't stay but a few minutes. They said they were going to Canada. They were so cheap they didn't want to pay for anything. Besides, I think I scared them away."

"Oh!

"I charge five dollars a day and two bucks or something for a ride to the store. I see you're not hungry. Are you OK?"

"Yeah, I'm fine. I just had supper at the Three Points Roadhouse."

Before I could say another word he says, "You look terrible. Take a bath in my whirlpool. Five bucks for fifteen minutes. I have to charge for everything as it all costs me so much to keep up the place. I'll turn it on and in five minutes it'll be ready. I'll give you a towel."

"OK." Soon, I was in the warm midst of the whirlpool.

Jack comes in and declares, "Look, aren't you glad. Look how black the water is now. I bet you feel like a million dollars."

"Yeah, it's great!" I put on clean underwear, comb my hair, get dressed and come out to the living room.

We chat for about three hours, til close to midnight, about all kinds of matters. Most of the conversation revolves around his experiences as a youth, going into the navy during the war, deep sea diving, guard dog training, his marriage, and his exploits with the motorcycle club, The *Shaggers*, a motorcycle club he claimed he started. He goes on with his philosophy on life and how he survived the hostile world he lives in. Jack refers to the signs outside. I explain it had been too dark to read the signsoutside. He shows me the PCT register going back several years with entries of hundreds of visitors during the hiking season. He shows me a manuscript of his biography written fairly recently. He offers to let me have a copy of it. Both of us exhausted. I retire to the garage, where I quickly go into a deep sleep, but not before wondering about the significance of this man's existence.

Monday, May 1, 7:00 AM: A Morning with Jack Fair.

I am hesitant to leave this time of day I decide to put off the walk through the desert for the time being until I feel the temperature is such that I can do it without heat exhaustion or dehydration. I utilize the time to read and try to take in the significance of the statements Jack is making with his signs. He must have about thirty signs posted on his house, all related to common themes of dealing with life's stressors ranging from dealing with women, children, crime, violence, the police, illness and death.

Soon Jack steps out of the house. He seems somewhat more civil than the night before. He invites me in. I make some tea. He inquires if I would like a ride to the market. I decline, saying that I am doing fine with what I have. Besides he has all kinds of snacks and goodies to eat, at a fair price. I let him know that I would like to stay until the temperature begins to drop.

The morning is spent continuing the intense conversation carried on the night before. By now, I have had the opportunity to review his art work, read their contents and have prepared answers to what I expect his questions would be.

"You're shocked aren't you."

"Sure, was that your intent?"

"Yeah, I want people to know about real matters."

This conversation went on for about an hour or so describing his unique way of looking at the world. He describes man's condition as taking a tough position or being taken advantage of. He went on to discuss how he developed his "tough" position on life and death. He attributes his stance based on a "messed up relationship with my mother." He says he learned from her that he couldn't learn to really trust anybody.

Soon, he tires out. He decides to take an afternoon nap. I tell him, I plan to leave about four O'clock or when the thermometer begins to drop from 92 degrees. He agrees to store a box of supplies of cold weather gear contributing to my pack weight. He gives me a copy of his biographical manuscript which I put into the box. I tell I will probably drop by in a week or so by car and pick up the box and manuscript.

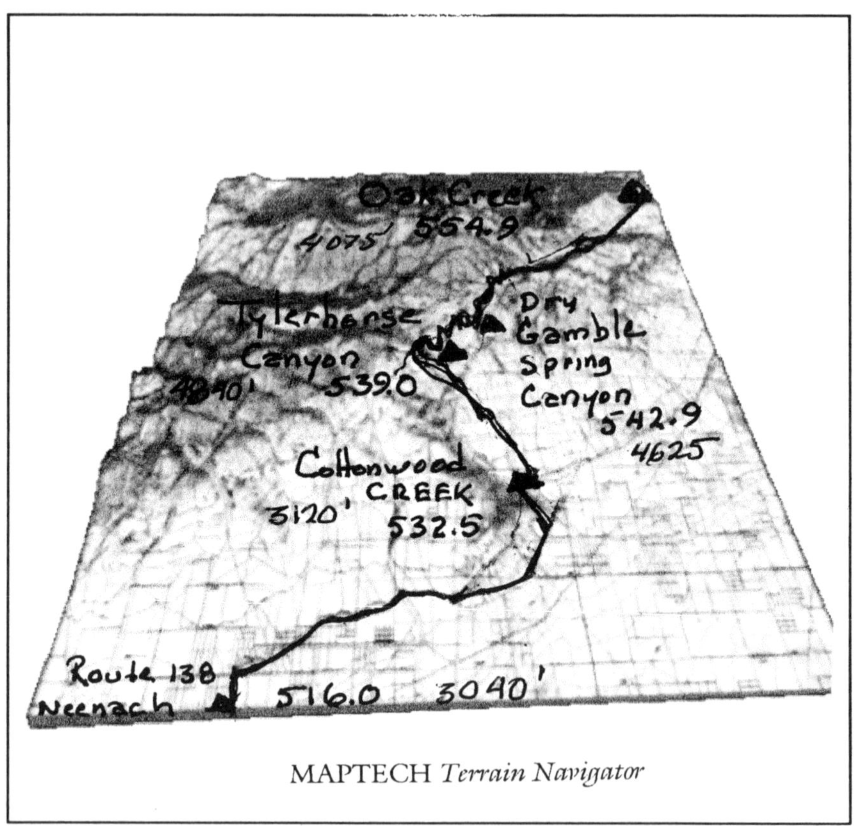

MAPTECH *Terrain Navigator*

Through the Mojave Desert to Tehachapi Pass

Chapter 26

THROUGH THE MOJAVE DESERT
TO TEHACHAPI

Neenach....The L.A. Aqueduct....Cottonwood Creek ...Lost
in the high desert? ....Tylerhorse Canyon...Dry Gamble Creek
....Oak Canyon and Willow Creek ...The Ranch Motel....
Tehachapi Airport....A memorable flight home

May 2, 4:30 PM: Departing Jack Fairs Home, Neenach, El 3040, Mi
516.0

My intent was to cross the desert after the heat of day, to do the walk during the evening and early morning. This part of the strategy works. But It may have worked out better if I had not lost the trail. If being lost is (a) not knowing where you are and also (b) not knowing how to get where you want to go, I was lost! You'll see how I handled this situation just north of Cottonwood Creek where the desert meets the Tehachapi Mountains.

The thermometer eventually begins to drop. When it drops to ninety degrees, I decide it is time to leave. By 4:30, I am on my way. Jack is probably sound asleep,

Being unsure of any water for the next 24 miles, I fill up with four liters of water and head north on the PCT, across Neenach school, closed at the time. The sprinklers are on, but inside a fence. The gates are closed securing any otherwise available water.

In about a mile I come upon the wide, deep and flowing California Aqueduct. Signs say to stay away. But I am aware that I could crawl down, collect some water at a slight risk of falling in.

In about another mile or so, the highly exposed trail turns northward, now following the underground Los Angeles aqueduct directly north along an adjacent dirt road. The LA aqueduct is a huge underground pipe that crosses underneath the larger California Aqueduct at the point where the PCT turns north. Along the way are a number of desert homes, seen from their rear, typically on large lots, some with horses nearby the road. I see an occasional person tending to their work. No one bothers to wave. People that drive by the opposite way wave as they leave their trail of dust behind.

The dirt road-trail crosses into Kern County. The notable things growing in this environment are but a few scraggy Joshua trees, occasional clumps of sagebrush and widely scattered forms of chaparral by the roadside. Then in about a mile north the PCT turns eastward continuing to follow the course of the L.A. aqueduct. At this point the PCT follows the top of the concrete slab that covers the grand old pipe. At regular intervals, I pass locked chambers where one can hear the rushing water below. The sound only adds to the thirst already being experienced.

Suddenly, a car approaches from the opposite direction, westbound along the adjacent aqueduct road. He stops. He says, " Hello! It looks like you're doing the Pacific Crest Trail."

"Yeah, I've started from Mexico last year and now started from Acton on my way to Tehachapi."

He reaches down and hands me a cold can of beer.

"I'm sorry, but I don't think I should have this now."

"Don't matter, drink it whenever you want. Take it with you."

"Thanks."

He points out, "Up the road a piece is a water hole, next to a private home where a road cuts to the south, not far. Should you need it, go for it. No one will mind."

"Thanks for the beer and good wishes."

9:00 P.M. Somewhere along the L.A. Aqueduct El ca 3100, Mi 523

It's dark. There is no moon. No sound except for my foot steps and my swaying pack. So far, no signs of animals nor insect. It becomes quite dark. I begin to walk onto posts and bumping into things. I try to avoid wandering off the aqueduct roadbed to a ditch. When I do,

I try to avoid stepping on a horned toad. They are all around. It is too dark to see the house the man described. I find a place to sleep for the night, a flat area off to the south about twenty yards from the noisy concrete slab. I'm too tired to cook. I gratefully drink that can of beer and fall into a deep asleep.

May 2, Tuesday: L.A. Aqueduct

Up at 3:30 AM. With the help of my single triple A-energized battery driven flashlight, I head east and wait for dawn's first light. Soon enough, light appears. The hours pass by quickly, aided by the change of scenery due to the rising sun and changes in light revealing small ridges and the moderate slopes of the desert terrain.

11:00 AM: Cottonwood Creek; El. 3250, Mi. 533.0 - 0.0

I reach the water hole, a trough, at Cottonwood Creek well before noon, before the full heat of day.   The flora changes little, becoming more sparse as the trail leaves the lower areas to reach even drier climes as it approaches the Tehachapi Mountains.

The area here offers the first rest bit since leaving Neenach. Here, at the creek, a water trough can be seen emptying it's running contents into the streambed of cottonwood creek, now with a trickle of water in the midst of the wash. There are concrete, bunker-like huts overlooking the stream bed as if this is a gauging station. Though the facilities are locked, some shade is provided by small concrete overhangs.

1:00 PM: North of Cottonwood Creek; Here's One way to Get Lost!

A lot trails. None marked as PCT. The trails and roads are rocky. I take the widest trail and find myself walking a mile or so before I realize that there are no foot prints where they would otherwise be seen if someone were to walk through. I check my topo map, take a bearing and conclude this dirt road parallels the PCT, now about a quarter of a mile or so to the east. I look east. I see a steep cactus laden ridge and several deep gullies that look difficult to traverse and what's more, it is marked off as private property. The 1988 topo map reveals a road spur not far ahead that meanders north-eastward. If looks like it will cross the PCT in about a mile. So rather than head back a couple of miles, I opt for this approach and continue to head north on the dirt road looking for the turn off to the right.

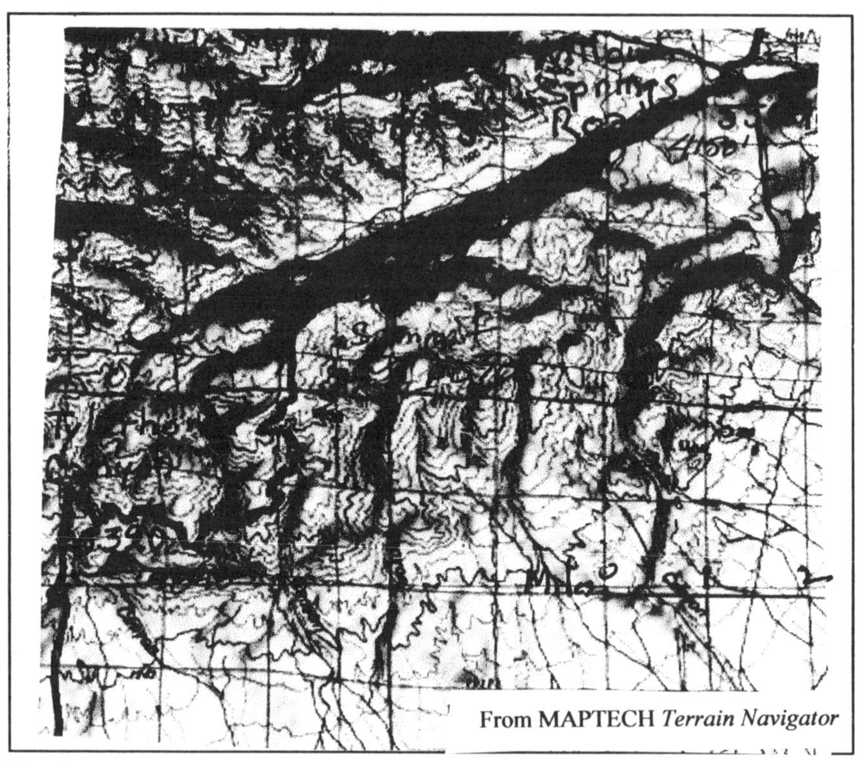

I head up a road by mistake and lose sight of the trail

Nuts! Ahead, is an imposing locked gate surrounded by barbed wire completely blocking the road. A sign says "No Entry, Trespassing Forbidden."

Just as I get to the gate to consider my options, a car approaches from behind me. The driver explains the PCT is indeed about a mile away, but does not know of a way to get there. I tell him I have some good, but old maps that indicate a dirt road will get me there. He opens up the gate and lets me through and wishes me luck. Soon enough, I reach the spur road that leads uphill and northeastward. The first trouble arises when the road comes to a T, an unexpected development that is inconsistent with the map. I try the southerly route. It seems to go nowhere. I return and head north on the T. This road meanders in several directions. I see a ranch. A house. There is somebody working. I dismiss the opportunity to check there. I continue walking an eastward dirt road. What happens next is that because of the distance traveled, I surmise I must have passed the PCT without recognizing the ill defined trail. Upon recognizing that I went too far east, I head northward, cross country, attempting to parallel the PCT looking for a place to head back west. The terrain does not permit westerly travel. The only landmarks are ridges too ill defined to get a meaningful compass reading. I see an occasional man made structures on the horizon that serve to maintain a reliable compass bearing.

Even with the help of the topo maps, It is not clear where I am. It is not clear which direction to go to get to the PCT. Furthermore, I conclude, even if I come across a trail or dirt road, there is a good likelihood I will not be able to identify the path as the PCT.

By now it is about the hottest part of day and I realize I am not only disoriented, but I am beginning to identify signs of dehydration. The wind has started to blow real hard, so hard, I cannot unfold the map and hold it still enough to read. I look for some shade and protection. There is none around! I see a Joshua tree a hundred yards away. I head for it. The cooling effect of the blast of wind creates a weird cooling sensation, feeling hot and cold at the same time. I am anxious to sit down in the shade and get some protection from the sun and wind. Finally, I reach the lone Joshua tree.

The wind is blowing hard. I have to fold the map in order to keep it from flapping about. I look for landmarks to get a compass fix and bearing. There are no identifiable peaks nor landmarks to get a compass fix. Nuts, Now what? Wait...settle down! Relax. Drink up. There's plenty of water left. I force down a lot of water. Though not hungry, I get something to eat. I feel somewhat better. I ask myself what is causing this disorientation. I know north and south. I can see signs of civilization down hill to the direct south. I tell myself to wait. Think this through. Not to give up yet. I settle down, rest, cool down, and down some more water and crunch on a power bar, I begin to feel less anxious.

I sort things out. I tell myself I will try extra hard to stay on the trail. If not sure I am on the right trail, to head back til I have a positive sign I am indeed on the trail or heading to it, even if this means walking south to Mexico! I recall how I saw somebody a few hundred years from the dirt road a while back, How come I didn't ask them for directions? It must be that I try too hard to avoid embarrassment. Yes! This is embarrassing. Fortunately, there's no one around to see how I got screwed up. No! No point in recriminating myself! I try not be so hard on myself.

I check my watch. It's 2:30 PM. I give myself a cut-off time. One and a half hours to go on looking for the trail. Should I not find the trail nor determine how to get to the trail, I will head back down hill. Either I connect with the PCT by 4:00 PM, or I head down the hill in a southerly direction to find some relief or transportation home.

Being there is no trail or road in sight, I resolve to walk cross country guided by compass. No landmark as a fix, I opt to maintain a generally northwesterly direction in hopes of picking up the PCT. In so doing, I go around gulleys, ditches and knolls. After about a half hour or so, I find that immediately to my north is a deep canyon, impenetrable. To my west is small ridge that blocks the horizon. To my immediate east, not more than a hundred yards I see a dirt road. It leads abruptly up a steep hill, to a knoll at the base of the mountains that I am almost upon. I figure I will take this road uphill. Should I gain sufficient height, I may be able to get a couple of fixes on a landmark and establish my exact position.

As I head up the road I am also hoping to see something that looks like the PCT. Upon gaining a couple hundred feet, I look to my immediate right and see a chasm a few steps away, of several hundred feet straight down! That's no good! I look north and I see the road heading up, then deteriorating and then winding down into a deep canyon below to the right. I scan to the west over another knoll. Lo and behold, I see what looks like a PCT emblem on a marker a couple hundred yards to the immediate west. Oh, for a pair of binoculars! There is also a chasm between there and here. I chance that what I see is indeed a PCT marker. Soon enough I'll get my answer. I know from the maps that the PCT takes a turn from its northerly track, eastbound to flank the mountain side to reach the head of Tylerhorse Canyon. Avoiding the impulse to do more cross country searching to the west, I head northerly along the road in hope that I will meet up with the trail as it veers eastward. I hope now that I am not north of the PCT and if not, my chances are good that I will strike the trail.

I am relieved to discover a trail. It is narrow, overgrown with chaparral, something that could pass for an animal trail. No footsteps. But soon I clearly see a marker ahead. No wonder I couldn't find the trail! I probably passed it more than once and didn't recognize it as such!

4:00 P.M., Tylerhorse Canyon, 538.7, El 4840

In about a half hour the PCT, after turning east, takes me to the head of Tylerhorse Canyon, the chasm that a while ago appeared below me to the east. Here, there is protection from the wind and sun, with plenty of shade, water to drink, a place to sit and clean up. It is an adequate place for an overnight.

In about fifteen minutes I am surprised to find that I am completely refreshed and anxious to move on. So, rather than spend the evening here, I head out to Gamble Spring Canyon, where I will spend the evening. This will permit me to get an early morning start on the climb to the summit tomorrow morning.

The tedious trek takes about two hours and I arrive at dry Gamble Creek. I note I have ample water for the evening and tomorrow morning as well. I spend a leisurely evening recuperating and pondering what I did that was wrong. I conclude I probably should have turned around as soon as I discovered I was not on the trail. Next time around, if I see someone, I won't hesitate to ask for directions or even advice. But I also did a few things that were good. I avoided much of the heat, maintained a modicum of fluid balance, used compass for maintaining a steady course, did some pretty good "dead reckoning" and put a time limit to my exploration.

Wednesday, May 3, 6:30 AM: Depart Dry Gamble Creek, 542.9, El 4625

The tread immediately ascends in eight switchbacks up the exposed side of the mountain, a final 1600 foot vertical distance to the summit between the Mojave Desert and Tehachapi.   Upon reaching the highpoint at 6,280 feet, the rest of the way seems easy. The trail winds along pinyon pines with ample shade, the first hint of being in the southern reaches of the Sierra. With that thought, my mood is uplifted. It's as if I reached some kind of barrier, traveling over 500 miles over desert and dry mountains. Yet, it is still dry. There is no water around.   There are many signs indicating private property in all directions.

Down to Tehachapi Pass
By Kim Parent & Jeff Hayash

Too soon, I hear the familiar drone of the wind turbine machines, reminiscence of the noise at the airport. As the trail descends, the noise gets louder and louder until I see that I am on the western boundary of a conglomeration of tall windmills, all whirling in the face of the prevailing 30 knot winds from the west. This situation continues until reaching the trail head at the bottom of Oak Creek Canyon where I stop and collect some water which I quickly treat with iodine tablets. I easily wait a half an hour for the chemicals to interact. A long the streambed I see the familiar flora and shade trees seen along the streams at lower altitudes throughout southern California. Here, are the cottonwood, sycamores, ash, and willows. All are dominated by large oak trees.

1:30 PM: Oak Creek at Willow Springs Road, 555.1, El 4150 - 0.0

Once filled up with treated water, I head up the dirt road to the highway. Alas, the road is blocked by a huge barbed wired gate with all perimeters wired so that exit is questionable. There are no signs of cars nor any activity anywhere.

Again I ponder the situation and take stock of things. I see no point to turning around and looking for an exit. I conclude I must be among the first of PCTers to come though and that must be why the road is still blocked. I eventually find a crawl through space. I manage to throw my pack over the barbed wire and crawl under it like I did in Basic Training through the infiltration course. In this case there were no machine guns going off. But I imagined what would happen if I were observed.

It was but a short walk to the highway. I stick out my thumb. In fifteen minutes, a car pulls up. The driver, Dave, a floor installer, was good enough to pick me up. He was on his way to put on some milage doing some bicycling. He insists on taking me to the post office, where I shared with him the method by which trekkers review and sign in the roster. He drives me by the airport to show me where it is. Dave then insists on dropping me off at a nearby motel. I keep his number. Should I ever need the services of a floor maker, I'll be sure to give him consideration. He sometimes gets to the L.A. area.

3:00 PM: Tehachapi, The Ranch Motel

I was informed that I could have a room if I were to wait for half an hour. I walk over to the airport, a few blocks away, and check it out. After settling down in the room, showering and re-organizing myself, I walk to the nearby restaurant, but find it closed. I walk over to a nearby mini-store. I buy some snacks and a quart of beer. I return to the room, call David at the airport and arrange a flight from Tehachapi Airport about noon tomorrow.

All is set. I cook a small dinner and ably nurse this quart of beer all night. This is the best beer I ever had, and the first time I ever drank so much alone.

Thursday, May 4, 10:00 AM: To the Airport - 0.0

After a most pleasant sleep in a real bed and another shower, I find a terrific place nearby for breakfast. After extending the time twice as long as required, I saunter back to the motel, confirm the flight, check out of the motel and backpacked the few blocks to the airport.

The airport office is physically open. There is no one around. I step inside, buy a drink and make myself comfortable, answering the phone when it rings. I take messages for the airport director, who I never have met.

Eventually, I hear an airplane, the second one in two hours. I look up and spot 6396V, our Cessna 172rg, a four seat airplane with retractable gear and a 180 horsepower engine with more equipment than is necessary to get me home. The plane taxis to me. Out steps David and Jeff Kertes.

They explain to me that Van put in a little box in the rear seat that has a GPS, a radio transmitter and an interfacing node that is supposed to send out our location over the air to his home computer, a live tracking of our flight. Wow!

I opt to fly the plane back. I choose to overfly the very route that I walked. Upon take off, I climb about fifteen hundred feet, continue east, find the trail head, then climb a little more as I follow the trail over the Tehachapi Mountains. Then over the Mojave. I over fly the trail to Three Points, then east along the Sierra Pelona Ridge to Agua Dulce, where I turn right to pick up the ILS which I follow out of Newhall pass to the field. It all happens so fast!

Upon landing, Van appears at the hangar, excitedly explaining the mission was successful. He shows us a printout of both flights, to and from Tehachapi. Jeff's flight north reveals a straight line from Van

Nuys to Tehachapi. My return flight follows the route of the PCT, from Tehachapi to Agua Dulce.

Jeff did not have adequate pocket change to return my payment for his time. He offers a beer at the Air Tel in exchange. Jeff concurs with me that we probably participated in an a general aviation landmark, successfully demonstrating live tracking through the global positioning system in a private aircraft. We probably were the first to successfully demonstrate live GPS tracking through radio transmission in a civilian private flying platform!

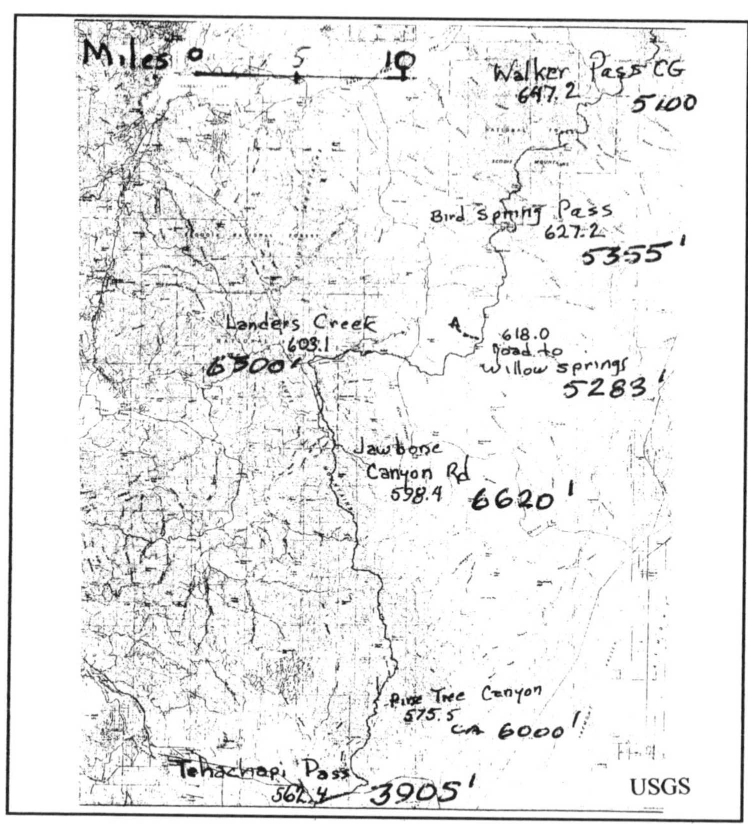

Section F: Tehachapi Pass at H-58 to Walker Pass at H-178
84.1 Miles

SECTION F

THE SOUTHERN SIERRA NEVADA:
H-58 AT TEHACHAPI PASS TO H-178 AT WALKER PASS

Prologue

How far south does the Sierra extend? At what point does one reach the Sierra? This matter depends more on one's perspective than where they appear on maps. For the northbound trekker it is really quite clear when they are first viewed and encountered.

On transiting westerly along the crest of The San Gabriel Mountains, my gaze was often focused on the wide expanse of desert to the north and the mountains beyond. Beyond the flat desert terrain lay an extended mountain range that filled the northern horizon. This view was of the continuous southern spine of the desert divide that separates the relatively moist climate of Central California from that of the arid deserts to the east. The views from the Angeles Crest called to mind how the southern spine of the Sierra protrudes from the Mojave to reach the distant horizon and the snow covered Mount Whitney chain of peaks. From that perspective, the southern spine of the Sierra starts from Antelope Valley in the northwest Mojave.

Upon reaching Cottonwood Creek, one begins to breech the southern spine of the Sierra, the local area known as the Tehachapi Mountains. Adjacent to the trail there was but little resemblance to the Sierra, anywhere in the immediate area. But in a few hours the trail summit, 6,000 feet was reached. It soon becomes apparent that the coolness of air and the scent of the mountains had replaced the dry desert air. Though in a transitional area, the horizontal view to the west became that of a rich conifer forest. There was no sign indicating such, but that unposted summit marked the beginning of the Sierra.

Walking up northward from Tehachapi Pass at Cameron Overpass of Highway 58, El 3830 feet, I began to definitely experience some of the features *expected* of the Sierra. Initially, pushing on up through to altitude, the switchbacks were exposed to the sun. It seemed then that the desert would never end. Upon reaching the first gap, somewhat higher than 6,000 feet, the extremity of the desert environment was now left behind for a while. The area again becomes transitional in nature. In shaded areas, it is conifers. In exposed areas, it is Joshua trees, yucca, manzanita, with ample sage, mesquite and cacti. The area differs from the desert because where there is shade and protection from exposure, there is a coolness of being in a montane forest.

As the trail diverted westward from the désert divide the climate is moist and forested. By the time one reaches the Piute Mountains, it looks like, feels like, and smells like the Sierra. Here, there are running creeks, and bubbly streams in canyons, signs of glaciation. Large Jeffrey pines dominate the scene.

But, too soon, the trail turns eastward towards the Sierra Crest where the flora regresses back to high and dry desert. Very dry. Water is scarce. Where there is a northeastern exposure, it is more tolerable, but still no trail access water. Here, the elevation of six and seven thousand feet is not enough to undo the dryness in the air and soil. This dry environment in the high desert existed for about twenty long miles while transiting the eastern ridges until reaching the Scodie Mountains. During this stretch, the nearest water source laid a mile or so off the trail and down several hundred feet in elevation. It was not until reaching the burnt forest of the Scodie Mountains that water was found on the trail, near McGyver Springs.

Chapter 27

North From Tehachapi Pass

May 14, 2000, Sunday Morning: Mojave

Jon and I drive together to Tehachapi Pass. We will head out together. The plan is for Jon will walk northward with me for a couple of days, then return to the car. I'll continue northbound to Walker Pass.

While dining at Denny's, in Mojave, we give some thought to the weather forecasts. The Times indicates very widely scattered short showers over southern and central California today and tomorrow. The Internet this morning revealed much the same, but more benign, perhaps scattered showers in the northern part of the sate. Along the way, the radio indicates a general nice outlook for the period. The skies around here and over the mountains to the northwest are clear. It is on the warm side with quiet winds.

Following breakfast we head up Willow Springs Road, which after a straight gradual climb begins to meander a bit around widely scattered chaparral through rather desolate areas, not far from Oak Creek Canyon where I dropped off from the PCT last week. Rather than pick up the trail here, I decide to drive head east through this somewhat rural area dotted with homes and ranches and leapfrog across the chaparral and oaks through the flats and rolling hills of Tehachapi Pass, thus permitting Jon to skip about seven miles of walking through the pass.

The PCT can sometimes be seen several hundred yards up and off to the right paralleling the road. Soon we approach Highway 58, a major thoroughfare between the Central California Valley at Bakersfield and the Mojave Desert and it's namesake City, Mojave. We cross at Cameron Overpass and secure our car in the shadeless area.

May 14, Sunday, Noon: Tehachapi Pass, El 3830, Mi 563 Sky 0.0

Though I have some rain gear, we are expecting warm weather. We carry about four liters each as we head down the well marked PCT paralleling the contour of the highway. The trail soon turns northward and upward requiring a bit of an effort, not without reward of view, to reach the first ridge. To the south, on the other side of this pass noted for its historical and still busy train travel, is a round mountain filled with windmills. They are all spinning about. It looks windy up there.

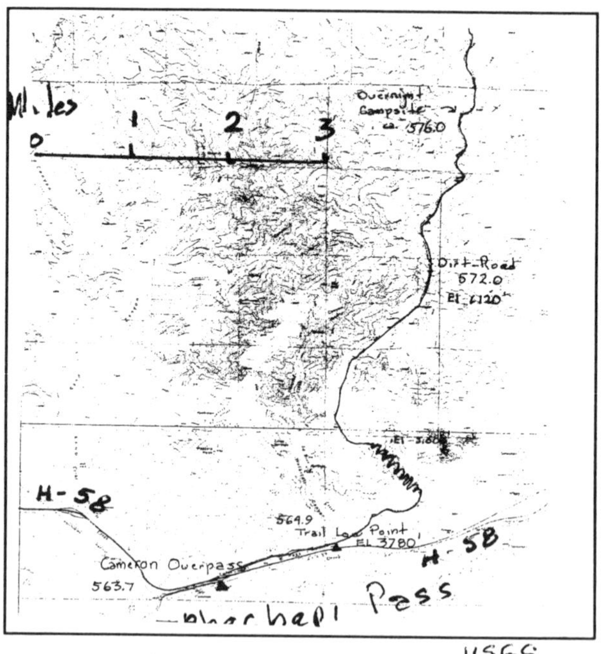

Tehachapi Pass to Head of Pine Tree Canyon

The way up this exposed face provides immediate views over the Mojave Airport and the buttes on the other side of the town. Aside from the low chaparral and grasses, the dominating tree is the occasional pinyon pine, small Joshua trees and an occasional juniper.

After eighteen switchbacks, looking like a seismograph .on the map, the trail reaches a balmy altitude of 5,000 feet, at which point the climb moderates somewhat til reaching the summit at 6,120 feet. The two hour or so walk to the top is quite dramatic with views of the overlapping ridges to the south, Waterfall Canyon to the west. The distant ridges to the west are covered with gigantic windmills, but too far to hear. Approaching the summit we experience a nice breeze that well compensates for the warm heat of the day, probably around 80 degrees here at mid altitude.

Despite the rapid climb, we find we are not unduly tired, quite likely because we are inspired by the dramatic views unfolding with each increase of altitude. There are deep ravines below us, narrow ridges to cross, groves of yuccas, Joshua, then finally to pinyon pines, a signal that we have reached the southernmost reaches of the Sierra forests. Some nice potential campsites are passed. Abandoned prospecting sites are approached and views of the higher mountains ranges to the north beckon us on.

Soon we descend gradually following the contours of the more north eastern exposure through narrow trails and high brush and pinyon pines. We find ourselves on an old jeep road that descend rapidly, passing more potential campsites. We urge ourselves on to where the Guidebook indicates a large tree, a "grey pine" on a flat offering several sites for camping. We soon spot the area. We see one pine tree. Without a word we start to look for a site.

7:00 P.M., A Campsite Above Pine Tree Canyon, Mi. 575, El. 5500 0.6

We note the sky is beginning to darken. There are some cloud build-ups to the west a few miles away. Now there is a hint of some rain. Jon sets up his area on a flat sandy area featuring a tarp held up with two sticks and guy lines providing some shelter should it rain. I look at the skies. I look at his area . I urge Jon to help set up a tube tent between two trees, settling down the corners and sides with large rocks found about the entire area. We agree to climb into the tube tent in the event we fear getting wet. After stowing extra equipment inside, I set up my bivvy bag on a sloping area that appears unlikely to collect water should it rain.

Despite my willingness to share my cuisine, Jon insists on not cooking. He easily eats his meal of dried veggies, crackers and assorted non-sweet snacks. I travel very light, so I am limited to cooking my soupy pastas that work for me on my makeshift lightweight stove. The sandy soil and existing small fire pit offers some convenience. I offer him samples. We have a pleasant chat but notice the dark overcast sky. We easily drift off into a sound sleep.

About midnight, as I step out to take a leak, I notice a drop or so of sleet. I hurry back to the warmth of the bag. The next thing I know, it is morning.

May 15, Monday, 6:00 AM, The Head of Pine Tree Canyon, El 5500, Mi 575. Sky 1.0

I hear the pleasant pitter patter of sleet falling on the erected part of the bivvy bag over my head and fight the urge to continue this blissful state of semi-consciousness. I step out, take my morning leak and notice that the ground is now turning pleasantly white with a dusting of snow and sleet. Most of the campsite area, though, is damp, not quite wet. I look over at Jon's area and note that the sides of his tarp cover is drenched with water, but that Jon seems nevertheless dry inside his bag. He indicates he is fearful he indeed could get wet. We decide to get dressed and pack our stuff and move along, one way or another. We postpone breakfast till we get moving. We get dressed in our rain gear and put everything together.

Meanwhile, the skies are completely overcast with fog limiting visibility to about 100 yards. The upper elevations, just a hundred feet above us can still be seen, outlined by a blanket of snow. We seem to be in the transition area between clearer visibility below us and clouds one hundred feet above. I take note that we are in a saddle. Both directions lead directly into the fog and snow. I find it hard to not get too distracted by the interaction of weather contributing to the beauty and wonder of the environment. I wish I had more time to just sit and observe this spectacular fluidity of nature.

To move northbound, because of the snow, means not getting into Golden Oaks Springs for a couple of hours. But at the moment there is no way of telling what kind of weather waits ahead. There occurs a temporary break in the overcast and fog. The clouds, coming from the west, seem to be stopping at the Sierra Crest, hardly moving into any of the desert regions to the immediate east.

We decide to walk cautiously northbound on the trail in hope of soon getting a bead on the weather picture. The trail immediately climbs and takes us into the fog and snow cover. It is snowing lightly increasing as we climb to higher altitude. The whole area soon becomes white. There is no way to draw a conclusion as to what lies in store for us northbound along the trail. Jon lets me know he wishes to return, alone, to the car at Cameron Overpass.

I don't leave the matter for Jon to decide. I say,

"Let's do a one eighty and head back to the car."

"Don't you want to go on?"

"Sure, but I'll just be worrying, particularly if the weather does not improve."

Jon replies, "I don't want to go on because it may be more difficult to get back later. But I can make it back easily enough. I can see the trail and know the way back."

"Yeah, that MAY be so, but I'm not even sure it's wise for me to go on under these conditions. I'm sure the weather will eventually improve, but when?"

"Won't you be disappointed again?"

"I'm used to it....I guess such uncertainties is what makes it such a wonderful adventure."

"We hesitate. We look around us. We appreciate the idyllic scene. I plant a picture in my mind wondering what it may look like when it is not all white. We turn our backs to the north, head down the hill to soon pass by our evening campsite.

Curiously, the trail remains free of snow. But everything else is completely covered with fresh snow. It is uncertain as to how long the trail will be easy to follow. I can't figure out why the trail is clear and the area immediately around it is completely white. We're not that special! Anyway, I figure it would be easy to get lost and disoriented should conditions not improve. Because of the various steep grades and drop-offs at various points it could well be life threatening should we get lost and feel compelled to move. Besides, I want to apply what I learned on the trek to Big Bear and remember how concerned Joel and I were when we couldn't locate Jon on the trail. A Map and compass under these conditions of poor visibility would be of little value. One solution would be to set up a campsite and simply wait for the weather to improve. But Jon does not have the time and I certainly do not wish to separate under such conditions. I am aware that serious mishaps in the mountains tend to occur more often when people separate, especially in poor weather.

So, now we pick up our pace downhill. In a short time we reach the saddle where we camped out. The saddle area remains just below the cloud deck, but the campsite is now entirely covered with a white blanket of snow and unrecognizable as such. Even with but an inch or so on the ground, what not long ago seems to be imprinted in memory, is entirely lost from recognition.

We follow the road uphill towards the summit, and soon re-enter the fog. Snow continues to fall lightly at the moment. The temperature must be hovering near the freezing mark. The trail, now a jeep road, remains clear though the area adjoining the road remains completely white. There is no clue as to what lies ahead weather-wise.

The steep dirt road turns muddy. Real muddy! Big clumps of mud accumulate on my boots. Walking up this steep hill with this extra weight is tiring. Jon is wearing jogging shoes, but not complaining. He says his feet are still warm. He says his hands are cold. Though I am securely dressed in cold weather gear, from head to toe, Jon had not prepared adequately for cold weather. He has no mittens and is wearing jogging shoes without gaiters. He does have a good jacket and shell pants, so there does not seem to be an immediate threat of hypothermia, just plain discomfort. Enough discomfort, though, to distract one from the beauty of it all. Yet, he'll stop, when the clouds momentarily part and look over the changing scenery.

Soon, we leave the jeep road and traverse the north side of the mountain where the trail becomes narrow and hard to follow. But fortunately, for reasons I do not understand, the tread remains snow free and readily identifiable. If it were covered by even an inch, we could lose the trail. Being alone would then make it quite a stressor situation.

We soon make it to the gap that brings us to the southern face. Now, suddenly, we are getting pounded by gale force winds with snow and sleet. It is hard to keep our balance especially on the narrow ridges that are even more exposed to the changing gusts. The winds are gusting up to forty knots from various directions. These crazy gusts over shadow the prevailing wind, which is about twenty knots. What happens now, on the narrow ridge top, is the winds suddenly appear coming from our left at 40 knots, then from our right at 40 knots. This causes us to walk low and use our hands.

Fortunately, the snowing stops. There is less snow on the terrain. We begin to move down under the clouds. Now, we see the dramatic cloud build-ups. We see the system is not just a local Sierra crest phenomenon. Buildups are covering all quadrants of the sky. We can also see in the sky above us how the wind shear that we are now experiencing is happening. The experience of swooping winds we feel on these exposed ridges occur following the development of updrafts caused by the thunder cells. It seems the air is first sucked up vertically, thus causing a vacuum of air that is not only immediate, but erratically replaced by air that passes over our locale. The sudden gusts interact with the more prevailing winds that generally cross westward from the cooler valley and mountains to the superheated air of the Mojave. We see and feel this interaction of forces resulting in wind shear with a resultant momentary vertigo and become aware of how it all contributes to the present danger.

The cloud cover permeates some of the desert, but blue skies are seen about ten miles to the east, beyond the desert terrain. I suppose the reporting stations in the populated areas are experiencing clear and warm weather. I conclude, partly for this reason, forecasting of weather in the southern Sierras is quite coarse for purpose of trekking.

Soon we reach the eighteen switchbacks. We find momentary shelter in an isolated protective areas, by a Joshua tree, a big rock, or sometimes being close to a protruding ridge. But as soon as we cross a ridge exposed to the west, we are hit by a blast of forty knots winds from various directions. Jon is more subject to the effects as his silhouette is larger; his backpack extends from above his head to his butt, whereas mine is from shoulder to hip.

Soon after the eighteen switchbacks, we reach lower and more level ground. Here, the winds subside. Now it is familiarly warm. We parade back to Cameron Overpass where we are relieved to see the car is still there and warm from the sun. We are soon off on our way home trying to comprehend the significance of our second experience together on the PCT.

Chapter 28

Jawbone Canyon to Walker Pass

The Piute Mountains, near Robin Bird Springs....
Willow Creek Springs....A stealth camp....Walker
Pass Campground....Kern Valley Airport.

May 22, Sunday

A week later, Jon and I drive up Interstate 14 to Highway 395 beyond Tehachapi Pass looking for a road to connect to the PCT beyond Tehachapi Pass. There does not seem to be any entry short of Derringer Grade that connects with the PCT near Robin Bird Springs, about twenty four miles north of where Jon and I turned around last week. After determining there is no easy short cut, we decide to check into the Bureau of Land Management ranger station on Highway 395 at Jawbone Canyon for maps.

We park at their modern facility. I decide to bring in my copies of the *Guidebook* and my USGS topo maps. The facilities are visitor oriented and we are impressed with the information and resources at their disposal. I browse around and look at their interesting collection. They ask me if I am aware of water resources in the area. I tell them I have information on trails and water sources in the *Guidebook*. I pick up some local maps geared fro drivers that can supplement mine. We drive the 20 west miles westward to the PCT. We pass a lot of desolate area set aside for off road vehicles. As we approach the Sierra crest, we pass the Skyline Ranch, a resort area that features a landing field for small aircraft. Here, we have to wait for some cattle to clear the road. At least this time I am in a car! The sun is starting to lower. We opt to quickly drive up Derringer Grade to find the trail. Soon, the road climbs sharply. The road winds around some streams. We soon leave the sparse chaparral and enter a forest of conifers as we approach the summit. We easily find the PCT near a gap, about half a mile by trail north of Robin Bird Springs, almost 20 miles north of where Jon and I turned back last week. Here, the white firs, large black oaks, tall Jeffrey Pines dominate the montane forest. It is getting dark. I pull out my gear. I set up in the duff under a huge Jeffrey pine.

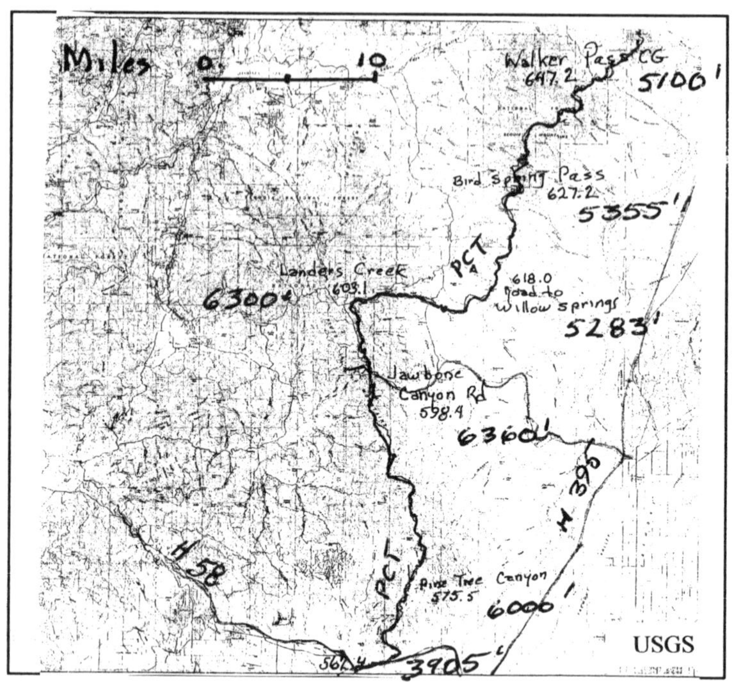

Jawbone Canyon To Walker Pass

As I check out my equipment, I cannot find my copies of the *Guidebook* and topos. We conclude I left them at the BLM ranger station. Too far to go back. Besides they are closed. I look at what maps I have and decide I should be able to navigate. I thank Jon for the trip and wish him a safe trip back home. I set up camp, polish up some leftover snacks from lunch. I recall my notes of yesterday, mentally review the route as I recall it and compare it to the BLM maps I picked up this afternoon. Temperatures are expected to be high. Lancaster will reach 102, as will Lake Isabella. By interpolation, I figure it could well reach into the nineties at lower elevations on the trail. But for now, it is quite nice and cool.

Monday, May 23, 6:00 AM: In the Piute Mountains, Jawbone Canyon Road, Near Robin Bird Springs, Mi. 598.4, El 6620 - 0.0

With anticipation for a pleasant morning, I put my gear together and head northbound on the PCT. The trail nicely meanders gradually downhill through forested slopes marked by a number of brooklets stemming from the ascending slopes a thousand foot or so higher on both the east and western sides. The trail cuts through various small canyons with numerous streams and springs bubbling with the sounds of gently moving cascading brooklets. Because I am fully rested and loaded with water, I cannot rationalize stopping so soon on the trail. I say to myself, "Can it get better than this?" The answer: "This is probably among the prettiest and most hospitable area I've seen yet. The seasonal springs appear active and the intermittent streams are running well. The trail continues to drop through mini-meadows, cienegas and past a number of inviting places to stealth camp as well as nearby improved campsites. Here, any thirst is caused by the sound and sight of running water, not the superheated air.

Soon, unbeknownst to me, I pass the last reliable source of water on the trail for 35 miles. I am aware and know there are indeed places up trail 14 miles or so, but one has to leave the trail for a good walk downhill to reach it. But with over three liters of water, I am confidant that I will make it to reach an off-trail supply without much thirst. Besides, I hope there remains a chance of finding some water some place along the trail. The streams are all moist; why not?

Once at Landers Creek, the trail turns eastward, closer to the Sierra crest and dry Owens Valley. The trail very gradually leaves the moist montane forest. Imperceptibly, each mile takes one into more xeric conditions. What makes the trek difficult now is the heat itself, lack of shade and the up and down pattern of the trail that varies from 4,500 feet through 6,600 feet, up and down exposed to the sun.

As the trail meanders eastward, a ridge ahead blocks the view of desolation and high desert ahead. Nevertheless, as the trail continues to the gap, pinyon pine and desert chaparral already replace the mixed conifers. Where it was moist and green with grasses and creek side plants, now even the pinyon pines and junipers are getting smaller and far apart. I recall the *Guidebook* telling of nearby water sources. But alas, I have no detailed information on hand. As the trail continues on the exposed flanks of St John's Ridge towards Pinyon Mountain, to my left is a unique bare peak, aptly named Mayan Peak, El. 6,108 feet, resembling the shape and barrenness of a Mayan temple that I climbed with Hannah in the Yucatan Peninsula in the southern portion of Mexico. This bare temple in the sky, with no growth on it all, serves as a beacon and landmark while one meanders south of it.

The trail now attacks the slopes of Pinyon Mountain. I take note that there seems to be no pinyon pines, nor any kind of tree other than an occasional stunted Joshua tree. Now panting in the heat of day, with not much for cooling except a drenched t shirt and bandana, I find that my water source is close to empty. I now cannot replace the amount of sweat loss even with unlimited water. I recognize symptoms of dehydration setting in. There is the sparse yellow-green urine, signs of heat exhaustion, some nausea, tiredness and lack of appetite, and a strong desire to crawl under anything that gives some shade and rest. Not soon enough I look down the mountain side and see a little pond. I recognize it, from maps I no longer have, as Willow Springs. Avoiding the tendency to make a short-cut, I follow the trail around Pinyon Peak, eventually get to the dirt road where a sign indicates the spring is one mile down.

7:30 PM: Road to Willow Creek Springs, Mi. 618, El. 5283 - 0.0

After what seems like an eternity of time, I finally step through this loosely compacted, sandy 1.8 mile section of road, a drop in altitude of 863 feet. As I approach the spring, I am excited to find clues of nearby water. The air smells of cow dung. Here are hoof prints, disturbed plants and soil, then bits of green grass, more tramping of soil and more clots of dung. Finally, I spot the pond. Yuk! Disgusting! The stink of the pond so matches the nearby stench that I don't even smell it. I reach for my iodine pills. I don't know how the cows survive this!

 I look around. I see a barbed wire fence forming an enclosure of a moist area of about 300 square yards. Inside is an area where stream side plants are growing, but no water is standing or moving. There are no trees around. The area reeks with the odor of cow dung seen all over the smelly place. As I hopelessly walk around to find a suitable spot to draw some water, I see what looks like a combined hand pump and faucet near the corner of the barbed wire fence.

I attribute it to good luck that I am able to get the pump to work and that there is clear, odorless water coming through. Without hesitation, I drink down the last remaining eight ounces of water and fill up my water bottles. I climb over the fence to the protected dried out spring area and set up the campsite in this small but relative pristine area. I tolerate the twenty minutes for the iodine tablets to do it's thing, then fix it up with something to mask the bleach taste.

After an hour or so, I find that I feel normal again, but not hungry enough to eat much of anything. Everything that I am carrying tastes too bland and dry to eat. I am just too plain tired out after putting on all these miles in the heat. I climb in the sack and become acutely aware that nature's best is not where man, his tools and domesticated animals trespass. Yet, I tell myself, were it not for the development of the trail, I would not have the opportunity to be out in this area. I contemplate the matter as I quickly fall asleep.

May 24, Wednesday, 6:00 A.M.
Departing Willow Springs, Mi. 618+ 1.8, El. 4420 - 0.0

No appetite to eat. I treat new water and trudge up the loose sandy road. One step back for every three up. Now, this one mile diversion seems more like a four mile diversion. All is uphill. Almost two hours is required to make it back to the trail. My neckerchief is already drenched completely and I am already down about liter of water.

The trail is un-relentlessly exposed, meandering around points when you hope it will go straight. I go from one shaded Joshua tree to the next, resting, catching my breath, taking in some water or flavored drink to cover up the iodine taste. I have come to know the signs of heat exhaustion and dehydration and know that I am beginning to experience these unwanted partners. I discover it is hard to drink this lousy tasting water. It nauseates me and brings on beginnings of the dry heaves. I decide to offset my final fate by resting under a large Joshua tree mid day and try to wait there til the temperature drops. But I can't sleep nor get a good rest as the terrain is rocky and the spines of the yucca are too sharp as I slip down into them when I do fall asleep. As the sun moves overhead, what was once shade becomes a blast of heat. I am also fearful of falling asleep.

I watch a small cloud approach from the north. I concentrate on its movement. It is beautiful. It is small at first, but seems to be gradually getting bigger. As the cloud approaches, a wonderful wind begins to cool my aching body. An updraft occurs that seems to form grotesque shapes, like how I feel inside. Is this a projection? Illusion or hallucination? As I am looking at the ridges to the south they appear to darkn. I look overhead and see clouds approaching the sun. The shade of the clouds gets closer and closer. The shade is now widely covering the area of the ascending trail ahead! I take stock of my situation, my water supply, and my body condition. A look at my watch lets me know it is barely pass three PM. I become inspired to go ahead. I urge myself on upward on the exposed trail. Sure enough, the clouds form a welcome umbrella for the next two mile jaunt to the next gap. Once there, I see the trail ahead is also well shaded by those great formations in the cloud. Soon, drops of rain fall. As I put on my jacket, it stops raining. A nice interlude. Now, it seems my luck has changed. Morale is up.

5:00 PM: Bird Spring Pass, Mi 624.7, El. 5355 - 0.3

The trail soon passes another abandoned mining site, some prospect digs, then leads to a viewful gap near a dirt road leading to a radio tower. One final spurt brings me down to dry Bird Spring Pass. Suddenly, at the bottom where the trail will cross a road to climb up the other side, is a little wooden sign. An arrow and something clearly written as "W A T E R ." About twenty yards in the direction of the arrow, laying in the shade of some tall sage is a collection of seven or eight large green jugs of water. There is no identification of how the water got there, who put it there, nor of the quality of the

Near Bird Spring Pass   Steve Kral

water. The multi-gallon containers have a forest-green government look to them. It may be planted by a BLM crew. Not pondering the how and whys, I fill up. I change plans to spend the night with these jugs, this time in a more relaxed mood. Certainly, my luck has changed! Realizing I developed an appetite, I settle down for a real homemade meal of the usual stuff that tastes unusually good and easily get into the sack and fall quickly asleep

May 25, Thursday, 6:00 AM: Departing Bird Spring Pass,
El 5355, Mi 627.2 - 0.0

Not hesitating to fill up on water, I readily put my gear together and find I am inspired now to attack the exposed mountain side at this reasonable hour and look forward to re-enter the Sequoia National Forest and Kiavah Wilderness that I deduce is just beyond the ridge above. Soon after leaving the dirt road there is another trail register. Upon entering my name, I note very little activity north or southbound. Just a handful of names thus far this year. Two of them I recognize, Doug and Scott who passed by several weeks ago.

On this southern exposure, the vegetation is sparse. Just a few straggly pinyon pies and an occasional Joshua. Temperatures are fine now. The heat of day is yet to come. Looking south into the pass, one can visualize settlers during the 1800s passing through the desert to the east to the more hospitable central California valley and coast.

Once over the first gap or two, a summit, 6,940 feet, is reached without announcement. Here are momentary views of Lake Isabella to the far west, numerous mountains and ranges, and desert views to the east. The Piute Mountains are seen to the south. To the north can be seen the higher Sierra peaks including the snow-clad Mt. Whitney chain. Soon the trail takes one into a nicely forested area where it meanders gently up and down through a mixed forest, mainly Pinyon Pines.

Then, too abruptly, I find myself enveloped in an immense area of a completely burnt down forest marked by blackened poles. Spikes are sticking out where once there were rich branches of green needles and cones. The ground cover is spotted with several species of low thriving green plants, appearing bizarre in contrast to the blackened spires that surround them. The PCT is hard to follow through this area. Several times I revert to compass and dead reckoning to follow the direction of where I believe the trail were to go if there had been no burn. There are no PCT markers. They were all destroyed. I do not wander far from where I believe the trail lies. The tread seems to wind prematurely onto the dirt road that continues on to McIvers Spring. Near the summit, before the spring and deserted cabin described in the Guidebook, is a small stream that passes over the dirt road. I fill up intending to unload the water later should a more positive source appear. Soon, a PCT marker appears revealing the tread to the left, going uphill. I turn off the road and follow the path through some pleasant transition flora and views of terrain in all directions. This view must signal the summit had been reached.

As I am briefing myself as to whether to continue on down trail to Walker Pass, I am aware of the gusting wind, now reaching about 20 knots. I see a spot that looks like a couple ancient walls next to one another a bit away from the trail overlooking vistas to the north. Here is a perfect protective stealth campsite for the evening.

6:00 PM: Camping at "The Ancient Fort," El. 6700, Mi 640 - 0.3

A leisure dinner and a rest is in order. It is easy to be leisurely now as I acknowledge this difficult leg is just about finished. Tomorrow, it is all downhill and I expect to be at Walker Pass in three hours.

The wind begins to blow harder. I feel secure in the protection of the "castle rocks." As long as I lay low, there is no blast to be felt. I lay low the whole night and find no trouble falling asleep.

Friday, May 26, 6:00 AM: To Walker Pass - 0.0

The trek down to Walker Pass is uneventful. The flora is somewhat rich as the trail meanders for the most part on the northern exposure where mixed conifers and a transitional forest flourishes. Here views can be seen above the well traveled pass between Lake Isabella to the west and Inyokern, and the Mojave Desert to the east. To the north can be seen some of the well known peaks of the Sierra, including Mt. Olancha and Mt Whitney, signaling more adventure and nice things to come.

Walker Pass Campground, 12:00 Noon
Mi. 647.2, El. 5100 - 0.0

Here, there are a number of picnic tables, each with a campsite consisting of a pit, nearby water faucet and sufficient shade. There are also stalls and feed for horses. Nearby, not far, is a road that circles part of the area enabling car camping and picnicking as well.

Anticipating hitching a ride, I head for a faucet in this almost deserted campground and go about giving myself a needed stand-up bath with my neckerchief serving as wash cloth and towel. I inspect my feet and find they are in pretty good shape considering the heat and rush to get through the arid areas.

I walk out to the road. In fifteen minutes I get picked up by a retiree, his wife and their guard dog. They reside in the Inyokern area and are on their way to recreate in the Kern River by Kernville. They drive me directly to the airport where they drop me off right at the restaurant and Unicom office. It can't be better. After expressing my appreciation, I head for the phone, call home and leave a message. I call the airport, reach David who complies with my request for a lift by air.

In about three hours, after a leisurely lunch, snacks and rest, in taxis our C-172 RG, 6396V, piloted by Frank Surfas, a CFI and a companion pilot who came along for the ride.

Unlike the last flight, where I flew out, I let Frank fly as I was tired and wanted to enjoy the view. Upon taxiing, we all notice an unpleasant ominous noise coming from what we agree are the main gear wheels. I recall the history of the plane, recalling that Jeff and I heard somewhat the same noise, but not as noticeable. As we taxi, we stop and walk with the plane moving the front gear up and down. We give David a call and conclude the bearings are dry.

We taxi out carefully to the very end of the field and take-off with our fingers crossed. It turned out the noise continued until airborne. I sit up front and navigate. Frank complies with my request to fly along the trail southbound to Tehachapi Pass. From the air, the trail looks uneventful, with little hint of the ups and downs, flora, and beauty and drama seen from within. In minutes, the area is overflown. Though the mountain area seems brown, they do not belie how dry it really is down there.

We approach the field slowly. The landing yields the same familiar noise from the gear. It turns out, upon inspection, the main wheel bearings were rusted from sitting too long following a rain.

SECTION G

WALKER PASS (H 178)
TO KENNEDY MEADOWS

Prologue

The challenge of this section lies in the fine tuning of management of water carriage. The trailhead at Walker Pass, 5,246 starts 1,500 feet higher than that of Tehachapi Pass. Views become more spectacular as the first summit is reached, in about an hour. Elevations remain mostly above 6,000 feet, but drops as low as 5,160 feet at Needle Creek, the first on-trail source of water, 14.3 long miles from Walker Pass Campground. Another climb occurs, first past some nice water sources, then over a gap to   cross a stream at Canebrake Road where there is a nearby campground and water fountains, 14.6 miles beyond the first water crossing of Needle Creek at Mi 676.1. Then up again through pleasant forest to a summit of 8,020 feet before dropping down into Rockhouse Basin where one is immediately greeted by an intermittent water source 12.4 miles after Canebrake Road. Should there be no water here, then reliable water can be found after an exposed 4.2. miles through the dried out basin until reaching the flowing and beautiful south fork of the Kern River. The trail follows along the river and other wet spots, to briefly return to some dry areas, long enough to appreciate the cold drinks and food available at the Kennedy Meadows Camp Store.

This area, with its flowing river, large campground, and fairly well equipped camp store, provides the northbound trekker with a closure in completing the trek through southern California. Here lies the gateway to the high Sierra.

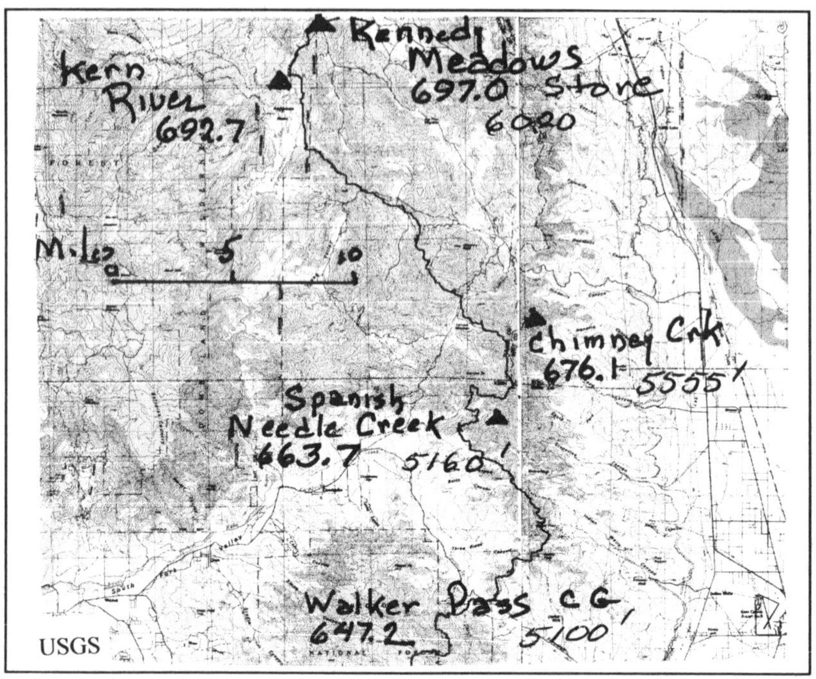

Walker Pass to Kennedy Meadows

Chapter 29
Walker Pass to Kennedy Meadows

Walker Pass Campground....Departing Walker Pass....At the trail head....Needle Creek....Chimney Creek Campground.... South Fork of the Kern River...To Kennedy Meadows.

June 12, Off to Walker Pass

Before picking up Van, I review the weather picture for the upcoming period. Forecasts reveal local temperatures to be somewhat above the norm. The southern Sierra look like they'll have lows of 46-66 with highs of 77 to 83. Lancaster expects a high of 95, Mammoth, a high of 74. I note Bishop, at 4,000 feet, comes in at 91.

We leave Highway 14, north of the city of Mojave, to travel westward up Highway 178 in a consistent eight mile climb to reach Walker Pass. We see the pioneer memorial and the nearby PCT marker indicating the trail head.

The trail can be seen winding up the exposed mountain side in a similar manner to that of the northbound trail from Tehachapi Pass, eighty four miles down trail. Whereas water was available 14 miles up from Tehachapi Pass, water is available 12.2 miles up from Walker Pass. A difference between the two trail heads is that here at Walker Pass the exposed ascent starts off about twelve hundred feet higher. The trail reaches its first summit at just over 7000 feet where hopefully cooler climes and hospitable segments occur a bit sooner. But water is a long 12.2 miles away.

7:00 PM: Walker Pass Campground, El 5100, Mi 747.2 - 0. 0.

We arrive at the driver rest stop and nearby spread out campground. As we arrive, I am astonished to find a group of fifteen or so backpackers congregating around two picnic tables. I immediately recognize them as PCT hikers. I have never seen so many hikers together. They seem to have a look to themselves. I guess it's the high quality clothing, Gortex, gaiters and their general demeanor, tranquil as can be imagined, with a "now its over look, but tomorrow is but another day." I continue to be in shock to see so many at the same time and in the same tired condition. A white van leaves as we arrive.

I introduce myself to the group indicating our car will pull out for Los Angeles tomorrow morning and will be available for anyone in need of ride. Furthermore I indicate there may be some stuff in the car, extra food and first aid stuff should someone be short.

While I socialize among the group, Van sets up his evening home in his large stand-up tent about thirty yards from the car and perhaps fifty yards away from the group. Van brings up his large double bed air mattress and fills up his tent with this and related gear. He sets up one of his lounge chairs facing the west.

I set up my site close to Van's area. I mingle some more with the hikers. All appear paired up in small, somewhat cohesive groups of two or four pairs.   There seem to several couples among this group including two Israelis, a couple from the east coast, one of which is hard of hearing and mute, and another couple or so that do not seem married, but simply platonic partners. The women all seemed paired with a man or two. The men are also paired up with one another as there are somewhat more men than women in the group. All appear in their late twenties or thirties, except for a lady that stepped into the van before it pulled off.

The Israeli couple speak a fluent Hebrew when together but were comfortable with English as well. He asked me what impressed with my trip last month to Israel. I told him that several images stayed with me. I was impressed with the various climate and resources, but indeed the greatest resource was that of the people. He was unaware of what was happening in the middle east, that the Israelis successfully pulled out of Lebanon, that the president of Syria, Assad had died following a summit meeting with Clinton a week or so before. Although surprised, he says he wants to forget all that now that he's on the trail.

Improvo, called such because he can put on a good mimic show at night, speaks with his hands. Kadoodle, a sculptress by trade, can communicate well with sign language. Hawkeye, a retired prison guard, wonders around socializing with everybody. Finch and Tweedledee are busy cooking while others are trying to sleep.

It becomes dark. Van and I retire to our areas, chat a bit. I drop off into sleep as he continues talking about his ventures with the tracking device he is building.

Tuesday, June 13, 6:00 AM: Departing Walker Pass, El 5100, Mi 647.2 - 0. 0.

As I rustle about, I wake up Van who responds by quickly getting dressed and getting the gear into the car. Everyone nearby is still inside their bags. We quietly drive off. Van stops at the trail head up the road a few hundred yards. We cross the street to read the monument erected to honor Walker and Fremont who pioneered the trail over the southern flank of the Sierra Nevada, mid century, 1800s.

I wave goodbye as I head up the trail. I look below as he speeds down the highway toward Interstate 14. The sky is clear. It is calm. The temperature requires a long sleeve shirt or sweater. I have with me three and a half liters of water and four days of food supply, the pack now at about 28 pounds.

I soon wonder when the first of the group will pass me along the trail. I soon conclude that it may quite a while as I find myself covering a fair amount of ground in good time as the trail is but only moderately steep and relatively easy to climb despite the length of the climb.

The ascent is rewarding. Views are outstanding from the beginning. Views become more splendid with the gain of elevation. To the immediate south is the dramatic Walker Pass that indistinctly merges with the desert to the immediate east. Soon, I look back over Walker Pass to ranges that I covered, the Scodie Mountains and the burnt out forests topping the ridge to the south. Looking eastward are the expanses of desert is the Naval Base of China Lake, communities of Inyokern and Ridgecrest. To the immediate north lie Mt Jenkins and

Owens Peak, both upward of 8,000 feet, both steeply protruding from the desert floor of Owens Valley to the east.

After much of the ascent appears a commemorative plaque honoring James Jenkins just before the PCT meanders around the east exposure of the peak, named after him. I walk out to a ridge overlooking the desert. I pull out some snacks and give myself a well earned rest. Here, the first of the group, Hawkeye and Tweedle pass me while I am resting. Later, Improvo and Madam Butterfly pass me. Then, not far behind, comes the Israelis.

Noon is approaching as I traverse the saddle between Jenkins and Owens Peak. The view is overlooking the lower Owens Valley to the east is awesome as is the desert environs. To the immediate west are the steep slopes to the summit of Jenkins Peak. The conditions become more xeric, the terrain now dominated by rocks and talus and small clumps of chaparral, mostly sage and more occasional dried out brittle brush, unrecognizable small plants and dried out grasses.

Not soon enough I reach a shaded gap, Mi. 656.3, where the trail turns westerly into shaded climes on the northern exposure of Mount Jenkins at the 7,020 summit at the saddle between Owens and Jenkins Peaks. Here, I find the group of four that passed me. They are sitting lying and huddling under the shade of a rocky overhang having a rest bit and snacking. We are all surprised despite the altitude how warm it is here. We chat a bit. They inquire if I plan to leave the PCT and scramble up to the top of Mt. Jenkins. I wonder what might have given them the impression I had such energy! They must be kidding. Anyway, it's a way of engaging one in a fun trail conversation.

Foreseeing the lack of water becoming a problem as the heat of mid day approaches, I leave them to continue downhill desiring to put some miles behind me before the next climb. My bandana is already wet and drenched, a familiar, but ominous sign that I am releasing more water than I can drink.

This immediate downhill portion is to the northwest, now into less exposed terrain. In contrast to the climb, the descent serves to ease the body sensation of heat . It is indeed relaxing as less energy is needed and less sweating occurs to cover distance. At the same time I have the comfortable cooling effect of a wet shirt and bandana resulting from the arduous climb. I nevertheless drink water as I can and must.

Now the flora is mixed. There is some chaparral and some conifers, more grasses and small plants as the soil now is relatively moist. A little bit of small animal activity is now noted, their movement is given away by the rustling sounds of the movement of squirrels and small birds disturbed by my movement. No animal tracks are noted. And no water.

Now it is three or four miles to Joshua Springs. I will make up my mind as to whether to make a water detour to Joshua Springs or continue on looking for water at the Needle Creek area, three or four miles further along on an up and down exposed portion of trail.

The trail too soon leaves the northern flanks of Mt Jenkins, becoming exposed again, but in a different way. The trail drops in elevation. The view now is to the southwest overlooking a basin and valley connected to Lake Isabella. It seems as if the heat is rising from the oppressive looking basin below.

I soon come upon the spur to Joshua Springs. Though a sign says a quarter of a mile, I see that it is downhill and goes through more exposed areas. I recall the trying experience at Willow Springs. With three or four miles to go and a liter of water, I conclude that I'll probably be better off going direct to the Needle Creek area where there is "supposed" to be water.

The day gets hotter as it approaches mid afternoon. The altitude drops. The altitude is now about 5,500 feet. The shade is scant. I find a shady place and set myself down to rest in the shade of a large Joshua tree, the only shade producer in the area and reluctantly decide to wait out the heat of day. I am reminded of the rough condition last week while climbing through to Walker Pass. Soon, the Israelis pass by. They offer that they also think there is water at Needle Creek. After a while I cool off a bit. I continue on. Now it is uphill over a knoll. It is slow going now and the trail covers a very exposed area. I soon become tired. It is so hot! I soon see another shady spot where I will have another rest in the shade. I continue this go and stop maneuver and take advantage of whatever coolness comes along. I am now assuming the temperatures to be in and around the mid nineties without signs yet of the afternoon cooling that I had supposed would occur at this altitude.

Looking at the nearby terrain I see how it is that the area is catching the rising hot air from the desert not far below. The trail now has dropped in altitude to only about a 1,000 feet above the desert floor alongside Lake Isabella. I recall weather forecasts of temperatures in the area to be in the mid-nineties. I had not anticipated that the high temperatures would reach this mountainous sector.

7:00 PM: At Needle Creek, Mi. 661.5, El. 5160 - 0.0

Not soon enough the trail picks up the contours leading to the many source branches of Needle Creek. Looking down below, I see the trail merging into a canyon that seems as though it could hold some cool, flowing water. The trail, however, parallels the canyon and seems reluctant to drop into it. Instead the trail continues to climb as does the canyon. The chaparral is getting thicker as the trail now seeks a northern exposure of a small ridge. Not far ahead, I see the trail meandering down to cross a streambed with cottonwoods, willows and various green plants. The area is dry. No sign of moisture even below the surface. Another streambed is crossed. It is also dry. Then, minutes later, the trail enters into a very dark area and what appears now to be the main canyon. A streambed is but a few yards below.

I immediately sense the dampness of the area. I sell the moisture. Then believe I hear the water. I search around and indeed find a streamlet with enough water flowing to readily fill up my empty bottles with clear water. At first, I don't care about the bugs and mosquitoes. But as I settle down, I realize they are all about me. I cover myself up, put on a head net and anxiously await the allotted time for the iodine pills to sanitize the potential cysts of giardia which I suspect to exist in this kind of water so near the cow dung that permeates the area near the stream.

As I settle down and make an evening out of it all, along comes Hawkeye and Tweedle. I guide them to the water source. Then along comes Kadoodle and her partner. It turns out she helps me set up my bivvy bag. They move along searching for an upper more hospitable place to stay and opt to fetch water further up another branch of Needle Creek. They stopped over at Joshua Springs where they filled up a few hours ago. They said it was hot and the sptring was in awful condition. I learn that two trekkers were so overcome by the heat and lousy conditions there that they were hallucinating.

Soon another two hikers, Mark and Matt drop in and settle for the night. It is now dark but the moon has yet to arise. Now, it is no help. Last night, the full moon was up at dusk. I am tired, and cannot carry on much of a conversation for very long.

Mark cries out!, "Do you hear that. Someone must be there!"

"Yeah," Matt concurs.

I think I hear sounds away in the dark. But I'm just too tired and sleepy to care at the moment. Soon, I hear Mark explaining, "It's a cow!"

Again, I am too tired to make supper. I take in some more liquids, I soon fall into a blissful sleep, but to be awoken a few times to take leaks after consuming so much recent water.

Wednesday, June 14, 6:00 AM: Departing Needle Creek, El 5160, Mi. 663.7 - 0.0

I quickly arise from the sack to avoid the insects that are attracted to the area. I delay breakfast for later and immediately prepare to leave. Mark and Matt are awake, but in their sacks. I say so long and tell them I am looking forward to them passing me on the uphill.

Perhaps it is the time of day, but the trail seems much more pleasant. Now, filled up with water, I quickly leave the moist area and get back into the exposed mountain side. I soon pass the Israelis, still in their tent and Katdoodle who is meandering and conversing with them as they prepare to get up. The trail begins its earnest climb to the first saddle. The trail switch backs several times across various branches of needle creek, several flowing with water. At the moment there does not seem to be a need for me to fill up as I made sure I was well hydrated before leaving camp and filled up with water.

The trail continues to climb to about 7000 feet to a gap revealing the heights to the north. Here, there are views of jagged Spanish Needle, Lamont point, Lamont Peak, and several others at about 7000 to 8000 feet within several miles. I arrive at the Sierra crest and reach a dramatic overlook of the desert to the east. I settle down here on a rock perched high on a ledge where I survey a good portion of the Mojave Desert. What I see below must be well over one hundred degrees. Here, it is probably in the high eighties or low nineties, but with a cool breeze that has a great cooling effect when wearing drenched clothing. I find some shade and have a leisurely lunch while I relax and attempt a call home. I do get through to Hannah. Hannah confirms that Jon expects to arrive at Kennedy Meadows Sunday, early evening.

The trail from this point heads down to Chimney Creek Campground where there should be water. It is, however, about eight miles away. I take stock of my water, find it on the low side and decide to move on while I still have it.

The trail immediately takes the northeastern side of the hill now, becoming more wooded, thereby cooler with more shaded opportunities. Yet, it remains hot. Sweat continues to pour out at a faster rate than input of water. Pondering this predicament, I move on downhill a bit faster taking advantage of the possibility of putting more milage on with less energy and sweat.

Suddenly, a day hiker appears coming uphill in the opposite direction. He tells me he is camping out at the campground and hopes to make it to Needle Peak and back before dark. He asks about short cuts and I advise him there does not seem to be any and the area looks pretty inhospitable for overland walking. He assures me there is ample water at the campground.

Soon, the trail begins to level off and turns northerly and reaches a broad saddle before continuing down again. Here, I come across a back packer not seen with the larger group, Scott Cannery, who says he has been on the trail before. He speeds up his pace a bit. I see him wandering off trail to a shady area.

5:00 PM: Chimney Creek Campground at Canebrake Road, El 5555, Mi. 676.1- 0.0

The trail passes a dry streambed and undulates up and down towards Canebrake Road and the campground. Not soon enough the trail reaches Chimney Creek with its flowing water. Just as I am about to jump in, I look up and see on the road, the white van that I saw at Walker Pass Campground. I start to walk up to the road and to the campground. Out steps a tall white haired man from the truck. He dramatically says, "I'm Paul. Head up the road a piece. There we'll have barbecued salmon. There is ice cold watermelon, grapes, as much beer and soft drinks as you can drink and all kinds of goodies to go along with it! Come on up. It's just a piece up the road."

I am so exhausted, dehydrated and in a state of disbelief that I head up the road, stop in the first shady spot and there try to digest what is happening.

Paul sees me hesitating, calls out for me to wait. He drives by and picks me up! We drive up a hundred yards or so to the campsite which now houses some of the same group that I had met at Walker Pass a couple nights ago. Arriving into the campground, I hear everyone cheering on my arrival. I wave my fist in the air in acknowledgment as I get out of the car and head for the water barrel. This scenario reoccurs as several trekkers arrive in Paul's van. All appear exhausted and dehydrated in various degrees. All are also in some form of disbelief of what is happening around them!

All of us recover in a matter of an hour or so and settle to an evening of pleasantries over a case or two of cold soft drinks and beer. What a blast! In comes Scott. In comes Lara. In comes Applejohn. Finally, in comes Lorraine, Paul's new wife of one year.

The reason for the angel-like activity is that Paul is providing stop over service, not just for his new wife, but for the entire group of about sixteen people that are accompanying her on her trek from the Mexican border. It turns out that Lorraine is an employee of the Pacific Crest Trail Association and has decided to put on some milage this year. It was his van that I saw depart from Walker Pass the other night.

The evening culminates in a pot luck dinner of several courses, various kinds of dishes made from dehydrated food, pasta, soups, rice and beans, all organized by Lorraine. None of our productions come close to the treat of the barbecued salmon made by Paul and the cold watermelon he kept on ice. All this is followed by more ice cold drinks. The stories continue, unabated. All seem plausible. The highlight of the evening is the narration of "The Ultimate High," a piece of poetry given by heart, by Hawkeye, a lengthy poem of someone traveling about seeking counsel on how to obtain the ultimate high. His rendition was memorable. How he managed to recall the whole thing was a surprise to all of us, including himself.

June 15, Thursday, 7:00 AM: Departing Chimney Creek Campground, Mi. 676.1 El. 5555 0 0.0

Some hikers left last night taking advantage of the full moonlit warm evening and a few had left earlier this morning. Most had taken up Paul's offer to drive a good proportion of their gear to Kennedy Meadows, thus permitting the opportunity to "slack pack" from here to Kennedy Meadows. Applejohn and Scott opt to ride in to Kennedy Meadows with Paul as they felt they had not recovered well enough from their bout with the heat yesterday to walk off so soon. I am in no hurry to leave. I plan to wait for Jon at Kennedy Meadows. I help Paul to clean and secure the area. Upon doing so, I enthusiastically take up his offer to take with me a few cold, Kosher pickles. Lorraine is preparing to leave and I assume she will soon whiz by me on the trail.

Waving goodbye, I head down the quarter of a mile of dirt road to pick up the PCT. The trail immediately heads up a canyon to parallel above a stream that seems to be flowing downhill towards the campground. Though uphill, the segment is pleasant this time of day, meandering through pleasant flora, leaving the more typical kind of chaparral behind for mixed plants thriving in a high riparian forest.

Up from behind me comes Lorraine at a pretty good clip, slows down and chats a bit, then continues up with her steady fast slack packing gait. Soon, after about two miles from the campsite, I spot

Fox Mill Spring, Mi 678.1, 6580'. I decide I am well loaded and do not bother to stop. Passing abandoned mine sites, I continue the gradual, pleasant and moderate ascent to the summit. Up from behind I hear the clatter of trekking poles. Coming up rapidly are Hawkeye and Tweedle. They really speed along with their poles in full motion. They explain how crappy conditions were at Fox Springs.

Without fanfare, a couple of summits and gaps are attained, each with a grand view of nearby area. The trail seems to level off somewhat at about 8,000' meandering through a very pleasant forest.

Between trees and nearby ridges I see, a mile or so ahead, a carpet of chaparral forming Rockhouse Basin. The northwest perimeter is marked by domed peaks and spires. The Mt. Whitney chain appears again, looming larger. There are but scanty bits of snow near the top. The trail now takes leave of the Chimney Peak Wilderness and enters into the 1994 extension of Dome Land Wilderness.

I find that I keep on passing Hawkeye and Tweedle. They travel fast, but often stop and take advantage of the many scenic spots that occur in greater number.

After passing them, I set myself down at a shaded overview of a deep canyon containing a tributary of the South Fork of the Kern River. The trail continues to drop following the contours of the canyon to lead down a mile or so into dry looking Rockhouse Basin. On its western flank lies the South Fork of the Kern River.

Though my water supply is running out, I hope for water upon reaching the basin where I assume the trail will soon cross this tributary, a mile or so from the Kern River. Eventually, the tributary is found at the point in which the trail reaches the basin. But, alas, there is no water. I pull out my hand spade and dig for it. I find some moistness, but no water. I again notice early signs of dehydration. I also note that I now have only half a liter of water left. The next certain water is now about four or five miles across an exposed hot area, not a pleasant undertaking with but two cups of water left and still thirsty.

As I am taking stock of options, along come Hawkeye and Tweedle. They are similarly low on water, but more energetic than I. Having checked my maps, and having time to think the matter through, I tell them, "I am in no hurry to get to Kennedy as I will have to wait there for my son to arrive." I go on to say, "I believe I saw water in the streambed up trail."

Tweedle says, "Yeah, I thought I did, too."

"I'll opt to follow the stream bed down until I eventually find water. If not, I'll wind up a bit over a mile at the Kern and fill up there and figure out a way to make it back to the PCT."

They are anxious to get to KM, about 11 miles from here. They compare thoughts. They decide they have enough water and in good enough shape to attempt the crossing of the basin to the Kern River, about five miles ahead, then to consider going on to KM. They have been anxious to make their timetable by being at KM on what they consider is "Ray's Day," the day by which to be in KM if one is attempting to reach the Canadian border before the weather prohibits negotiating the trail at more northern latitudes.

We wish one another luck as they trudge through the basin and I head back to the dried out stream. Just after about twenty yards, I find a pool of clear water with trout swimming about, trapped in the pool as it is drying out. It is heavily guarded by swarms of bees, hornets and large flies with yellow wings. I quickly fill up and leave the area before being stung a few times. Not by the bees or hornets, but by those large flies. Their sting goes through the t shirt. Though bothersome for about five or ten minutes, the sting and itching sensation soon subsides.

I consider the trade-off of being nauseated by the iodine taste of the water, which may in turn contribute to more symptoms of dehydration or facing the possibility of having symptoms of giardia in a couple of weeks. I choose the latter. After guzzling down a liter of this fresh cool water, I will carry a couple of liters on my back to accompany me through the basin while I hope to easily reach the banks of the Kern River.

I move on now, after a total rest bit of about half an hour and head through the hot sandy tread through the low chaparral and shadeless area of the Rockhorse Basin. It looks like a dried out meadow. The trail actually follows the eastern perimeter of the basin, crossing a number of dried out stream beds. It is very barren. Glad I filled up, I readily reach the far side of the basin whereupon the trail turns westward heading towards the Kern.

6:00 PM: On the Banks of South Fork of Kern River, Mi. 692.7, El. 5760 - 0.0

What a paradise. The spot I settle on is a swath of smooth clean sand directly on the banks of a smooth flowing part of the river, about twenty feet wide. Despite the richness in flora, there are no insects about here; no moths, bees, hornets nor flies, nothing! Right near the bank are several large smooth rocks, still warm from the sun. The inviting rock is contoured like a lounge chair. It is so easy to rest! I wash myself. I slip down and dunk myself in the water and shortly return to rest on these warm rocks as I try to keep from falling asleep. The reason why there is an absence of insects must be because of the multitude of birds seen siting around. All are quiet as if satisfied with dinner.

I too settle down with a rather large cooked dinner and congratulate myself for making the decision that led me to this wonderful place. The night is uneventful and with the exception of the gentle lapping of the river and occasional rustle from a nearby animal, all is tranquil.

June 16, Friday, 8:00 AM: Departing the Kern River Campsite, Mi. 692.7, El. 5760

The trail follows stream side for about a mile, then meanders eastward as it climbs away into noticeably warmer climes as the trail straddles some small streams and meadows. Soon, I find myself sweating again, drenched in the heat even though it is now only nine or ten in the morning. Not soon enough, the trail leads nearby some private property and approaches the highway.

I opt to head up the highway where a sign indicates the camp store to be about a mile away uphill. Trudging uphill along the exposed hot roadbed is quite trying but well compensated by the anticipation of purchasing a cold drink at the store, placing a call, bumping into some familiar backpackers and hearing their story on how they made it though the heat.

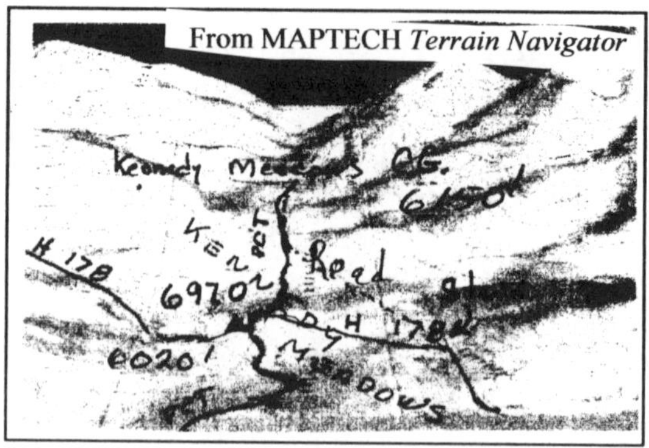

Approaching Kennedy Meadows

Chapter 30

At Kennedy Meadows

The Camp Store....Kennedy Meadows Campground
....Dinner at Irelans, A tribute to Paul....Meadow Ed
...A whiffleball Game...Northbound....

The Camp Store, Kennedy Meadows, Friday, Near Noon, El 6050,
Mi. 697.0 + 0.7

It is noon as I approach the Kennedy Meadows General Store. I see from afar the porch of the store is full of backpackers. Among them are Kadoodle, Madam Butterfly and Improvo, the Two Israelis, Richard and Heather from England, Finch and Lara, all lounging about on chairs and benches on the covered deck. Some have their legs propped up. Some are eating snacks or drinking something. Those not sitting are sorting out the contents of their supply boxes or rummaging through the hiker boxes. The contents of packs are all spread around. All are clearly enjoying conversing with one another as they share their experiences of completing the trek through Southern California. I polish of a cold Squirt as I await my turn to use the radio telephone inside the store.

Everyone is either relaxing or busy at organizing things or cleaning something. Two young ladies are nearby at the outdoor water faucet cleaning out the inside of their packs. I watch how they do it. They hose out the inside, swish around the water, then turn the pack upside down and let the remaining water that hadn't leaked out, flow out. I do the same for mine. My Kelty Cloud doesn't leak.

This is indeed a general store. Though it was the trekkers that caught my attention, there are about thirty more people milling about the store. Most are outdoor sports enthusiasts, campers, many with kids.

Some commercial people drop off a delivery. A few people are in who actually reside in the general area. An occasional car stops by as people are heading out or returning from their own outdoor adventure. A friendly, jovial couple are waiting in anticipation for a hiker to appear. Everyone appears to be in a good mood and caught up in the excitement and accomplishment of the backpackers. Backpackers seem to rule the day.

Later that afternoon, Kadiddle holds out a red T-shirt and asks us to sign our name on it along with the opportunity to contribute a few bucks for Paul's efforts at Chimney Creek Campground.

I find out that the two backpackers found in a state of delirium while at Joshua Springs seem to have recovered. Applejohn and Scott, who were driven in by Paul, are somewhere about, and seem OK. Hawkeye and Tweedle made it in last night about ten O'clock, probably still sleeping in camp.

Afer a couple of soft drinks, I confirm by phone that everything is OK and that Jon is expected to drop in Sunday evening. I come to the conclusion that there is nothing pressing to do but to continue having fun for the next day or so waiting for Jon to arrive.

In comes a back packer. He is wearing a long sleeve shirt and long pants. His beard is longer than mine and is clearly over 70 years of age. It must be Mike. As soon as he enters the porch, I introduce myself. He speaks with a marked English accent. I tell him his friends, who I had just met, are just around the porch. They have a reunion.

Soon, another pair comes traipsing in. Sweat and all. Some cheer as they recognize the pair of young men. The pride exists in everyone.

Friday Afternoon: Kennedy Meadows Campground, El 6150, Mi 699.4 - 0.0

The camp store is three long exposed miles to the U.S. Forest Service Campground in Kennedy Meadows. Rides are regularly offered to all that want a ride to the campground. A family member to one of the backpackers drives me to the area where we find Paul and the group that spent the night together at Chimney Creek Campground.

I hear word that Meadow Ed is in. I must meet him right away. I met him last year on the Devils Slide Trail on the climb from Humber Park, above Idylwild, while unwittingly trekking up into the storm. I immediately recognize him, tall, rotund, a white beard, fair complected with a broad smile that permeates his being. This is the Trekker angel I heard so much about last year. He seems to turn up at the most unexpected places. I am most anxious to hear his stories and what prompts the man to do the wonderful things he does for hikers along the PCT.

Well, I kind of find out, at least to a point whereupon I am for the moment, satisfied. He has put on a lot of miles on the PCT and continues to hike portions of it, doing so for the last several years. I get to know him, largely by observing him, the best way for me to really know someone. I discover he knows a heck of a lot of people around the area.   He also carries a register of hikers he meets at various points on the PCT, classified by year. He offers them a couple of hiker boxes of food and supplies which they are free to take. He provides rides, first aid supplies, water and a a lot of trail information and intuition about the adjusting to the demands of long distance hiking. He is knowledgeable about the trivia, lore and water holes and details along the PCT. But what is most impressive is that he knows many hikers today and other trail angels and supporters that have been doing the trail for years. At the moment he is planning to walk northbound through to Horseshoe Meadows or Kearsarge Pass..

I stay near his campsite where three radio hams are setting up. I watch them set up their facility. One fellow, by the name of Gordy, "Blister foot," as he is called, takes out a large slingshot, puts something into it, takes aim beyond a tree and lets go. In a moment, a line is spent over branches of trees. This line is modified to form an antennae for their transcribing center, set up in the rear of a pick up truck. He later tells me he earned that nickname by being susceptible to having blisters on his feet. He now has it beat. He is planning to walk northbound in a couple of days after his fellow hams pull out to go home, Sunday.

They set up their equipment. In a couple of hours they have a radio station set up and are communicating on various frequencies to people around North America. They're at it all day and all night. One of the threesome is transmitting or listening all the time. They are such fanatics! They keep me up much of the night. I find what they are doing interesting and learn a great deal just by listening and watching what they do.

I share the site with Applejohn. It turns out he is from the northern part of England . He is 65 years old who has started out from Mexico. He also had a coronary bypass. We compare notes on how we are adapting to the demand of the trail. He is one of the fellows that experienced heat exhaustion and/or dehydration symptoms on the way to Chimney Creek Campground who elected to drive in to KM with Paul. His description of what was going on was quite similar to mine, but a little more severe. He seems to be recovering nicely and expects to trek northbound tomorrow after a day's rest. Applejohn speaks with a clarity of diction, like halfway between an Oxford and BBC type of English that characterizes professional people. He is retired from working with computers and software interfaces.

Finch, his younger hiking partner, comes from Michigan, is very laid back, reserved, but knowledgeable about outdoor skills. He also is planning on making it to Manning Park this season. Most everyone hiking is planning on being in Canada by September. With the confidence that comes with putting in 700 miles already, it seems that everyone that wants to do so should make it.

Dinner at Irelan's, 7:00 PM:

That night our immediate hiking group at the campsite is offered a ride to the local restaurant in town, Irelans, down the highway a mile or so east of the camp store. Upon arrival there, we see Paul and the group of 12 or so hikers that appeared at Chimney Creek Campground. We all dine together on the porch on a buffet of bean soup and salad with an entree of broiled teriyaki chicken and potatoes. There is plenty of beer to drink and an ice cream cone for those that so wish one.

Before the beer is finished, Katdoodle, the same person that helped me with the bivvy bag the other night, gets the attention of the group of the "diner-hikers." With some embarrassment, she displays the red shirt and calls up Paul, the trail angel of the moment.

To everyone's delight Paul struggles but succeeds in reading off all of the entries inscribed on his shirt. The leftover funds are given to him as a gift, a token to offset some of his costs. All these parties and dinners no doubt are costing him a fortune. But he obviously is enjoying it all and his mood is contagious.

After dinner and after the ride to the campground, Mark enters our site and wonders if anyone knows the whereabouts of a camera he misplaced. He is upset because it belongs to a friend. The last he remembers seeing it was at the restaurant.

We wrack our brains to figure out who last saw the camera. After a revisit to the restaurant, it turns out he found it some obvious place. Everyone, including myself seems to be misplacing things and calling upon others to help recover the missed items. Nothing, it seems ever gets lost or stolen, just misplaced. A couple of times, someone retrieved a missing item of mine somewhere where it should not be. Richard lost his data book and Hawkeye misplaced his socks. This could be big trouble. I find a *Guidebook* in a box behind the camp store and recover a pair of wool socks lying near the outdoor shower.

In the afternoon a group of friends of the radio hams set up camp nearby. Two are hiking the trail. Another pair have just returned from Kearsarge pass where they climbed up the pass and left a food supply for the other two. We carry on a brief conversation before we all retire. We concur: no snow to speak of between here and Kearsarge Pass.

Saturday, June 18, Kennedy Meadows Campground

The morning is spent mingling in the world of the radio hams met when I arrived at KM. I become more familiar with the three hams and where they are from. Blister foot and the pair of trekkers that came in late yesterday depart to get an early start on the trail.

Several other parties trek off this morning. As our campsite is out of the way of the trail head, we are not aware of their quiet departure. I find that I am spending the entire day at the campground area, going from one site of backpackers to another in this large campground. In previous years backpackers found themselves in one large sector of the campground. It would be more fun we were in the same general area. Those wanting exclusion could easily arrange the opportunity.

I get to know more about Meadow Ed. He recalls our meeting last year while he was going down the Devil's Slide Trail to get out of the snow and when he met me going up, into the snow. He says he couldn't figure out why I would want to do such a thing. We recall the experience. What could I say? I explained how it turned out for me. He explains how it was also a challenge for the others to get through during that stormy period above Idylwild.

Sunday, June 19, Mid-day: The Kennedy Meadows Whiffleball-Baseball Game

A number of hikers continue to leave the area. A couple of backpackers trek in from the north. They explain they came south from Kearsarge Pass. They indicate there was no snow along the trail..

Sometime in the early afternoon upon returning from the camp store, getting a great outdoor shower, I find myself watching a zany form of a baseball game, whiffleball-baseball. I join in this zany impromptu game, played with a stupid plastic bat and lightweight plastic unique ball, that when hit barely has any power to it. But if hit expertly, can nevertheless travel a good distance. If hit with the ball, or even with the bat, I suppose, it does not hurt. Such is the advantage to the pitcher. Not only is the advantage to the pitcher, but he/she can easily get the ball to curve unpredictably right at the plate, or to send one to the plate that will permit the person to whoop one away.

Most of the initial group is out playing, Matt, Mark, Lara, Finch, and David. I join them in the out field, hoping no balls get that far. They occasional do. If so, I retrieve it from the gully behind. One out is all that the batter is allowed and there is no need to run to any of the bases.

When a person scores a hit, it is counted as a run. There are no balls. But three strikes and you're out. Each time someone strikes out or flies out, we rotate. It is a lot of fun to see one another in a situation other than carrying a pack.

Soon, Richard and Heather, both psychologists, can't stand by merely watching. They join in the game with us. Being from England, they know nothing about baseball, just cricket. They soon figure that "out" is not the opposite as "in" and "strike" refers to a bat and not to a work attitude. They do extraordinary well. This game, with no time out for beer, goes on for hours. Soon, though, it is time to prepare for supper and the game slowly comes to an end, with no one in particular, the winner. This is the first time in all my life, I've ever played a game not caring about who won.

That night the group sets out to party at the other restaurant down the road. I elect to stay in the campground and while away the evening at the campsite with Meadow Ed

That afternoon, I meet Willy, who has come up from Mexico taking still pictures along the way. He is staying in the immediate area adjacent to where Meadow Ed has set up. As our area has been vacated by the hams, I move my gear up to their spot. We soon plan dinner together. Ed will provide the chicken and potatoes he had stored in a friend's large recreation vehicle, not far away. Ed arranges for the owner to nuke the potatoes while Willy prepares the chicken and I prepare the salad. We hope that Jon will appear in time. If not, too bad for Jon. I join in with Ed to share the beer we stored up. With our help, Willy sets up the fire pit and prepares our entree, barbecued chicken, for the feast.

Willy barbecues several pieces of chicken carefully dripping onto the pieces a prepared teriyaki sauce. The smaller pieces of chicken, the legs and small wings are fried in a previously prepared bath of oil, onions and my dehydrated garlic. All this takes place while Ed and I look on. One of the pans has teriyaki, the other has the garlic sauce. The components of the meal are all ready at the same time. We dig into it. I find out later that Ed was a cook and chef at some prestigious resorts. No wonder it was so good!

Jon appears just as we finish off the last remnants. As I thought, he stopped over at Colonel Sanders and polished off some chicken on his own. So, justice prevails!

We did share some remaining beer and pleasantries sitting around the table while it got dark. We are all anxious to turn in, and did so at the late hour of ten O'clock with the almost-full moon on top of us.

Monday, June 19, 7:00 AM: Northbound.

The morning is spent getting our gear together for the trek northbound. Meadow Ed has re-arranged for a friend to await his arrival at Onion Valley as he also plans to continue northbound on the PCT and trek down from Kearsarge Pass.

Jon and I fill up our backpacks. We drive to the trail head at the north end of the campground. We disembark, secure the jeep and head for the register where we enter our names and trek on to the higher Sierra Nevada.

SUPPLEMENTS

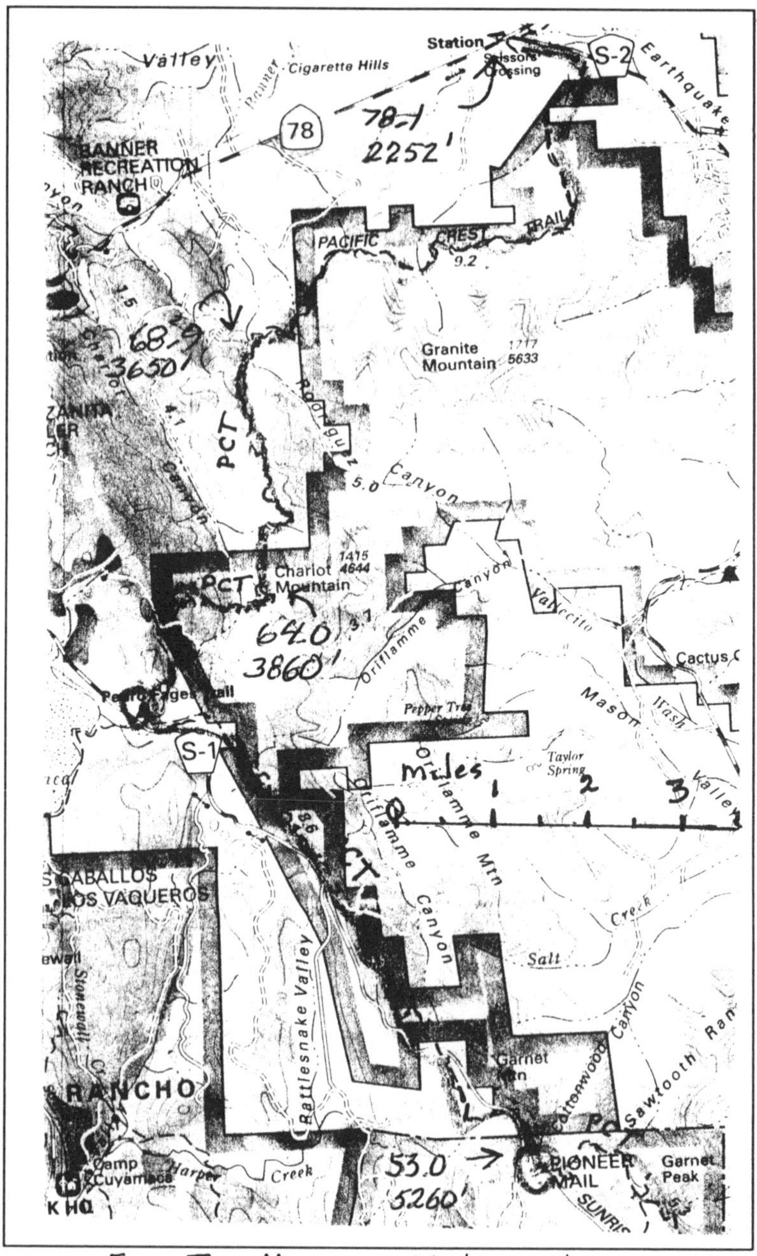

From Tom Harrison Photography

Pioneer Mail Picnic Area to Scissors Junction
53.0 - 78.1 (25.1 miles)

SUPPLEMENT A

Campo to Lake Morena Revisited
Pioneer Mail Picnic Area to Scissors Junction

Lake Morena Campground....Campo....Hauser Creek....
The 2001 PCT Kick Off at Lake Morena....Mount
Laguna...Pioneer Mail Picnic Area....Chariot Canyon
....San Felipe Creek....Julian....Scissors Junction
....Warner Springs....Home of John Angle near Kamp Anza.

The leg from Pioneer Mail Picnic Area to Scissors Junction was missed in 1999, being not prepared for the snow. The leg was finally completed following the Pacific Crest Trail Kickoff at Lake Morena in 2001. Being there, I could not resist re-doing the nearby leg from Campo to Lake Morena.

April 24, 2001, Wednesday, 4:00 PM: Lake Morena Campground, El 3065, Mi 20.2 - 0.0

"Meadow" Ed Faubert and I arrive at Lake Morena to participate in the upcoming 3rd annual Pacific Crest Trail Kick-Off put on by people from ALDA West and PCTA. It is not clear what will occur nor how it will work out. But we expect a lot of fun as we know we will renew trail acquaintances.

Meadow Ed, as he had been doing for several years, will be pitching in by way of providing water drops and information to trekkers starting on their northbound trek. My contribution will be providing shuttles for trekkers wishing rides to various nearby trail heads and answering questions about the southern California portion. Trail angels, family and well wishers are expected. We soon agree to walk a leg he had missed, Campo to Lake Morena.

April 26, Thursday 9:00 AM: Campo 1.5 - 0.0

Ed and I are dropped off by "Mad Monte" Dodge on his way to pick up some trekkers from Lindberg Airport in San Diego. Perhaps his nickname is related to his great inventions, one being a stove made from Coke or beer cans, a type I now use.

As soon as we step on the tread, Ed is identifying plants. I try to to remember their names and all the details. We identify about thirty wild flowers in the first mile or so. As the exposure changes, so does the flora, by quality and kind. We observe three different species of lupine, two species of yucca , differences in forget-me-nots, and I learn to differentiate chamise from ribbonwood. At the first creek, mile 3.9, below the more obvious cottonwoods, sorrel, willows and baccharis, we see and gobble up celery, miners lettuce, water cress and pepper, all within three feet of one another right where the trail crosses the creek.

After this restful, refreshing and educative stop, we start the climb up and around the southeastern exposures. The flora reflects the more xeric conditions. The view of the ranches below, the basins to the southeast and the border wall compensate for the diminution of rich plant life. As the trail turns west and goes over the first gap to traverse the plateau at about El. 3,400 feet at mile 9.0, the trail goes through a rich glade of chamise. There is nothing else in view but a few scrub oaks and manzanita, all of the same height. The trail then turns north out of this glade heading for Hauser Canyon.

Meanwhile we are traveling slowly. It is past 2 PM. It is getting hot now with little shade. We have become low on water and are looking forward to reaching the depths of the canyon where we were told the creek is bubbling. It is now 4:00 PM when we look over the lip and see the depths below. My gallon of water supply has dwindled down to about a pint as we head down the final stretch. Ed seems to be drinking less and has a liter or so. As we approach the dirt road he offers me some water. At the same time we see a couple of bottles of water laying on the trail. We take one. We share it and quickly polish it off. We wonder who we can thank.! More trail magic.

The trail follows the easterly descending road to where the trail suddenly picks up dropping us north (El 2810, Mi 15.0) through a thicket of now familiar wild flowers and rich chaparral to reach the riparian grassy area below.

5:00 PM: Hauser Creek, El 2320, Mi 15.7 - 0.0

There is no creek to cross. There is no sound. It is almost dry. No one is to be seen. No movement. No animals. There are no signs of recent travelers. There are but two puddles, one still and the other has some running water, an inch deep and three inches across. No other water is in immediate sight. We do not hesitate to scoop up as much we can to filter the water later with Ed's suction tube device. After we're done, there is only a stream of one inch. We readily drink what's left of Ed's leftover water and it is soon gone while we filter several liters. Ed scarfs down some cold snacks. I cook up the same meal I had two years ago at the same spot: green pea soup with dehydrated beans and beef jerky. Ed sets up his campsite in a seemingly routine manner. We name all the plants in sight, crawl in our sacks and fall asleep as dusk comes to an end.

April 27, Friday, 6:00 AM: Hauser Creek - 0.0

After coffee, we trek up the hill identifying one plant after another. We make it to the top of the first gap in just over an hour, one third of the time that was required for me two years ago! Just after crossing the final summit, El 3495, Mi 18.2, we find a couple of day hikers resting in the shade overlooking the views. Ed goes on ahead while I chat with the hikers. They each own a ranch nearby. She is cutting up a yucca. She cuts out the green skin, revealing a six inch white solid pulp. She cuts them into lengthy quarters and offers them to me. He explains that it tastes good, but to expect a dry kind of sore throat about thirty minutes after eating it. This effect should pass shortly. I polish off a quarter. Delicious. It has a texture and moisture of sugar cane, approaching the sweetness. They explain that they cut it some more, like French fries, heat it till a boil, then throw out the water and boil it again. Then it can be eaten as is, or prepared in various ways. They also eat the flowers. I was surprised to discover that the flowers taste quite well picked as is. They explain that it goes well fried in eggs.

10:00 AM: A friendly meeting with a large rattlesnake

Soon after catching up with Ed, I find myself in the lead, about ten steps in front. As I am telling him about my experiences with the two ranchers, and as I am looking back to explain a point or two, he suddenly stops and for the first time, yells out, "STOP."

I freeze.

He calls out, "Look out, a snake!"

Instantly, I see it. Instantly I am aware of the characteristic rattling sound. Instantly, I catch my breath. "Yikes, it's a monster!" It is positioned perpendicular to the trail, halfway across, with its rear several feet out of sight. The diameter of its body must be three inches or more. It is shaking, trembling and raising its head facing me eye to eye. In a split second, I turn around and accelerate up trail looking back. I run right into big Meadow Ed. I can't get by. He just stands there enjoying the excitement. I squeeze by. I am amazed. He's just standing there. Ed says, "It's a rattler."

"Yeah, tell me! Listen to that rattle."

"It's heading back."

"Yeah, the monster is going backwards!"

"It sure was a big one."

"Ed says, ha! Hiding behind me. I know your style. Just wait til I tell everybody."

"What can I say! I was lucky to get around you. You almost blocked the trail!"

We were laughing the whole way to Lake Morena..

12:00 Noon Friday April 28 through Sunday, April 29: The Kick Off

Arriving at Lake Morena, we change over to serve as trail angels, a task that Ed is known for. Getting some trail behind us helps our morale. Now, we are ready to help. From that time on through Monday, Ed is ready to provide pictures, log books, sketches and some original poetry about matters at hand to anyone so inclined to look or listen. And they do. He offers some group sessions on where water may be found for the next two or three hundred miles. Donna

Meadow Ed at Lake Morena

Saufley continues on for the next hundred miles or so. Mad Monte and Bob Thompson offer great "workshops" in making stoves out of soft drink cans, an improvement beyond that of Roy Robinson's innovation, both certainly better than my Coke stove that runs on 150 proof rum. All that watch are in a trance as they transform a beer can into an efficient stove with denatured alcohol as fuel. I pitch in by shuttling trekkers to the border or some nearby trail head, down or up trail. Lorraine and Paul Downer provide a table full of PCTA merchandise, books, PCTA cups and memorabilia for review and sale. A hundred trekkers are milling about. Trail angels have coolers filled with soft drinks and snacks for the taking. Dinners and breakfasts are catered by the PCTA, and ALDHA-west. Ron Moaks, PCT 1997 and editor of the PCTA *Communicator,* is interviewing Brian Robinson, Roy's son, who is in the midst of trekking the AT, CDT and now the PCT this calender year, 2001. Roy, who has done the AT and much of the PCT, watches with pride.

Saturday night is highlighted by a novel gear contest. Led by Greg Hummel and Al Reynolds, a contest of "no rules" of who can exhibit and explain the most novel piece of self inventive equipment.

PCTA *Communicator*

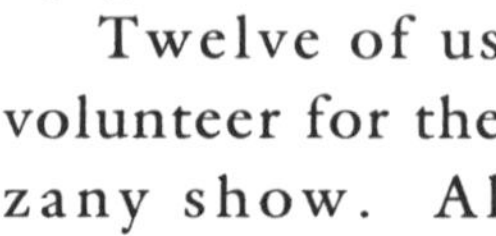

We learn of Roy Robinson's latest stove

Twelve of us volunteer for the zany show. Al presents a self-designed pack that sets on the hip with no weight on the shoulders. Ann presents a novel stove stand. Sheila presents a sun resistant crazy hat. Roy Robinson presents a shelter half that hangs on tent poles. Lightning Bolt, with his exaggerated southern accent, presents his super lightweight cookware set. I present my stretchable band that measures distance on a topographic map, irregardless of latitudinal changes. We all win prizes. My category is for the "lightest, but most useless!" My prize is a stove made by Monte from a Coke can. While we're engaged in all this fun, Jason Kramer agrees to pick Ed and I up at Scissors Junction, Wednesday evening at six thirty to take us to our car at Mount Laguna. Meadow Ed still will do this leg with me, a third time for him.

April 29, Sunday, 4 PM: Mt. Laguna P.O. and Resort, El 5980, Mi 42.9 - 0.0

Ed and I drive and arrive at the resort. Several trekkers are sitting outside meandering about as we pull in. They seem to be deliberating on where to stay overnight until they can get to their supply boxes when the post office opens Monday at 8:00 AM.

I go inside and engage the proprietor who permits me to park the car in their area for the next two days. In the meantime, I bring up the topic of the illegal emigres passing by. I am told that the Coyote who was associated with the eight people that died on their northbound trek in 1999 was caught and indicted for second degree murder.

Meadow and I pick up two trekkers, Ben from Vermont and Ray, from Mariposa, California who will join us for supper at our campground site. We find a delightful spot adjoining a large meadow and watch for the animal life as we barbecue our frankfurters. We are impressed with Ray's knowledge of the Sierra.

April 30, Monday, 8:00 AM: Pioneer Mail Picnic Area, El 5260, Mi 53.0 - 0.0

We leave Mt. Laguna Campground at 7:00 AM and drop off water at a couple of strategic spots for Ray and Ben. Ben drops us off at the trail head at Pioneer Picnic Mail and drives the van to the resort for us to pick up.

At Pioneer Mail, the trail leaves the desert divide and the pine forest for good as it heads generally northeast around Garnet Mountain overlooking Oriflamme Canyon and Oriflamme Mountain beyond. The trail drops in altitude after the first short climb. After nine miles of rather pleasant walking, we reach Mason Valley Truck Road where there is supposed to be a cistern of water. Alas, it is empty. No water in the general area. We are not concerned about ourselves, but with others who may be counting on water being here. Ed leaves a note explaining that we could not find any water in the area and where water may be found off trail.

3:00 PM: Chariot Canyon, El 3860, Mi 64.0 - 0.0

Upon reaching Chariot Canyon we spot a water cache of five gallons awaiting us on the trail. Probably courtesy of Charlie, who helps with trail maintenance and water drops. There is sufficient shade for a number of sites; we choose the most attractive, a site with tall oaks and willows and cut off logs suitable for sitting. The immediate area is full of miners lettuce, which Ed and I devour. Nearby is baccharus, willow, scrub oak, manzanita, prickly pear, grasses, and several beautiful wild flowers that get our attention but cannot identify, a small clump of tiny flowers, about the size of forget-me-nots mixed in shades of yellow and orange, like tiny mallows. A trekker tellsus he spotted water upstream about 200 yards. We relax, casually set up our site and chat with arriving and passing fellow trekkers met back at the Lake Morena Kick Off.   In comes Ann, from the east coast. In comes Hariott from Vancouver. In comes Brian Robinson. In comes Ben. Others pass

Jack, Ed, Brian and Bill at Chariot Canyon

through as I head upstream to search for water. Harriot efficiently sets up her tent, then cooks with cold water. She is a part-time "angel" often helping trekkers as they arrive in Canada. Her accent is pleasantly Germanic and responds with humor when I try to practice my German. We tend to group up, within hearing distance, somewhat mindful that there may be illegal immigrants in the area. Temperatures are pleasant as we all call it an evening at dusk..

May 1, Tuesday, 7:00 AM: Departing Chariot Canyon, El 3860, Mi 64.0 - 0.0

Harriot is up and out, as are Ann and a few others that may have stayed overnight as we crawl out of our sacks. Despite the upcoming heated descent, Ed and I are in no hurry as we are looking forward to being picked up at Scissors Junction the following evening.   As we wander about, we automatically put our stuff together and find that we are nevertheless anxious to get moving. Soon, we fill up on water and trek up the road a few hundred yards to begin the short transverse climb over the ridge to reach Rodriguez Canyon (El 3650, Mi 68.9).

As we round the bend, we see ahead a group of trekkers, crowded, relaxing in the shade of the only scrub oak around. Here, are Nick, Swiss Miss and her partner, and couple more trekkers whose names I've missed. Here, those wandering about are looking for water in the cistern just above the trail crossing of the dried creek, but finds it secured. Still loaded with three liters of water and finding but little shade, I head out before the others. As the trail descends and rounds xeric Granite Mountain, cholla and prickly pear appear more frequently. Soon there is agava and an absence of many of the wild flowers seen in the moister areas above. Yet, in shaded and more protective areas, can be seen a number of flowering plants seen more frequently in cooler climes.

Enough shade for one person
Peter Haskell

Mostly descending, but with ups and downs, the heat soon becomes oppressive. Wherever there is a bit of shade can be found trekkers. Below a scrub oak or chamise. I pass Nick. He passes me. Down comes the large group that pass me. I pass them later. Down comes Ann and Monte. I meet up with them later. We all sit under an overhanging rock formation, a recluse overlooking one of the most xeric areas in southern California, dry earthquake Valley and the barren San Felipe Hills which these trekkers will encounter as I did in early April, 1999, either this evening or after a rest bit in Julian. Down trail a couple of miles we can see our destination for the afternoon, Scissors Junction where a deserved rest bit awaits all of us under the bridge where we expect a stream to be flowing. Then, down comes Meadow

Ed. I wait for Ed to cool down. As Monte leaves, he claims it is twenty degrees warmer outside the cool protection of this rock cavern. Ed and I saunter down the hill, steeply at first. The trail levels off somewhat as the trail takes us on a slow, almost straight line to the paved road where we will parallel it for another mile before coming to the streambed and bridge. Along this final stretch, the trail narrows as a plant we cannot identify drives us mad as its branches stick out and scratch exposed limbs of our bodies. No one gets scratched twice!

3:30 PM: San Felipe Creek, El 2252, Mi 77.9 - 0.0

As we approach the road, we see a cache of water. Having shared my water with others along the descent, I arrive with only a half liter left. Ed and I then visit with the group of ten or so trekkers sitting in various places including a bizarre shaded area adjoining dirty San Felipe Creek under the highway overpass. I discover the cellular phone works. I make contact with Sandy Kramer who says she will contact Jason who can pick us up from Ramona in a couple of hours. I offer Wayne a ride to Ontario Airport and Harriot a ride to Warner Springs tomorrow morning between eight and nine, assuming Jason picks us up, drives us to our car to enable us to return tomorrow morning to pick them up. Soon, Jason appears. Ed and I drive off in his small crowded vehicle. He kindly drops us off at the Mt. Laguna Lodge. We pick up the van. We spend the night at Mount Laguna Campground.

Waiting for the day to cool down
" Meadow Ed" Faubert

May 2, Julian , 7:30 AM - 0.0

Ed and I throw our gear in the van, pay our fee of $14.00 and head out for Julian for a well deserved breakfast. We find the city deserted. As we drive around, we find the first place that opens, a small specialty café across from the old local two room jail house that Hannah and I visited a few years ago. After a wonderful breakfast sandwich, less the meat which I pass on to Ed, we depart looking forward to arriving at Scisssors Crossing on time.

8:30 AM: Scissors Junction, El 2252, Mi 77.9 - 0.0

We pick up Harriot and Wayne as planned. Two trail angels from San Diego have dropped off about twenty gallons more of water. They noted that 32 gallons of water were consumed in the last two days. I help them unload and load up the empty containers in their car. Their motive: compassion. I recall the lady serving salad at the dinner line Saturday night at the Kick Off. I learn that she made the delicious salads

Jim, Ann, Hal, Harriot and Wayne

herself. I find this out as they leave. I wave them down. They stop. I explain, "You guys deserve a thank you from someone."   They acknowledge the recognition and laugh as they start their drive home.

9:00 AM: Warner Springs: post office, gas station and store, El 3040, Mi 110.6 - 0.0.

As we pull into the area, we see Art walking towards the post office. I offer him a ride. We pull in to fill up with fuel. There is Grizzly, Brian and the "honeymooners," a couple that had been recently married and spending their recent married life together on the trail. Harriot and Wayne join the scene. Ed packs up Ben's parka in a box and I bring it to the post office for Ben to pick up tomorrow. We soon pull out and drive to Anza where Ed will spend a few days at the home of Paul Miller, manager of Kamp Anza, a private campground and recreation vehicle site offering a rest for PCT trekkers.

11:00 AM: Home of Paul Miller near Kamp Anza - 0.0

Paul and his wife live on small acreage site in Anza Valley facing the Santa Rosa Mountains, a couple miles or so off from the PCT. Paul shows me his cultivated rose garden with numerous varieties. On each plant is a metal plate identifying the plant, each with a name of one of his "favorite" trekkers that had passed through. Here, I find plates inscribed with Swiss Miss, Mad Monte, Meadow Ed and several others who I had met on the trail during this year and the last two. He senses I am a friend to Meadow Ed and others as they have trekked northward. He becomes more friendly and invites me to stay or return. It is hard to leave as I review his log book and entries made by trekkers over the last few years that have dropped in. He tells me he plans to redevelop the area and make it more hospitable next year. Ed plans to complete a section over the northern portion of the San Jacinto Mountains next week. I take his supply boxes with me and wonder when our paths will cross again. Wayne and I drive off, leaving Meadow Ed with John. The conversation continues non-stop with Wayne as we drive to find a hotel near the airport. I drop him off at the Hilton, where he plans to shower, bathe and pamper himself a while before heading to the east coast. I drive home, looking forward to seeing Hannah and relishing the time to reflect on all that happened this last week.

SUPPLEMENT B
TRIP SUMMARY

The table provides a summary of when I passed through various areas, the distance traveled, and companions along the way.

Two legs were "leapfrogged," and made up later. The first was the loop around Baldwin Lake near Big Bear and the other was the leg between Summit Valley and Cajon Pass. The legs are included in their geographical sequence with dates noted.

A number of area along the way of the PCT were circumnavigated by foot. They required, for one reason or another, to go off the trail to return to it later. For this reason, the distance walked varies from the PCT milage.

Areas skipped in terms of continuity without "making it up" as of this date, include (1) a stretch from north of Sulphur Springs to near Mount Pacifico, four miles, (2) Over Tehachapi Pass, from Willow Springs Road to Cameron Overpass, about seven miles, and (3) from the head of Pine Canyon to Jawbone Canyon Road, about twenty four miles -- a total of thirty five miles.

Location/Destination	Date	PCT Marker	Miles Walked	Comments
Mexican Border	3-11-99	0.0	-	Dropped Off
Hauser Creek	3-12-99	15.7	16.7	Solo
Lake Morena	3-13-99	20.2	5.5	Solo
Boulder Oaks	3-14-99	26.1	5.9	Joel/Solo
Boulder Oaks	3-25-99	26.1	-	Droppped Off
Cibbits Flat	3-25-99	32.0	8.3	Solo
Burnt Rancheria	3-26-99	42.2	10.4	Solo
Mt. Laguna Resort	4-4/8-99	42.9	-	Dropped Off
Sunrise Highway	4-7-99	47.4	4.5	Hannah/Bill/Ron
Pioneer Picnic Area	4-7-99	53.0	5.6	Solo
Pioneer Picnic Area	5-1-01	53.0	-	Meadow Ed
Chariot Canyon	5-1-01	64.0	11.0	Meadow Ed
Scissors Junction	5-2-01	78.1	14.1	Meadow Ed
Scissors Junction	4-27-01	78.1	-	Dropped Offl
San Felipe Hills	4-8-99	87.2	9.1	Ron/Bill
Barrel Springs	4-9-99	101.9	14.7	Ron/Bill
Warner Spr Airpt	4-10-99	110.6	1.7	Ron/Bil/Flight Outl
Warner Springs	4-18--99	112.4	-	Dropped Off
Combs Mountain	4-19-99	130.2	17.8	Solo
Above Anza	4-20-99	147.0	16.8	Solo
Highway 74	4-21-99	153.7	7.7	Solo/Picked Uo
Highway 74	4-24-99	153.7	-	Solo/Dropped Off
Cedar Springs	4-24-99	164.4	12.7	Solo
Near Apache Peak	4-25-99	176.0	12.1	Solo
Idylwild	4-26-99	180.2	9.2	Solo/Walked-Idylw
Humber Park	4-28-99	180.2	-	Solo/Dropped Off
Wellman Trail Jcn	4-28-99	182.2	4.5	Solo
Stealth Camp	4-28-99	182.2	1.8	Solo
Humber Park	4-29-99	180.2	5.0	Solo/Ride-Idylwild
Idylwild	4-29-99	180.2	-	Picked up
Idylwild St Park	5-4-99	180.2	-	Dropped Off

Location/Destination	Date	PCT Marker	Miles Walked	Comments
Black Mountain	5-5-99	192.2	12.5	Solo
SanGorgonio Pass	5-6-99	212.0	21.6	Solo/Picked Up
Whitewater	5-13-99	221.1	8.1	Joel/Jon/Dropped
Mission Creek	5-14-99	237.4	16.3	Joel/Jon
Coon Creek CG	5-15-99	248.0	10.7	Joel/Jon
Big Bear City	5-16-99	257.9	15.8	Joe/Picked up
Oaks Camp	12-24-00	257.9	-	Dopped off
Van Dusen Canyon	12-24-00	276.3	18.4	Solo/Drove Off
Van Dusen Canyon	5-25-99	276.3	-	Joel/Dropped Off
Little Bear CG	5-25-99	287.0	10.7	Joel
Nr Deep Crk Bridge	5-26-99	298.0	17.4	Joel/Solo
Mojave Dam	5-27-99	314.2	16.7	Joel
Summit Valley Store	5-28-99	322.9	8.9	Joel/Picked Up
Summit Valley Store	12-03-00	322.9	-	Drove
Silverwood Lake	12-03-00	331.6	12.0	Solo
Cajon Pass	12-04-00	344.7	20.1	Solo
Summit Valley Store	12-04-00	344.7	6.0	Solo/Drove
Cajon Pass	6-02-99	344.7	-	Solo/Dropped Off
Lytle Ridge	6-02-99	359.0	15.3	Solo
Wrightwood	6-3/5-99	365.9	11.9	Solo/Snowed In
Guffy CG	6-11-99	366.8	-	Joel/Drove
Grassy Hollow	6-11/13-99	372.9	6.1	Joel
Above Vincent Gap	6-13-99	376.0	3.1	Joel
Vincent Gap	6-13-99	376.5	0.5	Joel
Islip Saddle	6-13-99	388.1	11.6	Joel/Jon
Cooper Canyon TC	6-14-99	397.2	9.1	Joel
Sulphur Springs CG	6-15-99	406.9	9.7	Joel/Drove
Near Mt Pacifico	7-11-99	408.5	1.6	Joel/Jon/Drove
Top of Mt Pacifico	7-22-99	413.6	-	Dropped Off
Messenger Flats CG	7-23-99	431.0	18.4	Solo
Soledad Canyon Rd	7-24-99	444.1	13.6	Solo/Picked Up

Location/Destination	Date	PCT Marker	Miles Walked	Comments
Soledad Canyon Rd	4-27-00	444.1	-	Dropped Off
Agua Dulce Area	4-27-00	454.9	10.8	Solo
Spunky CG	4-28-00	471.3	20.4	Solo
Lake Elizabeth Rd	4-29-00	485.2	16.9	Solo
Neenach-Jack Fair	4-30-00	516.0	22.0	Solo
Gamble Spring Cany	5-01-00	542.9	29.9	Solo
Willow Spring Rd	5-02-00	555.1	12.7	Solo
Tehachapi	5-03-00	455.1	-	Solo/Hitched
Tehachapi Pass	5-14-00	563.7	-	Jon/Drove
Head of Pine Canyon	5-14/15	575.0	11.3	Jon
Tehachapi Pas	5-15-00	563.7	12.0	Jon/Drove
Jawbone Canyon	5-23/24	598.4	-	Dropped Off
Willow Springs	5-24-00	618.0	22.0	Solo
Bird Spring Pass	5-25-00	627.2	11.2	Solo
Near McIver's Spring	5-26-00	641.0	13.8	Solo
Walker Pass CG	5-26-00	647.2	6.2	Solo/Hitched
Walker Pass CG	6-12/13-00	647.2	-	Dropped Off
Spanish Needle Crk	6-13-00	664.4	17.2	Solo
Chimney Creek CG	6-14-00	676.1	11.7	Solo
S. Fork, Kern River	6-15-00	692.7	16.6	Solo
Kennedy Meadows	6-16-00	699.4	7.7	Solo

TOTALS: 699.4   721.6

SUPPLEMENT C
CHAPARRAL

Chaparral is a term depicting a wide variety of hardy plants that flourish in the deserts and plains throughout western North America. More than 900 plant species have been found in this habitat, of which about 240 are mostly woody evergreen shrub. According to Kircher and Morrison (1998) on any given site there are usually about 20 different shrubs to be seen. Their deep roots help to prevent erosion. Most species regenerate quickly after burning. The community of plants were important centers of food, fiber, timber, medicine and dye.

Trekking through the area reveals how these plants vary because of differences in elevation, exposure, slope, latitude, fire history, and soil. Along the trail in southern California, chaparral is seen on desert plateaus, 2000-4500 feet and on exposed southwestern slopes up through 6000 feet or more. In the highlands, the chaparral growth is typically overtaken by the transitional forests that start at about 4500' in our latitudes. On the protected northeastern slopes that block out the afternoon sun, the chaparral is overtaken by the transition forest often down to 3500'. The higher the ridge, the more the effect.

Qualifying Plants

Brodiaeae, buckwheat, cactus prickly pear, California poppy, chamise, ribbonwood, ceanothus (buckbrush), chia, chickweed, coffeeberry, creosite bush, chinquapin (bush chinquapin), chokeberry, coffeeberry, flannelbrush, forget-me-nots, grasses, groundsel (baccharis), holly-leaved cherry, hyacinth, Joshua trees, juniper, laurel sumac, manzanita, mesquite, monkey flower, Mormon tea, mountain mahogany, mustard, pepper grass, pinyon pine, poison oak, prickly pear, rabbitbrush, sagebrush, scrub oak, squaw currents, toyon, yerba santa, yucca

Plants qualifying as chaparral, such as the above, have small, evergreen, thick, stiff leaves. Many have leaves with waxy outer surfaces. The roots are long, to reach into rocky subsoil for scarce water. They are well suited to survive not only the protracted rainless, hot months, but also to maintain life in areas of low annual rainfall and/or a rapid runoff from flash floods as well adapt to thin poorly developed soils. Their main defense against loss of precious water is a near-dormancy life phase during the hot and dry summer periods. Their leaves and stems do not wilt in the face of heat. Almost all photosynthesis ceases during hot periods, but the stiff evergreen leaves are ready to resume photosynthesis within minutes of a rainfall. It is a wonderful experience, awesome, to trek through such an area that has been long dry immediately after a rainfall. Aiding the situation is the small size of the leaves themselves and often the addition of a waxy coat or hairy insulating cover. Many of these plants are edible, provide a nutritious food and provide a source of water should an emergency occur.

Not only can chaparral thrive with scant water resources, but they also win out by thriving in the face of fire. All of the most widespread species reproduce well in the aftermath of fast moving range fires. Fires actually benefit these species. I noticed this dramatic effect while trekking through the Scodie Mountains, just south of Walker Pass. It was almost as if black spires of burn trees were sticking out of a jungle! Many actually contain flammable volatile oils that promote fires. Before the advent of the white people, wildfires burned the Southern California chaparral every 5 to 8 years! Not only does fire exterminate encroaching species, but it returns valuable nitrogen to the soil, thus promoting growth. Some species, like scrub oak and ceanothus, need fires to weaken their seed coating to allow germination.

SUPPLEMENT D

IDENTIFICATION OF PLANTS

1. Wildflowers and Shrubs   388
2. Grasses   412
3. Deciduous Trees   413
4. Evergreen Trees
        Junipers,   419
        Pines   420
        Firs   424
        Incense-Cedar   425
5. Toxic Plants   426
6. Safe Families   427
7. Where Plants were seen   432

Key for Consumptive Value

Ed   Edible; for emergency
Ck   Edible when cooked
Dr   Has a use when dried (flour, fruit, etc)
Gd   Good Tasting
Nu   Nutritious
Rw   Eaten Raw
Sal   For Salads
Tx   Toxic or poisonous
Rx   Medical use
Wt   Emergency water source
Bev   Into a Beverage

The codes are based on my review and interpretation of works by:
(1) Charlotte Bringle Clarke, *Edible and useful Plants of California*,
1977, (2) Christopher Nyerges, *Guide to Wild Foods and Useful Plants*,

1999, (3) Lee Allen Peterson, *A Field Guide to Edible Wild Plants of Eastern and Central North America,* 1977, (4) Steven Foster and James A Duke, *Medicinal Plants and Herbs of Eastern and Central North America.,* 2nd Ed, 2000, and (5) Gregory Tifford, Edible and Medicinal Plants of the West, 2001.

Note that all plants are subject to disease and external toxicity and that edibility is always seasonal. All should be positively identified before consumed..

1. WILDFLOWERS AND SHRUBS

Agave, Desert Agave, Century Plant, Maguey, *Agave deserti, f. Agavaceae*

First seen along the northwest slopes of Granite Mountain. A commonly cultivated desert plant. Readily identified, 2-3' high, distinctive thick fleshy leaves spreading out from the bottom with stickers on its edges and tips. Ed, Bev, Rx,

Amaranth; Pigweed, Redroot *Amaranthus retrflexus* Amaranth Family *f. Amaranthaceae*

These annual plants occur throughout the U.S. and along cultivated and populated areas along the lower foothills and on people's yards at the lower elevations. The short leaves are glossy green, oval shaped, alternately arranged on the stems, pinnately veined with wavy margins. The flowers are inconspicuous, in bristly dense spikes. When dead, they give the plant an unkempt, weedy appearance. These "weeds" have highly nutritious leaves and tender stems that can be eaten raw in salads or lightly cooked and serve well as a nutritional supplement around the world, especially in third world countries (Tifford, 1997). Nyerges (1999) suggests chopping the greens, add onions, heat, season, and "sit down to a delicious, better-than-spinach meal." Ck, Gd, Nu, Rw, Sal,

Baby Blue Eyes, Waterleaf Family *Hydrophyllaceae*

These pretty blue flowering plants can form a blue carpet, as it did during June on the slopes of Blue Ridge. First seen on Hauser Mountains. <u>A low plant, 4-12", with pale or clear blue, bowl-shaped999 flowers that bloom singly on slender stalks growing near the ends of slender, leaning, branched stems.</u>

Baccharis (See Groundsel-Tree)

Barrel Cactus *Ferocactus acanthodes* Cactus Family *Cactaceae*

This easy to spot, solitary plant is found on the PCT only on the lower slopes of the southern spine of the San Felipe Hills upon leaving scissors Junction. They are native to the deserts of California, southern Nevada, southwestern Arizona, and northern Baja. <u>They are readily recognized as a single columnar, barrel-shaped mass of spines about 1 ½ feet in height here. The flower is yellow or reddish. The fruits are fleshy, yellow and scaly</u>. Rw, Wt, Rx

Bladderpod *Isomeris arborea* Caper Family *Capparaceae*

Found along washes, brush, especially in alkaline soils <u>Not really noticeable unless they have "podded" or have yielded a yellow flower which appears in many short racemes, on a strong-smelling, dense shrub with palmately compound leaves. The fruit pod is 1-2" long, plump, on a long stalk.</u>

Blue dicks (See brodeiaea)

Brittle brush *Encelia farinosa* Sunflower Family *Asteraceae*

Found on dry exposed slopes. Has a brittle stem. When broken has a fragrant resin. The dense pale hairs on the leaves help to reflect heat. A <u>round, silvery-gray, leafy bush with bright yellow or silvery white flower heads that bloom in loosely branched clusters often form an umbrella effect of yellow topping. Height is 3-5', flowers are 2-3" wide. Leaves 1 1/4-4" long, ovate, hairy.</u> Flowers in March-June. The resin was chewed by Indians and used as incense in the churches of Baja. Rw, Gd, Rx

Brodiaea *Brodiaea ssp* Reported to be Lilly Family *Liliaceae* and in Amaryllis Family *Amaryllidaceae*

Wild hyacinth, wild onion, blue dicks. *Dichelostemma puchellum* Amarylis Family *Amaryllidaceae*

The hyacinth is another one of the plants easy to miss. A grass-like plant grows on hills throughout California in early spring, about 12-24" high, often leafless.   The flowers, in clusters of about ten with each flower having six petals, are deep violet, bluish , lavender to white. The little bulbs, eaten raw, are quite palatable. According to Dale (1986), the Indians and the children of early settlers called them grass nuts. *Pulchellum* is Latin for "beautiful."

Of the Amarylis Family, 29 native to California. Depicted in texts as having a common a grass-like appearance with flowers on ends of long stalks, six narrow petals and varying in color. According to Clarke (1977) most are quite edible, but there is a white flowered variety, *Zigadenus venonosusm* Death-Camas, variety that is poisonous.

Buckwheat (See California Buckwheat)

Bush chinquapin (see chinquapin)

Cactus (See agava, prickly pear, barrel cactus and cholla)

California Buckwheat; *Eriogonium fascicujlatum*   Buckwheat Family
Polygonaceae

These herbs appear as shrubs, vines, rarely trees, with swollen
joints. Tiny pinkish flowers, in dense cotton-ball-like terminal
heads. The flowers, reddish or purple to cream colored, are
symmetrical, in racemes, in spile-like clusters, or in heads.
Cherished by bees. The family grows in a number of climes,
from lower elevations well into the mountains. Alpine varieties
are usually dwarfed. The coloring of the flowers may change as
they mature. The Desert Trumpet; Bladder Stem; Indian pipe
Weed that range in southern California, tend to be spindly with
1 or a few leaflets, erect stems, with tiny yellow flowers on very
slender stalks. The stem has a pleasant sour taste. Dried stems
were used by the Indians as tobacco pipes.   Rw, Ck, Rx

Cattail *Typha latifolia*

Found alongside springs and marshes. Noted at Fox Mill
Spring, between Walker Pass and Kennedy Meadows. The
sausage-shaped spike of the cattail grows in shallow water. The
brown cylinder is in fact a flower head without petals. The
male flower, blooms for a short period. It appears at the tip of
cylinder fall off after pollination. They can be boiled and eaten.
Gd, Ck

Ceanothus, greenbark ceanothus, buckbrush, tobacco brush, coffee
brush, mountain lilac, California lilac

Ceanothus spinopsus, Buckthorn Family *Rhamnaceae*

Over 40 species of ceanothus appear throughout California, up
to 7000' and regularly seen on the PCT north through

Washington. *Ceanothus*, in Greek means spiny. They have <u>tiny flowers with a flattish central disk</u>. The so-called California lilac, sometimes called deer brush, is found along the southern parts of the trail, are a white-flowered shrub. <u>In general, they have an openly and loosely branched shrub, rigid branclets, with thin one-veined, oval leaf no more than an inch wide, gray bark, three to 12 feet tall. They have tiny white or pale blue flowers in 6" conical clusters</u>. Other varieties such as the Squaw Carpet (Ceanothus prostratus) a more close to the ground type, have leaves that are sharp and light green in color. The flowers are bluish or lavender in color and found in pine forests. Others in the Ceanothus family, for example the Tobacco Brush, occurs on open wooded slopes at 3,500 to 10,000 feet. Another one is the Snow Bush, found on open flats and slopes at 3,000 to 9,500 feet from the San Jacinto Mountains north through the Sierra Nevada.

Chamise, ribbonwood, greasewood *Adenostoma fasciculatum*

This shrub or small tree appears at the Mexican border behind the monument marking the southern terminus of the Pacific Crest Trail. They are 16-30' in height. Kircher and Morrison (1998) refer to chamise as the archetype and primary indicator of California chaparral. Chamise has been reported to practice a kind of chemical warfare in which water that runs of its leaves poisons the soil around the plant, preventing other species from germinating. The shrub varies a great deal in it's overall appearance, sometimes appearing scraggly as it does in the more southern region, but one next to it might be quite handsome and rich-looking. There is a rich glade of chamise on the northeast exposure to the San Felipe Hills. Evergreen with leaves nearly linear, but thin and rounded. At times, soft to the touch. Flowers in July-August, with <u>showy, crowded, compound clusters several inches in height. Fruits, small, dry and 1-seeded</u>. May Be Toxic! Tx-

Cherry (See holly-leaved cherry)

Chia. *Salvia columbaria*

Common below 4000' in open spaces, chaparral and in the foothills of southern California. <u>Stems are 6 " to 2' high.</u> <u>Unique large flower head cluster of blue or purple whorls</u>. Grows on dry hillsides or in sandy washes, where it blossoms in early spring. After the blossoms have passed away, <u>the easily</u> <u>identified dried stems and heads remain standing</u> all over the hills, shaking out the little gray seed in abundance. These seeds, were of economic importance to the Indians. In ancient Mexico and along the Pacific coast, the plant was cultivated and used as highly nutritive substance (Dale, 1985). Used like corn and an important cereals. The seeds were roasted, then ground. It is exceedingly nutritious. In 1966 it frequently commanded six or eight dollars a pound (Parsons, 1966). Ck, Gd, Nu, Rx

Chickweed *Stelleria media* Pink Family *Caryophyllaceae*

<u>These scrawny, small clustering plants</u> appear throughout California, a common weed in shady places, including fields, gardens and lawns. <u>They have a unique line of hairs running</u> <u>down the side of the stem. The leaves are oval. They only</u> <u>grow ½ - 1' high. The tiny flower is white with 5 petals; each</u> <u>has a deep cleft giving the illusion of having ten petals</u>. The entire visible plant is edible raw. A brief cold water rinse is all that is necessary. It can be cooked and prepared like spinach. It is also nutritious.   Rw, Sal, Ck, Nu, Rx

California Coffee Berry *Rhamnus californica* Buckthone Family *Rhamnaceae*

First seen in the lower Laguna Mountains. This plant is readily seen and identified. It stands out from the many dull plants along the trail. <u>The leaves are brighter green than others around, alternately arranged from 1- 2 ½" long, narrow and oblong in shape and with the margin of very small teeth or serrations. The fruits are 2-3 seeded, first green, they turn bright red and finally black in midsummer.</u> Yes! According to Nyerges, a coffee-like drink can be made by roasting and grinding the seeds. But, with large quantities, like two cups, can lead to diarrhea and abdominal cramps. Ck, Rx, Tx-

Creosote Bush Scrub *Larrea Varicata*

A dominant shrub appearing over large areas of desert from southern California to Inyo and Kern Counties up to about 5000'. As a whole, they are <u>strong-scented evergreen shrub with opposite leaves. Flowers are yellow with petals 5-8 mm long and twisted. Small fruits covered with white hairs</u>. They were frequently employed by the Indians for medicinal purposes. The Cahuilla groups made a tea from the stems and leaves, whish was thought to cure a variety of ailments including colds, infections, and bowel complaints. Tea was also considered a decongestant and a general health tonic. Often sweetened with honey. To relieve congestion, thee Cahuillas boil leaves in a pot or bowl and cover their head with a blanket to inhale the steam. Creosote was in the U.S. pharmacopoeia from 1842 to 1942 used as an expectorant and pulmonary antiseptic. Ck, Rx

A unique and rare species found near the trail going through Antelope Valley, along the California Acquaduct below the Tehachapi Mountains, with specimens up to 11,000 years! According to the *Guidebook*, p 174, a special type, uniquely observed in the Antelope Valley, has an estimated age of 11,000 years. This special plant can be seen, should one trek through the desert by day, along a stretch of the Los Angeles aqueduct. It is described as a green, glossy-leaved creosote-bush. They appear evenly spaced. Each plant secretes a toxin, washed to the ground by rains, that poisons nearby plant growth, thereby allowing it enough root space to gather water. The carbon dating puts it much older than the well-known bristlecone pine seen on the White Mountains, to the east of the Sierra Nevada across Owens Valley.

Chinquapin, bush chinquapin *Chrysolepsis sempervirens* , *Castanopsis sempervirnes*

Found on dry rocky slopes and ridges in Montane forests from 2500-11,000'. Seen in the San Jacinto and San Gabriel mountains and in the Sierra Nevada from Kern County and northward. It is described as ill smelling (Munz, 1972). Steeped leaves as tea <u>The shrub is 2-8' high with oblong, almost toothless leaves are golden or rusty-wooly beneath, 1-3" long. Flowers of the Bush Chinquapin are ill-smelling, yellow at first, and make spiny burs which become 1" thick</u>. Used as an external wash for fevers due to colds and flue. Also as an astringent. Nuts are sweet, edible and roasted. Rodents, particularly squirrels, gather them in fall. Clarke (1977) has a recipe for shortbread made from chopped chinquapin nuts. Rw, Ck, Gd, Nu, Rx

Chokecherry *Prunus virginiana*

Appears in damp places in woods and on brushy slopes and flats near streams below 8200' mostly in the mountains from San Diego Co north through mountain ranges and Sierra Nevada to Washington. Occurring in chaparral, foothill woodland and yellow pine forests. <u>The shrub is 1-5 m high, smooth gray-brown bark. Wide green leaves are oblong, 3-8 cm long, finely toothed. Flowers in clusters, 5-10 cm long at ends of short branches, with white petals. Fruit is a small cherry hanging in strings, round 5-6 mm thick, dark red or black; palatable when fully ripe</u>. Blooms May through June with fruits in summer.

Tea from the inner tree bark was used to check diarrhea and nervousness. Boiling can remove the hydrocyanic acid. Popular with birds and animals. Recipes for jam and syrup. Rw, Ck, Gd, Nu, Sal, Rx

Coffeeberry (See California coffee berry)

Coreopsis Sunflower Family *Asteraceae*

Coreopsis ssx

Seen along the Laguna Mountains while descending towards Chariot Canyon. Dahlia-like, <u>shiny green flower head with ray-like 8 bright yellow petals characteristic of sunflowers.</u> .

Coreopsis gigantea

This plant, according to Schaeffer's *Guidebook* (1996), appears only between Walker Pass and Kennedy Meadows in Canebrake Canyon. <u>It resembles a small tree, with a soft woody stem that branches near the top, where feathery leaves grow and large yellow flower heads bloom in clusters at the ends of long leafless stalks.</u>

Currants

Squaw currant *Ribes cereum* f. *Saxifragaceae*

<u>The red berry is about 6mm in diameter, with several small seeds. This erect shrub, up to 3' in height,</u>. The tree blooms June-July, with fruit appearing in the summer. There are 30 species of currants and their close relatives, the gooseberries in California. All are considered edible, though not always palatable. They are easily recognized by their characteristic leaf shape, which resembles a maple leaf with rounded points. ERG

Gooseberries *Ribes Saxifrage. Saxifragaceae*

Found near water holes or along stream beds and in dry or open areas in higher elevations. Gooseberries have thorns, while the squaw currant is thornless. Leaves are alternate and palmate. Flowers vary from golden orange to pink, to deep red. The fruit, the gooseberry are oblong and in favorable conditions they reach ½" in diameter. Sometimes the fruits are covered with soft spines, which must be removed before eating. Upon ripening they turn red or bluish black. Wt, Rw, Ck, D, Gd.

Flannelbrush *Fremontia* Cacao Family *Sterculiacae*

Found along the California border, a spreading shrub with many large saucer-shaped, yellow-orange flowers, 1 ½ -2 ½ " wide. The sepals are petal-like, ovate, with long hairs in pits at base. Leaves are ½-3" long, dark green. The plant grows from 5-30'. It ranges much of California to central Arizona.

Forget-me-nots pop-corn flower Plagiobothrys nothofulvus. Borage Family *Nievitas*.

Appears throughout the state. Taken singly they are not showy, but often cover fields presenting the appearance of light snowfall. A tiny group of flowers often packed with commercial gift, floral displays. Loosely branching, up to 18 inches in stringy heights protruding form a depressed group of long drooping leaves. The name "nievetas," is Spanish for the diminutive of *nieve*, snow. They have a delightful fragrance.

Groundsel-Tree *Baccharis pilaris* Composite Family

The tiny tree-like plant varies in size, 1-12' high. Upon exposed, wind swept hill it is low and close-cropped, but in more favorable localities where the soil is rich and climate more genial, it responds to become a picturesque shrub and tree-like.

While on the trail It can easily be missed as it flowers in the fall The very small yellow flowers are at the very end of the branchlets. Leaves are short, 1-2" long, alternate and leathery. When fully flowered, they have an umbrella shape.

Holly-leaved cherry prunus ilicifolia)

On dry slopes and fans below 5,000 ft, especially in chaparral, from Baja California through coastal mountain ranges. I have eaten the cherries, they do not ripen until late summer and therefore have yet to experience them on the trail. They grow 1-8 m tall, with gray or reddish-brown twigs. Irregularly curled leaves are oval, 2-5 cm long, with sharp teeth on edges. Flowers are white, 2-3 mm long. Fruit ranges from red to yellow, 12-15 mm long, with thin, sweetish pulp. Blooms April through May with fruit ripening in summer and fall. The Cahuilla Indians favored this cherry, abundant in the San Jacinto Mountains. They used the kernel, primarily, extracting it from the pit, crushing it into a mortar, leaching it in a sand depression, and boiling it into a soup. The fruit was pressed to make a drink, and the bark was used to make a tea for treating colds. Hikers enjoy nibbling on the thin, sweet pulp. The kernel is dried, crush and leched by nut fanciers. A sweet sauce may be made with the thin pulp by simmering it in a little water and adding lemon and sugar to taste. They can be eaten as picked, bearing some resemblance to the common cherry, somewhat bitter and lacking the familiar sweetness of a bing cherry. Rw, Ck, Dr, Gd, Sal, Rx

Hyacinth (See Brodiaea)

Joshua Tree *Yucca brevifolia*

This easy to spot high desert specimen is the tallest and most tree-like of the yuccas. It also has the shortest leaves, 6-13" long, only 1/4 - ½" wide, <u>bayonet-shaped, spine-tipped with upright clusters of showy white blossoms. Most species have cylindrical, fleshy fruits 3-5" long.</u> Though reported to grow in the 2000-6000' range, they can be seen growing at higher elevations, e.g. in the flats adjacent to Big Bear Lake and on both sides of Walker Pass in the southern Sierra. This yucca is found in dry soils from 2,000 through 5,000 feet typically, but found in the southern Sierra up to 7,000 feet. There are areas along the trail from Tehachapi Pass to Walker Pass where, for miles, the only shade along the way is the Joshua tree. Wt, Rx

Laurel Sumac *Rhus laurina*

This shrub or tree is very common throughout southern California, growing up to 15 feet.<u> It's easily identified by its curled leave are 2-5" long, 1-2" wide, with fold along he mid rib. An unpleasant odor is produced when the leaves are crushed. Fruits are white.</u> Seen often as part of the more dense chaparral along the PCT from the Laguna Mountains through the San Gabriel Mountains. The fruit heads provide a food source for deer and quail.

Lupine Lupinus *desiflorus* Pea Family *Benth*

Many varieties thrive in southern California., each with <u>distinctive coloring</u>. All are in the pea family. <u>Leaves are crowded with 5 - 10 leaflets, palmate, linear-spatulate, usually less than an inch long.</u> Considered as a whole, since the species has a number of forms, it is found on dry stony slopes and benches between 4,000 and 8,500 feet from the San Bernardino Mountains to Oregon. The first encountered were on the slopes of the Hauser Mountains<u>, bluish-whitish fragrant flowers, 6 - 10" high,</u> probably *Lupinus bicolor,* <u>with flowers less than half an inch long, but very showy.</u> Some central and eastern U.S. varieties are poisonous. It seems best to leave these pretty plants alone. The seeds of wild lupine, *Lupinus perennis* are poisonous. Some lupines are toxic whereas others are not. According to Foster and Duke (1999) botanists have trouble distinguishing between the toxic and non-toxic varieties.

Mallows, tree-mallow *Lavatera assurgentiflora* Mallow Family

The typical Mallow plant, cheesewood, is seen in vacant lots, spreading and branching out up to three feet, seen as typical mounds of greenery, 1-3' high. Some types have gray leaves with an arrowhead-like shape. The lower <u>two lobes of the leaf form a perpendicular angle to the stem, with no regard to the angle of the stem. Flowering, depending on type can be white, yellow or red</u>. According to Nyerges (1999), there are no poisonous varieties in this family and according to Peterson (1977) all mallows are edible. They can be cooked and eaten like spinach. The tender young leaves can be used okra-like to thicken soups and stews. Raw fruits can be eaten as is, having a nutty flavor. In Mexico the leaves are chewed to alleviate minor sore throats. Used also as a poultice on sores and swellings. Ck, Rw, Rx

Manzanita - *Arctostaphylos glauca f. ericaceae*

A most spectacular grove, the richest and healthiest I've seen, appears about a mile or so north of Lake Morena, just before the trail ascends up the ridge that separates the lake from Cottonwood Valley. <u>A tree-like shrub 3-25' high with reddish-brown bark.</u> May be found in full bloom, when its dense crown of <u>pale foliage, surmounting the rich purple-brown stems,</u>. After the blossoms have passed away, the shrubs put forth numerous brilliant scarlet or crimson shoots. The name, itself comes from the Spanish, manzana, apple, and the diminutive, ita,—was bestowed by the early Spanish-Americans, who recognized the <u>resemblance of the fruit to tiny apples.</u> The species, A. patula, high in Kern County have berries more palatable.. Some are bony and quite unsatisfactory. Bears are fond of them and the Indians ate them raw and pounded them into flour. The leaves can be made into a tincture valued for colds (Parsons, 1966). Parsons describes the largest manzanita, upon the estate of Tiburcio Parrott, in St. Helena, Napa County. In 1966, it was 35 feet in height, with a spread of branches equal to its height, while its trunk measures 11 ½ in circumference. Rw, Ck, Dr, Rx

Mesquite, honey mesquite *Propsopis grlandulosa*

Common in washes and low ground below 3000 feet. in the Mojave Desert. But seen along the trail in exposed areas at altitudes upward to 5,000'. <u>A Low tree or large shrub with several trunks 3-7 m high. Deciduous with compound leaves with 7-17 pairs of leaflets 1.5-2.3 cm long. Flowers are small and greenish in slender spikes</u>. Blooming is in April through June. with pods ripening in the fall. Historically, an important food source. Beans are from pods, pleasantly sour., Were bartered. Collected and dried. Ground into flour. Used for a drink. The blossoms were roasted or made into tea CD

Miners Lettuce: indian lettuce *Montia perfoliata*

A green plant, <u>less than a foot high</u> on the northeastern exposure in moist soil and in shady areas. I picked them along the northern slopes of the Sierra Pelona Mountains. <u>The leaf is up to 2"</u> growing out of a stem in its middle. When I see em, I eat em. The flower-racemes look as though they might have pushed their way right through the rather large saucer-like leaf just below them. The plant flowers March-July. According to Parsons (1966) the succulent leaves and stems were greedily eaten by the Indians, from which it is called "Indian Lettuce." I learned to avoid the stems and flowers which added a little too much flavor. They have long been grown in England, where they are highly esteemed for salads.   Rw, Gd, Sal, Ck,

Monkey Flower; Snapdragon Family *figwort*

There are many species of monkey flowers, several seen throughout southern California.

The Scarlet Monkey-Flower

 Red flowers, stems 1-3' long. Opposite, saw-toothed leaves. Appears along stream banks and moist places below 8.000', blooming from April to October.

Mimulus Tilingii

Yellow flowers, with 2-lipped, 1"+ long with brown spotted ridges in the throat. It occurs on the wet sides of the San Jacinto Mountains from 6,400-11,000'. Bright green leaves, 1" long. Stems, 6-16", few flowered.

Meadow Monkey Flower

Yellow delicate flower with the 5-petals easily loosened. Leaves are 3-veined and vary from smooth to quite hairy. In meadows and wet grassy banks from 3000-11000' in the San Jacinto Mountains.

Fremont's Monkey Flower

Pink or purple flower with yellow or white inside, 5-petaled, 2-lipped. 2-7" high.

Mormon Tea, *ephedra.*

Common on dry slopes and hills below 4500 feet throughout the Mojave Desert   Looks broom-like, <u>seemingly leafless shrub, 1.2 m high. Jointed stems are pale green when young, with a white bloom, turning yellow or gray with age. Scale like papery leaves are very small and occur in pairs which fall off, leaving gray bases.</u> Fruiting structures are small male cones 4-8 mm long, yellow to light brown with protruding stamen; female cone is light brown to yellow-green. Blooms March to April. Hab: Warm, arid regions: Uses Brew green or dry twigs in boiling water, a tonic for kidney and stomach disorders. Stems were chewed to relieve thirst while seeds were roasted and ground into flour or make a bitter bread or mush. Roots ground into flour and sprinkled it on sores. The drug ephedrine is obtained from a Chinese species. Ck, Dr, Rx

Mountain Mahogany *Cercocarpus*

A common shrub upon the interior hills of the Coast Ranges on the drier slopes up to 10,000'. Recognized by its <u>wedge-shaped, leathery dark green leaves, prominently veined, toothed midway, and notched at the summit. Height to 25'.</u> Heaviest and hardest wood in California. The dense wood will sink in water. Not related to the tropical mahogany trees. Its flower without petals, are green and inconspicuous; but the long, solitary plumes of its little fruit are very noticeable and pretty.

Mustard, Black *Brassica nigra* **Mustard Family** *brassicaceae*

Common on dry hillsides and waste places throughout the state and along the trail. Widespread partly because the U.S. Forest Service planted them on burns to retard erosion, and partly because the mission fathers used to spread the seeds to mark the trail from one mission to another   They are not black! <u>Flowers</u>

are showy yellow in elongated racemes. Fur petals, 7-8 mm long, and 6 stamens, 2 shorter than the other. Fruit is an elongated, slender pod 1-2 cm long in maturity, with a beak at the tip which is empty of seeds 1-3 mm long. Flowers April through July. The plant stands erect, 0.5-2.5 m high and is an annual. . The same plant from which commercial mustard is made. The best leaves to use are the lower ones. Because of the strong flavor, they should be cooked for about 20 minutes in water and served with butter or a seasoned, and with a mild dressing. The greens become quite strong when warm weather sets in, so they are best gathered when young. High in Vitamins, especially, A, B and C, The unopened flower buds can be eaten like broccoli, boiled in salt water for just a few minutes. To make prepared mustard , collect the pods, allow them to dry, then obtain the seeds. Grind them in a food chopper or mill and roast in an oven until browned. Mix this flour half and half with commercial powdered mustard, moistening with a mixture of half vinegar and half water. Mustard plasters can also be made by using the ground 3 seeds half-and-half with flour and water. Clarke has five recipes, a cream of mustard soup, a mustard dip, mustard and collard greens, and Danish Mustard. Rw, Ck, Gd, Dr, Nu, Sal

Ocotillo *Fouquieria splendens*) Ocotillo Family *fouquieriaceae*

Easy to spot in dry rocky places below 2500 feet, 10-15 feet tall, resembling nothing more than a bundle of giant, green pipe cleaners. First seen approaching the San Felipe Hills, the only one of its family to exist in North America. It is not a succulent; does not store water. Instead it drops its leaves during the dry season and grows them quickly after each rainfall, perfectly adapted to their searing desert environment. Much of the year, ocotillo's branches look like spiny, lifeless stalks. In just 2-3 days after a rainstorm, the branches sprout vibrant green clusters. Almost as quickly, the leaves wither and die as ground water becomes scarce. In this manner ocotillo may leaf out 6-8 times a year. They are used in Mexico for "living" fences; cut stems are planted in the ground where they will re-root if watered. The powdered root is used to treat swellings, for bathing to reduce fatigue. May be soaked in equal amounts of water overnight for a beverage. Ck, Dr, Rx

Penstemon; climbing penstemon; mountain pride, scarlet honeysuckle *Penstemon cordifolius f. Figwort.*

May be seen along the streams of the first 25 miles. There are many varieties of the figwort family snapdragon. They are characterized by <u>wand like branches and stem with heart-shaped leaves, suggestive of the garden fuchsia. A brilliant foliage in many colors, including bright red, that encircles the stem of some varieties and then tops it.</u> The name penstemon comes from the fifth stamen, which is usually different from the others, having no anther but sporting a thick golden beard. The leaves are cordate or ovate, 1' or less in length.

Peppergrasses *Lepidium ssp* Mustard Family *cruciferase*

Found as weeds of roadsides and waste places toothed or deeply multi-lobed long leaves with spike-like clusters of tiny 4-petalled flowers. RSCN

Western Peppergrass *Lepidium montanum*

Found in dry, open places in deserts, occurring with creosote bush, sagebrush, pinion, and juniper. From southern California to southeastern Oregon and east to Wyoming and Texas. Rw, Sal, Ck, Nu

Wild Peppergrass, Poor man's pepper *Lepidium virginicum*

> Widespread in waste places along roadsides below 7000 feet. Many-branched, about <u>2' in height.</u>, familiar plant. <u>Leaves are incised and lanceolate.</u> Flowers occur in racemes with numerous small 4-petaled <u>white blossoms.</u> Petals are 4 in number. Fruit is a small pod, nearly heart shaped. Blooms in spring and summer. Stem is often hairy. Leaf is more sharply toothed. Used by natives for medical use. Prepared like mustard. Rw, Sal, Ck, Nu, Rx

Yellow Peppergrass *Lepidium flavum*

> Seen in the lower flats of the desert<u>. The stems, brittle at the joints and lie on the ground. Only the dense, short acemes of yellow flowers are turned upward. The seeds have a peppery flavor</u>. Rw, Sal, Ck, Nu

Phacelia, desert bell. *Phacelia campanularia*) Waterleaf Family *hydrophyllacae*

> <u>A short, but stiff, erect, leafy, glandular-hairy plant with dark blue, bell-like flowers in loose coil at the end of a branched, open flower cluster. Height is 8-30" with leaves 3/4-3" long, ovate.</u> The edges are shallowly lobed and sharply toothed. Found on dry sandy or gravelly places in deserts throughout southern California. In a spring following a wet winter, thousands of these plants will bloom forming masses of deep, rich blue.

Poison Oak *Rhus diversiloba*) Sumac Family *anacardiaceae*

> This bothersome plant occurs throughout much of the southern California sections. I did not see any poison oak higher than

5000'. The plant appears in the relatively moist areas, often as the trail rounds an intermittent stream beds on a slope and in canyon beds. It likes the company of other similar looking shrubs. The plant changes its appearance from season to season. <u>In spring and summer, the plant has shiny green leaves, each divided into three oval, lobed leaflets. Toward fall, the leaves and stems turn reddish</u> and the small whitish flowers become smooth berries. In winter and early spring the plant is harder to recognize.

The *Guidebook* points out that the it is, with the exception of mosquitos or flies, the most consistent nuisance along the trail. For the allergic, the rash in most people leads, at worst, to a few days of insane itching and irritation. It may, however, completely incapacitate a luckless few.

On occasions when I made contact with poison oak with marked scratches, as when helping to pull a water line to fight a fire above Carbon Canyon in Orange County--while wearing a tee shirt, I had no reaction, i.e. no rash nor itching. Yet at other times, I may have barely touched the plant and endured a two days annoying rash. The best approach is prevention, to avoid contact with it and anything around the plant.

There are a number of ways to deal with it once contact is made. Water helps to inactivate the toxin, and alcohol helps to extract the oil form the skin, as does soap. Scratching and rubbing exacerbates the condition by permitting it to enter the skin. The local Indians of last century had various ways to treat the rash, including poultices derived from nearby common plants.

According to Nyerges (1999) The juice of the stems can be enlisted as an aid useful in treating warts. The Yuki Indians placed the leaves directly on rattlesnake bites to counteract the venom. Nyerges relates a number of nearby plants that were said to be used for treating the rash including the yellow juice of the aloe vera plant, leaves of mugwort, yerba santa and chickweed. Rx, Tx

Prickly Pear *Opunta* Cactus Family *cactaceae*

Appears often along the lower elevations of the trail; most readily seen along the exposed southwestern slopes. The mature pear appears purple or red, <u>sometimes even yellow. They grow from the tips of the green oval fleshy and spiny pad. All are edible</u>. The fruits need to be twisted off or cut from the pads, then carefully peeled and enjoyed fresh. According to Nyerges (1999) when peeled and put in the refrigerator, they taste like melons. Since the water content is high, they can be cherished when water carriage is at issue. Wt, Ck, Rw,

Rabbit Brush

There are a number of variants that grow on mountain sides and flats from 3,000 to 11,000 feet, from southern California on north to Siskiyou and Modoc counties. They are noticeable in areas in the San Bernardino Mountains and north of Walker Pass. An aptly named shrub less than <u>2 feet high with twigs covered with felt-like wool. Flowers in racemes or spikes</u>. They bloom in the late summer and fall.

Ribbonwood (See Chamise)

Sagebrush *Artemisia tridentata*

This<u> aromatic shrub resembling terpentine</u> is found in the desert areas and exposed areas up to 8,000', north to Siskiyou county. The evergreen shrub is <u>0.5-3 m high with a silvery leaf</u>. Blooms August to October. Used for flour.. Used to make flour and batter. A treatment for sore eyes and colds, a hair tonic and to alleviate stomach disorders. A popular barbecue wood.. Ck, Dr, Rx

Gray-ball Sage; desert sage *Salvia dorrii*

A handsome plant, pretty in leaf as well as flower. Up to four feet in height. Flowers May-July, with flowers about ½ inch long. On dry flats and slopes, often associated with sagebrush. East of Cascades and Sierra Nevada from Washington to southern California; east to central Arizona, Utah, and southwestern Idaho. It is this sage referred to in Zane Grey's classic, western Riders of the Purple Sage.

Black sage *Salvia Mellifera* Mint Family *labiatae*

Common among the chaparrals. Grows from 3-6'. Leaves are narrowly oblong, 1-2"long. Flowers are lilac-colored united petals about ½" long, in whorls. When dried can be used for flavoring in soups like garden sage. Leaves can made into a strong-tasting tea. Best gathered when the plant is not flowering. Sage honey comes largely from this variety. Rw, Ck, Dr, Rx

White sage (Salvia apiana Mint Family *labiatae*

A close relative of the garden sage, 3-6' tall with conspicuous whitish-gray leaves. The fresh leaves are slightly sticky and have a distinct aroma. The leaf margin is only slightly toothed with minute teeth. Flowers are white. Ck, Dr, Rx

Scarlet Gilia; skyrocket; desert trumpets; skunk flower *Ipompsis aggregata* Phlox Family *polemoniaceae*

Appears on the upper slopes of mountains as the chaparral overlaps the transition to the montane forest. Showy bright red or deep pink at the tops of sparsely-leaved stems, expands to five petal points, in clusters. 6-84" in height. They can't be missed when flowering. Leaves mostly 1-2" long, densest near the base, pinnately divided into narrow segments (like a feather). They have a slightly skunk-like odor in the leaves.

Scrub Oak (See Deciduous Trees)

Skyrocket (See scarlet gilia)

Snow Plant, *Sarcodes sanguinea*

Found in the coniferous forest, protruding from the duff, southern Oregon through southern California. Seen first one in late spring, in the area south of Big Bear, elevations above 7,000. And occasionally through the higher San Gabriel Mountains as well. Once seen, never forgotten. They quite bright in color in stark contrast to the duff associated with a montane forest. This unusual plant Requires soil produced by the slow decay of leaves. They are stout, fleshy, entirely bright red. Height   8-24", flowers April-July. Corolla bell shaped, ½ - 3/4" with 5 round lobes

Teddy Bear Cholla *Opuntia Bigelovii* Cactus Family *cactaceae*

Look for them coming down from the Laguna Mountains to the desert below. They are native to southern Nevada, Arizona and California. It generally has a central stem with many short lateral branches, of which the central ones are erect and others horizontal or semi-erect. The branches are light green, 2-6" and diameter of 2". Sine the spines almost completely cover the stem, the plant gives off a pale golden color. Flowers are borne on the tips of the stems at the top of the plant, 1 ½" long. The fruit is yellow and pear shaped.

Toyon,, Christmas berry, California holly, native holly *Heteromeles arbutifolia* Rose Family *rosaceae*

Many toyons cover the Hollywood hills and Santa Monica Mountains, as they do around our home. Found as a <u>shrub and small tree, 15-30' tall. They may be missed before it blossoms.</u> The berries become obvious in the fall. <u>Leaves are oblong, leathery and even toothed, 2-3" long, dark green on top and lighter underneath.</u> Flowers are white, 5=-petaled, 1/4" wide. The flowers are followed by the <u>conspicuous 1/4' red-orange fruits in large clusters.</u> Edible raw, but somewhat bitter, astringent and dry tasting. For best results, the berries should be lightly baked, steamed or soaked in water, and then cooked. Berries can be crushed and sweetened to make a wild "applesauce." Because they contain some cyanide, it is best to not make a tea. Rw-, Ck, Tx-

Wild Hyacinth (See Brodiaea)

Yerba Santa *Eriodicyon californicum*

Seen along the trail at altitudes between 3500-6500'. An aromatic shrub, evergreen, with shedding bark and weedy growth. Leaves alternate, somewhat <u>leathery and oily in appearance, 0.5-1.5 dm long and</u> often toothed. <u>They are sticky above and light-colored below</u>. Flowers occur in terminal branched scorpiod cymes, lavender to white, tubular or horn-shaped, 9-15f mm long and have 5 small loves and 5 stamens. Blooms from May to July. Common below 5500 on dry slopes almost everywhere, occasionally higher, as observed in the San Gabriel Mountains. Used as a remedy for colds, grippe, and asthma. Smoked (non-nicotinic) or made into tea. Leaves and flowers were steeped for tea and drunk for ailments such as stomach ache and rheumatism. The "holy herb" also was used by the Spanish Californian as a poultice on aching or sore areas.

Mashed leaves were often applied to cuts, wounds, abrasions and fractured bones to keep swelling down and as an aid in mending as well as relieve pain. Top make tea, tear up 2-3 fresh or dried leaves, and pour boiling water over them. Cover and let steep. Chewing the fresh leaves at times produce a refreshing taste in the mouth. The bitterness first experienced may soon be dissipated. Leaves can be dried and smoked. Wt, Ck, Dr, Rx

Yucca. Spanish bayonet - *Yucca Mohavensis,*

First seen on the PCT before Campo, becoming more varied in appearance as one climbs the Hauser Mountains. <u>They even appear stream-side on the exposed side, such as along Holcomb Creek. They are a shrub-like plant with a single or few short stems surround by narrow stiff leaves. Some sit flush with the ground while others may have a trunk.</u> Flowers are fleshy with red-purple tinges. Fruits ripen in August. The flower, is approximately 6" long, fleshy, resembling a short banana in shape, blooms May-June. Appears on dry slopes, 3000-6000 feet, mountains of southern California. All parts used by Indians. Ripened fruit was eaten raw or roasted, usually with the bitter outer skin removed. Young flowers said to be used in omelettes, added to tomato or onion soup, added to tossed salads or deep fried like squash blossoms.
Rw, Ck, Dr, Sal, Rx

2. GRASSES

Grass *Gramineae*

All grasses, St. Augustine, rye, bluegrass, crabgrass, oats, rice, corn, barley, millet and sorghum are edible. Grass seeds can be roasted, ground into meal for bread or cakes. Or soaked in water to be made into mush. The very young, newly emerging grass shoots under 6" can be eaten raw in salads or cooked. Generally these have little flavor. Mature grass is too fibrous and tough for human consumption. However they can provide lifesaving nutrition if one is willing to chew them. The grasses are best used before the jointing stage. Once the jointed stage is reached, the vitamin and protein content are quickly loss. Grass picked at or before the jointing stage has approximately 40% protein, compared with approximately 4% protein at the mature stage. Most cereal grass joint about 3 weeks after being planted. Grass picked at this stage can be eaten in a survival situation or can be dried and powdered and added to other staples. According to Nyerges (1999) 99% of grass seed is entirely safe to eat. The seeds of Darnel (lolium temulentum) and some sorghums are said to be toxic. Cyanide, the usual cause of their toxicity, can be eliminated by cooking or thoroughly drying the grain. Since only a few grains have this toxic characteristic, all that is necessary is to cook or dry the grain. Ed, Rw, Ck, Wt, Sal, Rx some may be Tx-

3. TALL DECIDUOUS TREES

ALDERS; white alder *Alnus rhombifolia*; also *Alnus incana*

Though a northern plant, found mostly along our streams and damp soils, complimenting willows and cottonwoods up to 8,000'. They grow to 65'. 3'. Tiny brown cones ½-3/4" long. Simple leaves, ovate-eliptical i shape, cvordate at the base, with the margins sharply double toothed, dark green and glabrous on top and whitish gray and pubescent below. Fruits are tiny achenes.

ASH, OREGON, *Fraxinus oregona*

The leaves are large, compound, 5-7 leaflets , in opposite pairs, slighylt toothed toward the tip and downy on the underside.

<u>They grow up to 80'.</u> Fruits have lancelolate wing and in a dense cluster. They flourish in cool, deep soils in temperate climes. Mainly in valleys and lower slopes. But seen in Sierra and San Bernardino Mountains. These trees are frequently planted along streets and parks. The wood was used by Indians for canoe paddles.

CAROB, algaroba, locust bean, St. John's bread *Ceratonia siliqua*. *f. leguminosae*

Widely cultivated in California. An evergreen tree with thick crown, native to the eastern Mediterranean. <u>Leaves compound with 2-3 pairs of oval, shiny leaflets, often with a notch at their tip. Flowers are small, borne on the old wood. No petals and 5 stamens. Pod is like a thick bean pod, 10-26 cm long, leathery, and filled with sweep pulp between seeds.</u> Color of pod is dark red-brown. Pods produced in fall but often hand on the trees until much later in the year. Pods long used for both human and cattle food. Dried pods contain 50% sugar, sold in some cities like candy. The U.S. imported ,250,000 pounds in 1935 for flavoring dog biscuits and chewing tobacco. It is often sold now as a substitute for chocolate in many products and as a "health food." In preparing the delicious product, the hard seeds must first be removed. Best accomplished if the pods are picked before they harden. Otherwise soaked. To make Carob meal, pare off the stem end, then place the entire pod in water and grind it to bits in a blender. Simmer the meal for about 10 minutes and strain. Discard the water and spread the meal thinly on a cookie sheet or screen to dry in a warm place o of pilot-lit oven. When dry, the mean can be ground in a hand grist meal or flour mill to a fine powder. The powder, the can be added to mild and heated for a cocoa substitute or used in recipes calling for chocolate. GCDNRx

COTTONWOODS

Both grow along stream beds. Leaves tapered, toothed.. Seen on the relatively moist areas on the banks of streams that cut through otherwise dry areas throughout Southern California, but also in the mountains in moist shaded areas, along willows, poplars, elms and sycamores. Inner bark tea used as a female tonic; the bark contains the aspirin like compound, salicin (Foster and Duke, 1999, 329). Salicin , when taken into the body, is transformed into salycilic acid, providing many of the properties of acetylsalicylic acid, common aspirin. Rx

Fremont Cottonwood *Populus fremontii*

> 50-75' Diameter, 1 -3'. Mature bark is dark, thick withy deep furrows. Leaves wider and shorter

Black Cottonwood *Populus trichocarpa*

> 60-80' Diameter, 2 -3'. Twiges spicy scented when crushed. Leaves 4-8", more oval shaped and longer, very fined toothed

OAKS

California abounds with oaks, with 9 species of tree sized and 12 scrub oaks. Five hybrids are known. Several varieties are seen along the trail at all elevations below 8,000. The type varies much with altitude, soil conditions and exposure. The types tend to be grouped together. All have end buds clustered on the tips of their twigs, are fan veined, flowers appearing in My and early June. Acorns begin development shortly thereafter. The first oak seen on the trail is the small, aptly named, Scrub Oak. It resembles the larger oaks, but is smaller and more scraggly. The scrub oak permeates much of the PCT and seems to contribute to the chaparral throughout all of southern California. Sometimes they resemble trees and other times seem more stunted than the surrounding chaparral. The beautiful and stately Black Oak seems to herald the climb into the conifer forests in the Laguna, San Bernardino and San Gabriel Mountains. Immediately below the montane forests, can be found the Interior Live Oak with heights 30 to 65 feet and on drier slopes up to 7,000 feet. The Canyon Live Oak with heights of 20 -65 feet, sometimes looks more like a shrub, but easily differentiated from the scrub oak by virtue of its full features. Often, it seems, they hybrid with one another to form kinds that in part resemble one another, particularly the smaller oak trees.

Before acorns can be used, the bitter and constipating tannin must be leached out. This can be accomplished by rinsing chopped or ground nuts in water until they are no longer astringent. Some of the nuts are naturally sweet and do not require this process. The Black Oak is one of the sweeter acorns, but still requires some leeching. Some Indian tribes used them medically, allowing the meal to accumulate mold, which was scraped off to use for boils, sores and inflammations. Native Americans converted acorns into a food stable by grinding the nuts and pouring hot water through the flour to leach out the tannic acid. According to Petrides, in some parts of Mexico, roasted acorns are used as a substitute for coffee. The Spanish names, *roble* is often applied to deciduous oaks and *encino* to evergreen. CRxT-

Scrub Oak *Quercus dujosa*

> They appear as <u>miniature oak trees</u>. All along the southern California portion of the PCT. Along with the Chamise, the very first shrub or tree noted at the southern trail terminus. Sometimes the are quite small, like along the way to Campo and beyond, whereas at

other times, they reach several meters high. But regardless of their size, they always blend in well with the chaparral that they become hardly noticeable.

Interior Live Oak *Quercus wisliozenii*

Appear in groves on inland grasslands. Seen on the grasslands between Barrel Springs and Warner Springs, around Agua Dulce, and Tehachapi Pass. They flourish on dry slopes reaching <u>heights of 30-65'. They are dark barked with short-pointed flat leaves only 1-2" long, shiny and hairless</u>.

Canyon Live Oak *Quercus chrysolepsis*

Covers a similar area as does the interior live oak. It often appears as a shrub. <u>Heights of 20-65'. The trunk is grey. The acorns are somewhat larger and longer than the interior live oak</u>.

California Black Oak *Quercus kelloggi*

<u>At higher elevations up to 9000'</u>, often sharing the montane forests with conifers throughout the length of the trail in southern California where they reach <u>up to 40-100'</u>. In fact , they seem to herald the forest as one leaves the chaparral to ascend the various ranges. <u>They have longer leaves 4-7" long, dark green leaves with 5-7 bristle- tipped lobes. The acorn is the largest</u>.

SYCAMORE, California *Platanus racemosa*

Among the first deciduous trees noted on the trail, near Campo and up through the Hauser Mountains and Laguna Mountains, where they can be seen in the more moist soils and alongside cottonwoods and willows in the first streams. They are long lived, up to 600 years, <u>tall, from 130-165 feet</u>. They are seen on the PCT on the cooler, deep alluvial soils often on stream banks and canyons up to 4,000 feet. Their leaves, branches and barks leave their mark on the trail. <u>The bark is light green, whitish, or mottled, flakes off in irregular puzzle-like pieces, exposing yellowish and whitish under-bark</u>. <u>There are 3-5 leaf nodes, typically 5, somewhat resembling the maple, but the nodes are more indented with the sections of the leaf more pointed and mostly toothed</u>. The characteristic fruit balls vary from 3-7 per stalk. The wood is hard, coarse-grained used for boxes, barrels, cabinet works, furniture and especially, butcher blocks. The twigs are eaten by deer and muskrats. The trunk and branch cavities are sought for nests and shelter by wood ducks and racoons. American Indians used inner-bark tea for dysentery, colds, lung ailments, measles, coughs; also as a "blood purifier" and emetic and laxative; the bark was once suggested for rheumatism and scurvy (Foster and Duke,1999, p 316) Rx

WILLOWS, *Salix ssp*

Willows are catkin-bearing plants with 3 bundle scars. Recognized by their <u>slender leaves</u>. Many willows are only shrubs, some far-north and high-altitude species being only a few inches tall. Identifying the kind of willow is often a difficult task. The most common in our area is the <u>black willow</u> <u>*Salix nigra*), with heights of 30-100' and trunk diameters of 1-3', the sandbar willow salix exigua) with heights to 20'</u> up top 8000', the arroyo willow *salix lasiolepsis*) with heights up to 30' limited to canyons leading to arroyos. The wood is of some commercial value but is not highly regarded even for fuel, charcoal or posts. The leaves provide browse for livestock; many birds and mammals eat the willow twigs, buds, leaves, or fruits. Willows tend to be seen along with cottonwoods, sycamores and alders along streams in otherwise dry areas providing a welcome rest stops. The inner bark contains salicin. The tea is supposedly good for headaches. The branches make a good walking stick. If they are slightly bowed and flexible, they can serve as walking poles as they can spring one along the trail and reduce fatigue. Rx

4. EVERGREEN TREES

JUNIPERS

Small, slow-growing trees, but lead a long life, commonly found in dry climates. Though having similar looking leaves as the cedars and cypress, their scale-like leaves , they can be easily recognized by their hard fruits, blue when young, maturing to either blue or reddish brown. When the fruits appear blackish, they become juicy and resinous. The wood is durable and usually aromatic. When they are large, they are used for "cedar chests." Indians and early pioneers ate the raw fruits of some, and also made them into a flour, perhaps cooked with other foods to make them more palatable. The berries have been used to flavor gin. Dr, Ck, Bev

California Juniper *Juniperus californica*

A shrubby tree of deserts and foothills of California and western Arizona and Baja. Leaf scales are yellow-green, mostly paired, blunt and with a gland dot. Twigs tend to be rounded rather than 4-sided. Fruits 3/8 - 5/8" in diameter and reddish with a white bloom when mature, though sometimes bluish at first. Several trunks, brown to gray that shed. Heights 10-20' with diameters of 1-2'. Seen on dry soils below 5000'. Dr, Rw, Ck, Rx

Western Juniper *Juniperus occidentalis*

Many seen on Mount Laguna, San Bernardino Mountains, Tehachapi Mountains, and north of Walker Pass to Kennedy Meadows. Most dramatic in the dry areas below 6000, in Kern County. <u>Height typically to 10-25' but occasionally higher mixing with firs and pines. Sometimes with a single trunk.</u> They grow in dry rocky soils to 10,000'. <u>Berries bluish, changing to reddish, oval, 12-18 mm long.</u>, produced in spring and summer. The berries are used as astringents. Preserved by drying, then ground and baked into cakes or made into mush. Berries have been roasted, ground and made into a beverage. Ck, Dr, Rs, Bev, Rx

PINES

Pinyon Pines *Pinus monophylla*

First seen closely in the San Bernardino Mountains mixed with other conifers. Long stretches north of the Piute Mountains abound with pinyon pines, often providing the only shade. A <u>Small tree, 5-15 m tall, usually with a divided trunk and rounded or flat top in age. Needles occur singly, are rigid and pale gray-green, 2.5-3.5 cm long. Cones are 3.5 - 5.5 cm long with four sided scales.</u> Nuts ripen with crops produced only every other year under ideal conditions. They appear scattered in dry rocky places 3500-9000 feet. A prominent tree on the exposed sides of the lower southern base of the Sierra and on the eastern side of the Sierra crest where it thrives between the desert below and the montane forests above. It provides the largest of the pine nuts. These nuts were important for Indians. Green cones were usually knocked down and set on fire to remove the pitch. Seeds were then easily removed form the opened cones, shelled and parched for future usage, pounded into cakes or eaten fresh. Pinyon seeds are very rich and supply considerable protein and fat. They contain 3000 calories per pound. The gum of the tree was used for chewing to ease sore throat, applied to burns and sores. Rw, Ck, Nu, Rx

Coulter Pine *Pinus coulteri*

The first wild pine to be seen walking northbound up the southern California slopes, from the basin or deserts to the transition forests, will be the Coulter pine. Sometimes a bit scraggly, they first appear in Long Canyon in the Laguna Mountains, at 5,000 feet. They are easy to spot as they uniquely have the super large, massive, 4-5 pound, light-brown distinctive cone. The cones stay on the trees for years before they plummet down. Should one seek refuge under a mature tree, take care to wear a helmet, as they become missiles potentially causing havoc to anything alive. Coulter pines grow to 40-60 feet with trunk diameters of 1-2'.

Foxtail Pine *Pinus balfouriana*

Doesn't appear along the trail until the most northern portion of the southern California region and in fact rather localized to the south-central Sierras and later in the Klammath Mts in Trinity and Siskiyou counties. They are found in the higher elevations, 6500-7500 feet and oftentimes along the trail reach up to the timberline. Identifying characteristics are their aptly named short spruce-like cluster of brighter green needles along the entire limb, 1-1 ½" in length. Their cones are 3-4" long, dense, without prickles and shaped

<u>like a hand grenade.</u> What really makes them identifiable is their location, in areas where there is little competition by way of other tall trees. They live to be about 350 years.

Jeffrey Pine *Pinus jeffreyi*

A common pine tree seen along the PCT at altitudes between 6,000 to 9,000' where they grow to 100-130' sometimes <u>up to 180' with a diameter of 2-4 or more.</u> They are found throughout all higher mountain ranges in California, usually overlapping, but mostly above the Ponderosa. What makes them easy to identify are their <u>unique vertically scaly bark and furrows that emanate a distinctive pleasant vanilla scent</u>. The cone is egg-shaped as is the Ponderosa, but larger, lighter and stiffer cone scales. It can hybrid with the Ponderosa and Coulter pines, as ours at our Santa Monica Mountain home, El. 1200 feet, where it has become a huge tree, higher and larger than any I've seen elsewhere among this group of pines.

Limber Pine *pinus flexilis*

Seen near the summit of Mt. Baden Powell, in the San Gabriel Mountains. They appear scraggly and widely spread out from one another, but less distant than the Bristle Cones pines. Grows slowly up to 75 feet, usually less. At 15 years, 15 feet: At 40 years, 30 feet. Branches are windy. Leaves stiff, dark green, 2-3 inches. Cones are egg-shaped, 4-6" long. <u>Endures wind and dry soil</u> better than most pines. Mts of North America.

Lodgepole Pines *Pinus contorta*

Though prevalent throughout the Pacific northwest, can can be along the PCT through southern parts of the state. I've seen them in the higher portions of the San Jacinto Mountains and San Bernardino Mountains. Identifiable by their medium-dense 2" long, almost round cone that tend to stay on the trees, a dark trunk, furrowed, but not vertically so. They grow 60-100', reported up to 115'., with trunks 1-2' in diameter. They are used as walls to form log cabins.

Ponderosa Pine *Pinus ponerosa*

The most widely distributed pine in the western U.S. and commercially the most important pine in the West. They appear from 3,000-5000 feet in the more protective areas, higher than the Coulter, in areas favorable to the Jeffrey pine. The trunk bark has a resinous odor as opposed to the vanilla-like odor of the Jeffrey. They have a 3-needle grouping of long 10" needles, a dull colored short, egg-shaped cone of only 3-6" that do not stay very long on the tree. Height of 60-130' but reported up to 260'. Typical trunk diameters are 2-4'.

Sugar Pine *Pinus lambertiana*

A tall, columnar, stately tree that characterizes a rich forest, seen along the PCT at the higher, cool slopes and deep soils at elevations, 4000-9000'. Not as common as the Jeffrey and Ponderosa. pines. Distinctive qualities are the long, 11-20", brighter colored cones, sweet small of the trunk without the resinous odor of the Ponderosa nor the vanilla aroma of the Jeffrey and its great height of 180-200 feet; some reported to be as high as 250'. The mature trunk bark is a quite dark brown or dark gray, in vertical ridges. The wood is prized for cabinetwork, veneer backing, house interiors and shingles.   CD

FIRS

Like spruces, firs are found in cold climates. Needles are short. From a distance they closely resemble spruces, especially, the Douglas fir. They differ from spruces in that the cone extends upward.   The needles when plucked leave a smooth circular scare on the twig. Although the big cone Douglas Fir and red fir occur in the Sierra, I do not recall seeing any other fir than the white fir from Campo to Kennedy Meadows.

White Fir *Abies concolor*

The most common fir tree along the PCT, perhaps the only true wild fir to be seen in southern California. Grows from Baja to Oregon and eastward to Colorado and New Mexico. They are easily spotted within the confines of the montane forest where they share the lower southern California montane forests with the Coulter and Jeffrey pines and cedars at elevations not exposed and above 4,500 feet.

The white fir seems to change its appearance as it matures, thus giving the impression that there are more than one species of fir to be seen in a given area. . In southern California Mountains, I've noticed that the trunks of the younger, shorter than 50' tend to have a smooth light grey or white trunk, whereas the more mature trees have a quite dark trunk, neither resembling one a nother in texture. They attain a height of 100-

180', some reported to reach 210'. Some live to 350 years. They share the lower southern California montane forests with the Coulter and Jeffrey pines and cedars at elevations not exposed and above 4,500 feet They hybrid further the north with firs limited to the northwest Pacific states and British Columbia. Their needles are bluish or greyish-green, minutely haired or smooth, 2" long, rounded or bluntly pointed at the tip, with 2 bluish-white bands on undersides. Cones greenish or purplish, 3-6". Will endure more heat, drought, and air pollution than other firs. Their twigs are eaten by deer and grouse, their seeds by squirrels and chipmunks. The woods lack odor, and as such has been used for butter making and storage.

SPRUCE

None of the spruces were seen along the PCT in southern California. According to Petrides (1998) spruces are limited to cold climates north to the limit of trees, becoming dwarf in Alaska. But not found in the Sierra, nor in southern California. Cones hang. Spruces have single needles, not clustered. Spruces sharply steeple-shaped, evergreen trees with short and stiff needles, quite sharp, are mostly more or less 4-sided. The needles grow all around the twigs.

INCENSE-CEDARS   Incense-Cedar *Calocedrus decurrens*

Easy to identify. The only "cedar" to be seen along the PCT in southern California. They also are to be found further north on the trail throughout the Sierra and Cascades. They grow in the northern California coastal range and north well into Oregon and live up to 500 years. Their short, 3/4-1" cone is inverted and erect. They grow to 60-80' with reports to 150'.

<u>Diameters are 3-4' up to 7'. When very close, they appear like the redwood tree, similar looking swollen trunk and leaves.</u> Whereas the juniper has fruits, our cedars have cones, woody and brown. They range in elevations varying form 2000-8000'. The wood is durable and fragrant; used for fencing, shingles, cedar chests, and wooden pencils.

OTHER TREES

Holly leaved cherry, Joshua trees, manzanita, mountain mahogany, chamise, scrub oak, yucca are listed with the shrubs and wild flowers

5. AVOIDING POISONOUS PLANTS

Of the thousands of species of plants that grow wild, relatively few can be considered dangerously poisonous. Peterson (1977) surveyed the area and found that cases of fatal poisoning attributed to plants are extremely rare. Livestock poisoning occurs more frequently (Clarke, 1985). Nevertheless, guidebooks indicate the necessity to positively identify the plant and to contact plant societies, botanical gardens, or state conservation agencies for a list of rare or threatened plants in the immediate area should questions occur (Foster and Dude, 2000).

Rules of thumb

..Learn to recognize plants in your area

..Most cases of poisoning involve small children

..Do not use any plant that you cannot positively identify as edible, particularly true with roots, shoots, berries and mushrooms

..Do not assume that plants that superficially resemble edible plants are themselves edible

..Avoid plants that have been sprayed with insecticides, or that grow in contaminated water or along margins of heavily traveled highways.

..Be certain which parts of plant should be collected, at what season, and proper ways to prepare them.

..Sample unfamiliar edible plants sparingly at first.

..There are no foolproof tests for determining either edible or poisonous plants. Animals are not reliable indicators.

6. SAFE FAMILIES

There are a number of entire families of plants in southern California that are safe and free of toxins. Christopher Nyerges (1999), in his recent book, Guide to Wild Foods and Useful Plants, included an appendix which serves as a relatively easy guide to recognize plant families that are nontoxic and primarily edible. Any species within the families are, within specified limits, safe. According to Nyerges it isn't always essential that you know each particular plant species before you can consider it safe. There are several entire groups of plants that are either entirely nontoxic or mostly nontoxic with some qualifications. Nyerges points out one should be certain that the given plant is a member of one of these families before sampling any part of it. I've included the family groups whose members have been seen on the PCT throughout southern California.

CACTUS FAMILY *cactaceae*

Cactus plants are perennial succulents, herbaceous, or woody. There are believed to be 2000 species worldwide. All the cactus flesh and fruits can be eaten if they are sufficiently tender, readily available, and palatable. Most of the young cactus pads, once peeled, can be eaten raw. In some cases, cooking will improve the flavor and texture. The fruits are edible raw or cooked, once peeled of their outer skins. Be careful to remove all spines before eating. A small number of relatively scarce cacti, including peyote and desert rock, are extremely bitter and if eaten in sufficient amounts, can cause a narcotic or hallucinatory effect. Some Eurphorbia, which resemble cacti, exude a thick milky juice when cut, are poisonous.

Examples:

> barrel cactus ferocactus)
> prickly Pear Opuntia)

CHICORY TRIBE OF THE SUNFLOWER FAMILY *Compositae*

The sunflower family has a daisy-like flower head. They can be annual or perennial herbs. The sunflower family is one of the largest plant families, divided by botanists into 11 or 12 distinct groups called "tribes." One of these tribes is the chicory tribe, characterized by being herbs with alternate or basal leaves and milky juice. The flowers are clustered into heads, all perfect. Each ray flower is five-toothed at its apex, an easy-to-make observation. The entire above-ground plant can usually be eaten raw; they may need to be steamed sometimes for improved palatability. The seeds can be eaten.

Examples:

> chicory *Cichoreum)*
> dandelion *Taraxacum officinale*
> Hawkweed *Hieracium*
> Malacothrix
> sow thistle *Sonchus*
> Wild and cultivated lettuce *Lactuca*

MINT FAMILY

Includes mostly aromatic herbs or low-growing shrubs with square stems and leaves that are always simple and opposite. Worldwide, there about 3,5000 species. The seeds of many can be harvested and used in bred products, ground into flour, or used in tea. CAUTIONS: Do use the leaves for tea if the flavor or aroma is unpleasant. One member, wooly blue curls Trichostema lanatum), has been used to stun fish in small pools of water. Do not use wooly blue curls for tea.

Examples

> horehound, true mints such as peppermint, spearmint, bergamont mint, pennyroyal.

MUSTARD FAMILY Cruciferae)

All members are herbs with alternate leaves and flowers in terminal racemes. There are four distinct sepals and four petals in a cross or x-form. Worldwide there are 3,2000 species. Mustard gives a spicy flavor to salads and make a good steamed vegetable or spinach-type dish. The flowers, unopened flower buds, and many of the tender fruits can also be added to salads or cooked foods. CAUTIONS: Older plants tend to be quite bitter, so they usually need to be cooked to be palatable. Avoid the tough and woody specimens, thus inedible.

Examples

> Bladderpod, broccoli, common mustard, hedge mustard, pennycress, peppergrass, shepherd's purse, squaw cabbage, sweet alyssyum, tansy mustard, toothwort, turnip, wallflower, watercress, wild radish, winter cress

OAK FAMILY *Fagaceae*

Includes oak trees, beeches, chestnuts and chinquapins. About 900 species worldwide. Most are trees, some are shrubs, and most have deciduous leaves. Refer to Acorns in the appendix for how acorns are processed for use. CAUTIONS: You must leave out the bitter tannic acid before you use them.

PURSLANE FAMILY Portulacaceae

Annual or perennial succulent herbs whose entire leaves can be alternately or oppositely arranged, or mostly basal. The flowers are perfect (contain both stamen and pistil). The fruit is a capsule. There are 580 species worldwide. The entire above-ground plant can usually be eaten raw; it may need to be steamed sometimes for improved palatability. The seeds can be harvested and eaten.

Examples:

miner's lettuce, bitterroot, desert purslane, pussy paws.

ROSE FAMILY *Rosaceae*

Consist of herbs, shrubs and trees, all with alternate leaves. The calyx is four-or-five lobed and there are usually five petals. Cultivated roses contain many more petals. Fruits are variable, ranging from a pod, an achene, a drupe (such as a plum), a cluster of drupelets, such as blackberry, or a pome, such as an apple. Worldwide there are about 3,000 species.

Many leaves of this group can be eaten, some raw, some when cooked. The petals can be eaten as well as the fruits, if fleshy and palatable. The group contains most of the commonly recognized berries, the bulk of cultivated fruits, all roses, and many wild plants. CAUTIONS: The leaves of some of the group contain cyanide. An indicator of this is the bitter-almond aroma that emanates when the leaves are crushed. Do not make tea form such leaves. Also the seeds of many of the fruits (apples, cherries and apricot) contain cyanide. There is rarely a problem consuming these seeds or nuts in small to moderate amounts, but poisonings have occurred when eaten in large amounts.

Examples:

> apples, blackberries and raspberries, cinquefoil, Cvotoneaster pannosa, pears, service berries, stone fruits including peach, cherry, apricot, almond, plum, all wild and cultivated roses, strawberries, and toyon.

WALNUT FAMILY *Juglandacaeae*

Worldwide there about 60 species, mostly walnuts. These are deciduous trees with pinnately compound leaves. The fruit is a two-lobed, hard-shelled nut enclosed in a sheath. The nuts of all can be eaten, though in many cases a rock or hammer is required to break the thick, hard shell. CAUTION: Only eat mature nuts. When collecting the freshly fallen walnuts, the husks can stain hands and clothing.

Examples:

> bitternut, black walnut, butternut, English walnut, hickorynut, pecan.

7. WHERE PLANTS WERE FOUND

Mexican Border North to Lake Morena

Chamise, scrub oak, manzanita, ribbonwood, yucca, cottonwoods, willows, baccharis, sorrel, miners lettuce, celery, water cress, pepper, live oaks, sycamores, ceanothus (lavender), mallows, forget-me-nots, blue dicks, mallows, lupine (hoary), California poppies, Majita poppies, paint brush, heliotrope, kudo vine, Mexican sage, ceanothus, amarinth, nettles

Up and Over The Laguna Mountains

Chamise, manzanita, Live-forever, pearly everlasting, thiistle, yerba santa, beavertail cactus, iris, snowberry, yellow violets, baby blue eyes, huckleberry-oak, manzanita, Coulter Pines, Jeffrey pines, black oak, poison oak, mountain mahogany, hoary-leaved ceanothus brush

Down the Laguna and Granite Mountains

Yellow Pasquel, wallflower, yarrow, baby blue eyes, miners lettuce, columbine, clarkia, low buckwheat, rabbitbrush, teddy-bear cholla, heliotrope, laurel sumac, chamise, fox tail grass, popcorn flower, brodiaea, larger junipers, agave, tumbleweed, mustard, baccharis, yucca, prickly pear, penstemon, yellow dandelion, scrub oak, ash, cottonwood, willow,

Up and Over The San Felipe Hills

Ocotillo shrubs, barrel cactus, occasional live oak. Buckwheat, rabbitbrush, sage, mesquite, chamise

Warner Springs to San Gorgonio Pass

Chamise, ceanothus, ribbonwood, ocean spray, sumac, sagebrush, mountain mahogany, holly-leaf cherry, yerba santa, baccharis shrubs, sycamores, cottonwoods, chia, white forget-me-nots, beavertail cacti, squaw brush, brodiaea, sycamores, willows, Coulter pines, oaks, chamise, Coulter pines, live oaks, chamise, oaks, live oaks, Coulter pines, Mojave yuccas, rabbit brush, cacti, white firs, black oak, white fir, incense-cedar, Jeffrey pine, lodgepole, manzanita, western white pines, Coulter pines, yerba santa, buckwheat, holly-leaf cherry,. Scrub oak, manzanita, yucca, scarlet gilia

San Gorgonio Pass to Cajon Pass

Mojave yucca, bristlebrush, rabbit brush, creosote bush, cacti, laurel sumac trees, phacelia, chia, popcorn flower, fiddleneck, foxtail brush, baccharis, alder, willows, cottonwoods, chia, yerba santa, catclaw, bladderpod, Joshua tree, yucca, cacti, alders, incense-cedars, Jeffrey pines, interior live oaks, mountain mahogany, manzanita, pinyon pines, Jeffrey pines, white fir, lupine, purple sage, lodgepole pine, juniper, mountain mahogany, white fir groves, pinyon pines, buckwheat, ephedra, Mormon tea, Joshua trees, pinyon pines, sagebrush, rabbitbrush, pinyon pine, junipers, cedars, Jeffrey pines junipers, black oaks, mountain mahogany, buckwheat, flannelbrush, cedars, spruces, holly-leaf cherry, willows, cottonwoods, alders, baccharis, willows, cottonwoods, chamise, buckwheat, flannelbrush, chamise, buckwheat, yerba santa,

Cajon Pass to Agua Dulce

sunflower, chamise, cacti, chia, big cone spruce, mountain mahogany, juniper, black oak, white firs, whitehorn, bitter cherry, live oaks, ocean spray, Jeffrey pine, white fir, lodgepole pines, limber pines, manzanita, sagebrush, white firs, ceanothus, white fir, sugar and ponderosa pines, interior live oak, mountain mahogany, interior live oaks, mountain mahogany, hoary-leaved ceanothus, flannelbush, yerba santa, Jeffrey pines, rabbitbrush, interior live oaks, ponderosa pines, Coulter pines, brodiaea, lush grasses, big cone spruce, incense cedar, black oaks, Jeffrey pines, ponderosa pines, oak, spruce, Coulter pine, yerba santa, chia, fidddleneck, false willows, watercress, sycamores, lichens, yerba santa, buckwheat, willows, Baccharis shrubs, squaw brush, flannelbrush, poison oak. Buckwheat, sagebrush shrubs, junipers.

Agua Dulce to Highway 58 Near Tehachapi

chamise, foxtails, yellow mustard, grape vines, bunch grasses, interior live oaks, canyon live oaks, interior live oaks, big-cone spruces, Coulter pines, incense -cedars, oaks, big cone spruces, black oaks, brodiaea, baby blue-eyes, iner lettuce, big cone spruce, Coulter pines, black oak, scrub oak, manzanita, buckwheat, Joshua trees, rabbitbrush, junipers, pinyon pines, Coulter pines, junipers.

Highway 58 Near Tehachapi Pass to H78 at Walker Pass

pinyon pines, sagebrush, baby blue eyes, Jeffrey pines, black oaks, white firs, mistletoe, black oaks, willows, golden oaks, manzanita, wallflowers, blue-purple lupines, pinyon pines, blue penstemon, pinyon pines, sagebrush, buckbrush, belly plants.

Section G: H 178 Walker Pass to Kennedy Meadows

Blue chia, lupines, forget-me-nots, willows, cottonwoods, pinyon pines, Jeffrey pines, sugar pines, white firs, black oaks, rabbit brush, sagebrush, coreopsis, willow, wild rose, sedges, watercress, junipers, pinyon pines, agave, baccharis,

SUPPLEMENT E

Water, Water Everywhere, But Nothing to Drink! On Water Carriage and Body Hydration

Distant water sources through southern California....How many containers to fill?....Signs of dehydration on the trail.... Loss of judgement is an early symptom....A little bit of theory ....Importance of early detection....Offsetting the impact of dehydration

Walking the PCT throughout Southern California through late Spring requires covering long distances between water sources. Trekking northbound on the PCT typically requires ascending southern slopes which are often exposed to the sun and without shade for many miles. The ascent becomes more challenging when conditions are warm or hot.

Water Sources Through Southern California

Table 1 presents a summary of the distance between known water sources, northbound on the Pacific Crest Trail throughout southern California. The data was compiled by reference to the *Pacific Crest Trail Data Book* tempered by observations of my own travels through southern California along the PCT throughout the spring and early summer of 1999, 2000 and 2001, relatively dry years.

Table 1
Water Sources From Mexico To Kennedy Meadows

Distance Between Water Sources

Miles Between Sources	Number of Occasions	Total Occasions
1-6	***** ***** ***** ***** ***** ***** ***** ***** ***** ***** ****	54
7-10	***** ***** ***** *****	20
11-14	***** ****	9
15-19	*****	5
20+	***** *	6

There are forty occasions trekking through southern California when water sources are greater than seven miles, 40% of the PCT in the southern sections. There are eleven occasions when water sources were beyond 14 miles apart. Six hauls longer than 20 miles include (a) a 23.8 mile trek through the Anza Borrego Desert including traversing the San Felipe Hills, (b) a 23 mile exposed and generally uphill stretch from Agua Caliente Creek (five miles north of Warner Springs) to Tule Creek, (c) a 22 mile mixed altitude jaunt through the northern San Jacinto Mountains down through exposed areas to Snow Canyon Road to a water fountain (d) a 23 mile uphill ascent between Cajon Pass and Guffy Campground above Wrightwood, (e) an exposed 23 mile up and down trek from Agua Dulce over the eastern section of the Sierra Pelona Mountains to the Ranger Station at San Francisquito Canyon, near Green Valley, and (f) A 28 mile exposed stretch from the moist

Piute Mountains to McGyvers Stream on top of the Scodie Mountains, unless one goes off the trail for a few miles in between.

The distance over the Mojave desert is 17 miles, from Neenach, to Cottonwood Creek. Because of easy terrain, comfortable conditions at night and early mornings, the exposed leg does not seem to present much of a problem as one might otherwise suppose.

Critical periods occurred with medium distances of 8-14 miles through exposed areas requiring ascents during conditions of unexpected heat after midday, with dry winds or no winds at all. It was traversing these medium distances in the southern Sierras that a significant number of us experienced serious troubles in 2000. We all had the experience in crossing deserts where we had sustained ourselves during hot and dry conditions. Such conditions occurred in late spring through the southernmost exposed slopes of the Sierra, north of Tehachapi Pass and again north of Walker Pass on the way to the West Fork of the Kern River, just south of Kennedy Meadows.

How Many Water Containers to Carry? How Many to Fill?

It is apparent that conservative planning should consider more factors than temperature and distance. One may consider ranges of anticipated weather conditions, trail grade, available shade from trees or cloud formation, changing temperatures, breeze, kind and quality of clothing one has available, the weight of the pack on the back, one's level of endurance, time of day, and an appreciation of how much milage you, and any companion, can comfortably put on a given day. Any of these factors can interact with the others to cause one to rapidly cross limits of safety.

According to Hackett (1993) The decrease in the relative humidity of the cold, dry air of mountain environment, combined with rigorous exercise, results in additional marked fluid losses. Normally, the respiratory passages moistens all air inhaled, but does not reclaim the moisture in the air exhaled. One to two liters of water (without salt) can be lost this way each day at moderate altitudes. Sweating also takes place more freely in the dry air with loss of body salt.

When trekking long distances, the object of drinking water is not so much to offset the sensation of thirst, but to keep the level of body hydration under control. Here, experience in long distance trekking or related experiences when water must be carried, can help. Consider that water weighs two pounds per quart (plus the weight of the container). When doing multiple ascents over exposed ridges on a warm day, one is not likely to drink water anywhere near a rate necessary to compensate for water discharged by sweating.

Indeed, the additional carriage of water creates an added stressor. An election to camp overnight amidst a dry site results in more water consumption. The time spent overnight, along with cooking, adds time and output of energy before reaching the next water source. The longer the time spent on trail, the greater is the uncertainty of what weather lies ahead..

Some long distance trekkers find it helpful to cover long distances at a high rate of speed, thus avoiding highly exposed area thus avoiding a dry overnight campsite. Experienced thru-hikers with light packs, can sometimes handle such conditions in southern portions of the PCT by covering 25 or even up to 35 miles per 24 hour period, thus enabling them to reach their supply point in a comfortable period of time.

Covering such distances per day, of course, enables one to complete the entire PCT in one year. One can do so averaging about 16 miles per full walking day. This figure also allows for a good number of additional full or partial layover days. But in practice, one decides for themselves, prior to each leg, a strategy as to how to cover distances between legs. In southern California, options for water carriage is critical. Each individual must decide for themselves what will work for them considering their goals. It may boil down to how many containers to carry? How many to fill with water?

Signs and Symptoms of Dehydration on the Trail

The following body, behavioral and psychic signposts are associated with abnormal body dehydration.

<table>
<tr><td colspan="2" align="center">Table 2: Symptoms of Dehydration on the Trail</td></tr>
<tr><td>bloated feeling in the gut</td><td>fever</td></tr>
<tr><td>circulatory shock</td><td>sensation of heat</td></tr>
<tr><td>confusion</td><td>sparsity of urine</td></tr>
<tr><td>coma.</td><td>Dark colored urine</td></tr>
<tr><td>constipation</td><td>Vomiting/dry heaves</td></tr>
<tr><td>decrease of sweating</td><td>diarrhea</td></tr>
<tr><td>dry skin</td><td>dry throat and tongue</td></tr>
<tr><td>weakness/drop in performance</td><td>nausea</td></tr>
<tr><td>loss in general judgement</td><td>dizziness, light headedness</td></tr>
<tr><td>feeling of impending blackout</td><td>irrelevant focus of awareness</td></tr>
</table>

postural change in blood pressure and/or pulse (>20% upon sitting after lying)

Compare with signs and symptoms of panic reaction, circulatory shock, apoxia, altitude sickness, hypothermia, heat exhaustion and heatstroke.

Psycho-Physiological Reactions to Lack of Water:

When we don't get enough water, tissues of the body dry out as water moves from the vast reservoir among and inside body cells to be injected into the bloodstream. The cells, and the tissue of which the cells form, begin to shrivel and malfunction. Brain cells are the most susceptible to dehydration and thus poor judgement and mental confusion will be among the first signs or symptoms.

Loss of Judgement May Be Among First Symptoms of Dehydration

But there is more to it. At first I was puzzled as to how it was that loss of judgement was the first observable major symptom of dehydration at the exclusion of many other signs and symptoms. I'll try to explain how it can happen. A little bit of theory is needed here.

A Little Bit of Theory

There are three types of body signals associated with body reactivity to stressor events. An event or signal becomes a stressor when the event is followed by two kinds of body responses, an excitatory stress response (EXCITOR) and an inhibitory body reaction (INHIBITOR). The function of the INHIBITOR is to cease its hold on body reactivity and thus permit specific EXCITORs to occur and do their thing. The stressor in our scenario is lack of water to accommodate tissue need. When this event occurs, inhibitory and excitatory body reactions coordinate to offset the impact of low water levels.

A situation likely to occur during a dehydrated body state is a premature failure on the part of an INHIBITOR to permit conditions that will lead to replenishment of water to the cells that are competing in need. In our outdoor scenario, a likely systemic reaction to this initial failure will be an over-compensatory excitatory reaction in a way similar to circulatory shock, that produces hypoxic-like symptoms long before the slower parade of symptoms associated with dehydration. Like hypoxia that occurs during simulated high altitude flight without added oxygen, the changes in judgement and performance is first noticeable by others, way before it is recognized by the pilot.

The first sign that one is approaching a dehydrated state in the midst of strenuous outdoor environment can very well be a deficit of judgement in making effective tactical and strategic decisions at a time when good judgement is needed most.

Deficiency in Electrolytes

Compounding the problem, dehydration is often accompanied by a deficiency in electrolytes. When electrolytes are deficient, water doesn't move as readily from the large reservoir of cells into the bloodstream. Here we have another stressor event. Water is held in body reservoirs impeding entry to the blood stream. A number of over-compensatory events can immediately occur including a blood pressure drop causing light-headed-ness, and sensations of impending blackout, particularly upon standing (orthostatic hypotension). Should the water and/or electrolyte losses continue, blood pressure will fall dangerously low, resulting in more over-compensatory action such as circulatory shock that may cause severe damage to organs, such as the kidney, liver and brain. All this can occur even though there are untapped reservoirs of water throughout the body and even if one quenches one's thirst.

Importance of Early Detection

For such body events to take place, one would quite likely be alone and in a non-forgiving environment. What we need to know, especially at times we travel by ourselves, is that we must recognize some of these body events taking place in ourselves before we become incapacitated. Yes, we can more readily observe such symptoms in others, psychic disturbances such as dizziness, exhaustion and loss of judgement. These can well be among the first body activities to become dysfunctional. So, should we become aware of the existence of any of the above signs or symptoms in ourselves or among others, let these signals serve as cues for us to act quickly to offset or reverse the course of dehydration.

Offsetting the Impact of Dehydration

For mild dehydration, drinking of sufficient water over time, may be all that is needed. However, when both water and electrolyte losses have occurred, salt (especially sodium and potassium) must also be replaced. In other cases, all that may be necessary to offset the impact of poor judgement is to modify tactics and strategies in order to finish the leg in a more satisfactory manner. This may be a simple matter if two or more trekkers are hiking as a group. However, if one is trekking solo, special care must be taken to assure early a Pleasant outcome.

Table 3: Preventive Measures to Avoid Dehydration

Attend to water carriage; not too much as the weight contributes as a stressor; and certainly carry not too little between water sources.

Drink fluids before thirst sets in.

Take special care and planning when alone.

You may not be aware of your symptoms even though obvious to others.
Be on the lookout for others who may be symptomatic.

A simple bit of advice to a hiker may offset a major problem.

When short on water avoid panting, especially in dry air.

Adjust clothes to minimize sweating.

Monitor color of urine and take preventive measures when discolored.

Adjust pace to offset overall heat production when trail is exposed.

Carry some salty foods: not necessarily tablets, but if so, a tablet with eight ounces of water.

Collect sweat and utilize as a cooling device, e.g. a wet neckerchief over the head or about the neck and shoulders

When temperatures will soar, get up early; plan to rest in a cool area.

Should dizziness occur, only a bit of time may be needed for the body to re-accommodate it's signaling mechanisms. A sign for a rest and to take stock of options.

ABBREVIATIONS

ALDHA	American Long Distance Hiking Associatiion
BLM	U.S. Bureau of Land Management
CG	Campground
El	Elevation in feet
EXCITOR	Excitatory stress reaction; body action that directly ameliorates the impact of a stressor event.
FBO	Fixed base operation, ground facility supporting aircraft operations
FS	U.S. Forest Service
GPS	Global positioning system, used here as a portable hand carried device used for navigation
GHA	Green Hornets Aviation
GVL	Green Valley Lake, located in the San Bernardino Mountains
INHIBITOR	A body Inhibitory reaction to a stressor event.
KM	Kennedy Meadows campground and store
PEST	Proactive excitatory stress reaction. A body stress reaction that occurs as a result of change in body signaling. A normal and expected body response due to change in action..
H	State Highway, e.g. H74, highway 74
I	Interstate, e.g. I10, interstate 10
Mi	Milage, distance along the PCT from Mexican border
PCT	Pacific Crest Trail
PCTA	Pacific Crest Trail Association
STRESSOR	An internal or external event prompting a defensive body reaction
USGS	U.S. Geological Survey, used to describe topological maps with contours with latitude and longitude

+	plus miles over and beyond milage on the PCT, e.g + 0.4 indicates four tenths of an additional mile walked
-	Less miles trekked on the actual PCT trail, e.g. - 0.5 indicates a half mile was skipped
0.5	Refers to proportion of overhead clouding.

GLOSSARY

Plant Descriptions

alternate leaves	Leaves on a stalk that alternate, non-symmetrical
furrowed	Refers to a tree bark, series of rows
lancelated	Spearlike in shape, a leaf considerably longer than its width
leaflets	A subdivision of a complex leaf. Appears like series of leaves
ovate	A shape of a leaf; oval; the broader end is at the base
palmate	A leaf shaped like the palm of the hand
pedicle	A stem from a stalk supporting a flower
pinnate	Arranged in rows
racemes	A long flower cluster, individual flowers appear on long stalks with pedicle
spatulate	A leaf shaped like a spade
spikes	An elongated flower cluster without pedicle
umbel	Shaped like an umbrella
whorled	Circular leaf arrangement on a stalk

Body Reactions as Used in Text

apoxia	Lack of oxygen to brain tissue
dehydration	Critical lack of water in body cell tissue
endorphins	Brain substances that bind to opiate receptors and raise the threshold to pain
EXCITORS	(Original term) Body activity that directly offsets the impact of a stressor event
heat exhaustion	Fatigue resulting from over heating
heat stroke	The body does not adapt to heat (serious)

hypothermia	Loss of effective production of protective body heat
INHIBITOR	(Original term) Body control mechanism permitting excitatory stress reactions to ameliorate the impact of a stressor
PEST	(Original term) Proactive excitatory stress reaction; follows any change in body adaptation

Miscellaneous Terms Used in Text

marker	Trail identifier; a sign or imprint
Shabbot	Jewish sabbath; Friday evening through Saturday through dusk
waypoint	A landmark manually entered into a GPS receiver usually based on latitude and longitude and designated by address (a name).
SILOGRAM	Name of our family corporation, "MARGOLIS," spelled backwards
Silogram	A number of unique devices I designed, e.g. a stretchable ruler to measure longitude on a map.

REFERENCES

Angier, Beradford. *Feasting Free on Wild Edibles*. Pyramid Books, New York: 1966, 1975.

Berger, K. & Smith, Daniel R. *The Pacific Crest Trail: A Hikers Companion*. The Countryman Press: Woodstock, Vermont, 2000.

Brown, Vinson. The Sierra Nevadan Wildlife Region. Naturegraph Company: San Martin, CA, 1954.

Burn, Barbara. *North American Wildflowers*. The National Audubon Society Collection. Bonanza Books: New York, 1984.

Chandler, Philip et. al. *Taylor's Guide to Trees*. Houghton Mifflin: New York, 3rd Ed., 1987.

Clarke, Charlotte Bringle. *Edible and useful Plants of California*. University of California Press: Los Angeles, 1951.

Clarkson, Quentin D. *Handbook of Field Botany*. Binford and Mort: Portland, Oregon, 1961.

Coffey, Timothy. *The history and Folkore of North American Wildflowers*. Houghton-Mifflin: New York, 1994.

Dale, Nancy. *Flowering Plants: The Santa Monica Mountains, Coastal Mand Chaparral Regions of Southern California*. Capra Press in Cooperation with The California Native Society: Santa Barbara, 1985.

Downs, Allen. *The Great Allen Downs Adventure on the Pacific Crest Trail*, Self Published, 2000.

Foster, Steven and Duke, James A. *Medicinal Plants and Herbs of Eastern and Central North America.*, 2nd Ed, HoughtonMifflin: New York, 2000.

Henderson, Brad. *Wildflowers of the San Bernardino Mountains.* Irvine Press: Lake Arrowhead, Ca, 1999.

PDR Medical Dictionary, 1999, p 468.

Hackett, Peter H. *Mountain Sickness: Prevention, Recognition and Treatment. American.* Alpine Club: Golden, Colorado, 1993, p53f.

Henderson, Brad. *Wildflowers of the San Bernardino Mountains. San Bernardino Mountains* Land Trust, Irvine Press: Lake Arrowhead, CA, 1999.

Kircher, John & Morrison, Gordon. *Field Guide to California and Pacific Northwest Forests.* Houghton Mifflin: New York, 1998.

Lanzara, Paola and Pizzetti, Mariella. *Guide to Trees to Trees.* Simon and Schuster: New York, 1987.

Terrain Navigator, 2001. California Terrain Coverage (Compact Discs), Maptech: Andover, Md: www.maptech.com, 2001.

Margolis, Harold J. *Inhibitory Control Theory*, Silogram: Los Angeles, 1991, p268.

Merck Manual of Medical Information, Home Edition, 1997, p665.

Munz, Philip A. *California Mountain Wildflowers.* University of California Press: Los Angeles, 1972.

Niehaus, Theodore F. and Ripper, Charles L. *Pacific States Wildflowers.* Houghton Mifflin: New York, 1976.

Nyerges, Christopher. *Guide to Wild Foods and Useful Plants*. Chicago Review Press: 1999.

Pacific Crest Trail, Mexico to Canada, Data Book, PCTA, 1997.

Parson, Mary Elizabeth. *The Wildflowers of California*. Dover Publications: New York, 1966.

Peterson, Lee Allen. A *Field Guide to Edible Wild Plants of Eastern and Central North America*. Houghton-Mifflin: New York, 1977.

Petrides, George A and Petrides, Olivia, *Western Trees*. Houghton-Mifflin: New York, 1998.

Pizzetti, Mariella. *Guide to Cacti and Succulents*. Simon & Schuster: New York, 1985.

Plants and People of the Sonoran Desert: Trail Guide. Desert Botanical Garden: Phoenix, ca 1986.

Robinson, John W. *Trails of the Angeles: 100 Hikes in the San Gabriels*, Ed. 1998, Wilderness Press: Berkeley, 1971.

Ross, Cindy. *Journey on the Crest*. The Mountaineers: Seattle, 1987.

Schad, Jerry. *101 Hikes in Southern California: Exploring Mountains, Seashore and Desert*. Wilderness Press: Berkeley, 1996.

Schaeffer, Hjeffrey P. et. al. *The Pacific Crest Trail, v1: California*. Wilderness Press: Berkeley, 5th Ed., 2000.

Schimelpfenig, Tod and Lindsey, Linda. *Wideness First Aid*. National Outdoor Leadership School and Stockpole Books, 2nd Ed. Lander: Wyoming, 1992 pp 305-309, 133-188

Semb, Gearge and Patricia.. *Day Hikes on the Pacific Crest Trail.* Wilderness Press: Berkeley, 2000.

Spellenberg, Richard. *The Audubon Society Field Guide* to North American Wildflowers. Alfred A Knopf: New York, 2001.

Tilford, Gregory L. *Edible and Medicinal Plants of the West.* Mountain Press: Missoula, Montana, 1997.

Topo! Southern California Terrain Sections (Compact Discs) Sunflower Productions: San Francisco, 1997.

Townsend, Chris, *The Backpackers Handbook*, 2nd Ed, Ragged mountain Press: Camden, Maine, 1997.

United States Geological Survey (USGS) Maps of various scales.

INDEX

Foliage... Peaks, ridges and ranges....Landmarks
and places....Events and topics....Trails....
Animals encountered....Names of trekkers & others

Foilage

agava 377, **388**
alder tree 92, 120, 143, 144, 146, 179, 180, 187, **413**, 419, 433
amaranth 37, **388**
ash 319, **413, 432**
baby blue eyes **389**, 432, 434
baccharis 143, 144, 179, 193, 303, 385, 389, *397*, 432, 433, 434,
barrel cactus 61, **389,** 391, 428, 432,
blue dicks (see brodeiaea)
brittlebrush 229
brodiaea 385, **390**, 432-434,
buckwheat, 124, 167, 348, 357, 385, **391**, 432-434
California black oak (see oaks)
California buckwheat (see buckwheat)
California coffee berry (see coffee berry)
California poppy 226
canyon live oak 244
carob tree **414**
cattail **391**
ceanothus 36, 81, 84, 143, 179, 180, 198, 203, 385, 386, **391**, 392,
    432-434
chamise 7, 10, 11, 13, 14, 20, 21, 37, 67, 143, 202, 370, 377, **392,**
    408, 416, 426, 432-434
cherry 124, 385, 393, 395, **398**, 426, 431, 433
chia 138, 169, 180, 198, 385, **393**, 433, 434

chickweed 385, **393,** 407,

chinquapin 385, 390, **395,** 430

chokeberry 168, 197, 199, 385, **395**

cholla 20, 37, 377, 391, **410**

coffeeberry **393**

coreopsis (sunflowers) **396,** 434

cottonwood 20, 22, 24, 26, 34, 37, 143, 180, 193, 282, 288, 311, 319, 323, 350, 370, 413, **415,** 418, 432-434

Coulter pines 42, 43, 77, 84, 97, 124, 132, 304, **421**-425, **432-434**

creosite bush 385, **395**

currants **396**

desert trumpet 230

Fir (white fir) 146, 147, 155, 262, **424,** 433

flannelbrush 385, **397,** 433, 434

forget-me-nots 14, 19, 61, 370, 376, 385, **397,** 432, 433

foxtail pine **421**

Gooseberries 396, **397**

grasses 19, 20, 38, 41-43, 67, 83, 87, 95, 143, 175, 179, 180, 189, 202, 204, 239, 282, 283, 303, 326, 336, 348, 371, 375, 385, 390, 402, 405, 406, **412,** 413, 417, 429, 432, 434

greasewood **226,** 231

groundsel (see baccharis) 385, 389, **397**

holly-leaved cherry tree 226, 231, 234, **398**

hyacinth 226, 230

incense-cedar **426**

interior live oak 244, 256

Jeffrey pine **422**

Joshua tree 108, 144, 169, 312, 315, 324, 326, 327, 331, 336, 338, 340, 349, 385, 398, **399,** 426, 433, 434

juniper 62, 134, 140, 154, 140, 171, 174, 239, 326, 336, 385, 387, 405, **419,** 420, 426, 432-434

laurel sumac 37, 385, **399,** 432-434

limber pine 254, **422,** 434

lodgepole pine **423**

lupine 19, 239, 263, 370, **399,** 400, 432-434

mallows 19, 37, 376, **400**, 432

manzanita 20, 21, 26, 36, 37, 41, 42, 66, 81, 84, 124, 147, 178, 171, 199,202, 203, 256, 262, 324, 370, 375, 385, **400**, 401, 426, 432

mesquite 35, 41, 142, 186, 193, 204, 385, 324, **401**, 433,

miners lettuce 20, 370, 375, **401**, 432

monkey flower 226, 236

mountain mohagony 132, 143, 147, 168, 170, 171, 174, 239, 261, 385, **403**, 432-434

Mormon tea 226, 236, 256

mountain mahogany 94, 107, 109, 112, 161, 226, 237, 250, 255, 256

mustard 14, 37, 202, 204, 385, **403-406**, 429, 432434

oak trees **416**

ocotillo 61, **404,** 405, 432

penstemon **405**, 432, 434

peppergrass 20, 370, 385 **405**, 406, 429, 432,

phacelia 138, **406,** 433,

pinyon pine 98, 109, 196, 201, 226, 256

poison oak 93, 119, 140, 142, 161, 226, 239, 256

ponderosa 179, 261, 422, **423**, 434

prickly pear 36, 99, 132, 169, 171, 375, 377, 385, 391, **408**, 428, 432

rabbit brush 136, 137, **408**, 433, 434

ribbonwood (see chamise) 370, 385, **392,** 408, 432, 433

sage/sagebrush 14, 62, 81, 83, 166, 167, 186, 198, 202, 256, 312, 324, 348, 385, 405, 408, 409, 432-434

scarlet gilia **409**, 433

scrub oak 20, 21,. 37, 42, 62, 64, 65, 81, 84, 124, 170, 198, 370, 375-377, 385, 386, 415, **416**, 432-434

skyrocket(see scarlet gilia)

snow plant **410**

spruce 84, 261, 421, 424, **425**

sugar pine 148, 261, 434, **423**

Sunflowers (see coreopsis) **396**, 428, 433, 389

sycamore 22, 282, 289, 319, 415, **417**, 419, 432-434

teddy bear cholla (see cholla)

toyon **411**

willow tree 20, 22, 95, 144, 146, 179, 192, 193, 109, 143, 288, 289, 303, 311, 319, 337, 349, 375, 413, 415, **418,** 432-434
yerba santa 124, 132, 202, 385, 407, **411,** 432-434
yucca 20, 36, 42, 124, 132, 136, 144, 146, 169, 171, 180, 186, 324, 327, 338, 370, 371, 385, 398, 399, **412,** 432, 433

Peaks, Ridges and Mountain Ranges

Antsell Rock 101
Apache Peak 99, 100
Bertha Mountain 179
Blue Ridge 203, 214, 216, 218, 237, 238, 240, 255, 257
Butterfly Peaks 99
Cleghorn Ridge 131, 202
Combs Peak 77, 79, 83-85
Cornell Peak 111
Delamar Mountain 177, 179
Fuller Ridge 107, 118, 121, 138
Gold Mountain 171, 179
Granie Mountain 60
Hauser Mountains 1, 13, 15, 18-21, 33, 35-37
Jeppesen Mountain 148
Kratka Ridge 261
Laguna Moungtains
Lions Peak 99
Mayan Peak 336
Morena Butte 22
Mount Baden Powell 203, 237, 239, 242, 244, 250, 251, 252, 255, 422
Mount Baldy 203, 238
Mount Grinnell 95
Mount San Jacinto 95, 218, 219
Mt Islip 256
Mt Jenkins 347, 349
Mt Pacifico 268, 270, 271

Mt Whitney 341
Mt Williamson 261
Owens Peak 348
Palm View Peak 99
Pine Mountain 238, 255
Pinyon Peak/Mountain 336
Piute Mountains 335
Pyramid Peak 99
Red Tahquitz Peak 101
San Andreas Fault 203
San Bernardino Mountains 84, 85, 90, 92, 95, 99, 105, 225, 241, 380
San Bernardino Peak 148
San Felipe Hills 29, 51, 58-61, 65, 186, 377
San Gabriel Mountains 50, 131, 203, 228, 237, 255, 256, 259, 267,
    271, 273, 278, 285-287, 299, 323
San Jacinto Mountains 84, 85, 90, 92, 95, 99, 105, 225, 241, 380
Santa Ana Mountains 118
Santa Rosa Moungtains 66, 77, 79, 84, 100, 225, 379
Scodie Mountains
Sierra Pelona
Spitler Peak 100
Table Mountain 89
Tahquitz Peak 101, 102, 107, 118
Tehachapi Mountains 303, 310, 313, 321, 323
Ten Thousand Foot Ridge 148, 149
Telegraph Peak 217
Throop Peak 255
Wright Mountain 203, 238

Landmarks & Places

Acton 277, 284-286, 312
Agua Dulce
Angeles National Forest 298, 299
Arrrastre Trail Camp 155

Baja 4, 9, 37
Banner, town of 58
Banning Pass (San Gorgonio Pass) 85, 106, 126, 135
Barrel Springs 59, 61, 66-68
Barton Flats 147, 148
Bear Springs 178, 299, 300
Bird Spring Pass 338, 339
Borrego Springs 51, 66
Boulder Oaks 19, 25-27, 29-32, 34, 55
Bouquet Canyon 299, 300
Buckhorn CG 259
Burnt Rancheria CG 29, 35, 40, 44, 50, 241
Cabazon 105
Cajon Pass 130-132, 172, 184, 184, 196, 199, 203, 204, 209, 210,
    214, 218, 224
California Aqueduct 311, 312
Cameron Overpass
Camp Lacky 123
Camp Seeley 195
Campo 1-4, 6,8, 12, 13, 17-19, 24, 27, 47, 50, 92, 120, 213, 226,
    260, 278, 369, 370
Caribou Creek 171
Cedar Glen 185, 192, 202
Chilao Flats 255, 264, 265
Chimney Creek CG
Chimney Peak Wilderness 355
Cibbits Flat CG 29, 31-33, 35, 38-41, 45, 80
Cleveland National Forest 255
Cloudburst Summit 264
Coachela Valley 84, 95, 96, 101
Coon Creek 133, 146, 149-152, 156, 241
Cooper Canyon 259, 263
Cooper Canyon Trail Camp 259, 263
Cottonwood Creek 313
Cottonwood Valley 26-28

Crab Creek 173, 179, 181

Crab Flats 178, 180-182

Crestline 195, 199, 202, 205, 218

Crystal Lake 261

Cucamonga Wilderness Area 217

Deep Creek 186-193

Deep Creek Hot Springs 131, 183, 188, 191, 229, 235

Deer Springs 118, 120, 154

Eagles Roost 261

Elizabeth Lake Canyon 303, 304

Escondido Canyon 281, 288-290

Fred Canyon 35, 38

Gold Canyon 131, 137

Grassy Hollow Visitor Center 214, 229, 234, 237, 238, 241, 243, 251,

Green Valley 299, 301-303

Green Valley Ranger Station 303

Green Valley Lake 147, 148, 163, 164, 166, 173, 180-182, 184, 205, 235, 299, 301-303

Guffy CG 217, 219, 220, 237, 238, 240

Holcomb Creek 185

Holcomb Creek Crossing Trail Camp 131, 173, 178, 180, 182, 183,

Horse Thief Canyon 131, 199, 202, 203

Humber Park 78, 95, 102, 103, 105, 106, 112, 361

Idylwild 103-106, 114, 115, 117, 118

Idylwild State Park 117

Indian Canyon 282

Inspiration Point 240, 257

Islip Saddle 257, 260, 261

Jackson Flat CG 238, 242, 251

Jawbone Canyon 333-335

Julian 57, 58, 369, 378

Kearsarge Pass 361, 363, 364, 366

Kennedy Meadows 224, 281, 343-345, 351, 354, 358-360, 363, 364

Kern River, south fork 342, 343, 345, 355-357

458   INDEX

Kern Valley Airport 333
Kiavah Wilderness 339
L.A. Aqueduct 311, 312
Lake Hemet 100
Lake Henshaw 71
Lake Hughes 303
Lake Isabella 335, 340, 341, 349
Lake Morena 1,12, 13, 18, 19, 23-27, 37, 104, 145, 241, 369, 370, 372, 373, 376
Lamel Springs 242, 253
Little Bear CG 178
Little Horse Thief Canyon 131, 202, 203
Little Jimmy Trail Camp 256
Live Oak Springs 95, 97-99
Long Canyon 42
Lower Shake CG 304
Lytle Ridge 203, 209, 214, 216, 218
Mount Pacifico CG 271-277
Mattox Canyon 282, 286
Messenger Flats CG 266, 277, 280
Mexican border 6-16
Mission Creek 141-146
Mojave Desert 136, 185, 192, 193, 199, 218, 239, 248, 256, 262, 279, 291, 299, 303, 310, 311, 318, 321, 323, 325, 326, 331, 341, 345, 351,
Mojave Dam 193, 199
Mojave River 192, 193
Moreno Valley 118
Needle Creek 343, 345, 348-351
Neenach 298, 299, 305, 307, 311, 313
North Fork Ranger Station 280, 281, 299
Oak Creek, 319
Oaks Camp 156, 165, 166
Palm Springs Tramway 111
Paradise Inn 91

Pine Canyon 216, 304, 305
Pine Tree Canyon 327, 328
Pines Motel, Wrightwood 222, 227, 228, 235
Pioneer Mail Picnic Area 34, 48, 49, 53, 54, 58, 369, 375
Posta Valley 44
Ranch Motel, Tehachapi 311, 320
Rattlesnake Canyon 261, 262
Red Dome 139
Ridgecrest 347
Robins Nest RV Park 282, 286
Rockhorse Basin 356
Saddle Junction 78, 94, 95, 100, 102, 107, 112, 113
Salton Sea 34, 51, 84
San Bernardino National Forest 95, 131, 147, 148
San Francisquito Canyon 303
San Gabriel River 238, 241, 255
San Gorgonio Pass 77, 95, 117, 122, 124, 127, 130, 1231, 133
Santa Clarita River 285, 286
Scissors Junction 34, 58-60, 369, 374, 376-378
Sequoia National Forest 339
Sheriff's Substation at San Bernardino 157f
Sierra Pelona Valley 288
Silverwood Lake 131, 185, 192, 199-201
Skyline Ranch 333
Snow Creek 121, 124, 126-128, 135
Snow Forest Ski Resort 113
Soledad Canyon 277, 278, 281, 284-286, 288
Spunky CG 299-301
Strawberry Canyon 109
Strawberry Junction and TC 95, 118-120, 241
Sulphur Springs CG 259, 260, 264, 267, 268, 271
Summit Valley 131, 132, 168, 185, 192-194, 196, 198, 199, 204, 235
Summit Valley Country Store 185, 192-194, 196, 199, 204
Tehachapi Airport 311, 320
Terwilliger Valley 83, 88

Teutang Canyon 131, 138
Three Points 255, 257, 259, 260, 264, 271, 278, 299, 304, 305, 308, 321
Tule Creek 77, 85, 86, 260
Tylerhorse Canyon 311, 317
Upper Shake CG 304
Vallecito Valley 51
Van Dusen Canyon 165, 166, 170, 171, 173, 175, 195
Van Nuys Airport 95, 115, 116, 233
Vasquez Rocks 282, 285, 287-289, 299
Vincent Gap 239, 251, 252, 257
Walker Pass 281, 322, 323, 325, 333, 334, 341, 343-345, 347, 349, 352, 353
Warm Springs 188
Warner Springs 1, 2, 49, 59, 60, 66, 68, 71-73, 76, 77, 79, 117, 121, 294, 369, 376, 378, 379
Warner Springs Glider Port
Wellmans Divide 102, 108
West Palm Springs Village 127, 136, 225
Whitewater Creek 131, 133, 139, 141
Willow Creek (south slope of Mt. San Jacinto) 109
Willow Springs 336, 337
Windy Gap 256
Wrightwood 209, 213, 216-221, 223, 224, 227-229, 237, 257-259

EVENTS AND TOPICS

Blizzards 108, 237
cellular phone, use of 68, 72, 124, 127, 134, 156, 158, 162, 192, 196, 234, 242, 252, 256, 286, 378
Dehydration 220, 290, 308, 315, 336, 338, 355, 356, 362, 436-442
Forest fire/s 197, 238
gales 51, 63, 331
GPS 6, 18, 29, 320, 321
heat exhaustion

heat stroke
Hypothermia 40, 55, 110, 220, 221, 330
Internet and trekking
lightning strikes 267, 269, 374
motorcycles on the trail 91, 178, 280, 308
Search and Rescues 154, 155, 157, 158
sleet 9-11, 13, 63, 65, 328, 331
snow 24, 27, 28, 39, 40, 45, 47, 49-55, 57-59, 65-67, 81, 83, 85, 97,
    98, 100-103, 105-114, 118-124, 126-128, 135, 138, 148, 158, 166,
    168, 176, 217,-222, 224, 226-228, 237-240, 242, 254, 255, 264,
    272, 281, 294, 323, 328-331, 340, 355, 363, 364, 369
snowing 109, 219, 329, 331
thunder 107, 216, 218, 267-271, 331
tornado 63
water carriage 435-440
water sources on trail 435f
water sources, distance between 435f

Trails

Acorn Trail 214, 217, 219, 220, 227, 234, 237
Bear Creek Trail 186
Devils Slide Trail 78, 102, 106, 112-114, 118, 361
Marion Ridge Trail 118, 119
Mt San Jacinto Trail Spurs 95, 102,
Mt. Waterman Trail 264
Palm Springs Tramway Trail 101, 112
Silver Moccasin Trail 255, 256, 259, 264

Animals Encountered

bears 153, 197, 199
birds 117, 119, 333-335, 338, 339
cattle 23, 27, 29, 32, 59, 67, 69, 70, 88, 89, 126, 333, 337
dogs on the trail 134, 155, 223, 267, 293, 296, 307, 308, 342

foxes 115, 35
mules 248
rattlesnake/snakes 81, 82, 125, 126, 261, 262, 372
squirrels 176
wild cats 195, 225

Trekkers, Angels and Others

Allen Downs 99, 104, 113, 115, 225
Alaskans, The two
Al Reynolds 374
Art at Warner Springs
Andy at Whitewater 139
Ann 374, 376, 377
Batch (Calvan Batchelder) at Idylwild 96, 97, 104
Ben, at Mount Laguna 374-376, 379
Bill Jennings
Billy, from Laguna Beach 51, 53, 54, 57, 59, 65, 66, 68, 69, 71-73
Bob, near Mount Pacifico 278, 305, 373
Brian Robinson 373, 376, 379
Charlotte Clews at Idylwild 104, 113,
Cory, on the slopes of Mt. San Jacinto 120
Dana, on the slopes of Mt. San Jacinto 120
Dave, Camp Host, Spunky CG 301, 319
David Long, at wrightwood 228, 229, 235, 258
David Margolis, 114, 223, 252, 320, 342,
Dave, motorist from Tehachapi 319
Deputy Sergeant Cartrell, SBSD at Big Bear 159, 161
Deputy Karen, SBSD at Big Bear, 160, 162
Deputy Scott, SBSD at Big Bear, 156-160
Donna, at Idylwild 104
Donna Saufley 281, 293, 295, 373
Doug, at Agua Dulce 293, 294, 296, 297, 303, 304, 340
Finch, near and at Kennedy Meadows 347, 359, 362, 364
Godie (Blisterfoot) 361

Greg Hummel 374

Grizzly 379

Hannah 27, 46, 49, 54, 56, 58, 73, 90, 95, 102, 103, 114, 116, 127, 133-136, 148, 158, 162, 166, 171, 176, 180, 182, 189, 190, 192, 194, 195, 223, 225, 229, 230, 234, 235, 237, 258, 267, 270, 271, 283, 285, 286, 336, 351, 378, 380

Harriot, from Vancouver 376, 378, 379

Hawkeye 347, 348, 350, 353-355, 360, 363

Heather, from England 359, 365

Homer, at Silverwood Lake 200

Improvo, from Ashland 347, 348, 359

Jason Kramer, from Julian 374

Jack Fair at Neenach 305, 308

Jeff Saufley 295-297

Jennifer, from Virginia 224-226, 229, 230, 232-234

Jim, Flight instructor at Warner Springs Airport 73, 74

Joel Margolis 3-7, 25-29, 133-164, 166, 167, 173-184, 185-195, 238-244, 251-272, 331, 381-383

Jonathan Ley, at Idylwild 104

Jonathan Margolis 114, 115, 133-159, 162-164, 209-212, 242, 252-258, 267-271, 325-332, 333-334, 354, 365, 366

Kadiddle/Kadoodle, at and near Kennedy Meadows 356, 359, 368, 369

Lara, from Ventura

Larry, at Summit Valley 168, 190, 194-197, 205, 235, 269

Leena, at Whitewater 139

Lightning Bolt, from Georgia 374

Lorraine Downer 354, 355, 373

Lynn Kyndall, Search and Rescue, San Bernardino

Malcolm, at Wrightwood, 224, 226, 228

Mario, at Boulder Oaks 50, 290

Marlene, from Virginia 224, 226, 229-234

Matt, near and at Kennedy Meadows 350, 351, 364

"Meadow" Ed Faubert 104, 106, 107, 359, 364-366, 369, 372, 374, 377, 380

Mike Hall, at Kennedy Meadows 359, 360
Monte Dodge 370, 373, 377, 380
Nathan Ley 113
Neal, at Wrightwood 224, 226, 228
Paul Downer, TA from Sabastopol 352-354, 359, 360, 362, 363, 373
Ray, from Mariposa 374, 375
Rebecca, on the slopes of Mt. San Jacinto 120, 194
Rebecca Williams from Truckee 120, 194
Richard, from England 359, 363, 365
Rinaldo, from Laguna Beach 51, 53, 54, 57-59, 62, 65, 66, 68, 71-73
Rob Bedichek 104, 105, 114, 133, 225
Ron Moak 373
Roy Robinson 373, 374
Scott Williamson 293, 294-297,299, 303 340
Sean, Dispatcher, Green Hornets Aviation 33, 223
Sheila, from Oregon 374
Todd, at the North Fork Ranger Station 281, 282
Tom Marshall, Pilot at Green Hornets Aviation
Tweedle, at and near KM, 348, 350, 354-356
Van (Johan Van Nimwegen) 30-32, 37-40, 45-47, 49, 54, 56-59, 68, 79,, 80, 90, 91, 93, 96, 100, 103, 105, 106, 116, 117, 119, 127-129, 133, 135, 223, 271-277, 320, 321, 345-347
Wayne Wichert 379, 380,
Willy Colour 365
Yip (Andrew Yip) 104, 113